ESSENTIAL PRINCIPLES OF BUSINESS for CXC

2nd edition

Alan Whitcomb & Sybile Hamil

LONGMAN

Publishing for the Caribbean

Pearson Education Limited
Edinburgh Gate, Harlow,
Essex CM20 2JE, England
and Associated Companies throughout the world.

Carlong Publishers (Caribbean) Limited,
P.O. Box 489,
33 Second Street,
Newport West,
Kingston 13,
Jamaica

Lexicon Trinidad Limited,
Boundary Road,
San Juan,
Trinidad

© Alan Whitcomb with Sybile Hamil 1995, 2000
All rights reserved. No part of this publication
may be reproduced, stored in a retrieval system,
or transmitted in any form or by any means, electronic,
mechanical, photocopying, recording, or otherwise,
without the prior written permission of the Publishers.

First published 1995
Second edition 2000
Eighth impression 2005

Printed in Malaysia, PP.

ISBN 0 582 40053 8

CONTENTS

Acknowledgements vi
Preface vii
How to use this book viii

Chapter 1
BACKGROUND TO BUSINESS
1.1 The development of economic activity 1
1.2 Scarcity and choice in a modern society 4
1.3 Caribbean economic problems 4
1.4 Economic systems 7
1.5 Types of production 9
1.6 Interdependence of industry 11
1.7 Things to do 12

Chapter 2
ORGANISATION OF PRODUCTION
2.1 Production levels 15
2.2 Factors of production 16
2.3 Location of business 19
2.4 Business size 19
2.5 Technological change 24
2.6 Things to do 25

Chapter 3
BUSINESS ORGANISATION
3.1 The role and functions of a business 29
3.2 Management 30
3.3 Organisational structure 34
3.4 Small and large businesses 38
3.5 Management information systems (MIS) 39
3.6 Things to do 42

Chapter 4
TYPES OF BUSINESS
4.1 Private and public enterprise 45
4.2 Limited liability 45
4.3 Private ownership 45
4.4 Special business relationships 50
4.5 Business growth 53
4.6 Government-owned businesses 54
4.7 The role of government agencies 56
4.8 Things to do 58

Chapter 5
RECRUITMENT, SELECTION AND TRAINING
5.1 Recruiting employees 63
5.2 The personnel department 65
5.3 Staff orientation and training 66
5.4 Welfare of employees 66
5.5 Staff records 66
5.6 Dismissal and redundancy 67
5.7 Things to do 68

Chapter 6
MOTIVATION OF EMPLOYEES
6.1 Job satisfaction 71
6.2 Wages 71
6.3 Working conditions 73
6.4 Things to do 76

Chapter 7
INDUSTRIAL RELATIONS
7.1 The importance of industrial relations 80
7.2 Trade unions 80
7.3 Collective bargaining 81
7.4 Industrial legislation 81
7.5 Restrictive practices 82
7.6 Pressure groups 83
7.7 Things to do 83

Chapter 8
MARKETS
8.1 What is a market? 87
8.2 Financial markets 87
8.3 Commodity markets 88
8.4 The consumer market 88
8.5 Channels of distribution 89
8.6 A common market 89
8.7 Things to do 90

Chapter 9
THE MARKETING DEPARTMENT

9.1	What is marketing?	93
9.2	The marketing department	94
9.3	Marketing mix	94
9.4	Product life cycle	96
9.5	Merchandising	97
9.6	Price determination	97
9.7	Competition	100
9.8	Public relations	101
9.9	Trade associations	101
9.10	Things to do	102

Chapter 10
MARKET RESEARCH AND ADVERTISING

10.1	Aims of market research	106
10.2	Types of market research	107
10.3	Market research in action	108
10.4	Functions of advertising	108
10.5	Forms of advertising	109
10.6	The advertising campaign	110
10.7	Is advertising wasteful?	111
10.8	Consumer protection	112
10.9	Things to do	113

Chapter 11
LOCAL TRADE

11.1	The chain of distribution	117
11.2	Wholesale trade	117
11.3	Functions of wholesalers	118
11.4	Services provided by wholesalers	118
11.5	Elimination of the wholesaler	118
11.6	Retail trade	119
11.7	Types of retailer	120
11.8	Patterns in retailing	122
11.9	Selling on credit	123
11.10	Mark-up and profit margin	124
11.11	Setting up a retail business	124
11.12	Things to do	125

Chapter 12
THE OVERSEAS MARKET

12.1	The importance of international trade	130
12.2	Balance of trade	131
12.3	Balance of payments	132
12.4	Methods of selling abroad	133
12.5	Difficulties faced by exporters	134
12.6	Free trade restrictions	134
12.7	Regional and foreign economic institutions	135
12.8	Things to do	139

Chapter 13
BUSINESS DOCUMENTATION

13.1	Transactions	143
13.2	Making enquiries	143
13.3	Purchasing	145
13.4	Despatch	146
13.5	Charging	146
13.6	Foreign trade documents	151
13.7	Stock records	152
13.8	Business contracts	153
13.9	Things to do	158

Chapter 14
TRANSPORTATION

14.1	The importance of transportation	163
14.2	Choice of transport	163
14.3	Methods of transport	163
14.4	Containerisation	167
14.5	Transportation terminology	168
14.6	Things to do	168

Chapter 15
COMMUNICATIONS

15.1	The importance of business communication	173
15.2	Internal methods of communication	174
15.3	Business meetings	175
15.4	Business correspondence	176
15.5	Postal communication	176
15.6	Telecommunication	178
15.7	Things to do	178

Chapter 16
THE STRUCTURE OF THE BANKING SYSTEM

16.1	Caribbean banking	185
16.2	The central bank	185
16.3	Commercial banks	186
16.4	Merchant banks	186
16.5	Other specialist banks	187
16.6	Things to do	187

Chapter 17
BUDGETING AND BANK ACCOUNTS

17.1	Budgeting	191
17.2	Bank accounts	192
17.3	Cheques	192
17.4	The bank statement	194
17.5	Things to do	195

Chapter 18
BANKING SERVICES

18.1	Standing order	198
18.2	Direct debit	198
18.3	Credit transfer	198
18.4	Bank cards, credit cards and money cards	200
18.5	Electronic funds transfer	201
18.6	Borrowing from a bank	201
18.7	Miscellaneous bank services	201
18.8	Things to do	202

Chapter 19
BUSINESS FINANCE

19.1	The balance sheet	208
19.2	Cash flow	209
19.3	Costs and revenues	210
19.4	Break-even	210
19.5	Capital	211
19.6	Turnover	212
19.7	Profit	213
19.8	Return on capital invested	214
19.9	Things to do	214

Chapter 20
STOCK EXCHANGES

20.1	Selling new shares	219
20.2	Selling second-hand shares	219
20.3	Securities traded	220
20.4	The return on shares	221
20.5	Factors affecting share prices	221
20.6	Speculation	222
20.7	How a stock exchange works	222
20.8	Striking a bargain	222
20.9	The importance of stock exchanges	223
20.10	Things to do	224

Chapter 21
INSURANCE

21.1	The insurance industry	227
21.2	The purpose of insurance	227
21.3	Uninsurable risks	228
21.4	The principles of insurance	229
21.5	Types of insurance	230
21.6	The insurance contract	232
21.7	Things to do	233

Chapter 22
NATIONAL ACCOUNTS

22.1	The standard of living	237
22.2	National income	238
22.3	Gross national product	240
22.4	National expenditure	241
22.5	National debt	241
22.6	Growth and development	242
22.7	Things to do	243

Chapter 23
TAXATION AND INFLATION

23.1	Principles of taxation	247
23.2	Functions of taxation	247
23.3	Methods of taxation	248
23.4	Economic effects of taxation	249
23.5	Inflation	249
23.6	Things to do	251

Chapter 24
THE ROLE OF GOVERNMENTS

24.1	The responsibilities of governments	255
24.2	Government assistance to entrepreneurs	256
24.3	Government intervention in business	257
24.4	Social services	258
24.5	The role of government agencies	259
24.6	Governments and the labour force	260
24.7	Things to do	261

Chapter 25
THE SCHOOL-BASED ASSESSMENT

| The SBA | 266 |

| Index | 273 |
| Answers to objective tests | 279 |

ACKNOWLEDGEMENTS

The Publishers are grateful to the following for their permission to reproduce photographs:

Anne Bolt for pages 55 (top left), 55 (right), 121 (left), 121 (right), 165 and 167; Canadian Imperial Bank of Commerce, The Bahamas for page 200; Ford Motor Company Ltd. for page 25; T. Geddes Grant (Barbados) Ltd. for page 117; Life File Photographic Library/Sue Davies for page 29 (middle right); Popperfoto for page 235; David Simson for pages 29 (bottom right), 120 (top left), 120 (bottom left), 120 (right), 128, 166, 173 and 181 and Philip Wolmuth for pages 29 (top right), 29 (left) and 55 (bottom left).

The Publishers are also grateful to the following for their permission to reproduce artwork:

Peggy Clifford pages 1, 2, 3, 46, 47, 53, 82, 109, 154 (top), Caricom Export Development Project, Barbados for page 134 (taken from *Buyers Guide 6th Biennial Trade Exposition, April 1992, Kingston, Jamaica*) and Chartered Institute of Marketing (UK) for page 116.

PREFACE

This book is intended for use as a basic text for students preparing for the CXC examinations in Principles of Business and other related examinations. The book will also be useful for those who may not be taking examinations but have an interest in learning about the world of business.

The aim of the book has been to present comprehensive coverage of the syllabus in a readable and interesting style that will appeal to the full range of abilities. Wide and constructive use of illustrations is an important feature of the book.

Each chapter of text is supported by a variety of activities, containing varied degrees of difficulty, that will help the student to form revision notes, and practise objective tests and stepped structured questions. Also included are exercises that encourage independent research.

The activities at the end of each chapter give a variety of opportunities for 'differentiation', allowing the learning material to be directed at varying degrees of student ability. The **Search and find** work could be tackled by all students, perhaps with the teacher deleting questions related to topics that are considered unnecessary or which some students will find too difficult. This type of activity helps the student produce revision notes. The **What do you know?** exercise is a relatively simple objective recap test that most students will enjoy completing. The other objective test takes the form of the classic multiple choice test. There is also a collection of **Structured questions** at the end of each chapter. These are '*stepped*', that is, each sub-part becomes progressively more difficult, thus allowing all students to achieve introductory questions whilst stretching the more able person in later sub-sections. The weighting of these questions is indicated by the mark allocation suggested. Many of these questions are related to data which adds interest and aids learning. A **Key words** exercise requires the student to show their understanding of important business-related words used within the chapter. The final activity consists of a variety of **Research assignments**. These are intended to be tackled by the more able student as investigative learning, often giving the opportunity for research and providing evidence of independent thought. They provide a useful selection of ideas to encourage individual research and contribute to **School-Based Assessment**.

The answers to the objective tests are contained at the back of the book and these can be cut out by the teacher if this is seen as desirable.

HOW TO USE THIS BOOK

Each chapter of the book is written in a clear, direct style. When a complete chapter has been carefully read, the **Things to do** section can be tackled. This section contains a variety of activities aimed at reinforcing and testing the learning that has taken place. This important part of each chapter contains the following elements.

1 **Search and find**   The student is required to write out a series of questions and answers to formulate revision notes on the theme of the chapter.

2 **What do you know?**   This simple revision exercise consists of ten sentences with key words omitted. The student is required to write out the sentences and insert the missing word, which can be chosen from a list at the end of the test.

3 **Multiple choice**   This section consists of ten multiple choice questions requiring a selection of one appropriate answer from four alternatives.

4 **Key words**   The student is required to find out the business-related meaning of ten key words used in the chapter, and then include them in a separate sentence to show they understand their appropriate use.

5 **Structured questions**   The questions that form this section are structured and weighted for progressive difficulty. In this section, the total marks available for each question are given in brackets.

6 **Research assignments**   Each chapter ends with this, the most challenging section, which consists of a selection of assignments that can be used as a basis for individual research.

Chapter 1
BACKGROUND TO BUSINESS

1.1 The development of economic activity

Direct production

All people have three basic NEEDS — food, clothing and shelter, and many of the activities we engage in are aimed at satisfying those needs. Activity which results in the satisfaction of our needs is often referred to as 'economic activity', therefore, people are sometimes called 'economic animals'.

Early people had a simple way of life. They would provide all of their needs themselves without the aid of others. This is called **direct production**. They would hunt animals and gather plants and berries. They were living in a **subsistence economy** — providing just sufficient to survive, but not to improve their way of life.

In time people learnt to plant seeds to grow what they wanted, and to pen animals. This resulted in less time having to be spent in searching for food. Early people were now able to improve their way of life by building a permanent home, and by making tools to improve ways of satisfying their needs. One of the results of these improvements was that people found they were producing more goods than required. They were producing a **surplus**. They began to exchange goods for the surplus of others.

Barter

The exchange of one thing for another without the use of money is called **barter**, and this was the way the earliest form of trade took place. An important *advantage* of the barter system of trading was that it made it possible for people to dispose of any surplus they had, and at the same time obtain a wider variety of things they needed. This helped people to improve their way of life and it also allowed them to **specialise** in producing the things they could do best. This increased their **productivity** and resulted in more surplus and further **wealth**. It may seem that the barter system of trading was a simple way to trade but there were a number of *disadvantages* caused by problems of the system.

Problems associated with the barter system

A double coincidence of wants People not only had to find someone who wanted their surplus, but the person they found had to offer what they wanted.

An exchange rate Having found others who wanted what they had to offer, early traders still had to agree on the quantities of each other's goods that were to be exchanged. Imagine the difficulty in deciding how many chickens to exchange for an axehead.

Divisibility of goods Some rates of exchange did not make it possible to trade because some goods could not be split into smaller parts. For example, if one axehead was worth half a live pig, then it was not possible to trade with only one axehead because you cannot have half a pig and also keep it alive.

Storage of wealth Many goods which had been exchanged could not be saved for use at a future date because such items as food could not be stored for a long period of time.

Fig. 1.1 Exchange by barter

Money

The development of money solved many of the problems of barter. When we talk of money today we cannot help but think of coins and notes, but money was not available in this form to early man. Other things were used instead. These included such things as shells, dogs' teeth, beads, grain, spearheads, hides, arrowheads, fishhooks and

BACKGROUND TO BUSINESS

Fig. 1.2 Goods used instead of money

animals. They were used as we would now use money. Even today many things are used instead of money in some parts of the world, and when a country's economy collapses people tend to change back to using goods instead of money because they do not trust money any more.

The characteristics of money
For something to be considered as money, or in place of money, it must have the following qualities.

- It must be *durable* — It must be hard wearing
- It must be *acceptable* — People must agree to its use
- It must be *divisible* — It must be possible to divide it into smaller units if necessary
- It must be *portable* — It must be convenient to carry

The use of money meant that people could *sell their surplus* of goods in exchange for money and use the money to *buy their needs*. Money acted as a medium of exchange. Trade became much simpler.

Eventually metal became a popular choice for money in any part of the world where it was common. Metal was:

- long-lasting
- able to be divided into smaller units and sizes
- scarce.

Some metals such as gold and silver were scarcer than others, and money made from these was of greater value.

The functions of money

- A medium of exchange — *Money makes the exchange of goods easier and makes barter unnecessary*
- A measure of value — *Money can be used to state prices for goods*
- A store of value — *Money can be saved, whereas to save goods may be inconvenient or impossible*
- A standard for postponed payments — *Money can be earned at one time and spent at another*

Indirect production

When early people exchanged their surplus by barter with others they were engaging in **indirect production**: in satisfying their needs in co-operation with other people.

A result of co-operating in this way was that people's basic needs were more easily satisfied. They now found that it was also possible to obtain things they wanted which are not essential to life. Further improvement in their way of life took place. In modern society, people's needs and wants have changed. Today we need a variety of products and we want things such as music and fine arts.

In modern industrial society most people satisfy their needs by cooperating with others to produce (indirectly) the needs of everyone. Sharing work in this way is known as the *division of labour* or *specialisation*, since people are

Fig. 1.3 Division of labour

FIRST

SECOND

THIRD

FOURTH

FIFTH

SIXTH

Fig. 1.4 Example of division of labour

specialising in doing a part of the whole process and dividing the labour between many, which benefits everyone. There are two ways of looking at division of labour.

Division of labour by product

This refers to people doing what they do best in exchange for money, and then using the money earned to buy the goods and services of others. We can see examples of this aspect of division of labour in all the working people we know. All workers are specialists.

Division of labour by process

By organising production into many stages or processes, workers become more specialised in their work, and consequently they produce more. For example, in a car production factory we can see a complete production line attended by many workers, each making their own contribution to the end product.

Advantages of specialisation
- Workers become more expert in their jobs.
- Jobs become simpler and easier to learn.
- Output per person increases.

- Machinery and automation can be used.
- Workers can more easily change jobs.
- Unit costs are reduced.

Disadvantages of specialisation
- Repeating a single task can become boring.
- Individual crafts and skills are lost through mechanisation.
- Greater use of machinery can cause unemployment.
- Production can easily be stopped by strikes.
- Slow workers may be unable to keep up with others.

1.2 Scarcity and choice in a modern society

Today, specialisation has spread world-wide, with not only individuals but whole communities concentrating on doing what they do best. But in order to specialise in this way, exchange must take place if everyone's wants are to be satisfied. The bus driver works for wages, but needs food, so the wages are exchanged in order to satisfy his needs. This involves making choices. In other words, the bus driver has to choose between keeping his wages, or putting them in the bank, and buying food. Or he might have wished to purchase a luxury item, but just had to choose between buying that item and buying food.

Whenever we go shopping we are involved in the basic economic activity of making **choices** because we have scarce resources. We may have to choose between buying a T-shirt and a cassette which we want. Or we may have to choose between a cassette player and a camera. We have **unlimited wants**, but we have **limited resources** (money) available. Consequently, we not only have to make a choice, but we also have to form a **scale of preference**. We have to put what we want into some order of priority.

Scarcity and choice are not only problems that have to be faced by individuals. Businesses and governments have to solve these problems also. Businesses have to decide how to use their limited resources to best effect for the benefit of the shareholders. For example, a business may have to decide between ploughing back most or all of its profit into the business, and paying its shareholders large dividends (or any dividends at all) for a particular year. Governments also have to decide what use to make of the limited resources they have available to the best benefit of the community. For example, some of our Caribbean countries have limited supplies of foreign currency, yet a large amount of goods must be imported in order to support the various sectors of the communities. The governments have to choose between buying basic food

Fig. 1.5 Our resources are limited but our wants are unlimited. We have to make choices

items such as wheat and corn which are important staples, and caviar, which is a luxury item. Or the governments have to decide whether to invest the scarce foreign money in the buying of raw materials for the manufacturing sector, or to invest the money in the buying of consumer products.

The success with which individuals, businesses and governments make choices and use their scarce resources has a considerable influence on the quality of life of us all. This is sometimes referred to as the basic **economic problem** — how to use available resources in a community to the best benefit of society.

1.3 Caribbean economic problems

The economic problem

Caribbean countries, like many other developing countries, face a number of difficulties. These include overpopulation, unemployment, limited natural resources, a largely unskilled labour force, and technical and scientific knowledge that is inadequate to meet the demands of modern society. These weaknesses are perpetuated by an inadequate infrastructure. A major result of this is insufficient inflow of foreign currency, thus making economic development difficult to sustain.

Because Caribbean economies are closely linked to and dependent upon the economies of developed countries, any economic difficulties experienced by those economies tend to be felt in the region's economies also.

Industrialisation

Industrialisation refers to business activities such as production or manufacturing. Thus we speak of the clothing industry, and the motor industry. Machine technology plays a major part in the transformation of raw materials into finished or semi-finished goods. This technology has to be financed through carefully planned investment and government support, sometimes through pooled resources. The major heavy industrial activities undertaken in the Caribbean region are in the areas of oil drilling and oil refinement, natural gas extraction, bauxite mining, production of petro-chemicals and electronics.

Industrialisation has several consequences:

- The creation of jobs for both skilled and unskilled workers.
- Pressure is put on governments to ensure foreign currency is available to buy manufacturing materials and equipment.
- Goods are produced for the local as well as the overseas market.
- Governments earn revenue through taxation.
- More people are employed in manufacturing, which can mean less people being available in agriculture.
- There are possible adverse environmental effects such as pollution and contamination.

Industrialisation results in a number of problems for the region. These are now summarised, together with examples of possible solutions.

Disposal of industrial waste

Governments and companies need to develop policies that are implemented and carefully monitored to acceptably dispose of industrial waste. Additionally they have to consider where the residue from one industry could be used in another, and ensure that capital is available to implement such a process. For example, perhaps the clay left over from bauxite production could be used to make bricks for the construction industry.

Primary production dominance

Many Caribbean countries find it difficult to be more than primary producers, mainly because of lack of capital, technical knowledge and the availability of people with the necessary technical skills. Governments need to invest greater resources into research directed towards establishing how their primary resources could be utilised in other ways. Petro-chemicals are a typical example that countries could continue to investigate.

Economic and social conflicts

The capital-intensive nature of productive activity, especially in the modern industries, results in high levels of efficiency but it does not contribute to alleviation of the high level of unemployment and other regional problems. Governments and companies need to find ways whereby both economic and social issues are addressed.

Opportunity costs

Heavy industrial activities use much energy. Consequently, Caribbean countries face large energy bills if productive activity is to be fostered. The cost of this energy means that other much-needed goods and services must be foregone. Governments need to determine whether or not the opportunity cost involved is justified.

Plough back

Industries need to be encouraged to plough back a greater proportion of their profits into the business sector to generate more employment.

Light industrial activities are also important to the Caribbean region. These include:

- craft production, especially for the tourist industry
- garment construction
- sugar production, flour milling
- food processing.

Problems encountered in the light industrial area are particularly related to **distribution**. For example, countries find it difficult to break into the international market. Although the region boasts a number of free zones, from which a number of manufacturing companies operate, these are mainly dominated by foreign-operated companies that produce goods especially for particular developed countries. For example, particular lines of clothing are produced for well-known designers for the international and other markets. Governments, therefore, need to continue their lobbying for participation in non-traditional markets.

Governments need to help these light industries to improve their products. For example, the craft industry needs not only funds, but also training for those involved in order to improve the quality of the products. This will increase their chances of participating successfully in the international market.

Unemployment

A large proportion of labour in the Caribbean is tied to agriculture and, because of the seasonal nature of some agricultural products, there are times when people are left unemployed. For example, sugar cane planting and harvesting is seasonal, and a large amount of labour is employed at these times. When the season is over, the workers return to their small-scale farming activities, or to casual work, or no work at all.

Perhaps governments could provide incentives for hoteliers who are willing to develop and market a tourism package for locals to encourage them to take their vacation in the local resorts rather than go overseas on trips which requires the use of much foreign currency.

Much of the local farm products could be produced by the farmers and sold to the tourism sector.

The **population growth rate** also has an effect on employment. Rapid population growth rate results in rapid growth in the labour force and, with the lack of availability of jobs, this poses many **social problems**. In this sense, unemployment can be said to create major **social costs** and also wastes **economic resources**. There are several **types of unemployment** in the Caribbean region:

Seasonal unemployment

This occurs in industries such as tourism and agriculture where the seasonal nature of the service or work leads to people being made unemployed at the end of the season's activities.

Casual unemployment

This occurs where persons only work occasionally. They have no set jobs and work mainly doing 'odd jobs'. Such people are classified as **casual workers**. Persons in this situation could be employed by governments to brush and clean drains and gullies.

Cyclical unemployment

This is sometimes referred to as **demand deficient unemployment**, because it arises from a general lack of demand for goods and services. Governments could create special works programmes, thus providing employment. From the payments received these workers will demand goods and services. Thus, they bring life back into the economy.

Structural unemployment

This type of unemployment occurs where industries face structural decline through lack of competitiveness. For example, when a product, skill or process becomes out of date or unfashionable, the resulting fall in demand leads to a fall-off in jobs in the industry. Governments could provide incentives such as having no duty on raw materials purchased by these firms enabling them to produce goods competitively, and thus keeping persons employed.

Frictional unemployment

This form of unemployment is temporary and voluntary. The lapse of time between a person leaving one job and finding another is referred to as **frictional unemployment**.

Residual unemployment

This is associated with persons who only work to achieve a particular goal and then leave the work scene. It also refers to persons in the potential workforce who suffer from some disability that prevents them from being gainfully employed.

Migration

Migration refers to the difference between the total of people entering a country (**immigration**) and the total of those leaving (**emigration**). It is not just the number of people who enter or leave the country that is important: the **skills** they bring with them or take from the country is a significant factor. The knowledge and skills taken out of a country is sometimes referred to as a '**brain drain**'. This is a major problem for the Caribbean region. The 'brain drain' has an important effect on economic growth and development.

Governments can help to alleviate the problems of unemployment and migration by:

- encouraging families to observe family planning, and to recognise it as a means of survival.

- developing and pursuing policies regarding the location of industries. This could include providing incentives to businesses to locate in areas other than urban areas.

- improving social amenities in 'relocation areas' to encourage people to live in such areas.

- encouraging more self-help programmes, including training in skills as well as in entrepreneurial skills.

- providing loans for small business ventures.

Education and economic development

The quality of the workforce of any country depends upon the quality of the education it has received. As Caribbean countries have moved away from their concentration on primary production towards the secondary and tertiary production referred to earlier in this chapter, there has been a need to raise the level of scientific and technological education in order to match the thrust for economic development. Particular attention has been given to technical-vocational education and the raising of industrial awareness.

A variety of educational initiatives have contributed to the aim of making education address the needs of modern industrial society. Skills training programmes have been designed to assist young people to achieve skills relevant to the work situation. A number of these training programmes were funded by the Canadian International Development Agency (CIDA), and the United States Agency for International Development (US AID). In addition, local chambers of commerce have also played a part in helping young people to gain an understanding of how businesses work.

Many other programmes exist, providing entry-, middle- and high-level skilled personnel to meet the needs of the public and private sectors in the Caribbean.

Education makes an important contribution to production because it helps to provide:

- a productive workforce
- skilled personnel required by employers
- economic growth through the training of people
- development of a creative, innovative workforce.

In addition, it is generally recognised that there is a relationship between education and population growth. Education assists in the regulation of family size and therefore assists in the long-term objective of reducing inequalities in our societies.

Caribbean governments have been investing in education. The University of the West Indies and the Caribbean Examinations Council are examples of the commitment of the governments of the region to education collectively. Individually, countries have been investing a large proportion of their budgets in education. More recently, CARICOM addressed the matter of human resource development as a strategy for economic development. Thus, much effort is being made to develop the human resource of the region.

However, governments need to ensure that education programmes are not only designed to take care of today's problems of the region, but that they also address the need to prepare their people for life in the new millennium.

Tourism

Tourism plays a crucial part in the economic life of some of the islands of the Caribbean. Visitors come mainly from Europe and North America, and also from Japan. Tourists are drawn by the natural environment — nice weather, good beaches, attractive mountains, springs, rivers and beautiful gardens.

Caribbean countries earn large amounts of foreign currency from tourism. This is needed by governments to pay for imports and to meet foreign debts. Tourism also provides employment for a large number of local persons. As was mentioned earlier, locally produced craft items are sold in the tourist industry.

Infrastructural developments that are put into effect to meet the needs of the tourist industry (e.g. road networks) also benefit the local community.

Whilst tourism brings its benefits, such as foreign exchange, employment and markets for some locally produced goods, it also has its negative effects. For example, land tends to be lost for structural developments, and agricultural workers leave the land to join the tourist trade labour force. Some critics argue that tourism contributes adversely to the spread of prostitution and drug problems. A less obvious adverse effect of tourism is that it can be said to add to the imports bill, because goods are imported to suit the tastes of the tourists.

1.4 Economic systems

The processes of production, exchange, scarcity and choice that we have looked at so far all take place in a political framework. The decision of what to produce or what choices to make from the limited resources available is influenced by the political situation within which the decision is made. No two countries are organised in the same way, but they all have to solve three basic problems, as follows.

- *What should be produced?* For example, what quantities of food, machinery or services should be produced?

- *How should production be organised?* What is the best way to combine the factors of production? Should automated or manual methods be used? What technological equipment (e.g. computers) is required? Where should the production take place?

- *For whom should production take place?* Should everyone be entitled to an equal share of production, or should some receive more than others?

Economists distinguish between four different economic systems which answer the foregoing questions. The first of these described here is a subsistence economy.

Fig. 1.6 These three basic questions must be answered by every society

Subsistence economy

A subsistence economy is one where there is little specialisation and little trade. In such an economy people tend to live in family groups and grow most of their own food. It is called a 'subsistence economy' because people do little more than subsist — they can provide only the basic necessities to live. This was the form of economy that was a feature of the life of early people. Today more advanced forms of economy exist.

Other economic systems differ according to the extent to which the government interferes with the economy. There are three basic approaches adopted by governments in dealing with the economic problem: free market economy, controlled economy and mixed economy.

Free market economy

In a free market economy there is little or no government interference in the economy. It is based on the private ownership of the factors (means) of production and the means of distributing goods and services. **Market forces** are allowed to determine how resources are allocated. Sometimes such economies are referred to as market economies, unplanned economies, free enterprise, laissez-faire or capitalist systems.

There is no example of a 'pure' free market economy because governments play an important part in the running of all countries. The nearest to a true free market is probably the USA, although the UK has recently moved considerably in this direction. Some Caribbean countries have been moving towards the free enterprise system. Such countries, for example Jamaica and Trinidad and Tobago, have taken steps to sell state-owned enterprises, remove subsidies, and allow the exchange rate to float.

Advantages of free market economy
- Free competition stimulates innovation and keeps prices down.
- Individuals are completely free to use their income and labour to their best advantage.
- Consumers decide what will be produced by influencing market forces.

Disadvantages of free market economy
- It encourages inequalities of wealth.
- Advertising can be used to create an artificially high demand for products.
- The more powerful businesses may buy out the smaller ones, thus reducing competition.
- Wealthy people are more able to purchase and influence the market than the poor.
- Companies may be tempted to restrict supplies to keep prices artificially high.

Controlled economy

In a controlled (or command) economy all the economic decisions are made by the government. The state decides what to produce, how it is to be produced and how it should be allocated to consumers. In other words, unlike in the free economy, it is the state that decides what the community needs and, therefore, demand is not influenced by the consumer. China and Cuba are examples of controlled economies.

Advantages of controlled economy
- The state ensures that the needs of the whole community are met, and not just the needs of those with the most wealth.
- State control eliminates wasteful competition.
- The state will provide goods and services that private enterprise would be unwilling to provide.
- It is not possible for a private monopoly to develop.

Disadvantages of controlled economy
- Free enterprise and competition are discouraged.
- Too many non-productive government officials are required to administer the system.

- Centralised production may not respond quickly enough to changing conditions and needs.
- Creativeness and efficiency are not encouraged.

Mixed economy

A mixed economy is a combination of elements from a free economy and a controlled economy. There is a public sector controlled by the government which provides goods and services that the state feels it can manage most efficiently, and a private sector in which individuals risk capital in producing goods and services for profit. Most Caribbean countries have mixed economies.

Globalisation

'Globalisation' does not really, as yet, have a precise definition. However, it can be seen as the intensification and spread of world-wide social, economic, cultural and political relationships among countries. Globalisation began with the development of international trade and has continued to grow. Cane sugar, an agricultural product of the Caribbean for many centuries, brought many peoples, cultures, and systems of operation together. Thus, globalisation can be seen as the linking of distant localities in such a way that local activities are shaped by events occurring thousands of miles away.

A major benefit of globalisation is the provision of high quality goods and services at a cheaper rate. This is achieved through the **economies of scale** which firms contributing to globalisation enjoy. In contributing to the process of globalisation, firms not only provide goods and services economically, but they also provide employment for people who may have otherwise been unemployed.

The impact of globalisation has had some adverse effects on small economies of the Caribbean. Large international firms that can produce high quality goods and services at a cheaper cost set a challenge to small firms that are producing similar goods and services. For example, international firms in the area of clothing and textiles have made great in-roads into the Caribbean market. Thus small firms are finding it difficult to compete.

From the foregoing it will have been seen that globalisation has opened the way for greater cooperation between countries, but it has also challenged Caribbean countries to examine the contribution they can make to the global market place.

1.5 Types of production

Earlier in this chapter we compared *direct* and *indirect* production. With direct production we said that individuals or small groups satisfy their wants entirely by their own efforts, unaided by others. However, indirect production, which is a feature of developed societies, involves specialisation, working for wages, and using the money earned to buy goods and services provided by others. Indirect production can be divided into three categories: primary production, secondary production and tertiary production.

Primary production is concerned with the extractive industries, secondary production with the manufacturing and constructive industries, and tertiary production with the provision of services.

```
                        Production
         ┌──────────────────┼──────────────────┐
Primary production   Secondary production   Tertiary production
extractive industries  manufacturing and     service industries
                     constructive industries
   ┌──────┐                                    ┌──────┐
Farming  Mining                             Commerce  Direct
  Fishing                                            services
```

Fig. 1.7 Family tree of production

Primary production

Primary production is concerned with the extraction of basic materials provided by nature, which are either above or below the earth's surface. The extractive industries are farming, fishing and mining. Without these much subsequent production would not take place.

Agriculture is an important primary production in most Caribbean territories. Sugar cane as well as many tropical fruits are grown. The following are other examples of primary production in the region:

Anguilla	fish
Barbados	fish oil
Belize	timber
Grenada	spices
Guyana	timber, bauxite, rice
Jamaica	bauxite, coffee
Leeward Islands	cotton, vegetables
Trinidad	oil, pitch
Windward Islands	spices, cotton, arrowroot

BACKGROUND TO BUSINESS

Fig. 1.8 Extractive industries

Secondary production

Secondary production consists of the manufacturing and constructive industries. These industries take raw materials (obtained by the extractive industries) and change them into finished goods.

Manufacturers may make the whole finished product or make a part or parts which will be put together and made into a completed article, for example, aluminium converted into pots and pans.

The construction industry takes raw materials and partly-finished products and changes them to an end product, for example, buildings, roads and bridges.

Tertiary production

When goods leave the producer they do not usually pass directly to the consumer. They have to be transported, stored, insured, advertised and sold by traders. These and the many other commercial activities make up tertiary

Table 1.1 *Comparison of types of production in the region with types of production in other parts of the world*

Types of production	Caribbean	Other countries					
		Nigeria	Brazil	Chile	Canada	UK	USA
PRIMARY PRODUCTION (extractive)	Agriculture *sugar cane, cotton, timber, rice, arrowroot, spices, coffee, bananas, citrus* Fishing Mining *bauxite, ore, oil, pitch*	Agriculture *nuts, rubber gum, timber, cotton, coal, peanuts* Mining *tin, coal, oil*	Agriculture *coffee, tobacco, corn, cotton, sugar cane, cocoa* Mining *iron ore, bauxite, ore, salt, lead*	Agriculture *grapes, citrus, rice, corn, peas, beans* Mining *copper, iron ore, nitrate, silver, coal*	Agriculture *wheat, oats, barley, tobacco, timber, vegetables* Mining *gold, natural gas, copper, nickel, iron, zinc, lead*	Agriculture *barley, oats, wheat, potatoes, vegetables, fruit, hops* Mining *natural gas, coal*	Agriculture *barley, wheat, corn, cotton, tobacco, soyabeans, potatoes, vegetables* Mining *coal, oil, natural gas, copper, iron ore*
SECONDARY PRODUCTION (changing primary goods into finished goods)	Manufacturing *rum, molasses, fish oil, processed coffee, processed foods, milk, garments, asphalt, furniture, sugar* Construction *buildings, bridges, roadways*	Manufacturing *textiles, leather goods and hides, pottery* Construction *buildings, bridges, roadways*	Manufacturing *sugar, processed coffee, textiles, processed foods, pharmaceuticals, chemicals, electrical equipment* Construction *buildings, bridges, roadways*	Manufacturing *wines, processed foods, leather goods, copper ingots* Construction *buildings, bridges, roadways*	Manufacturing *machinery & equipment, paper & paper pulp, petroleum refining, wood products* Construction *buildings, bridges, roadways*	Manufacturing *iron & steel, motor vehicles, transportation equipment, food processing, brewing & distilling, leather goods, textiles* Construction *buildings, bridges, roadways*	Manufacturing *iron & steel, processed foods, machinery & equipment, motor vehicles* Construction *buildings, bridges, roadways*
TERTIARY PRODUCTION (direct services)	Commerce	Commerce	Commerce	Commerce	Commerce	Commerce	Commerce

10

Fig. 1.9 The Red House, Trinidad: seat of parliament

production, and make change of ownership from producer to consumer possible. Tertiary production is sometimes called the service industry, but more often it is referred to as **commerce** and **direct services**.

Commerce can be divided into two clear areas: **trade** and **services to trade**.

- *Trade* is the buying and selling of goods in order to change the ownership. This can be divided into local trade and foreign trade.
- *Services* assist the buying and selling of goods, for example, banking, finance, insurance, transport, communications and advertising.

Direct services are the activities provided by people that do not change the ownership of goods but which are essential to the well-being of the community, for example, tourism, nursing, teaching, dentistry and acting.

1.6 Interdependence of industry

Industries depend on each other for goods and services. The tourist industry, for example, depends on the agricultural industry for supplies of food, and so some farmers sell their products — vegetables, citrus, among other products — directly to the hotels. The tourist industry is a large earner of foreign currency, and so the banks (including the central banks) depend on the earnings from tourism in order to meet the needs of individuals who, like businesses, require foreign currency to purchase raw materials from overseas. The raw materials are usually needed for the production of craft goods, hence the productive or manufacturing sectors also depend on the foreign currency earnings from tourism to an extent.

Let us now briefly summarise what we have learnt in this chapter.

- *Direct production* is characteristic of underdeveloped countries. It involves a considerable degree of self-sufficiency, and people live at subsistence level.

- *Indirect production* is a feature of all advanced economies, and this form of production is most common today. It involves people co-operating with others to obtain their needs.

- *Specialisation* is an essential part of indirect production and it involves people doing what they do best. Facilities for exchange must exist for specialisation to take place.

- *Tertiary production* or commerce describes the activities that are positioned between the producer and the consumer. These provide the means of buying and selling goods and services. They play a vital part in enabling people to specialise, earn wages and then buy their wants. They also play a major role in co-ordinating and promoting the activities of producers. We will now examine some of the ways in which this is done.

Traders, such as retailers, help producers by distributing their products. Exporters sell locally produced goods overseas. This not only provides work for producers, but also brings in foreign money that is needed to pay for the import of raw materials and finished goods that we cannot economically produce at home. In this way, home producers are able to specialise in manufacturing products for which they are best suited.

The services to trade also play an important part in co-ordinating the work of producers and distributing their products. For example, finance provides the capital necessary for a business to buy the assets it needs and also for consumers and businesses who wish to buy on credit. Banking makes transfer of payments between buyers and sellers possible. Banks also provide a variety of other services that make it easy for payments to be made, and therefore encourage production and trade to take place. Insurance solves some of the risks involved in producing and trading, such as the danger of loss or damage to goods or equipment. Transport provides the physical link between producers, traders and consumers, and gets goods to the market in good condition. Advertising helps producers and traders to make consumers aware of the availability of goods and services. Various communication facilities enable businessmen to communicate with each other and their customers at the various stages of production and distribution.

From the foregoing we can see that commercial activities are essential for production to take place, but also that commercial activities would not be needed if it were not for specialisation making exchange necessary. In other words, primary, secondary and tertiary production are interdependent.

1.7 THINGS TO DO

This section contains a variety of exercises to help you create revision notes, to test your understanding and to prepare you for examinations.

Search and find

Write out the question and the answer by referring back through the text to form revision notes.

1. What is direct production and why does it limit the quality of life?
2. Why is the production of a surplus important?
3. What is barter and what are the problems of trading in this manner?
4. How does money solve the problems of barter?
5. What qualities are necessary for something to be used as money?
6. What are the functions of money?
7. In what way does indirect production require people to co-operate?
8. How does specialisation help to create a surplus?
9. Explain the difference between division of labour by product and division of labour by process.
10. List the advantages and disadvantages of division of labour.
11. Why is exchange so important for specialisation to take place?
12. Why are we all required to make choices and form a scale of preference?
13. Why is making wise choices important to individuals, businesses and whole countries?
14. Describe some of the industrial problems that exist in the Caribbean region.
15. Industrialisation has yet to realise its full potential in the Caribbean region. What reasons can you put forward for this?
16. Why do you think light industries are important to the Caribbean region?
17. Describe the different types of unemployment.
18. What is 'migration'?
19. What do we mean by 'brain drain'? Does it matter?
20. How can governments help to overcome unemployment?
21. Why is education important to economic development?
22. 'Tourism has benefits and costs to Caribbean society'. Explain this statement.
23. State the four basic problems that economic systems have to attempt to solve.
24. What is a subsistence economy and why is it not a satisfactory way of life?
25. 'The free market economy and a controlled economy are very different.' Explain this statement.
26. What is a mixed economy?
27. What do you understand by the term 'globalisation'?
28. In what ways does 'globalisation' present a challenge to the Caribbean region?
29. Why is primary production also referred to as the extractive industries?
30. How does secondary production rely upon primary production?
31. Why is tertiary production so important to the other forms of production?
32. Distinguish between trade and the services to trade.
33. What are direct services? Give four examples of occupations that provide a direct service and say how they contribute to the quality of life.
34. In what ways are primary, secondary and tertiary production interdependent?
35. Give examples of primary industries in the Caribbean territories.
36. What are the basic economic problems that face the Caribbean region?

What do you know?

Write out the complete sentence and insert the missing word, which can be chosen from the list at the end of the questions.

1. ..... production means producing all of your needs without the help of others.
2. In a subsistence economy, just enough is provided in order to .....
3. One of the difficulties of barter was that of agreeing an ..... rate.
4. ..... makes the exchange of goods easy and barter unnecessary.
5. A problem of specialisation is that repeating a task can become .....
6. One of the advantages of division of labour is that workers become more ..... in their job.
7. We are all involved in the basic economic activity of making a ..... because of scarce resources.
8. Forming a scale of preference involves putting things we want in order of .....
9. In a free market economy there is no ..... interference.
10. Free competition stimulates innovation and can help to keep ..... down.

Choose the missing words from the following:

| priority | expert | survive | money | choice |
| boring | direct | government | prices | exchange |

Multiple choice

Select the appropriate answer, a, b, c or d.

1. Choice is a basic economic activity because:
   a) interest rates are too high
   b) resources are scarce
   c) incomes are too high
   d) inflation is too high.

2. Farmers, fishermen and miners are examples of people who work in:
   a) primary production
   b) tertiary production
   c) commerce
   d) secondary production.

3. A mixed economy is one which consists of:
   a) the provision of free social services
   b) more than one political party
   c) both public and private enterprise
   d) no private businesses.

4. Which of the following is not a function of money?
   a) a measure of value
   b) a substitute for cheques
   c) a store of value
   d) a medium of exchange

5. State which of the following is a feature of a controlled economy:
   a) the factors of production are privately owned
   b) the purchasers of goods determine demand
   c) there are private and public enterprises
   d) the state decides what the community needs.

6. Which of the following workers is employed in the tertiary sector?
   a) builder
   b) miner
   c) shopkeeper
   d) farmer

7. In a 'free' economy the most significant force in the distribution of goods is:
   a) the banks
   b) the state
   c) the shops
   d) the price system

8. Which of the following words can be applied to the economic system of the Caribbean?
   a) laissez-faire   c) centrally planned
   b) mixed   d) capitalist

9. Which of the following is a service to trade?
   a) farming   c) construction
   b) advertising   d) fishing

10. Which of the following is the odd one out?
    a) indirect production
    b) specialisation
    c) division of labour
    d) direct production

Key words

Find out the business-related meaning of each of the following words. Write a separate sentence for each word to show your understanding.

resources	scarcity	wants	needs
consumers	surplus	monopoly	competition
substitute	community		

Structured questions

1. a) Primary production is sometimes referred to as the extractive industries. Why is this? (2)

b) Name the three extractive industries. (3)
c) What is secondary production? Name the two main categories into which this form of production can be divided. (4)
d) Name five of the elements of tertiary production. (5)
e) 'Tertiary production is very different from the other forms of production, but it is just as important.' Explain this statement. (6)

2 a) Define barter. (2)
b) Briefly explain three of the problems of barter. (2)
c) Explain how money solves most of the problems of barter. (2)
d) Spearheads, teeth and shells have all been used as money in the past. What common features do they all have that made them suitable for this purpose? (3)
e) Why did metal become a popular substance for use as money? (3)
f) Clearly describe the basic functions of money. (8)

3 (a) Describe each of the following economic systems:
   (i) subsistence economy (4)
   (ii) free market economy (4)
   (iii) controlled economy (4)
   (iv) mixed economy (4)

(b) Give examples of countries of the Caribbean region which utilise *two* of the economic systems described in (a) above. (8)

Research assignments

1 Explain to an imaginary visitor from China the main differences between the economic system that exists in his or her own country and that existing in a Caribbean country of your choice. Include evidence that supports your report.

2 a) Imagine yourself to be a manufacturer of furniture. Describe how you would use division of labour in the production of a specific item of furniture.
b) One of the disadvantages of specialisation is that work can become boring for the worker. Suggest ways that you would try to overcome this problem.
c) What evidence can you give that proves that division of labour operates successfully in your locality?

3 What is division of labour? Show how this must lead to commercial activities, using specific examples and evidence from local businesses to illustrate your answer.

4 Explain why the success of industry is influenced by the effectiveness of commerce. Use specific examples from local businesses to illustrate your answer.

Chapter 2
ORGANISATION OF PRODUCTION

2.1 Production levels

Aims of production

Production refers to the creation of goods and services, i.e. the creation of utilities. The purpose of production is to provide people with the goods and services that they need or want to consume. **Needs** are things that are essential to human survival. There are three primary needs:

- food
- clothing
- shelter.

Production also provides the many things that people *want* to consume, but which are not necessary for survival. These things help to make the quality of life better: for example, televisions, cars and books.

In Chapter 1 we said that production can be divided into three main sectors: primary, secondary and tertiary. It can also be classified according to the levels of operation. These levels are dependent upon the resources available, and the extent to which the country has developed to exploit those resources. There are three basic levels of operation: **subsistence**, **domestic** and **surplus**.

Subsistence level

This level of production meets only the basic needs of the country in which it takes place. In other words, sufficient is produced only to enable the population to survive, but not enough to improve the way of life. This is the kind of problem faced by many of the underdeveloped communities of the world.

Subsistence economy is a term usually applied where agriculture is the main source of production. In other words people live almost entirely by what can be obtained from natural resources, and this could lead to a very poor quality of life. Usually the subsistence level of production is inefficient and very dependent upon the climate and weather. Periods of drought or other climatic problems result in severe hardship. Fortunately, the subsistence level of production is not as common today as it has been in the past.

Domestic level

At the level of domestic production everything is produced locally, that is, in the home country. This level does not involve any imports from foreign countries. Both human and natural resources are employed and the whole economy is dependent upon what it can produce from these resources.

Some developed countries, such as the USA, try to grow all the food they need because they have the resources to do so. The governments of developing countries, including the Caribbean region, encourage domestic production in order to make full use of the resources available in their country, e.g. the promotion of self-sufficiency in agricultural produce.

Small farmers in Barbados and St Christopher, for example, grow a high proportion of the vegetables and fruits available locally. The Windward Islands and Jamaica produce bananas for the world market. However, because many small farmers also engage in banana farming, large amounts can be obtained on the local market. A number of other islands produce yams, potatoes and cassava which serve as staple foods. Animal rearing in Guyana, Trinidad and Tobago and Jamaica assists in the provision of protein and other dairy products for the local markets.

Surplus level

Developed countries, such as the USA, Britain and Germany, have a wide variety of resources and exploit these to the full. They also have advanced technology which enables them to take full advantage of their resources.

Such countries are able to achieve a level of production which not only satisfies domestic consumption, but also produces a surplus that can be exported to other countries. This results in a better quality of life for the population because there is access to a wider variety of products, prices are competitive, and more can be earned from production.

The various Caribbean territories are at different stages of development in their levels of production, although they have developed beyond the subsistence level. Their operations at domestic and surplus levels vary. CARICOM and the CBI (Caribbean Basin Initiative) are two organisations which aim to encourage industrialisation throughout the territories.

The Caribbean Community, usually known as CARICOM, consists of Trinidad and Tobago, Jamaica, Guyana, Barbados, Anguilla, Antigua, Barbuda, Belize, Dominica, Grenada, Montserrat, St Kitts and Nevis, St Vincent, St Lucia and The Bahamas.

CARICOM is a 'Common Market'. That is, it is a group arrangement whereby there are no import duties on trade between one member state and another, and no restrictions on the quantity that can be exported or imported between member states. In addition, member states have agreed to impose the same rate of import duty on goods from outside CARICOM. An important objective of CARICOM is co-ordinating industrialisation in the region and assisting development. CARICOM is dealt with in greater detail in Chapter 12.

2.2 Factors of production

In Chapter 1 we learnt that there are only scarce resources to meet our unlimited wants. The scarce or limited resources which are used to produce the commodities people want to consume are collectively called the **factors of production**. They are:

- land
- labour
- capital.

Entrepreneurship is sometimes listed as a fourth factor. Each of the factors receives payment or reward in return for the contribution it makes to production. Land receives rent, labour wages, capital interest, and entrepreneurship is rewarded with profit, although some factors actually receive more than one return.

The factor of land

Land as a factor of production includes not only the land itself but all natural resources found in the earth and sea. Land includes mineral deposits such as bauxite, oil, iron ore, gold and diamonds. It embraces sunshine and rainfall, rivers, ponds and lakes, the seas and oceans, deserts and forests. Land in this sense includes:

- geographical surface area
- rivers, lakes and seas
- minerals and chemicals.

Land is fixed in supply. In other words, the supply cannot be increased, although the quality of the soil may be improved by the use of fertilisers, drainage, land reclamation, contouring and reafforestation. The search for minerals below the surface of the land and sea continues.

Production cannot take place without land. Primary, secondary and tertiary production and all economic activity involve the use of land.

The natural resources of the Caribbean region include minerals such as bauxite, oil, natural gas, gold, diamonds, clay, limestone, gypsum, manganese, sand, silica, marble and many others. Some of the physical forces which are harnessed for energy production include lakes, rivers and the wind. And of course the climate is a natural resource which helps to promote the tourist industry.

Table 2.1 *Natural resources of the Caribbean region*

Natural resource	Country	Example usage
Bauxite	Jamaica, Guyana	Refined as aluminium, used in pots and pans, machines and parts (e.g. aircraft parts)
Clay	Throughout Caribbean	Bricks, earthenware pots
Diamonds	Guyana	Jewellery, industrial diamonds
Forestry	Guyana	Furniture
Gold	Guyana	Jewellery
Limestone	Barbados, Jamaica, Trinidad and Tobago	Cement products
Manganese	Guyana	Metal and glass production
Natural gas	Barbados, Trinidad and Tobago	Energy fuel
Oil	Trinidad and Tobago	Petrol and by-products such as plastics and paint
Pitch	Trinidad and Tobago	Asphalt, shingles
Sand and silica	Throughout Caribbean	Building materials, glass
Sun	Throughout Caribbean	Solar energy

The factor of labour

Labour is the factor of production which is people's physical and mental contribution to the creation of goods and services. It is the factor that converts resources into goods and services that people want. This contribution to production is generally rewarded with wages, although sometimes profit or interest is the return received.

All production requires some labour. Even the automated factory requires workers to supervise machinery, program computers to operate equipment, and process paperwork. Therefore, it is important that there is an adequate supply of labour, with the required skills. In this respect, labour is often divided into three broad groups:

a) *Semi-skilled and unskilled*: jobs which involve little or no special training and usually involve working with the hands — drivers, cleaners, street sellers and some factory production line workers, watchmen, etc.

b) *Skilled*: engineers, mechanics, electricians, plumbers, trained machine operators, computer operators, clerks, junior supervisors, etc.

c) *Managerial and professional*: business executives, teachers, doctors, nurses, solicitors, architects, pharmacists, senior supervisors, etc.

These groups generally reflect differing qualities and levels of training.

Many businesses improve the quality of their labour force through education and training. This results in efficient use of the capital goods the business employs, and therefore contributes to the growth and development of the firm. But there are many other factors which determine the supply and quality of labour.

Determinants of the labour supply

Labour supply is influenced by several factors.

- *The size and structure of the population*: a large population will give a greater supply of labour. But a high proportion of very young or very old people will tend to reduce the supply of labour. These proportions will be influenced by school-leaving age, retirement age and birth rate.

- *The number of women at work*: this is influenced by many factors such as economic conditions in the country, wages, and attitudes towards working mothers.

- *Hours of work*: if there is a general trend towards a shorter working week (which is the case in developed countries), this has the effect of reducing the supply of labour.

- *Quality of the labour force*: it is not enough to have sufficient numbers of people available for work. They must also have the appropriate skills that are needed. If the required skills are not available the effect will be to limit the supply of labour.

- *Adequacy of health services*: it is important that adequate and readily available health services exist to keep the population healthy.

- *Mobility of labour*: the ability and willingness of workers to move to new jobs in other areas affects labour supply.

- *Government policies*: government commitment to training and other policies that help to improve the labour force and make it more mobile can have the effect of increasing the supply of labour in appropriate areas, and with the skills required.

One of the difficulties Caribbean countries have faced in relation to the supply of labour (particularly from the mid 1950s to the 1970s) is the effects of the migration of people to foreign countries. Whilst many of these migrants were unskilled, untrained and poorly educated, a lot of them were skilled and well-educated, including teachers, engineers and others. This 'brain drain' resulted in a shortage of labour in important skill areas in the region for many years, and thus restricted economic development.

Labour quality is influenced by the following factors.

- *Quality of education*: education plays an important part not only in producing a knowledgeable workforce, but it also contributes towards making people more mobile and adaptable to change.

- *Training facilities*: a shortage of workers with particular skills can be overcome by training more of these specialists through the education system or in-service occupational training.

- *Natural talent*: some skills are important but are natural talents and cannot be taught, although they may be increased by training; for example, acting, drawing or playing a musical instrument.

- *Health*: the standard of health of workers obviously affects their efficiency and productivity. Health is affected not only by living conditions, but also by working conditions.

- *Self-help and community work*: these have become an important aspect of the economic contribution of labour in the Caribbean region. Examples are projects in which the government provides materials and the community provides the labour. Organisations (e.g. Red Cross Society, Lions Club) use the self-help approach to help the provision of social or cultural facilities which the State does not provide.

Self-help or community organisations such as trade unions often act as potent pressure groups which try to influence the government to the benefit of the whole community.

Modern technology

Modern technology has resulted in increased automated methods and strategies being adopted by organisations involved in the production process. It is common today for machines to be programmed to receive, interpret and process information in the completion of a task. Take the **point of sale** in a supermarket as an example. Hand held and counter-top **scanners** read **barcodes** placed on packaging, transfer the information to the computer system, and once recognised, the prices are calculated and the customer is told how much to pay. For a cash payment the cashier receives the payment immediately. But if the customer chooses to pay by **credit card**, then another device comes into the process. The card is checked by the computer system to determine its validity before the transaction is completed by debiting the credit card company and crediting the shop (in due course). During all of this process, the computer system will be automatically updating the **stock records** of the shop, and even ordering replacement stock.

Human effort is needed to program, activate, monitor, and maintain technological equipment and systems. However, less human effort is now needed to carry out the many routine tasks in organisations. Consequently, people need to be retrained to manage technological devices, strategies, methods, procedures and concepts in modern society. This has implications for the **education** of the population and the **redistribution of employment**.

The factor of capital

Capital is the money and all other assets (possessions of value) which are employed in the process of production. Capital includes the buildings, machinery, equipment, stocks and many other things (producer goods) used in making the items we consume (consumer goods).

Capital in this sense takes two basic forms, fixed capital and working capital.

- *Fixed capital*: buildings, machinery and other equipment with a long life which are used many times over in the production of goods and the creation of further wealth.
- *Working capital*: stocks of raw materials, cash, bank balances and other items required for the day-to-day operation of the business and which are continually being used up.

Fig. 2.1 Can you identify the factors of production and enterprise in this illustration?

The entrepreneur

Some people argue that entrepreneurship can be considered as a fourth factor of production. Entrepreneurs are those who organise and co-ordinate the other factors of production. They are the owners of business enterprises who, by taking risks and making decisions, enable production to be carried out in anticipation of demand.

If entrepreneurs successfully predict future demand they are rewarded by a special form of income called **profit**. If, however, their judgement is incorrect they may get no reward or may even make a **loss**. For example, a shopkeeper may buy stocks of a new brand of confectionery, but has no guarantee of being able to sell them. There would be far fewer businesses in existence if there were not entrepreneurs around willing to take the risk involved.

In order to participate in entrepreneurship the entrepreneur must be willing to do a number of things.

- To raise capital, from savings or by borrowing, for investment in the business.
- To organise the various levels of labour required.
- To define and clarify business policy decisions so that all levels of personnel can understand what the firm is trying to achieve.
- To make any change necessary in the interest of the growth and development of the business.

Factors influencing business location

Industrial inertia - Sometimes firms stay at a particular site even though the original reason for siting in that area (e.g. near source of raw materials) no longer applies.

Raw materials - Closeness to raw materials or to the port where they enter the country may influence choice of site.

Transport access - Siting near to good road, rail, sea or air links can save in distribution costs or in the movement of raw materials.

Land - Availability of sufficient suitable land, at an economically viable price, in a suitable position will attract business.

Market pull - Businesses are attracted to sites close to where potential customers can be found; shops near where shoppers will be, hotels near tourist areas.

INFLUENCES ON LOCATION OF BUSINESS

Labour - Availability of suitable labour with a good no strike record. This will be influenced by availability of social amenities such as housing and medical facilities

Government influence - Some governments try to influence the location of businesses, e.g. to improve regional balance and reduce overcrowding in cities and towns.

Environment - Climatic conditions are important to some businesses, particularly those involved in agricultural products.

Fuel or power - Closeness to fuel or power are less important today than in the past, but some firms still need to locate near to sources such as water.

Linkage industries - Firms will locate near other businesses on which they depend, or near to other firms in a similar line of business.

Fig. 2.2 Factors influencing business location

2.3 Location of business

A major decision that all firms have to take is where to site their premises. A variety of factors will influence this decision, including the size of the organisation and the expected scale of its operations, but most choices of site are a compromise between several advantages and disadvantages. The summary chart, figure 2.2, shows the main influencing factors.

2.4 Business size

Economies of scale

The producer has to decide how to use the factors of production to the best advantage, because the chances of making a good profit depend upon how effectively the factors are employed. The entrepreneur also has to decide on what scale to produce and what size of business to operate, because the size of the business and the scale of production can also influence profitability. These decisions have to be taken by all entrepreneurs. Obviously, the entrepreneur should aim for the scale of production which yields the greatest profit margin.

Large businesses tend to dominate certain industries because their size gives them advantages over smaller organisations. For example, by producing larger quantities they can reduce their production costs. These advantages of size are called **economies of scale**. Sometimes business growth results in disadvantages; when this occurs it is referred to as **diseconomies of scale**. You should realise that there can be advantages in a business remaining small as well as advantages in being large.

In addition to economies of large scale and small scale, there are external and internal economies of scale. External economies of scale refer to the benefits gained by the whole of a certain industry, or the whole of society. For example, a particular invention may result in benefits to all firms in an industry, or to the whole of society. Internal economies of scale refer to the benefits gained by one particular industry. Internal economies of scale can be grouped into four categories:

- technical
- managerial
- marketing
- financial.

Technical economies of scale
Greater size allows more opportunities for division of labour, the use of machinery and automation, and other methods of increasing efficiency. It also allows a company to allocate more resources to research and development, which can result in further economies through increased efficiency and effectiveness.

As a firm increases its output and employs more workers there are more opportunities to divide work into stages and, consequently, workers become more efficient in their work. Dividing the work into stages in this way also makes it easier to introduce machinery and other labour-saving equipment.

Managerial economies of scale
Larger firms are able to employ more highly skilled personnel. Such employees will be attracted to the company not only by the higher salaries offered but also by the prestige of a larger organisation, and greater scope for advancement.

The employment of skilled specialists in charge of functions such as design and production results in the advantages of the division of labour. Small firms often do not have sufficient work to enable them to form separate specialist departments and, therefore, managers have to undertake a variety of tasks which can make them less effective.

Marketing economies of scale
Larger firms can purchase their supplies in bigger quantities than small firms. They can also engage in mass production and they save in advertising and distribution costs. The important result of these advantages is that such firms can market their goods more cheaply than smaller competitors, and obviously consumers will be more likely to give their custom to such firms.

Most firms see public relations as an important part of their marketing strategies, because if potential customers regard the reputation of the company as 'good' they will be more likely to want to give their custom to the firm. Large businesses are in a better position to sponsor sports and public events and offer attractive prize-giving competitions, thus promoting good public relations.

Financial economies of scale
A major advantage of being a large firm is that, because large firms own more assets, they find it easier to borrow money and they are more able to withstand financial pressures (e.g. of cash flow) than smaller businesses.

Banks and other lending institutions feel safer in lending money to large companies because they feel there is less risk involved. Similarly, creditors (e.g. suppliers) feel more confident in giving trade credit to larger firms than to smaller ones.

Large businesses

Both economies and diseconomies of scale can be examined by looking at the advantages and disadvantages of large-scale business.

Advantages of large businesses
- They find it easier to raise large amounts of capital.

- More capital is available for:
  — extensive advertising
  — research and development
  — employing specialist personnel
  — labour-saving machinery.

- Mass production allows greater possibilities of specialisation.

- They can obtain special prices and discounts.

The advantages of large businesses summarised in the foregoing list refer only to internal economies of scale, but there are also external economies of scale. Sometimes many related businesses in a particular industry are located in one place. This will encourage the provision of skilled maintenance and other backup services such as training facilities which benefit all members of the industry. In addition, all firms engaged in a particular industry may combine together for the purpose of advertising, research, or technical developments. Groups of industries will also attract good transport facilities, or special treatment from banks and other financial institutions.

Disadvantages of large businesses
- They can become too complex to manage.
- Lines of internal communication and management become unwieldy.
- Customers may find the large organisation too impersonal.
- Mass production can lead to boredom for workers and reduce quality.
- Workers find it easier to organise restrictive working practices.

The Law of Diminishing Returns

A firm cannot continue to grow indefinitely unless some factors change. If you continue to blow up a balloon it will eventually burst because the fixed factor (the balloon) cannot contain the varying factor (the added air). The same principle applies to a growing business. If the fixed factor is factory space and if the firm continues to add more workers, initially there will be more production, but eventually additional workers will result in less output per person as too many workers in a restricted space get in each other's way.

As a firm grows, it is subject to the Law of Diminishing Returns. When a firm is growing rapidly it experiences increased returns and rising profits. But there is a point in any productive organisation when diminishing returns will begin to operate. The additional output (marginal output) achieved as a result of the addition of a unit of labour begins to fall; therefore, the average output also falls. This is illustrated in table 2.2.

Table 2.2 *The Law of Diminishing Returns*

Units of workers	Total output	Marginal output	Average output
1	5	5	5
2	18	13	9
3	30	12	10
4	36	6	9
5	35	−1	7

Small businesses

In spite of the benefits of large-scale operations, small firms continue to exist because they have their own special advantages, and in some cases (e.g. direct services such as hairdressing) do not lend themselves to large-scale operations.

Many persons in the Caribbean engage in small business operations. This is one way of alleviating the unemployment problem. Small business entrepreneurship training programmes and centres, as well as small business associations, have been established in the Caribbean islands to assist and encourage small business operators.

Generally there is only limited management structure in small businesses and often the only management will be the owner(s) of the firm. This has its advantages in that there is less need for consultation when making decisions because the manager or owner performs all the important functions. But this person also requires a wider range of management skills than his or her counterpart in a large organisation.

Advantages of small businesses
- Closer communication exists between employees.
- It is easier to have good working relationships.
- Employees feel a personal involvement in the business.
- There is more personal contact between employees and customers.

Value of small businesses to a country
1. The small business provides employment, and thus utilises labour available.
2. Small businesses can respond to customers' needs faster than a larger business. For example, if a customer desired a variation to a product, a small, locally-based business can make adjustments to meet local market conditions. The ability to respond in this way to market conditions enables small businesses to continue to operate and create employment opportunities.
3. Small businesses contribute to the competitive spirit of the economic life of a country by competing with larger organisations, thus preventing them from having a monopolistic position.

Small business incubator
The idea of the small business incubator is relatively new, but centres have been established to provide:

- essential business services
- consultancy and training
- a flexible working space for the new businesses.

The incubator is seen as a tool that can be used to bring about economic growth in industrialising developing nations. A major objective of the incubator is to encourage innovations and the incubator will then provide some resources and training for the small to medium-sized businesses. The incubator will provide space, shared office facilities, advisory services, skills development in small business management, assistance and speed in securing office space, and access to 'seed money' through a loan scheme.

Small businesses are often born out of cottage industries (see below) or other community self-help projects. Many are family businesses with limited capital. These businesses often find it difficult to obtain a loan from the established financial institutions that tend to focus their attention on the larger, well-established businesses. However, small businesses have an important role in the economy:

- They contribute to the economic life of the country by providing employment.

- They provide a service that is needed by the population, especially in small communities that are not easily serviced by the businesses in the towns and cities.

- Because of the size of the business, customers' personal preferences are identified and met.

Cottage industries

A cottage industry is one of the extremes of small business. As the name suggests, cottage industries are carried on in the home, although increasingly they are to be found in community centres, parish halls or some other similar village facility. Frequently such businesses will involve handwork carried on at home but the term also applies to many other forms of employment, often where workers supplement their normal earnings in cottage industries after their day's work is completed.

Cottage industries originated as ways of increasing income without leaving home. They also satisfy the psychological need to use one's spare time productively. Today they are recognised as playing an essential part in the Caribbean economies.

People who have skills in handicrafts have for a long time successfully used free or relatively cheap local materials to produce a variety of goods, particularly to meet the demands of the tourist trade. This not only provides income for the producers of such items but also makes sensible use of their spare time. In some examples it can also provide employment for others who provide raw materials or who sell the finished product on behalf of the makers.

Cottage industries have continued to survive in the Caribbean because those involved have diversified and increased the range and scope of their products. Products produced by cottage industries include: pastries, straw hats, garments, embroidery, basketry, jams and jellies, string arts, flower arrangements, as well as direct services such as tailoring, beauty culture, catering, knitting, smocking and crocheting.

Throughout the Caribbean region various governments have tried to encourage production in this manner. For example, Caribbean governments may arrange major exhibitions and competitions, provide skills training, assist in the marketing of products, and may even make factory space available.

Apart from the aforementioned reasons for the continued existence of cottage industries, they have other important contributions to make to the economy of their countries. During a time of high unemployment they provide income and independence for many people. We also have to remember that the money earned by those engaged in the cottage industries is eventually spent — thus providing work for others.

Linkage industries

In Chapter 1 we said that there are three types of productive industries:

- *Primary*: those industries concerned with the extraction of basic materials provided by nature (farming, fishing and mining).

- *Secondary*: those industries which change raw materials and partly produced goods into some finished product (manufacturing and construction).

- *Tertiary*: the service industries (such as transport or tourism).

The linkages between these aspects of production are important because they facilitate a series of relationships between the productive sectors mentioned above. These linkages are of crucial importance to Caribbean development. For example, agriculture is an important economic base in many of the territories and the linkage industries make an agricultural-industrial drive possible.

A linkage industry is one that is linked with another. It is sometimes called a 'screw-driver' industry or a 'spin-off' because it has come about as a result of some other development. For example, canning and preservation of foods are 'spin-offs' of agriculture (forward linkage); one industry is producing the raw material for another industry. Conversely, manufacturers of farm machinery will supply to agriculture (backward linkage).

The linkage industries are important in the Caribbean at both national and regional levels because they:

- provide increased employment and an improved standard of living

- assist regional self-sufficiency (reduced dependence on imported goods)
- reduce wastage of the country's resources
- increase opportunities for combined research and development
- encourage more skills in the labour force
- forge closer Caribbean links at the social, economic and political levels
- promote earnings of foreign exchange.

Table 2.3 *Examples of industrial linkage in the Caribbean*

Crude oil (refining)	Petroleum, plastics, asphalt
Sugar cane	Candy, rum
Fruit	Canning
Bamboo	Baskets
Asphalt	Road-building
Livestock	Hides, leather goods

Benefits of local and regional linkages

The Caribbean Community (CARICOM) has been established to encourage economic development in the region. The organisation has been seeking ways and means of achieving its objectives and one of these is to establish linkages in terms of economic activity within the region. The argument is that if nations are to do well economically, then linkages between industries is a worthwhile alternative to current practices.

For example, Trinidad and Tobago is a major producer of pitch which is a by-product of oil — one of their major resources. Other islands could form linkages with this industry in order to obtain the raw materials for their own purposes. For example, with further processing, asphalt used in road construction can be obtained from the pitch.

Another example is the hospitality and tourism sector which is a major earner of foreign currency for most Caribbean islands. Because of the nature of the hospitality and tourism product, it is an area in which considerable cooperation and **linkages** are needed. For example, linkages can be established between the agricultural sector and the hospitality and tourism sector because large volumes of farm produce are consumed by this sector on an annual basis. Information about the quality, quantity and variety of the produce required by the sector is of importance to the farmers. Farmers would then be in a better position to produce to meet the product specifications of the hospitality and tourism sector.

The design and management of facilities are important aspects of the hospitality and tourism sector. Training of managers to develop these skills and competencies would complement their existing general management skills.

This type of training is best delivered by a building services engineer, allowing building services engineers and hospitality and tourism to work cooperatively.

Finally, craft items are produced by many local artisans for the hospitality and tourism sector. Yet, in the marketing of the tourist product, limited attention is given to this often small but important sector.

It is, therefore, clear that the opportunities for linkages at the local and regional levels exist, but a concerted effort must be made by the decision-makers to bring these sectors together so that they complement each other. In this way decisions can be made about how much of what is earned in one sector, for example, hospitality and tourism, should be ploughed back into other sectors such as craft and small farming, in order to improve the quality of their products. In other words, the backward sector could benefit from the modern or technologically advanced sector for their mutual benefit. This can only be achieved if a concerted effort is made by the decision-makers to forge the necessary linkages. This would help to reduce the incidence of **economic dualism** or prevent it. (See also Chapter 22.)

Regional linkages can result in:

- providing outlets for raw materials (at the primary and secondary levels)
- assisting in the development of the region at a faster pace
- assisting in reducing unemployment
- providing opportunities for countries to develop their expertise in the production of specific products
- giving the opportunity for the region, in the long-run, to compete in the global market-place
- preventing scarce resources from being used to obtain products from outside the region which could, with greater cooperation, be produced within the region. This would then leave the savings free to obtain products that are necessary, but for which there would be no clear comparative advantage if attempts are made to produce them locally or regionally.

The role of governments in developing regional linkage

Governments can contribute to the ideal of regional linkage by:

- outlining the benefits to be gained by CARICOM countries from regional strategies. Through CARICOM, regional strategies and policies could be identified and pursued.
- educating business organisations about the benefits to be derived from regional linkages. Encouraging

businesses to use the raw materials of the region, as well as buying locally produced goods. In this manner both local and regional businesses will be supported and helped to survive and develop.

- financing trade fairs at which both local and regional persons could be brought up-to-date on what is being produced in the region, and thus encourage businesses to obtain their supplies from both local and regional markets.

- ascertaining the skills and competencies needed for the industries and collaborating in providing the necessary training of the labour force to handle the tasks to be carried out.

- pooling resources in order to obtain the capital needed by various industries.

2.5 Technological change

The previous section of this chapter included examination of economies of scale. One aspect of this was technical economies. What we said was that the large size of some businesses enables them to use labour-saving machinery and automation. We will now look at this in more detail.

Automation refers to the use of sophisticated machinery which is electronically or computer controlled to carry out some form of production with the minimum of human intervention.

Demand for material goods has increased dramatically throughout the world, and many of these commodities are more sophisticated than ever before. The profit available to those who can produce goods and services most economically has always required businesses to look for the most economic way to meet this demand.

The most dramatic development that has assisted this has been the relatively recent innovation of and application of the silicon chip which has put computer technology within the reach of small businesses and even individuals.

Computers

Computers have had an important effect on businesses. A computer is an electronic information processing machine. It can handle databases and spreadsheets as well as operate as a word processor.

A computer can accept data from a user (input), supply information to a user (output), sort, select, store and retrieve information, and do calculations (process). The text or data may be in words or numbers. Computers operate on instructions (called a program) input by the operator.

A computer consists of the following main unit parts.

- *Keyboard*: an electronic keyboard used to feed information into the system.
- *Visual display unit* (VDU): a television-like screen (monitor) used to display text prior to printing.
- *Central processing unit* (CPU): sometimes called the computer's brain. It is the main part of the computer where the data is processed and the entire system is co-ordinated.
- *Memory system*: all computers have at least some internal memory, but this can be extended for long-term storage by recording data on to magnetic disks.
- *Disk drive*: a device that is used to feed in extended memory from disks.
- *Mouse*: a hand held device that is used to move an icon (graphic image) across the screen. The mouse usually has two or three buttons which are used to select objects on the screen. The action is known as 'clicking'.
- *Printer*: used to print out final text (hard copy).

Fig. 2.3 Computer system

Computers in business

The following are just some of the ways in which computers are increasingly being used in business operations.

Company registers of shareholders are constantly changing as a company's shares are bought and sold, and the current holders of the shares have to be paid their share of the company's profits. The registers of shareholders can be kept in the computer system and rapidly updated.

Stock records: automatic updating of records as stocks are removed from the warehouse or from the display shelves and checked out through the tills. The computer can automatically issue a warning when stocks fall too low, and valuation of stock is immediately available.

Accounts: the issue of invoices and statements of accounts and maintaining records of customers' accounts.

Payroll: the maintenance of a company's wages system can be operated by computer, including automatic deduction of income tax, etc.

Banking: banks use computers for automatic cheque clearing, keeping branch records, issue of bank statements and standing order payments, and operation of cash dispenser systems. They also use computers for immediate updating of customer accounts when deposits and withdrawals are made.

Word processing: computers can be used as word processors. Copies of letters, invoices, statements of account and other important paperwork can be keyed into a computer and stored for later retrieval for review on VDU or printout.

Production line applications: many machines in factories are used to perform repetitive tasks and, therefore, there has been an increasing use of computers to perform these tasks, for example in automated robotic welding.

The effects of the increased use of technology in production can be summed up as follows.

- Increased standardisation of production results in increased output and reduced costs.

Fig. 2.4 Robotics in a car plant

- Business risk is increased because sophisticated, expensive machinery must be purchased well in advance of the sale of products.
- If often results in the workforce being made unemployed.
- Leisure time can be increased by a reduced working week and a lower retirement age.
- The need for tertiary services is considerably increased.

Fig. 2.5 Some effects of automation. What next?

2.6 THINGS TO DO

This section contains a variety of exercises to help you create revision notes, to test your understanding and to prepare you for examinations.

Search and find

Write out the question and answer by referring back through the text to form revision notes.

1 What is meant by the term 'production'?

2 Name the three primary needs.

3 In your own words explain the difference between 'needs' and 'wants'.

4 What is the aim of production?

5 Briefly describe the three levels of production.

6 Give examples of the levels of production in the Caribbean region.

7 Give a brief description of each of the three factors of production.

8 In what way does self-help and community work contribute to the Caribbean economy?

9 Describe some of the factors that affect the supply and quality of labour.

10 Explain the difference between fixed capital and working capital.

11 To what extent would you agree that the entrepreneur can be considered a factor of production?

12 Give an account of what you consider to be the main influences on the location of businesses.

13 What do you understand by the term 'economies of scale'?

14 What are the advantages enjoyed by large firms? Why do large organisations also have disadvantages?

15 In what way does the Law of Diminishing Returns show the limits of large-scale production?

16 Why do small firms continue to exist even though large organisations have many advantages?

17 Why are cottage industries important to the Caribbean region?

18 What is a linkage industry? Why are they important?

19 Why do you think some people are apprehensive about technological change?

20 Word processors are making a considerable impact on office work. What is a word processor? Briefly describe the functions of the main parts of a word processor system.

21 In what ways are the functions of a computer wider than those of a word processor?

22 Describe four examples of the use of computers including at least one application to office work and one related to production.

23 Define automation. What are the possible results of automation?

What do you know?

Write out the complete sentence and insert the missing word, which can be chosen from the list at the end of the test.

1 The purpose of production is to provide people with the goods they . . . . . or want to consume.

2 There are some things that people . . . . . that are not essential for survival.

3 The . . . . . level of production meets only the basic needs.

4 The domestic level of production does not involve any . . . . . from foreign countries.

5 In order to be able to export, a country must be producing a . . . . .

6 . . . . . is the physical and mental contribution to production provided by people.

7 If an entrepreneur successfully predicts future demand they are rewarded with . . . . .

8 A major decision that all firms have to take is where to . . . . . its premises.

9 Large firms achieve bigger profits because they enjoy . . . . . of scale.

10 . . . . . refers to the use of sophisticated machinery and computers in production.

Choose the missing words from the following:

surplus	need	site	imports
profit	want	labour	economies
subsistence	automation		

Multiple choice

Select the appropriate answer, a, b, c or d.

1 Which of the following is a primary need?
a) money   c) land
b) transport   d) food

2 Which of the following is not a factor of production?
a) food
b) land
c) labour
d) capital

3 In a subsistence economy the main source of production is:
a) exports
b) manufacturing
c) agriculture
d) mining

4 Which one of the following will have the effect of reducing the supply of labour?
   a) a high birth rate
   b) a large population
   c) a high proportion of old people
   d) a low proportion of very young people

5 Which one of the following is the most appropriate description of entrepreneurs?
   a) the factors of production
   b) the consumers of goods
   c) the government
   d) the owners of business enterprises

6 Which of the following is a diseconomy of scale?
   a) extensive advertising is practicable
   b) labour-saving machinery can be used
   c) more capital is available
   d) lines of communication can become complex

7 Fixed capital includes:
   a) buildings
   b) stocks
   c) bank balance
   d) stationery

8 The Law of Diminishing Returns states that with additions to labour:
   a) marginal output rises
   b) average output rises
   c) marginal output falls
   d) total output increases

9 The labour force of a country is:
   a) all people below retirement age
   b) all persons who are employed or are available for work
   c) the total population
   d) all persons over the school leaving age

10 Automation in industry can result in:
   a) increased need for tertiary services
   b) employment of a larger workforce
   c) a more skilled workforce
   d) increased production costs

Key words

Find out the business-related meaning of each of the following words and write a separate sentence for each word to show your understanding.

profit	adaptable	talent	stocks
inertia	yield	complex	personnel
communication	management		

Structured questions

1 The tables 2.4 and 2.5 relate to a small firm which specialises in the production of hand-made dolls. The firm has varied its workforce in order to assess the optimum size.

Table 2.4 *Varying the workforce*

Labour force	Total output (per week)	Average output
4	200	
5	260	
6	324	
7	392	
8	456	
9	504	
10	540	
11	572	
12	576	

Table 2.5 *The different costs incurred by the firm during a five day working week*

Number of workers employed	10
Number of dolls produced	540
Weekly wages of each worker	$1100
Rent, rates, depreciation, etc.	$ 260
Power	$ 100
Raw materials	$ 500

a) Explain the difference between the terms 'output' and 'average output'. (2)
b) What does the wording 'optimum size' mean? (2)
c) What is the optimum sized labour force indicated by table 2.4? (2)
d) Calculate the average output of dolls for each of the different sizes of labour force. (3)
e) Using the given data draw curves on a graph to show average output. (3)
f) Give a reason why the firm may not wish to produce its maximum output of 576 dolls per week. (3)
g) If the dolls were selling for $10 each:
   (i) What would be the firm's weekly income? (2)
   (ii) Subtract the total production costs from the firm's weekly income to calculate the firm's weekly profit. (3)

2 a) What do you understand by the term 'automation' in relation to industry? (2)

b) Why have some people viewed automation with suspicion? (2)

c) What advantage does a word processor have over the conventional electronic typewriter? (2)

d) Briefly state the functions of the four main parts of a computer? (4)

e) Give a brief description of five contrasting business applications of computers. (10)

3 a) Define the terms below.
   (i) economies of scale. (2)
   (ii) diseconomies of scale. (2)

b) Select one product being manufactured for the tourist industry in your country, and explain to a manufacturer who could, but does not currently benefit from *large-scale* business, four benefits to be derived from such an operation. (8)

c) Since you wish to provide some amount of balance in your discourse with the manufacturer in (b) above, highlight four disadvantages which could result from large-scale business operations. (8)

Research assignments

1 Describe the economic factors you would consider if you were an entrepreneur choosing a site in the Caribbean to locate a medium-sized manufacturing business. Include in your report information and evidence to support your views.

2 a) What is meant by 'economies of scale'. Use specific examples from businesses in your region to illustrate your answer.

b) Using examples from your region, show why small firms are able to survive even though they do not benefit from economies of scale in the manner of large organisations.

3 Give an outline description of four firms within a 25-mile radius of your home, and offer explanations of the reasons they are situated where they are. Present copies of all correspondence between yourself and these firms.

4 What is meant by the term 'linkage industry'? Select one product from one sector and trace the linkages which result in its production. Provide evidence to show that you have personally researched a genuine linkage.

5 Consider the extent to which siting of any two businesses in your locality can be seen to be influenced by local or national government. Write a summary report containing evidence to support your findings.

6 Investigate the various types of cottage industry that are in operation in your local community. How do they benefit the economy?

7 How are computers being used in businesses in your community? Identify five sectors, for example, tourism, in which computers are being used. What evidence is there that their use of computers enhances their operations?

Chapter 3
BUSINESS ORGANISATION

3.1 The role and functions of a business

The main aim of any business is to make profits in order to give the best possible return to the owners for the money they have invested in the company. Businesses achieve this aim mainly through their major functional areas of production, finance, marketing and personnel.

Fig. 3.1 The functional areas of a business

Production

Finance

Marketing

Personnel

Production

The broad function of production is to satisfy human wants. In order to do this through the production of goods and services the firm will have to co-ordinate several areas.

- The purchase of stocks and raw materials.
- The design of goods.
- Research, development and experimental work.
- The manufacture of the company's products.
- The control of quality of production.
- The storage of the raw materials and finished goods.

We can see this reflected in the production of furniture. Consider a firm designing prototype furniture from raw materials it has purchased. It will research the market to investigate the best ways to market such items. This research will also reveal what need there may be to amend the design of the prototypes, and to produce samples to show prospective customers and obtain orders. Only then will full-scale production take place, during which quality control will be maintained to ensure that what is produced is of the required standard, and workers called **progress chasers** will make sure that goods are produced within the timescale required. The finished products will then be stored until they are required for the intended market.

Finance

Finance is required to form a business and to fund its operations. It is required, for example, to purchase plant machinery and raw materials, and to pay wages to workers. A business also needs finance to meet day-to-day running expenses and to meet maintenance costs.

There are four main sources of business finance (capital):

- savings of the entrepreneur(s)
- capital borrowed from a bank or some other financial institution
- capital raised by the sale of shares in the business
- profits of the business reinvested (**plough back**).

The finance of businesses is examined in more detail in Chapters 16, 19 and 20.

Marketing

The marketing function of business aims to anticipate consumers' demand in order that the right products are manufactured. Once the commodities have been produced it is the function of marketing to promote sales to the consumer. Marketing is not confined to goods alone; labour, capital, land and buildings must also be marketed as well as the many services that are needed. Chapters 8 to 12 examine marketing in detail.

Personnel

The personnel function of a business is to provide employment. Theoretically, the more businesses that exist, and the more successful they are, the greater is the number of personnel needed. However, in reality the provision of employment is far more complex than this simple view. For example, technological developments which lead to increased efficiency and business growth can also result in a reduction of the number of employees needed in a particular industry.

The integration of the two broad technologies of computers and telecommunications has led to increased efficiency and business growth. The revolution in electronics has transformed many of the traditional areas of employment. For example, many of the functions of office workers have been bypassed by computers and word processors. Methods of communication have also rapidly changed, with telecommunication making an even greater contribution, and the automated factory is now becoming more commonplace.

Part of the personnel function of business is the management of personnel: to recruit people with appropriate skills, care for their welfare, and ensure that where necessary in-service training is provided to update their skills. The personnel function is examined in Chapters 5, 6 and 7.

3.2 Management

Management functions

The functions of management can be grouped into seven areas.

- *Planning* involves looking ahead: making decisions and formulating policy on the intentions and objectives of the organisation, and the methods to be used to achieve the objectives. Planning assists the efficient utilisation of the firm's resources, and it emphasises preventative rather than corrective measures.

- *Organising*: ensuring that workers can get on with their job by making sure that people, materials and machinery are available in the right place at the right time. Good organisation involves planning what is to be done, who is to supervise it, time frames and the most efficient method of doing it.

- *Directing*: giving instructions to workers so that they are clear as to how their work should be done to best benefit the organisation.
- *Controlling*: supervising and checking the activities and performance of subordinates to ensure that instructions are being carried out properly and plans and methods are being followed.
- *Co-ordinating*: directing and integrating the activities of the team under management's direct supervision, and contributing to the overall co-ordination of the activities within the organisation in order to form a united strategy of operations to achieve the organisation's objectives.
- *Delegating*: involves assigning tasks or goals to subordinates whilst at the same time granting them the necessary authority to carry out the tasks. The subordinates must recognise their responsibility and accept their accountability for the expected performance.
- *Motivating*: encouraging other members of the organisation to carry out their tasks properly and effectively. Although extrinsic incentives such as wages help to motivate people, the ability to motivate others is very much dependent upon leadership qualities which are discussed later. Intrinsic incentives such as job enlargement and job satisfaction also help to motivate people. Motivation is examined in greater detail in Chapter 6.
- *Industrial relations* (the relationship between employees and employers) make an important contribution to the motivation of employees. Industrial relations is dealt with in Chapter 7.

Responsibilities of management

The foregoing functional areas of a business have to be co-ordinated and managed to ensure that the resources of the business are used to the best advantage.

All members of an organisation have some responsibility, even if it is only to have regard for their own safety and that of their work colleagues. But the higher in the hierarchy of the organisation that a person is, the greater will be that person's responsibility. Consequently, the greater degree of responsibility lies with the managers of an organisation, whether they are managing directors or managers of departments. Managers, in this respect, are those who have the responsibility to direct, control and co-ordinate others.

The management of an organisation is responsible to the firm's owners, customers and employees.

- *Owners*: to achieve the best possible return for the capital they have invested and to reinvest or 'plough back' sufficient capital in order to ensure sound future growth and development of the business.

    Managers will realise this ideal by maximising efficiency and creating a surplus (profit). Maximising **efficiency** involves 'doing things right' and being **effective** ('doing the right things'), which usually results in improved **productivity** (creating greater output) and a bigger profit. Producing a profit is evidence of being efficient.

- *Customers*: to provide goods or services of good quality, within the agreed period of time, and at a fair and economic price.

    Although legislation aimed at protecting customers exists (see Chapter 10), good managers recognise that considering their responsibilities to customers is good for **public relations** (improving public image).

- *Employees*: to provide the safest and most comfortable working conditions possible, to pay a fair wage and to secure future employment as far as possible.

    Provision of **training** for employees is a further responsibility of managers. Appropriate training is important because it helps the employees to achieve self-improvement, and this results in them becoming more effective as employees.

    It is also important that managers **communicate** effectively with employees — keeping them informed of the aims of the business and how it intends to achieve them. Communication also entails managers recognising and taking into account what the employee needs, not only to do their job well, but also for their personal development.

    Human relations are a further important tool in the management of employees. This refers to knowledge of the way in which groups work together, the needs of individual workers and the effect of different forms of supervision on employees. **Teamwork** is an important feature of this. Teamwork can have the beneficial effect of encouraging the development of a team spirit and a sense of common purpose.

The management also has some responsibility to the government, and to society. It fulfils its responsibility to the government by ensuring that the company is abiding by the law and behaving in a manner that is compatible with the country's trading practices both at home and overseas. Its responsibility to society is to ensure that the firm's operations do not cause harm to the general public, for example being environmentally aware.

In order to meet these responsibilities the management must organise and co-ordinate the work of others. The manager will, therefore, at times be required to:

- appoint and train new staff
- communicate company policy
- give instructions and set tasks
- assess performance
- discipline and dismiss staff.

Superiors are expected to be responsible for the actions of their subordinates. Although they can delegate the power or authority to carry out tasks to subordinates, the responsibility for actions cannot be delegated and ultimate responsibility always remains with the manager.

Leadership

People who are in a supervisory position in business need to have some understanding of group dynamics; that is, the way that people interact in a group situation. The extent to which people work effectively (or not) together affects the overall success potential of the business. In the business sense there are four basic elements of group behaviour: the group, an objective, the individual and the leader.

1 The group
Groups can be divided into two categories.

Informal groups have usually come together voluntarily (e.g. a music group), and the purpose of the group is not defined too specifically. There are no set rules (although an informal group may have an objective, such as to raise money for charity), and the leader will be chosen by the members of the group.

Formal groups are usually created for a specific purpose, such as a department in a firm. This type of group has a formal structure, a specific objective and an appointed leader. In fact, the leader may be the one who chooses the members of the group, and consequently enjoys the power of authority. People in businesses and factories generally work in formal groups, with expected standards of production and behaviour.

2 An objective
Because most groups in business are formal ones, they require a clear objective, for instance to formulate a marketing campaign for a new product. Unless the objectives are clearly defined (i.e. by the leader) the group will lose direction; the objectives will be liable to be misinterpreted.

3 The individual
Even though he or she is part of a group, each person still has to work as an individual in order to contribute to the group objective. However, this can result in a problem if the views of the individual, or his or her attitude or behaviour, are not in harmony with the rest of the group. Under such circumstances the importance of the objective may be sufficient to solve the conflict. Alternatively, it may be the skill of the group leader that will be the deciding factor.

4 The leader
Whereas the leader of an informal group may be chosen by the group members, with formal groups the leader is often appointed, as with a manager or chairperson. Such a leader may have the power to regulate the group's behaviour (e.g. they may be in a position to be able to direct someone to do something), but to use their authority in this way may adversely affect the group morale and attitudes. For this reason a good leader will try to identify the parameters within which the group can operate, often delegating some responsibility to members of the group.

Earlier in this chapter we saw that it is important that workers feel motivated. Wages are often assumed to be a motivating factor, but an unlimited amount of capital to provide wages cannot be guaranteed, and wages alone are limited in the extent to which they can be relied upon to encourage people to work hard and effectively.

The success of management and the ability to motivate others is very much dependent upon the ability to lead. But leadership qualities are difficult to identify and to define. Firstly, this is because they depend on the manager's own attitude towards the responsibilities delegated to him or her and to his or her subordinates. Secondly, the ability to lead is considerably influenced by the attitude of the manager towards the problems of his or her subordinates. Thirdly, some of the qualities required to lead others differ from one occupation to another.

To be able to motivate others, managers must also be inspired. They need to be committed to their organisation and must have an interest and pride in the products or services which they produce or sell. Leadership qualities are particularly revealed by the willingness of superiors to listen to, and understand, problems from their subordinates' point of view.

Styles of leadership

There are four basic styles of leadership and a leader may combine any of these.

1 Authoritarian or autocratic
The leader is the absolute authority on all matters, deciding what to do, and whatever others may think, it is done. It is often the case that this type of leader

frequently uses his or her position in authority to exert his or her will on others.

Such an approach to leadership is often effective, but it is not necessarily the most efficient approach. Although work may be completed in the way that the leader has specified, at the same time employee input and innovation is discouraged.

2 Participative or democratic
The leader will consult with those likely to be affected before making a decision, although the leader will reserve the right not to act on a majority view.

This style of leadership is popular because it enables workers lower down in the hierarchy to participate in the decision-making process. Consequently, they are more highly motivated and need less supervision.

3 Laissez-faire or free-rein
In this style of leadership the leader gives limited direction to workers. They are given general directions on the tasks to be tackled and then left to achieve them in the way they think is best.

There are circumstances where this style of leadership is appropriate (e.g. where the employee acts in a consultancy capacity), but generally, most employees prefer to work under some degree of authority from a superior.

4 Charismatic
A charismatic leader is one who influences and motivates others because she or he has outstanding personality or character. This type of leader is relatively rare. Those that do exist can be very successful in the extent to which they can motivate others to do things to support them.

Management communication

The success of any organisation is greatly influenced by the participation of all its members in its activities. We have seen earlier in this chapter that managers have an important part to play in co-ordinating and motivating all workers to achieve a common goal. But for all the workers to make a contribution, they need to know what goals they are expected to achieve. Experience has shown that people are more committed to involvement in an organisation where they are well informed of policies, and even more so when they have participated in making decisions.

Good communication is important in involving all members of an organisation in its activities. The most effective management communications require a two-way flow of information — downwards from management and upwards from employees.

Fig. 3.2 Two-way communication flow

Downward communication is initiated by management and is used to inform employees of the company's proposals, policies, decisions and progress. There are two main methods of downward communication, oral and written.

- *Oral*: direct command, discussions, meetings, loudspeaker, intercom, closed-circuit television, telephone.
- *Written*: letters, memoranda, notice boards, reports, company magazine, handbooks.

Upward communication may be initiated by employees but it is often 'collected' by management. For example, management may well require specific information from employees. This feeds back to management the views, suggestions, proposals and problems of employees. Upward communication can be 'collected' by direct and indirect methods.

- *Direct*: by managers talking to employees and elected representatives.
- *Indirect*: suggestion schemes, attitude surveys.

Teamwork

An effective tool of management is grouping people into teams. In a business, members of the organisation have a specific job to do, but they will also be a member of a group or team. For example, a sales representative will be a member of a group of people such as a marketing team.

The ability of a team to work together is important for two reasons:

1 When people work in a pleasant and cooperative atmosphere, they tend to work harder and more effectively.

2 A good team can achieve more in a shorter period of time than individuals or a weak team.

Managers need to choose team members carefully. A good team member will:

- listen to others and seriously consider their ideas, views and beliefs
- think carefully before speaking
- offer help and support and make suggestions when they are needed
- be prepared to accept constructive criticism from others
- put their own views in a calm and responsible manner
- act as a 'peacemaker' whenever possible.

Teamwork benefits employees because:

- it gives them a sense of common purpose and a feeling of 'belonging'
- they can consult experienced colleagues if they are unsure of something
- working as part of a group is easier than working alone.

Employers benefit from teamwork because:

- it enables workers to specialise which results in 'economies of scale'
- groups make 'top to bottom' communication better
- coordination of groups is easier than managing individuals
- the output of groups is greater than that of individuals.

3.3 Organisational structure

Chain of command

Many companies are organised in the form of a pyramid. The person at the top of the pyramid has the most authority, and the steps down the pyramid indicate less

Fig. 3.3 Pyramid organisation charts

authority. Each person in the pyramid is responsible to the person immediately above. The sections of the pyramid below the person in the managing position make up the chain of command. This shows the lines of communication between the person in the supervisory position and his or her subordinates. Each manager delegates work to the people below him or her in the chain.

Span of control

The number of subordinates a manager supervises, or the effective limit to the number of others that a manager can supervise efficiently, is sometimes referred to as the 'span of control' or the 'span of management'. There are a number of factors that influence the span of control, and they include the following.

- *The complexity of the work.* Some work is easy to check whilst other work demands closer supervision by the manager.
- *Self-discipline of workers.* Where workers are well motivated and have a professional approach a greater number can be supervised.
- *Method of communication.* Some methods of communication (e.g. face-to-face) are more demanding than others (e.g. electronic methods).
- *Frequency of supervision.* The more frequently that a manager needs to see subordinates, the more limited will be the span of control.

Fig. 3.4 Wide and narrow spans of control

- *Capability of the manager.* Some managers have more ability to lead and motivate than others, and this will extend their span of control.

If workers do not need close supervision then the span of control can be wide and flat. Where there is a need for closer supervision the span of control will be narrow and contain more people in sub-supervisory positions.

Fig. 3.5 Combined chain of command and span of control

Organisational structure

To be able to achieve its objectives satisfactorily, a firm relies on two types of relationship between personnel. These relationships are called the 'organisational structure' of a firm. One type is 'formal' and the other 'informal'.

Formal organisation is concerned with the official lines of communication followed by employees in carrying out management decisions. It allows those in charge to define objectives for each section or department to enable the organisation to achieve its corporate aims. Formal organisation helps to define responsibilities and to ensure that tasks are not duplicated but are co-ordinated between functions within an organisation, so that each department blends its activities with those of other departments to form a corporate strategy.

The functions found in organisations will vary depending on their type or size, and this will affect the organisational structure used. There are basically four types of formal organisational structure, and a business might incorporate more than one of these.

- Line organisation
- Line and staff organisation
- Functional organisation
- Committee organisation

Line organisation

This is a traditional form of organisation which involves a direct flow of authority, and responsibility is dispersed and delegated from top to bottom. The owner or chief executive will instruct those below her/him, such as departmental managers (sometimes referred to as **line managers**). They in turn will instruct the less senior employees who comply with the instructions (this is regarded as a **narrow span of control**).

Fig. 3.6. Line organisation in a small firm

Within this hierarchical form of organisation everyone has some responsibility. The higher the position in the hierarchy the greater is the responsibility, and this responsibility cannot be delegated. Tasks or objectives can be delegated, and so can authority or the right to use power. This right is defined by the hierarchy, and should correspond with position in the hierarchy.

The benefit of this method of organisation is that it is easy to understand, since it has an uncomplicated chain of command. Decisions can be reached quickly. It is particularly suited to a small business. However, this type of structure ties up the owner or chief executive with managing the relationships between departments and department managers, leaving little time for policy making and planning. At the lower levels, some employees may be over-aware, under this structure, of the 'lowliness' of their position, and they may therefore feel less 'job satisfaction'. It also restricts the inclusion of specialist personnel services which would be required by more than one department. A small firm could buy in specialist services such as legal advice and services offered by research agencies. This would be uneconomical for a large firm which could employ its own specialists. For this reason the pure line organisation tends to be less suited to a large firm; and mostly is seen in the small firms just described.

Fig. 3.7 Line organisation in a larger firm

Fig. 3.8 Line and staff organisation

Functional organisation

Frederick W. Taylor, regarded by many as the 'father of' of management theory, is credited with the development of the functional organisational structure. This structure is used in bigger businesses to divide functions such as finance, personnel, sales, and production into various specialist departments. In that sense, it is quite like a pure line organisation within a larger firm (see Figure 3.7), where specialist managers begin to emerge under the direct control of the owner or Managing Director.

But there is a crucial difference. In the functional organisation the individual departments and department managers are expected to communicate and instruct **each other** with respect to the functions they specialise in. The heads of department supervise, control and are responsible for the workers who perform their department's specialist function, but sometimes the head of a particular department may be acting under advise or instruction from another head of department.

In the functional organisation, therefore, work is divided so as to be done exclusively by those who are most specialist at it. The idea is that this should increase the efficiency of production of the company's goods or services.

But in this organisation the span of control is seen to be 'wide', because it is less clear how individual departments' ideas, methods and instructions mesh together to form an overall strategy that is for the good of the whole company. Conflict can come about if different departments disagree over a particular issue. An overly functional organisation is one where the Managing Director is not effectively managing the departments **as a group**, in order to achieve the company's overall goals. These difficulties with the functional-organisation structure have led to the now widely used 'line-and-staff' organisational structure.

Line-and-staff organisation

The line-and-staff organisation is a mixture of the line organisation and the functional organisation, and is common to many big international companies today.

The policies and overall aims of the organisation at the top management level are enacted as they would be in a line organisation. For example, the Managing Director may have many more regular and focused 'line' meetings with all the heads of departments, in order to develop an overall company strategy and to check that this strategy is on course. It is then expected that individual departments will be clearer as to how best to work with each other in enacting the top management's strategy for the company.

Therefore, the conflicts that might come about in a purely functional organisation are avoided. There is clear 'line' leadership from the top, which then allows the specialisms of individual departments to mesh together more effectively, creating the true efficiency that is the benefit of functional organisations.

BUSINESS ORGANISATION

Fig. 3.9 Functional organisation

In the most advanced form of line-and-staff organisation, managers even go so far as to give individual employees within their departments great autonomy over their daily work, requiring only that the employees report to them at the end of mini 'projects' they have been working on. This type of relationship is based on a great deal of trust, and is thought by many management theorists to get the best out of individual employees, who are expected to be motivated by the respect and freedoms they have been given.

Committee organisation

The committee organisation is based on the management principle of grouping specialists in committees to advise the executive and to assist it in developing policies and procedures. Some committees have authority to make recommendations to supervisors (**upward communication**), others are formed purely to receive information (**downward communication**), and some undertake management functions such as **policy making**. Some will be permanent working groups whilst others will be 'ad hoc' — set up to examine a particular problem and dissolved once they have achieved their goal.

Committees invariably slow up the decision-making process, but they improve morale by allowing employees to participate in it. The combined judgement of several specialists in similar or diverse areas promotes sound decisions.

Informal organisation

Some groups have an influence on an organisation, but their actions are not necessarily directed by interests of the business. Workers tend to form into informal groups based on their interests or skills. For example, a group of workers might get together to organise a social function. The reason for this grouping is not intended to benefit the organisation, although it may well have a good influence on morale, something in the firm's interest. In another example, workers might group together to express an adverse opinion about a new development the firm wants to undertake.

It is important for management to recognise the way in which informal groups work if they are to minimise the damage they can cause, or maximise the benefits to be gained by utilising such groups wherever possible.

Organisation charts

Organisation charts are illustrations which show the formal structure of an organisation. The chart shows the different positions in the business and indicates what is done by each part, or shows the links between various parts of the organisation.

The size of a business will obviously influence the structure and complexity of the chart. There are a variety of ways of presenting organisation charts. The method shown in figure 3.7 is a vertical organisation chart. This is the most popular, but there are others. For example, a pyramid organisation chart is shown in figure 3.3, and others in figures 3.12 and 3.13.

Fig. 3.10 Committee organisation

Fig. 3.11 A horizontal organisation chart

37

BUSINESS ORGANISATION

3.4 Small and large businesses

The internal structure of a firm is influenced by its size. The small business is organised fairly simply, whereas the larger company has a more complex structure and more divisions.

Small businesses

Small businesses cannot easily be divided into departments because they do not have the people or floor space to organise in this way. Consequently, workers in small firms tend to specialise less and they are required to have a wider range of skills and a broader knowledge of the way that the business is organised. This is because the workers are required to be able to carry out a wider variety of tasks, whereas in a large organisation they would have more opportunity to specialise in a particular activity. However, the variety of the work in a small organisation is considered to be an advantage by some workers.

Fig. 3.13 A circular organisation chart

Fig. 3.14 Company structure. A large business can be divided into separate departments, each with its own manager and internal structure

38

Large businesses

Large businesses are generally private or public companies, which are dealt with in Chapter 4. These types of organisation are owned by shareholders. The shareholders elect a board of directors to decide the general policies that the firm will follow. The board of directors will appoint a managing director to supervise the day-to-day operations of the business, and to ensure that the policies decided by the board of directors are carried out. A company secretary is also appointed to deal with legal matters such as contracts of employment, product guarantees and government legislation.

Business growth

As a business grows, it usually generates **economies of scale**. This means that as the business's size increases, its unit costs fall: the cost of each item the business sells is reduced because unit costs are more widely spread. Thus, it is cheaper to produce goods or services on a larger scale.

Internal economies of scale occur as a result of various factors within the business, and these factors are related to its size. For example, a larger business can afford to buy and use more expensive equipment (e.g. computers and robotics), and these reduce operational costs. Other internal economies of scale include being able to employ specialist workers, being able to buy in bulk, and finding it easier to raise finance and borrow money.

External economies of scale refer to the benefits gained by all the businesses in a particular industry. Sometimes, for example, businesses with similar interests locate in a particular area. This can benefit all such related businesses because other supporting businesses (e.g. those providing support services) will also locate in the region, making access to them easier. Similarly, skilled labour will move into the area to the benefit of all the businesses. In addition, such businesses may cooperate to create joint research facilities which again benefit them all.

Increased share of the market
When a business is becoming more successful it will be obtaining an increased share of the market, and it will be achieving this increase at the expense of its competitors. In order to satisfy the increased numbers of customers, it will have to expand the business to meet the increased demand it is creating.

Securing sources of supply
When a business has to rely on others to supply it with materials or services, it can be at a disadvantage. For example, if the supplier receives a better offer from other buyers, they may bargain for a better price. Similarly, when a supplier is finding that demand for its goods or services is particularly good, they will be more choosy who they will supply them to. A business may become large enough through expansion to create its own sources of supply and avoid having to rely too much on other businesses. For example, a manufacturer of canned food may expand into farming, thus becoming its own supplier (backward integration).

Securing outlets
Growth can enable a business to create its own outlets for its products. For example, a shoe manufacturer could expand to set up its own retail shops or mail order company.

Business growth and organisational structure

As a business grows in size it has various effects on the organisational structure. For example, whilst the growing company can employ more people, this can have implications for the organisational structure. It affects the chain of command and span of control examined earlier in this chapter. The possible problems this could create will influence the type of organisational structure the business will choose.

3.5 Management information systems (MIS)

What is MIS?

MIS is a modern concept that is rooted in **information technology** and **information systems**. A management information system is enhanced with computer technology and telecommunications technology. MIS can be said to be the development and use of effective information systems in organisations to support decision-making by management. Because of its link to the computer, the systems concept of **input-process-output** is an integral part of management information systems. Storage and retrieval complement input-process-output and thus makes the MIS more 'user friendly'.

The aim of a management information system is to provide accurate and timely information whenever and wherever it is needed in an organisation. This is to facilitate the decision-making process.

The major functions of an MIS include systems planning, organising, designing, overseeing and monitoring. The MIS team plans the system, organises the system to facilitate the day-to-day operations, designs the system to meet the needs of the organisation, oversees the total MIS system and monitors MIS centres within the organisation.

Characteristics of an MIS

Management information systems have the following main characteristics:

- *Provide reports* These are mainly standardised reports such as sales, financial and other reports as stipulated and required by organisations. They are regular recurring reports which are presented in summary form.
- *Static structure* The structure of an MIS is relatively static, mainly because the reports needed by organisations are standardised, and require limited change from week to week or month to month.
- *Stable technology* The MIS technology is stable. Procedures and methods may change mainly due to the updating of the system, but the basic technology remains the same.

Types of management information systems

1 **Transaction processing systems.** These are in common use today in supermarkets, stores, petrol stations and other similar sales outlets to handle **point-of-sale** transactions. Additionally, the processing of orders, especially those that are received electronically, is greatly enhanced by the transaction processing system. The automatic teller machine is part of the transactions processing system. Quick response of the system, reliability of the system, and stability of the technology are not just a few features of the systems, but also major requirements of the system.

2 **Decision-making support system.** This is a support system to enhance decision-making in organisations. This system operates in a less structured MIS environment. Therefore, in terms of its characteristics, it responds to ad hoc instructions since varied needs are to be satisfied, is more flexible and adaptable, and thus requires more facilities than the standard MIS system.

3 **Office automation system.** This system is designed to support office communication systems. It features a multi-media system that facilitates data processing, text editing, graphics, illustrations, voice and video communications for teleconferencing. Additionally, the system is structured and standardised. It requires flexible, adaptable and stable technology.

Office automation system applications include electronic mail, electronic bulletin boards, voice mail, image processing collaborative document processing and video-conferencing. A major requirement is a network system — local area network (LAN) to facilitate its operations.

4 **Executive support system.** This system supports management decision-making. Senior executives who need to make decisions on a regular basis utilise this system. The major characteristics are: high-level, aggregated and standardised information and data in areas such as sales and finance, among other types of reports that support decision-making. Often data must be taken from different sources in order to generate the required report. Important to this system, as is the case with other systems, is timeliness and accuracy of the data and information provided by the system.

Benefits of MIS to organisations

A number of benefits are obtained from a management information system. These include the following:

- It enhances communication and decision-making in organisations.
- It provides a good data base which enhances the timeliness and accuracy of information.
- It can contribute to the improvement of productivity since the 'turn round time' on tasks can be lessened considerably, providing of course, that persons are trained to use the system.
- It reduces the cost of labour since routine tasks can be carried out by a computer, thus requiring less labour-intensive inputs into production and services.
- It assists in the development of organisation policies.

Departments within an organisation benefit from the following:

- Standardised procedures in carrying out various tasks, or completing various assignments.
- Saving of space.
- Reduction in the cost of technology, thus funds from budget allocation can be used for other tasks.
- Improvement in the monitoring and maintenance tasks.
- Provision of staff training and updating.

BUSINESS ORGANISATION

Accounts
Records all payments in and out of the firm. It is particularly concerned with incoming and outgoing invoices, and maintaining the firm's money flow. Payment of wages is frequently included in the responsibilities of this department. The modern accounts department has an extensive data processing system backed up by computers.

Sales
To plan and organise the selling of goods or services offered by the firm. This department is one of the most essential because without it other departments would not be needed. Sales representatives provide an important link between the company and potential customers.

Legal
Most legal matters are dealt with by the company secretary, although a very large organisation might have a legal department. The department's activities include legal matters such as contracts, guarantees, insurance, compensation, etc.

Advertising
May be a separate department or it can be incorporated into the sales department. The aim of this department is to make potential customers aware of the goods or services the company offers and to encourage custom. Smaller firms may employ the services of an advertising agency to carry out this work for them.

Purchasing
The purchasing or buying department is responsible for all items bought by the firm. It obtains quotations from suppliers and issues orders, ensuring delivery is made on time. It also checks that prices, quality and quantity delivered correspond with the quotation and order. This department also deals with 'requisitions' which are written requests for supplies from other departments in the firm.

Transport
May operate the company's own fleet of vehicles, or alternatively it organises other forms of transport using agencies outside the firm. The function of this department is to arrange for delivery of goods to customers on time, in good condition, at home or overseas, and by the most economical method and route applicable.

Administration
Many firms have a general office concerned with co-ordinating the activities of the various departments of the firm. The administration department may include back-up facilities such as centralised filing, typing pool, mail room, reprographics and data processing. The administration department is frequently closely related to the managing director.

Production
Where the company is involved in production of some commodity, a production department may be used to co-ordinate the work of the factory unit. 'Progress chasers' may be employed to ensure that delivery schedules are adhered to, and 'quality controllers' can be used to maintain production standards and investigate complaints or deal with goods returned as faulty.

Personnel/Human Resources
Concerned with finding the right person for vacant jobs, dismissing unsuitable workers, dealing with resignations and providing references. It is involved directly in any induction training or staff training school the company operates. It maintains personal records of all employees and is involved in the welfare and happiness of all personnel.

Fig. 3.15   The departments of a large company

3.6 THINGS TO DO

This section contains a variety of exercises to help you create revision notes, to test your understanding and to prepare you for examinations.

Search and find

Write out the question and the answer by referring back through the text to form revision notes.

1. What is the main aim of a business?
2. How do the four functional areas of a business help it achieve its general aim?
3. Why is management an important aspect of a business?
4. Briefly describe the responsibilities of management.
5. Why do managers have more responsibilities than their subordinates?
6. Give at least three examples of the responsibilities you think a manager has to the government and society.
7. In what ways does management meet its responsibilities?
8. Describe the main functions of management.
9. Why is it important for a manager to have an understanding of group dynamics?
10. Explain the difference between informal groups and formal groups.
11. Why is it important that a firm's objectives are clearly understood by its employees?
12. Why is it that wage levels are limited in the extent to which they can be relied on to encourage people to work hard and effectively?
13. Why is it difficult to define the qualities needed to lead others?
14. List in your order of priority ten qualities you would look for in a potential manager of a medium-sized manufacturing company.
15. Briefly describe each of the four styles of leadership.
16. Why is communication an important factor in management?
17. 'Effective management requires a two-way flow of communication.' Explain this statement.
18. Why are there so many variations in the span of control?
19. How does chain of command differ from span of control?
20. Describe the four types of formal organisational structure.
21. Produce simple diagrams to illustrate the four types of organisation charts shown in this chapter.
22. Make an outline comparison between the organisational structure of a small business and that of a large business.
23. How does the function of a managing director differ from that of other directors?
24. Describe the functions of six departments in a large company.
25. Briefly describe the benefits of business growth.
26. Give two examples each of internal and external economies of scale.
27. Why does business growth affect organisational structure?
28. Define the term 'management information system'.
29. Give examples of the application of MIS.
30. How can MIS benefit an organisation?

What do you know?

Write out the complete sentence and the missing word, which can be chosen from the list at the end of the questions.

1. A major aim of a business is to make a . . . . . for the owners.
2. The broad function of production is to satisfy human . . . . . .
3. . . . . . is required to form a business and to fund its operations.
4. The . . . . . function of a business aims to promote sales of a company's products or services.
5. The . . . . . function of a business is to provide employment.
6. A greater degree of responsibility lies with the . . . . . of an organisation.
7. The managers of a business will organise and . . . . . the work of others.
8. There is an effective . . . . . to the number of workers a manager can supervise efficiently.
9. . . . . . groups have usually come together voluntarily.
10. . . . . . groups are usually created for a specific purpose.

Choose the missing words from the following:

formal	wants	marketing	personnel
finance	limit	co-ordinate	managers
profit	informal		

BUSINESS ORGANISATION

Multiple choice

Select the appropriate answer, a, b, c or d.

1. Which of the following members of a *large* company has overall responsibility for the day-to-day running of a business?
   a) chairperson of the board
   b) managing director
   c) company secretary
   d) sales manager

2. Which of the following is in direct control of a company's sales representatives?
   a) accounts manager
   b) personnel manager
   c) marketing manager
   d) chief buyer

3. Which of the following would not be a function of an accounts department?
   a) progress chasing
   b) invoicing
   c) payment of wages
   d) sending out statements

4. Which one of the following would not be a function under the direct control of the production manager?
   a) quality control
   b) progress chasing
   c) advertising
   d) workshop safety

5. Another name for the owners of a limited company is:
   a) personnel
   b) managers
   c) accountants
   d) shareholders

6. In which of the following four basic styles of leadership does the leader have absolute authority?
   a) democratic
   b) charismatic
   c) free-rein
   d) autocratic

7. Which one of the following managers is directly involved in primary production?
   a) bank manager
   b) factory manager
   c) farm manager
   d) office manager

8. Which of the following is used by management as a direct form of communication?
   a) meeting
   b) telephone
   c) memorandum
   d) intercom

9. In a firm, the manager with overall responsibility for staff training is the:
   a) marketing manager
   b) sales manager
   c) personnel manager
   d) chief buyer

10. Which of the following is the odd one out?
    a) transport manager
    b) legal secretary
    c) freight clerk
    d) delivery truck driver

Key words

Find out the business-related meaning of each of the following words. Write a separate sentence for each word to show your understanding.

prototypes   prospective   superiors
subordinates   supervising   motivate
complexity   objective   authority
delegation

Structured questions

1. Look at the illustration of a company organisation structure (figure 3.14) and answer the following questions.
   a) Which of the labels in the diagram refers to the owners of the business? (1)
   b) Only one of the labels in the diagram is an elected position. Name the elected position. (1)
   c) Which of the departments in the diagram would be responsible for issuing contracts of employment? State two other functions of this department. (3)
   d) Name the department that would carry out the following work and state the manager who would be responsible for the work of the department:
      (i) planning routes for company delivery trucks
      (ii) interviewing prospective employees
      (iii) sending out invoices. (6)
   e) Describe the work of three workers from the following list:
      (i) progress chaser
      (ii) wages clerk
      (iii) sales representative
      (iv) goods inwards clerk
      (v) quality controller. (9)

2. a) Name the department likely to be responsible for:
      (i) carrying out market research (1)
      (ii) ordering new stock. (1)
   b) Name the personnel likely to be responsible for:
      (i) deciding main company policy (1)
      (ii) preparation of a balance sheet. (1)
   c) Why is a company's transport department particularly important both to its sales department and to its factory? (4)

43

d) Rose Petal is the Production Manager of a medium-sized manufacturing company. She recently carried out a study of the way her department operates, with a view to identifying areas for improvement. Her main findings were:
- There is *insufficient delegation of decisions*.
- The supervisors in the factory workshops have *too wide a span of control*.

(i) Explain the statements in italic. (4)
(ii) How might Rose Petal's company be affected by these problems and what might she do to improve the situation? (8)

3 a) Why is management necessary, particularly in a large organisation? (2)

b) In what way would you say that management differs from leadership? (4)

c) The following list includes management personnel, other workers and documents associated with their work. Copy out the headings, and place each under the appropriate heading (the italicised items have already been put under their correct headings).

Management personnel	Other workers	Documents
sales manager	representative	quotation

personnel manager, legal clerk
quotation, requisition
transport manager, *representative*
chief buyer, welfare officer
delivery note, chief accountant
routeing clerk, guarantee
sales manager, order clerk
pay advice, company secretary
wages clerk, staff records (4)

d) Describe the work of each of the following business occupations:
(i) company secretary
(ii) welfare officer
(iii) routeing clerk
(iv) personnel manager
(v) representative (10)

Research assignments

1 Carry out an investigation into two local companies, one large and one small. Compare the advantages and disadvantages of their forms of internal organisation.

2 Give a detailed description of the functions of four departments of a large company you have access to and show how any one of them is dependent upon the other three.

3 Make a diagramatic 'map' of the organisational structures of a small and a medium-sized local firm with which you are familiar. Comment on the differences observed.

4 What evidence can you find of the existence of MIS in businesses? Does the size of the business have any relevance?

Chapter 4
TYPES OF BUSINESS

4.1 Private and public enterprise

In most Caribbean countries we say there is a mixed economy, because some businesses are privately owned and others are owned by the state.

The private businesses or enterprises are those that are owned by private individuals (that is, by *some* of the public). The main types of private enterprise are:

- sole proprietors
- partnerships
- private limited companies
- public limited companies.

There are also some organisations in which a special relationship can be observed. These businesses include co-operatives, holding companies and building societies. These special relationships are examined later in this chapter.

Public enterprise refers to industries and services owned by the state (that is, by *all* of the public) and run by either local or central government, for example, public utilities.

4.2 Limited liability

People who invest in businesses (**entrepreneurs**) face many risks. The obvious risk they face is that the firm does not make a **profit**, or, even worse, that it makes a **loss**. The most serious risk is that the business may go **bankrupt**, i.e. it cannot pay the money it owes to its creditors. Under such circumstances, if the business has unlimited liability, the owners of the business are not only liable to lose the money they have invested in the firm, but they can also have their personal assets (such as home and car) taken in order to pay off their debts. Although many small businesses have unlimited liability, larger companies would not be able to attract sufficient investors if everyone faced the risk of unlimited liability. For this reason, the status of limited liability exists.

The status of limited liability allows people to invest in a business without having to face the risks of unlimited liability which have already been outlined. When a business has limited liability the investor is only liable to lose the amount of money he or she has put into the business, and his or her private possessions cannot be taken if the firm fails. Thus a limited liability company is said to have a separate corporate identity, an identity all of its own and separate from the identity of the owners of the business. It can sue and be sued in its title name, which must include the word **Limited** (Ltd.) (or PLC if it is a public company).

Fig. 4.1 Business titles set in distinctive styles

4.3 Private ownership

The sole proprietor

This type of business may be operated by the proprietor (owner) alone or may employ several people, but the main feature of it is that it is owned by one person and tends to be a small business. There are many examples of sole proprietorships in the Caribbean.

TYPES OF BUSINESS

Do not fall into the trap of thinking of the sole proprietor only as a retailer. Any business, be it a small factory, window cleaner, removal firm, gardener or decorator, is a sole proprietor if it is owned by one person.

Sole proprietors tend to have only a few employees, and less machinery or capital than larger businesses. They also have less plant and fewer opportunities for economies of scale. Their market tends to be less diversified than larger businesses because their level of operations limits their output.

Figure 4.2 shows the advantages and disadvantages of the sole proprietor.

A small business like mine needs less capital	**but** I have to provide all the capital myself. It can be difficult to get a loan because I'm a bigger risk than a large company
When I make a profit it's all mine	**but** I have unlimited liability if the business goes bankrupt. If I am unable to pay my creditors, they can take everything I own
I'm my own boss, make all my own decisions, and I'm involved with every aspect of the business and all my clients	**but** There is no back-up if I'm unable to work for any reason, such as illness

Fig. 4.2 Sole proprietor advantages and disadvantages

Not surprisingly, the sole proprietor is more likely to fail than any other form of business and is particularly open to pressure from the larger types of business.

Most businesses try to expand in a natural attempt to make the business more stable and to give it greater continuity. One of the ways in which a sole trader may expand is by taking one or more persons into part ownership of the business to form a partnership.

Partnership

The law allows this type of business to have between two and twenty persons as members, although there are exceptions. A bank is not allowed to have more than ten partners, and certain professional firms such as accountants, solicitors and stockbrokers are allowed to have more than twenty partners.

This type of firm solves some of the problems faced by the sole proprietor. For example, because there are more people in a partnership there is more experience and knowledge available when making decisions, and sometimes one or more partners have specialist knowledge, such as accountancy to look after the financial side of the business. The partnership still has, however, some disadvantages.

Like the sole proprietor, the partnership generally has unlimited liability and each partner is fully liable for the debts of the business. By this we mean that should the business go bankrupt, the partners do not necessarily have to face the debts equally. For example, if a two-person business goes bankrupt and one partner has no personal possessions whilst the other has many, the creditors can claim the total debt from the wealthy partner. On the other hand, if both partners have sufficient personal possessions to meet the debts they will make equal contributions.

A **partnership deed** sets out the rights of each partner as to the division of the profits and so on. If such a deed does not exist then it is assumed that the profits or debts of the partnership are shared equally.

A partner may be willing to introduce capital into a business but may not wish to take an active part in the running of the business. Such a person is known as a **sleeping partner**. However, the sleeping partner will still have to meet his or her share of the debts should the business go bankrupt.

It is possible to have a limited partnership, but at least one partner must accept unlimited liability. Consequently, limited partnerships are relatively rare.

Some professional bodies do not allow their members to form limited companies. These include solicitors, doctors and accountants.

Advantages of a partnership

- Easily formed.

- More people to contribute capital than sole proprietor.

- Greater continuity than sole proprietor.

- Expenses and management of business are shared.

Disadvantages of a partnership

- Generally unlimited liability.

- Possible disagreements between partners.

- Each partner is liable for the debts of the business.

- Membership limit of twenty restricts resources of business.

Private limited companies

Any company which is not registered as a public company is a private limited company. This type of company must include the word 'Limited' (or Ltd.) in its title.

A private limited company is allowed to have a minimum of two members (shareholders). There is no upper limit. The capital of the business is divided into shares, but the shares cannot be sold on the Stock Exchange and they cannot be advertised for sale publicly. Therefore, new shareholders must be found privately; hence the term 'private'. The shareholders may or may not take part in the running of the business. If the company makes a profit it pays a 'dividend' on each share.

Some private companies may wish to keep control over the transfer of ownership of their shares. For example, a family concern might wish to ensure that ownership or control remains within the family. The private company may, if it wishes, write a rule into its articles of association requiring its members to offer shares for sale to existing members before attempting to sell them to non-members. Carefully audited accounts have to be kept for annual inspection. This can cause considerable expense.

Public limited companies

Private and public limited liability companies are sometimes called **joint stock companies** because each is an association of people who join together to contribute money to a joint or common stock, which is used in some form of business, and the profit or loss is shared among the contributors.

The public limited company must indicate its public status by including the letters PLC (or plc) in its title.

It takes a minimum of two persons to form a public company, and there is no maximum membership. Such companies are allowed to sell shares to the public. The transfer of share ownership is simple, and therefore the number of owners or shareholders can become very considerable. Consequently, this type of business can raise almost limitless funds.

We have more people to invest capital	**but** We are not allowed to sell shares to the public on the Stock Exchange. This may limit the capital we can raise. We may decide to restrict share transfer which would further limit capital raised
The burden of work and responsibility is shared rather than falling on one person or partnership	**but** It can take a lot longer to reach decisions and take action when many people are involved
Our liability is limited	**but** We must keep audited accounts

Fig. 4.3 Advantages and disadvantages of a private limited company

TYPES OF BUSINESS

Obviously, it would not be practicable for all the shareholders to take part in the running of the business, and therefore the shareholders elect a small committee called a **board of directors** to take decisions on their behalf, and this board elects a **chairman** to regulate their meetings.

Even the board of directors would consist of too many people for them all to take part in the day-to-day running of the business, so they appoint a person to carry out this task, and the appointed person is known as the **managing director**. Private limited liability companies also set up a board of directors, a chairman and a managing director.

Fig. 4.4 **Typical structure of joint stock company**

Look at figure 4.4, a diagram of one possible structure of a joint stock company. The business of this particular company involves the production and sale of goods. You will observe that the diagram indicates the election of the board of directors by the shareholders, and they in turn have elected a chairman and appointed a managing director. It can also be seen that three lines of activity emerge from the position of managing director, leading to the sections of the firm that control administration, finance and purchasing.

The administration department co-ordinates and supervises the activities of other sections of the firm, whose function it is to put into effect the policies determined by the board of directors. The finance and accounts department has a dual role to play. It monitors the debts owed to the firm by its customers and by the firm to its suppliers, and at the same time it closely watches the overall financial status of the company. The purchasing department buys supplies and raw materials to be converted into manufactured goods through the production stages of the firm.

The disposal of the finished products is the responsibility of the sales and marketing departments which may be divided into separate sections to deal with various target markets.

The public company has limited liability, and it obviously enjoys greater continuity than the other forms of business we have examined so far, but it also has several other advantages. As already explained, the public company can sell its shares to the public, and when this has been done, ownership of the shares can easily be transferred to new owners via the market provided by the Stock Exchange. This ease of transfer of share ownership encourages investors to provide capital to businesses, which they would have been reluctant to do were it not so simple to regain at least some of the capital invested.

Fig. 4.5 **Some examples of public companies in the Caribbean**

48

Advantages of public companies

Because they can advertise for capital from the public in the form of shares and debentures, public companies can obtain large quantities of capital and resources which can make them into large, strong business units. This is the main advantage of this type of business.

Their size enables them to enjoy economies of scale (advantages of size) such as:

- being able to purchase supplies in bulk, thus obtaining the most favourable terms, particularly in relation to price
- purchasing equipment which will save labour and expense
- finding it easier to borrow money and obtain credit.

Disadvantages of public companies

The main disadvantage of this type of business unit stems from its size. When a company is large it can become burdened by too much paperwork or *red tape*, employees and shareholders can feel too detached from the day-to-day activities of the business, and decisions made can take too long to be put into practice.

The public company, like the private company, has to send a copy of its audited accounts to the Registrar of Companies and to each of its shareholders. Therefore it is difficult for this type of company to keep its affairs secret.

The fact that shares can easily be transferred can also be a disadvantage to the business, because it allows the possibility of the firm being taken over by another company that has managed to obtain a controlling number of shares.

In addition, the management of large companies can become too impersonal and inflexible. It can also become inefficient and overstaffed, and therefore wasteful of resources.

Forming a limited company

All forms of private business must register with the Registrar of Business Names if they operate a business in a name other than the name of the owner. Even a sole trader, say, John Jones trading as John Jones Enterprises, must register.

When a company is being formed, it must register with the Registrar of Companies. This registration is carried out mainly by the presentation of two completed documents, the Memorandum of Association and the Articles of Association, by the promoters of the company.

Memorandum of Association

This document states the external relationship of the company, that is, its relationship with other organisations.

Fig. 4.6 Forming a limited liability company

The Memorandum of Association consists of six main clauses.

1. *Name clause.* This states the name of the company, for example 'Carter Electrical Engineering Company Ltd.' (The Registrar of Companies will ensure that two companies are not formed bearing the same name.) The memorandum of a public limited company has to state in a separate clause (clause 2) that 'The company is to be a public company'. The public company will indicate its status by the letters PLC at the end of its name whereas the private company will end its title with Limited (Ltd.).

2. *Situation clause.* This states the domicile (home) of the company; only the country where the registered office is situated is needed, for example 'Barbados'. The company can move its registered office within the stated country.

3 *Objects clause.* This states the object for which the company is established, for example 'to undertake the installation of domestic and industrial electrical appliances'.

4 *Liability clause.* This is a straightforward statement that the liability of members is limited by the amount invested in shares in the company.

5 *Capital clause.* This states the amount of capital with which the company is to be registered and the manner in which the capital is divided into shares, for example $200,000 divided into $1 shares.

6 *Association clause.* This is a declaration by the signatories stating that they wish to form the said company and that they are prepared to take up and pay for the number of shares shown on the form beside their names. The minimum number of signatories is two.

Articles of Association

This document outlines the internal relationships of the company, that is, the broad way in which the internal organisation will operate. It must be signed by the same people who sign the Memorandum of Association.

The contents of this document are more flexible than those of the Memorandum of Association, and they can easily be changed by the shareholders. However, any alterations to the Articles of Association must not conflict with the Memorandum of Association. Among other things, the Articles of Association show:

- the rights of shareholders
- the method of election of directors
- the way in which meetings are to be conducted
- the division of profits.

Miscellaneous statements and declarations

In addition to the Memorandum of Association and the Articles of Association, those forming a company must also make the following statements and declarations.

- *Statement of Nominal Capital.* This statement reflects the capital clause of the Memorandum of Association in that it shows the amount of registered capital and the manner of its division into shares.
- *Declaration.* Usually made under oath, through a solicitor, by the company secretary or a director confirming that all the requirements of the Companies Act have been met.
- *List of First Directors.* The names of first directors are listed. The minimum number for a private company is one and for a public company the minimum is two (not to be confused with *membership* minimum of two for a private company).
- *Statement of Consent.* Written by each of the proposed directors confirming that they are willing to act in this capacity.
- *Address of Registered Office.* States the specific registered address of the company (the situation clause of the Memorandum of Association only states the country). Any change in this address must be notified within 28 days of the change.

If the Registrar of Companies is satisfied that all the foregoing have been carried out correctly, he or she will issue a Certificate of Incorporation. A private company can now commence business and a public company can now proceed to raise capital.

Raising capital

The directors of the public company now attempt to raise the capital stated in the capital clause of the Memorandum of Association. This is done by issuing a **prospectus**. A prospectus is a private circular or an advertisement giving a frank outline of what the company hopes to do, and detailing the amount of capital needed in order to begin trading.

When the Registrar of Companies is satisfied that the company has met all the legal requirements, a trading certificate (also called a Certificate of Incorporation, as with a private company) is issued, allowing the company to begin trading.

The foregoing information related to the regulations involved in company registration and operations indicates how government intervention helps to protect shareholders:

- Use of prospectus.
- Objectives clause in Memorandum of Association.
- Annual General Meetings.

The financing of business is looked at in greater detail in Chapters 19 and 20.

4.4 Special business relationships

There are some businesses which, although they fall within the types of business we have already looked at, have some special relationship within their organisation.

Co-operatives

Co-operatives are special types of business organisations. They are incorporated financial institutions or other types of institutions owned and controlled by groups with specific interests, and thus have common goals and objectives. They aim to improve the economic well-being of their members.

The **characteristics** of a co-operative are determined by its type and purpose. There are four basic **types of co-operative**: consumers' co-operatives, marketing co-operatives, workers' co-operatives and producer co-operatives.

Consumer co-operatives are stores which share the net profits of the business among members. Britain was a world leader in the development of co-operatives, with the earliest consumer co-operative established by a group of Rochdale weavers in the UK in 1844. They became known as the 'Rochdale Pioneers'. Some co-operatives have formed their own manufacturing and wholesaling businesses, but they have come under increasing pressure from other chain stores. Only a limited number of consumer co-operatives are found in the Caribbean.

Marketing co-operatives are businesses where several individuals or small businesses combine to sell their goods or services. For example, a group of small farmers may establish a co-operative to sell their produce. They could also co-operate in this way to buy their supplies (e.g. seeds) in bulk, or to combine the use of some equipment. An example of this form of co-operation is the Christiana Potato Growers Co-operative.

Workers' co-operatives are businesses that are owned and run by their own workforces. For example, the crews of a bus company may actually own the company. In such cases the workers are highly motivated because it is in their personal interest to work as effectively and as efficiently as possible. These types of business are sometimes referred to as *people's co-operatives*.

Producers' co-operatives are involved in producing certain products. Farmers in a community may form a producers' **credit union**. They share workloads and often equipment also, take decisions about productive activity, and share profits.

Co-operatives are **financed** by their members. The co-operative sells shares to its members. Members can buy as many shares as they wish, but this does not mean that a member with a large number of shares will have more voting rights than someone with fewer. The democratic principle of 'one person, one vote' applies, that is, one vote to each member.

Shareholders receive a **dividend** if the co-operative makes a profit from its operations. The amount of dividend is related to the number of shares held. In other words, a larger shareholding will receive a greater dividend than a smaller shareholding. Dividends are generally small, since the major goal of a credit union is not to make a profit but to provide a service to its members. Dividends are shared out in proportions determined by the members who vote on the proposals at their annual meeting.

Earnings from a co-operative are not totally consumed in the payment of dividends. Most of these are ploughed back into the co-operatives to finance operational needs identified by the members.

Membership of some co-operatives is open to all members of the public who are of age. However, membership in certain types of co-operatives is restricted to people who have **common goals**. For example, the Teachers' Co-operative Society is open to teachers and not to the public at large; the service is designed specifically for teachers. Similarly, a producers' credit union would only be open to the producers it is established to serve (e.g. farmers).

A co-operative society is **controlled** by its members through the shares they have purchased and the **voting rights** mentioned earlier. The society is **governed** by a general meeting. At the annual meeting, members appoint a committee to deal with the operational activities. Committee members are drawn from the general membership. Some co-operatives employ professionals to manage their affairs.

Members, individually, **contribute** to the **share capital** of the co-operative society by purchasing shares. Additional amounts saved in the co-operative are used to buy shares. From the pool of these additional funds, loans are provided to members.

The **profits** or earnings generated by a co-operative require a fair system of distribution. However, members may do the following:

- Reserve the profits for use in the co-operative.

- Share the profit among members in the portions they have agreed.

- Establish a fund into which profits are kept for the benefit of members.

Advantages of a co-operative society

- Members benefit from the pooling of funds for the purpose of lending to other members.

- Even though the returns on investments are low, members have an opportunity to build the financial base of their co-operative society.

- Members have a say in what goes on in their society.

Disadvantages of a co-operative society

- Because the profit motive is not the major aim of a co-operative society, as is the case in other types of business, they tend to suffer from lack of resources.

- Limited resources reduce opportunities to undertake major economic activities for the benefit of members.

The **Co-operative Credit Union League** is the governing body for local co-operatives and credit unions. The League monitors the activities in co-operative societies. Thus, co-operative bodies are registered with this body. The following are some of the ways in which the League assists co-operatives:

- structure and management of co-operatives
- advertising and promotional activities
- planning and delivery of workshops and seminars
- publication of newsletters
- accounts and audit services
- insurance facilities
- financial services.

The Credit Union League is a member of the Caribbean Confederation of Credit Unions and also the World Confederation of Credit Unions.

Fig. 4.7 Well-known franchises operating in the Caribbean

Franchises

Franchising is another form of co-operation. It is co-operation between a big firm and a sole proprietor. In franchising, a well-known company allows someone to buy the right to use their products or techniques under their trade names. This is a fast-growing sector of the economy. In the Caribbean and many other parts of the world franchising is becoming particularly popular in the **'fast food' trade**.

Franchising offers a 'ready made' business opportunity for those with some capital who are willing to work hard. The potential entrepreneur (**franchisee**) pays to use the name, products or services of the major company (**franchisor**), which receives a lump sum and a share of the profits of the business (sometimes called **royalties**).

The franchisee receives the majority of the profits, but must also meet most of any losses. In addition to allowing use of their name, products, techniques or services, franchisors usually provide an extensive marketing back-up in return for the money they receive.

Fast food giants such as Wimpy, Kentucky Fried Chicken, Popeye's, Pizza Hut and Burger King are particularly well-known in the franchising sector, but the range of franchise activities is much wider than just fast food, and the following are just a few examples of this type of business:

- developing and printing of photographic films
- home tuning of car engines
- drain clearing
- car wash centres
- door-to-door ice cream sales
- bakeries.

Building societies

Building societies are also an example of a special business relationship. They act as intermediaries between 'small' savers who wish to invest funds and people who wish to borrow money to purchase or improve property.

Building societies lend by means of a **mortgage**, which is a long-term loan, often repayable over a period of twenty years or more. Most of the deposits of building societies are lent out in this way, but some of their funds have to be kept to meet demands for cash withdrawals.

It is usual for the deeds of the property purchased by the borrower to be held by the building society until the loan has been repaid. If the borrower defaults on the repayment of the mortgage, the society can sell the property to recover the debt.

Building societies have always competed with the commercial banks to obtain deposits from savers. In recent years they have begun to compete with banks also by offering many of the financial services that have traditionally only been provided by the banks.

Holding companies

For a variety of reasons, businesses sometimes form a temporary or a permanent combination to achieve a certain aim. For example, the combination of three or four businesses might usefully bring together several separate processes into one production or marketing unit.

This kind of partnership of companies is usually incorporated as a holding company. Each member company retains its legal entity but overall control lies with the holding company.

4.5 Business growth

Reasons for growth

Most of the large firms that exist today started as a small business and have grown. Many of today's small firms are tomorrow's big businesses. Businesses grow and expand for a variety of reasons.

- They are successful, and expansion is necessary to meet the demand for their product.
- They wish to make a greater level of profit.
- They are trying to gain economies of scale.
- They wish to reduce competition and become market leaders, maybe even gain a monopoly.
- They wish to secure their sources of supply or outlets for their products.

Expansion will only take place if the business can benefit and make extra profits.

Methods of growth

Basically firms can grow in four ways.

- By working existing plant and machinery harder, pushing it towards full capacity.
- By extending existing capacity or moving to a new, bigger site.
- By a **merger** with another company. A merger is where two or more companies voluntarily join together to form a single organisation. A **vertical merger** refers to two or more companies at *different* stages of the production process joining together, e.g. a bakery chain might buy a wheat farm. A **horizontal merger** is where two or more companies at the *same* stage of production join together, e.g. one grocery store joining with another grocery store.
- By a **takeover**. A takeover is different from a merger in that the company being taken over has not agreed to the two companies joining together.

Where a firm has acquired a number of other companies which retain their original names, it is known as a **holding company** (described earlier).

Fig. 4.8 How many times have I got to tell you? I'm not interested in a merger.

Directions of growth

Businesses need not expand simply by doing more of what they are already doing. Depending on the motives for expansion they can grow or integrate in a number of directions.

Horizontal integration. This is when a business extends its current operations, doing more of what it already does. It expands at the same level in the chain of production (e.g. a car manufacturer expands and builds another plant to produce more cars).

Chain integration is expansion to produce the same product, but for a different market (e.g. a car manufacturer producing more cars to sell in a new overseas market).

Lateral integration is expansion into a similar area of production, using similar techniques and processes but making something different (e.g. a car manufacturer expands to produce tractors or trucks).

Vertical integration. Vertical integration may be 'backwards' or 'forwards', or in both directions.

- Expansion backwards along the chain of distribution occurs when a business begins to produce the components and raw materials the business needs (e.g. a car manufacturer begins to produce tyres or windscreens for use in its cars).

- Expansion forwards involves extending along the chain of production, taking on the selling of the products (e.g. a car manufacturer opens up its own car showrooms).

Conglomerate integration is expansion into an area that has nothing to do with the current operations of the business (e.g. a car manufacturer begins to produce furniture).

Fig. 4.9 Integration

Multinationals

It is not unusual for expansion to take place across international borders. In other words, companies sited in different countries may combine to form a multinational company. The multinational is an enterprise that has subsidiaries or branches in more than one country.

The main objective of a multinational is to expand its operations into other profitable areas. It will do this in order to gain as large a share of the world market as possible, and to use its expertise and skills to the benefit of all the companies in the group.

The decision-making process is controlled by the parent company and implemented through its foreign subsidiaries. These subsidiary companies are either firms that have been set up by the parent company or they are foreign businesses which have been taken over. The parent company may own the subsidiaries completely, it may have a controlling interest (own majority of the shares), or it may just own a large and influential number of shares in the subsidiary.

Multinationals can bring **benefits to an economy**. Many of these benefits are gained from the multinational's wide experience across several countries.

- Reduced unemployment
- Introduction of new technology
- Improved training in latest skills
- Additional work for other companies.

The **disadvantages** of multinationals to an economy are that they:

- may import overseas personnel rather than recruit locally.
- may want to use working practices of another country, possibly resulting in industrial relations problems.
- may take their profits out of the country.
- can be difficult for governments to control because of their size and power.

Monopoly

Business in most democratic societies is based on the concept of free competition. Firms do not have the right to compete unfairly with rivals.

A possible result of the expansion of organisations is that they may end up in a monopolistic position. A monopoly exists when a company has so much control over the supply of a commodity or service that it is able to also control the price. In law, a monopoly exists when a company controls 25% or more of the total supply of a product. Whilst such a situation is beneficial to the firm, it can be against the interests of the consumer if the company abuses its power.

4.6 Government-owned businesses

State corporations

In Caribbean countries there are a few state-owned organisations, commonly referred to as **state corporations**. They are formed, out of necessity, by an Act of Parliament, mainly because the services required are not usually undertaken by private investors, even though everyone benefits in the long run. They have limited liability and, by an Act of Parliament, they can be dissolved. State-owned corporations are legal entities.

Types of state-owned corporations include public utility organisations such as the telephone, telegraphic and telecommunications, light and power, transportation, public broadcasting agencies, bureaux of standards, scientific research and environmental organisations.

State-owned corporations fall under the umbrella of the Central Government system, and thus under a Ministry of Government which is managed by an elected government minister. The government appoints a board of directors that oversees the day-to-day operations of the corporation. They are free to make their own business decisions, but these must be done within the context of the legal framework by which they are guided.

State-owned corporations do not exist to make profits as such, but to provide a vital service to the community or the country as a whole.

Advantages of state corporations
- The service or good is provided at a cheaper price.
- They provide employment for many persons and thus contribute to the economic life of the country.
- The community receives services which would otherwise not be provided, or would be provided at a higher cost to the consumer.

Disadvantages of state corporations
- A state-owned corporation usually provides a single, vital service to the country. Therefore, these organisations have a monopoly on the services provided.
- Because of the lack of competition, the organisations do not always provide the high quality of service that is desirable. Consumers sometimes have to accept mediocre service because they have no alternative choice.
- State-owned corporations often run into financial difficulties, because of the lack of entrepreneurial thrust of profit-making. Governments often have to inject large amounts of money into these organisations to keep them operational.
- Because of the inputs from governments into these organisations, political inputs have to be taken into consideration when decisions are being made. The political overtures interfere with the overall management of state-owned corporations.

Fig. 4.10 **State enterprises are run by central government**

Statutory bodies

A statutory body is an organisation formed by the government for a particular purpose. The organisation is a type of state-owned corporation, and thus has similar formation procedures, objectives, management structure, and advantages and disadvantages.

Nationalised industries

These are government-owned industries which are established to provide a particular service or to provide a particular good. Sometimes, too, the state takes over a private sector industry in order to ensure that the community is not deprived of an essential good or service. Often the industry taken over is a fledgling industry.

The government owns most, if not all of the shares in a nationalised industry. Usually, a chief executive officer is appointed by the state. This person reports to the appropriate minister of government under whose portfolio the organisation falls. The government usually begins by injecting into the organisation the required funds and other resources needed. However, the organisation is required to work towards economic viability in the long term.

Public and private sector motives

The main aim of firms in the private sector is to make a profit, which is the reward to the owners for taking the risk of investing money in the business. Traditionally, public sector organisations have not been profit-motivated to the same extent as private sector enterprises. Many people argue that some goods and services are essential and should be provided by the State either at a subsidised price or without charge. Others argue that the public sector is inefficient because it does not have the same profit motive as the private sector.

In recent years public sector organisations have been forced to adopt many of the profit-related features of successful private sector businesses operating in the same field of business as them. They have also been obliged to acknowledge political and public pressure to become more profit-conscious.

Regulatory practices governing establishment of a business

The regulatory practices governing the establishment of businesses refers to the rules and regulations by which persons who wish to establish a business should be guided.

Certain business operations must be duly registered with the **Registrar of Companies** and in some cases with government departments. A **certificate of registration** is issued, which must be appropriately displayed in the place of the business.

Different groups of business operators need different types of treatment.

- Professionals such as doctors, lawyers, accountants, pharmacists, and some engineers register with their professional associations. The governments permit such bodies to play a major role in overseeing the professional conduct of their members.

- Trades persons, such as electricians, by the very nature of their trades, have to be duly licensed. Electricians, for example, must sit and pass qualifying examinations before they receive their licence to practise unsupervised.

- Food handlers are required to obtain the food handlers' permits. These persons are required to take a medical examination to satisfy the authorities that they are in good health, especially related to situations in which there could be a serious spread of disease through the handling of food.

4.7 The role of government agencies

Caribbean governments operate within two broad structures. These are the **central government structure** and the **local government structure**. The central government structure is designed to reflect the higher levels of administration within the government, while the local government structure is designed to reflect the municipal or community affairs section of government.

Government departments

Because of the nature of some of the tasks needed to be carried out by governments, specialised areas such as departments, divisions, and agencies have to be established to handle them. For example, The Services Commission Division is responsible for matters related to staffing in the Civil Service as a whole, even though individual ministries have their personnel departments.

Another important department is the Department of Statistics. This department handles statistics for the whole country. All government offices need to submit the required statistics to this department so that the government can undertake informed planning.

Central government

Within this structure are the government ministries and departments and agencies to which the ministers of government are assigned. Figure 4.11 shows the basic structure of a ministry.

```
              Ministry of Education
                      |
        ┌─────────────┼─────────────┐
   School Services  Personnel   School Maintenance
    Department     Department      Department
```

Fig. 4.11

Each ministry has a permanent secretary who is a senior civil servant who handles the administration of the ministry as well as some departments, but who works closely with the elected and assigned minister of government. The permanent secretary is a servant of the people of the country and, therefore, is required to deliver a service for the benefit of the people.

A team of officers and other administrative staff are employed by government ministries to carry out the operational and management activities. The typical basic structure showing their position in the hierarchy can be seen in figure 4.12.

```
         Minister of Government
                  |
         Permanent Secretary
                  |
        ┌─────────┼─────────┐
     Officer   Officer   Officer
```

Fig. 4.12

The major **goal** of a ministry is to carry out the function that it has been assigned. This is done mainly through the implementation of the policies of government that are laid down for that ministry. It is the government ministry that is responsible for the implementation of government policies. Often, an **advisory committee**, a **task force**, or **consultants** may be appointed to assist with specific assignments or projects being undertaken by a ministry.

The **funding** of costs associated with the operations of a ministry are provided through **budget allocations** approved by the finance ministry. Sometimes projects are funded by **funding agencies**.

From the foregoing it can be seen that government departments are not established to make profits, but to offer services in the area in which it has been assigned, for example, health, education, works and construction, social welfare and finance.

Advantages of ministries and government departments

- They organise the implementation of government policies.
- They monitor activities in society to ensure they are within the legal framework.
- They assist the government to meet the needs of people.
- They make it possible to break down the major task of managing the country into manageable portions that can be assigned to departments, sections, divisions and individuals.

Disadvantages of government departments

- Government ministries and departments are subjected to change of government, even before a government's term of office has expired. Consequently, many policies, projects, assignments and other tasks are abandoned before they come to fruition.
- Government ministries and departments are constrained by resources and, therefore, so many well-deserving projects are designed but not implemented because of the limited resource allocation situation.
- Often, government ministries and departments lack the expertise necessary for their general and specific functioning because of the low salaries and wages that governments can afford to offer. This affects the quality of service that can be provided.

The local government or municipal authority

Local government is involved with **community affairs**. Municipality is concerned with local self-government. Thus, the people who live in towns, districts, parishes and cities have a say in how community activities are carried out, and even participate in the debate at the community level on how legislations are drafted and implemented. These functions are carried out by councillors and citizens invited to sit on committees.

Local government is part of the **public enterprise system** (see earlier). Members of the community with **voting rights** (those who are of voting age and are duly registered) elect their representatives through the local government election process.

The municipality is governed by a **Council**. The Council consists of all the people who were successfully voted into office in **Local Government Elections**; those elected become known as **Councillors**. From among the councillors, a **Mayor** and **Deputy Mayor** are elected. The councillors and the relevant central government ministers participate in the selection of people to hold these positions.

The Mayor chairs the **Parish Council meetings** and represents the community at various civic and other functions. The most important job of the Mayor is to present the people's concerns to the appropriate authorities. The **Ministry of Local Government**, and thus the minister in charge of the ministry, are directly associated with the municipal authority.

The council is assigned a **secretary**. The secretary provides services to the meetings as well as handling much of the administrative duties of the Council Office.

The councillors represent their communities at meetings. They also see to their overall maintenance. Since there are usually large numbers of councillors to effectively handle the various community activities, **committees** are established to undertake specific tasks. These committees consist of the people who operate at the 'grass-roots' of council activity and aim to ensure that the community's needs are clearly identified, that cases are well represented at council level, and that appropriate steps are taken, where possible, to deal with each case, and thus satisfy the identified needs of the community in the long run.

The municipal authority has **responsibility** for road maintenance, fire service, public health, garbage collection and disposal, poor relief, civic amenities such as parks and gardens, public cemeteries, the cleaning of water tables, gullies, culverts and the provision of water for domestic and other purposes.

Major **funding** for the municipal authorities comes from budgetary allocations channelled through the Ministry of Local Government. Other sources of funds include **grants** from the government for projects, receipts from **rates** and **taxes** levied on the public for certain services, for example, the use of public parking facilities, recreational facilities such as beaches, zoos, museums, the use of public markets for vending, and the provision of services which attract government **stamp duty**. The sums generated can be used as backing for loans needed by the municipality to finance its activities.

Advantages of municipal authorities

- Members of communities have a say in the decision-making process.
- Members of the community can contribute to policy decisions.
- Government policies are not just imposed on the community.
- Local needs are addressed at local levels.

Disadvantages of municipal authorities

- Resources are limited, therefore much of what needs to be done for the betterment of a community cannot be carried out.
- Central government is the main provider of funds to municipal authorities. Because central governments are elected for five year periods, many longer term objectives cannot be fully realised. Many projects have to be aborted after a change of central government, because the new government may not wish to pursue the policies of the out-going government. Often a new administration will decide they want resources channelled into other areas of need.

4.8 THINGS TO DO

This section contains a variety of exercises to help you create revision notes, to test your understanding and to prepare you for examinations.

Search and find

Write out the question and the answer by referring back through the text to form revision notes.

1. Why is it said that in most Caribbean countries there is a 'mixed economy'?
2. How does private enterprise differ from public enterprise?
3. Explain the meaning of limited liability.
4. Why is the sole proprietor the most common type of business? What are the advantages and disadvantages of this type of business?
5. What advantages would a sole proprietor gain by going into partnership?
6. Why are limited partnerships relatively rare?
7. Make a detailed comparison between private and public limited companies. Include a list of the advantages and

disadvantages of each of these forms of business ownership.

8   Give a description of the process followed in forming a limited company.

9   Give a brief description of the various forms that co-operatives may take.

10 Why can a franchise be said to be a 'ready made business'?

11 Why are building societies an example of a special business relationship?

12 What is a holding company?

13 What are the reasons for business growth?

14 Explain the difference between a merger and a takeover.

15 Describe the different forms of integration.

16 What is a multinational company?

17 Why are monopolies generally not in the public interest?

18 What is a state corporation? How does it basically differ from businesses in the 'private sector'?

19 What are the arguments for and against state ownership of business?

20 How do the motives of private sector businesses differ from those in the public sector?

21 In what basic ways would you say that the responsibilities of local government differ from those of central government?

22 What, if any, similarities can you see between central or local government and private sector businesses?

7   A ..... co-operative is owned and run by its own workforce.

8   In ....., a well-known company allows someone the right to use their products or techniques.

9   ..... integration refers to expansion into an area that has nothing to do with the current operations of the business.

10 ..... enterprise refers to industries and services owned and operated by government.

Choose the missing word from the following:

conglomerate	fail	franchising	private
external	mixed	public	worker
internal	deed		

Multiple choice

Select the appropriate answer, a, b, c or d.

1   Which of the following is likely to be a suitable form of business organisation for a group of solicitors?
    a) a co-operative
    b) a partnership
    c) a holding company
    d) a public company

2   A sleeping partner is one who:
    a) takes no active part in running the business
    b) has no liability for the debts of the firm
    c) is not included within a deed of partnership
    d) is a lazy member of the business

3   The owners of a public limited company are:
    a) the government
    b) the shareholders
    c) the local council
    d) the local community

What do you know?

Write out the complete sentence and insert the missing word, which can be chosen from the list at the end of the test.

1   In most Caribbean countries there is a ..... economy.

2   The sole proprietor business is more likely to ..... than any other type of business.

3   The partnership ..... sets out the rights of each partner.

4   The ..... company must include the word Limited or Ltd. in its title.

5   The Memorandum of Association states the ..... relationship of a company.

6   The Articles of Association outline the ..... relationship of a company.

4   The type of limited liability business which may restrict the right of share transfer is called:
    a) a co-operative
    b) a public corporation
    c) a public company
    d) a private company

5   Which of the following is not included in the Articles of Association when a company is being formed?
    a) the rights of shareholders
    b) whether the company is private or public
    c) methods of election of directors
    d) division of profits

6   Which of the following is the odd one out?
    a) Jones & Partners Ltd.
    b) R. Penny Ltd.

TYPES OF BUSINESS

c) Tare & Sons
d) J. Salesworthy PLC

7 Which of the following is an example of a marketing co-operative?
   a) a group of farmers co-operating to sell their produce
   b) a furniture factory where all the workers are owners
   c) a chain of shops sharing their profits with members
   d) a bus company owned by its employees

8 Limited liability means:
   a) the business cannot make a loss
   b) the firm is either a private or a public company
   c) shareholders are only liable for the money they have invested
   d) all employees are insured against accident

9 In law, a monopoly exists when a company controls what percentage of the total supply of a product?
   a) 25%
   b) 50%
   c) 75%
   d) 100%

10 The best definition of a multinational business is:
   a) a company selling many different products
   b) a business that has many foreign customers
   c) there are a chain of businesses in the home country
   d) one that has subsidiaries in other countries

Key words

Find out the business-related meaning of each of the following words and write a separate sentence for each word to show your understanding.

subsidiary   subsidise   royalties
continuity   proprietor   enterprise
bankrupt   divided   audited
assets

Structured questions

1 Refer to figure 4.6 on page 49. This shows the procedure followed in forming a private limited company and a public limited company. Answer these questions, which are related to the illustration.

   a) Many businesses, when in formation, have to register with the Registrar of Business Names. Why do they have to do this? (2)

   b) Explain the function of each of the following documents used in the formation of a limited company, including examples of the kind of information each contains:
      (i) Memorandum of Association (4)
      (ii) Articles of Association (4)

   c) What effect does the Certificate of Incorporation have on the identity of a business? (3)

   d) Why does a public company issue a prospectus, but a private company does not do so? (4)

   e) State three ways in which a public limited company can differ from a private limited company. (3)

—ESC—

ELECTRONICS SERVICES COMPANY LIMITED

St. John's, Antigua
Telephone: 694609

Directors: Al Simon, Priscilla Douglas (Managing), Mark Kirwan.

Fig. 4.13 Letter heading

---

2 Figure 4.13 shows the letter heading of a limited company. Answer the following questions related to it.

   a) How can you tell from the letter heading whether this is a private or a public company? (1)

   b) Who is the managing director of this company? (1)

   c) How does the function of a managing director differ from that of the other directors? (2)

   d) What do you understand by it being said that this company has 'limited liability'? (4)

   e) Give three advantages and three disadvantages of this type of business organisation. (6)

   f) If the firm that uses the letter heading were to expand, which type of organisation would it change to? What would be the advantages and disadvantages of making such a change? (6)

3 Examine the diagram of a company's structure (figure 4.14) and answer these questions related to it.

   a) There are two main forms of business organisation to which this diagram could be said to apply. What are they? (2)

   b) Name the groups of people in the labels missing from this diagram. (2)

   c) Explain the function of the two groups of people you have identified in part (b). (4)

TYPES OF BUSINESS

Fig. 4.14 Company structure

d) 'The chairperson is higher up in the company hierarchy, but has less day-to-day involvement in the running of the business than the managing director.' Explain this statement. (4)

e) Briefly but clearly explain the function of four positions in the above diagram which have not already been dealt with in this question. One of those chosen should be the company secretary. (8)

4 'Franchising is one of the fastest-growing sectors of the economy; over 20% of retail sales are accounted for by this form of trading, and the trend is growing each year.'

a) Give a brief description of what you understand by franchising. (2)

b) Franchising is particularly evident in the 'fast food' trade. What do you understand by 'fast food'? (2)

c) Name three major franchising companies. (3)

d) Give three examples (other than in the food trade) of services which are frequently provided by franchise companies. (3)

e) What are the benefits of franchise arrangements from the point of view of:
   (i) the franchisor (2)
   (ii) the franchisee? (2)

f) Give a clear explanation of the difference in the organisation of a normal sole proprietor business and that of a business with a franchise arrangement. Include mention of differences with regard to capital formation and the distribution of profits. (6)

5 a) What is a sole proprietor business? (2)

b) State two advantages of this type of business when compared with larger organisations. (2)

c) Two of the disadvantages of this type of business are that it has 'unlimited liability' and that it can suffer from 'lack of continuity'. Explain these two terms. (4)

d) Clearly explain two other disadvantages this type of business faces. (4)

e) How far would change from sole proprietor to partnership status help to solve the problems stated in parts (c) and (d) of this question? (8)

6 Diane Evans holds a majority shareholding in Easy Electronics plc, a company that owns a large chain of shops that sell a wide range of household electrical goods. Hightec Electrical plc produces a range of hairdryers etc. Hightec have been trying to take over Easy Electronics for some time. They have been openly buying ordinary shares on the Stock Exchange over the last year, but they have not managed to obtain sufficient shares in order to make a bid for the company. They have now offered to buy Diane Evans' shares at a price above the current market price.

a) What do the letters plc stand for? (1)

b) What implications do the letters plc have for companies? (2)

c) What is meant by the wording 'Diane Evans holds a majority shareholding'? (2)

d) What do you understand by the term 'take over' as used here? (2)

e) State at least three ways in which the takeover could affect the workers of Easy Electronics if it were to take place. (3)

f) What factors might Diane Evans take into account before agreeing to sell her shares? (4)

g) Suggest reasons why Hightec would want to take over Easy Electronics. (6)

```
   Mayor
     |
Deputy Mayor
     |
  Secretary
     |
  Councillors
     |
  Committees
```

Fig. 4.15 The basic structure of a parish council

7 The flow diagram of the basic structure of a parish council in figure 4.15 shows the various personnel involved in its operation. Answer the question related to the diagram.

a) What is a council? (1)

b) How do councillors obtain their positions? (2)

c) How does the work of a mayor differ from that of other councillors? (2)

d) What is the purpose of a committee? Give an example of a task that a committee might carry out. (3)

e) Describe two contrasting examples of the responsibilities of a parish council. (4)

f) In what ways does a parish council meet the needs of the local community? (4)

g) Why can the activities of a parish council be said to be just as important as those of central government? (4)

Research assignments

1 What is a nationalised industry and how does it differ from a business in private ownership? What are the arguments for privatisation of state-owned businesses? Which of these arguments do you support? What evidence is there to say your view is right?

2 Explain why a sole proprietor might decide to become a private limited company. How would such a change be financed? Give descriptive examples of local businesses that have changed in this way.

3 What is a limited company? Why has the limited type of company become the major form of business in existence today? What evidence exists that limited companies are the 'major form of business' in your locality?

4 Mrs Latter is the sole proprietor of a small factory producing soft toys. She is considering expanding her business by taking in some partners.

a) Describe as fully as possible the advantages and the disadvantages of expanding the business in this way.

b) Put forward a case supporting the view that Mrs Latter might also consider changing her business into a private limited company.

c) Investigate some local businesses that have changed their status in some way. How could Mrs Latter learn from the experiences of the businesses you have investigated?

5 Locate a well-established local entrepreneur who started his or her business from 'scratch'. What factors can you identify as making important contributions to its apparent success?

6 Make a diagrammatic 'map' of the organisation structure of a small and a medium-sized local firm with which you are familiar. Comment on the differences observed.

7 Select two competing businesses situated within your locality and show:

a) how they compete

b) why they are both able to survive in spite of the competition they are part of.

8 Make a survey of all the businesses within a clearly defined area in your locality and identify the legal structure (legal identity) of each. Present the information collected in some appropriate diagrammatic form (with a 'key' if necessary). To what extent are the firms investigated reliant upon the local transport network?

Chapter 5
RECRUITMENT, SELECTION AND TRAINING

5.1 Recruiting employees

Publicising vacancies

When a firm wishes to attract applications for a vacant position there are a variety of avenues open to it:

- school/college careers advisers
- job centres run by the government's training agency
- employment agencies run by private firms
- local careers officers
- newspaper advertisements
- friends and relatives.

Advertisements are the most common way of publicising a job vacancy and inviting applications. These advertisements are important to the firm; they must therefore be carefully formulated so that they attract the right sort of applicant. They must clearly state what is required, otherwise valuable time will be wasted investigating the suitability of applicants. They are also important to job hunters because they help to ensure that they only apply for the kind of job they really want.

To the firm:		To the applicant:
Job title	**OFFICE JUNIOR**	
Salary offered	**$120,000 pa**	Is the pay suitable?
Main characteristics of the work	To check invoices and calculate insurance and freight costs.	Will you enjoy the work?
Qualities required	Experience preferred but school leaver with Business Studies background considered.	Have you the qualities required?
Minimum qualifications	Neat handwriting, aptitude for figure work and minimum CXC in English and Mathematics required.	Do you have the right qualifications?
Fringe benefits offered	Subsidised meals Flexible hours Sports and social club Pleasant offices near to bus route	Are there any fringe benefits?
How applications should be made	Applications in writing to Mrs. B Singh, The Personnel Officer, Astor Publications Ltd., Emery Street, Christ Church, Barbados	What form of application is required?
To whom applications should be made		Is the job within convenient reach?

Fig. 5.1 Job advertisements must be clearly worded and carefully read by applicants

RECRUITMENT, SELECTION AND TRAINING

```
Telephone 268 6949                           4 Hill Walk
                                             ANCHOVY
Mr. P. Daley                                 St. James
Daley Designs plc
16 Market Street
Montego Bay
St. James


Dear Mr. Daley,                              12 May 199_

I refer to your advertisement in the 'Evening Post' inviting applications
for the position of general sales clerk, and I would like to apply for
the vacancy.

I am 16 years of age and I leave school at the end of this month.
I have completed examinations in the following subjects, for which I
am awaiting results: English, Mathematics, Business Studies,
Technology, Computer Studies and Art and Design.

I enjoy sport and I have represented the school in both hockey and
basketball. My other main interest is reading, particularly historical
novels.

For the past two years I have worked as an assistant in a local
hardware store, and I believe that this experience could make me a
suitable applicant for the vacancy you have available.

I hope you find my application of interest and I would be pleased to
attend an interview at your convenience. References are available
from my school and from my part-time job if you require me to
obtain them.

Yours sincerely

Kirsty Davies

KIRSTY DAVIES
```

Annotations:
- Your home address – note home town in capitals
- Name and address of the person you are writing to
- Date
- Say which job you are applying for
- Qualifications or examinations taken
- Personal interests
- Relevant past experience and why you think you are suitable
- Print your name under your signature

Fig. 5.2   Letters of application for employment should be carefully written, following the correct format

Letters of application

Prospective applicants should read the advertisement carefully. Not only will it give important information about the job and the firm, but it may also offer clues about what should be included in the letter of application.

In some cases it may be acceptable to type or word process a letter, in others the advertisement may state that the application should be in *first hand*, in which case the letter should be handwritten, preferably on plain paper. It is sensible to make a rough draft of the proposed letter before writing it out in an acceptable form. If the instructions do not tell you to write it, type it.

Curriculum vitae

Job advertisements today frequently ask for a curriculum vitae (cv) from applicants. A cv is a brief history of the applicant, including school attended, qualifications, relevant experience, etc. This should be typed to accompany the letter of application, thus making it possible to make the letter shorter and more concise. Sometimes names, addresses and telephone numbers of the **referees** are included at the end of the cv.

CURRICULUM VITAE	June Simon
ADDRESS	21 Court Street St. John's, Antigua
DATE OF BIRTH	12 October 1975
SEX	Female
PLACE OF BIRTH	St. John's
NATIONALITY	Antiguan
EDUCATION	Princess Margaret High School St. John's, Antigua 1987 to 1992
CXC	English language Mathematics French Biology History Business studies
INTERESTS	Reading Outdoor sports Music
WORK EXPERIENCE	Saturday job in family general store

Fig. 5.3   Example of a curriculum vitae

Application form

An application form is a standard printed form sent out by firms for applicants to fill out, providing specific information to support their application. The form may be sent to the applicant for completion prior to the interview, or it may have to be completed under supervision at the interview. There are two main reasons why firms use an application form as part of the recruitment and selection process. Firstly, it acts as a check on personal details, qualifications and experience, and it ensures that key information is included in the minimum space. Secondly, it allows selection panel members to make comparisons between candidates easily.

References

Most employers will require applicants to provide the names of persons (**referees**) willing to attest the character of the candidate. Written declarations (**testimonials**) from reliable persons testifying to the good character of the applicant may also be required. Referees should be contacted by the applicant for permission before their names are used on the cv.

5.2 The personnel department

The personnel department (sometimes called The human resources department) is concerned with finding the right person for each job, and if necessary giving him or her induction training. This department also deals with resignations, providing testimonials, and dismissing unsuitable workers. It maintains personal records of all employees and is involved in the welfare and happiness of all personnel.

Applications for employment are received and considered by the personnel department. This department is headed by the personnel manager.

Short list of applicants

From the many applications received in response to the advertisement, the personnel department lists a few of the most promising applicants and invites them to attend an interview. For this reason, the written application is very important if the applicant is to reach the next stage on the way to getting the job.

Interviews

Short-listed applicants for employment are invariably interviewed (usually in the personnel department) before any job offer is made. The aim of the interview is not only to assess the suitability of the candidate for the vacant position, but also to give the applicant the opportunity to seek further information about the job. During the interview the applicant may be required to complete an **aptitude test** designed to assess his or her suitability for the job available.

The interview is crucial for the applicant because it is at this time that the interviewer assesses the candidate's appearance, ability to communicate and general manner. Consequently, it is important to be thoroughly prepared for the interview. The following are tips for people who are called for interview.

Preparation for the interview
- Do a little homework about the job for which you have applied.
- Use your common sense about your appearance, and dress carefully.
- Take the letter inviting you for interview.
- Remember the name of the person you have to see.
- Know exactly where the interview will take place.
- Plan the route to get there.
- Arrive promptly for the interview.

During the interview
- Only sit down when invited to.
- Do not smoke.
- Try to be relaxed and confident, but not flippant.
- Concentrate fully on the interviewer.
- Be prepared to answer questions.
- Try to ask some sensible questions when you are invited to do so.
- Do not be over-familiar.

Questions to be prepared for
- Why do you want the job?
- What qualities do you have to offer?
- What are your ambitions?
- What do you do in your spare time?
- What do you read?

Questions you could ask
- What does the job involve?
- What hours are involved?
- What is the salary?
- What are the opportunities for promotion?
- What are the holiday arrangements?
- What fringe benefits are available?

5.3 Staff orientation and training

All new members of staff need to become acquainted with other members of the firm, as well as becoming familiar with the organisation of the business. Many firms organise an induction or orientation programme to introduce new employees to their workplace and colleagues. The induction programme will often be managed by the personnel department.

Staff training is often an important part of the introduction of staff to a new job. This will aim to help new employees quickly to become a useful part of the organisation by familiarising them with any new skills they need.

Staff training does not only apply to new employees. Sometimes existing staff will be transferred to other departments or other jobs which may require training in new skills. A large firm may operate its own internal training school, or alternatively staff may be encouraged to attend college courses to learn new skills.

5.4 Welfare of employees

Welfare refers to the concern for people's physical well-being. Social facilities, lighting and cooling or air-conditioning, hygiene and canteen services are all examples of things that contribute to the welfare of employees. These all come within the functions of the personnel department.

The personnel department may be responsible for the operation of the company's sports and social club, organising activities and events which encourage employees to mix socially. A member of this department may also have the responsibility of visiting employees who are sick, or those who have retired.

The firm may have its own **in-house newspaper** or magazine which is used to keep the workers up to date with events in which the company is involved, as well as providing a means of general communication.

Most firms recognise that good **working conditions** not only keep the employees happy, but also help to make them more productive and efficient. For this reason, firms try to provide good working conditions, but there are four Acts which are particularly concerned with staff welfare. These are dealt with, together with other aspects of working conditions, in the next chapter.

1. Factories Act
2. Contract of Employment Act
3. Health and Safety at Work Act
4. Employment Act

Find out when these Acts were passed in your island, and what are their main aims.

5.5 Staff records

The letter of application for employment, the curriculum vitae or the completed application form, together with the results of any aptitude test taken when the new employee joins the firm, form the basis of the employee's record. This information is held by the employer on a confidential file, usually in the personnel department.

Over the years the record is periodically updated with other information. For example, people in supervisory positions will occasionally write progress reports on their subordinates. These reports and other records of the employee's progress in the firm will include the following:

- punctuality
- health

- academic progress
- promotions and salary increases
- suitability for further promotion
- misdemeanours.

From the foregoing it should be obvious that the contents of personnel records are **highly confidential**. For this reason, people who work in the personnel department are expected to be discreet. In addition, the security of personnel records is of the utmost importance.

5.6 Dismissal and redundancy

Dismissal

In Chapter 6, reference is made to the **Contract of Employment Act**, which requires all employees to be given details of the terms of their employment. The Contract of Employment includes the length of **notice** (length of time as notification of ceasing employment) to be given by the employer and the employee. When a worker wishes to take up new employment elsewhere he or she is required to give a period of notice which allows the employer to look for a new employee. Similarly, if the employer wishes to dismiss the worker, a period of notice is generally observed, although there are exceptions to this, such as when the employee has been guilty of a serious misdemeanour. In such circumstances it is usual that certain steps are followed:

- oral warning
- written warning
- suspension
- dismissal.

Obviously, the employee may get instant dismissal for breaking important rules of the organisation, for example for stealing.

Today workers are protected against unfair dismissal by the **Employment Protection Act**, which requires an employer to show that there are good reasons for terminating the employment. An employee who feels that he or she has been unfairly dismissed can complain to his or her union or to the appropriate section of the labour ministry. If, upon investigation, it is found that the employer acted unfairly or unreasonably, an order of reinstatement of the employee will be issued to the employer. If the employer refuses to comply, then the matter will be referred to the **Industrial Disputes Tribunal** which will make the final decision.

Grievance procedure

An employee has a **grievance** in the following situations.

- An existing employer/employee agreement has been broken.
- A labour law has been violated by the employer.
- The employer has acted in an unfair manner.
- The health or safety of the employee has been put at risk.

The first point of contact for the employee is the **work supervisor**, who may be willing and able to offer a remedy for the grievance. In any case, the supervisor is likely to be the source of contact between the aggrieved person and the firm's management.

Should representation through the supervisor be inappropriate or unsatisfactory, the worker will contact his or her union representative, often another employee of the company. This person will be familiar with the rights of the worker and will act on his or her behalf, or direct the grievance to the union for advice and guidance. The union may even decide that the employee does not have a real grievance, and it is part of its function to advise the worker of this.

Redundancy

Redundancy refers to a situation when an employee loses his or her job because it no longer exists. This may occur because the business has been forced to cease trading, or because the firm no longer has the capacity to employ the same number of workers.

When an employee loses his or her job as a result of redundancy, he or she needs financial help to make the transition to new employment.

The **Redundancy Payments Act** requires employers to make a lump sum payment to employees being made redundant (as long as they have served for a minimum period of time). The amount of redundancy compensation depends upon the age, length of service and pay of the employee.

5.7 THINGS TO DO

This section contains a variety of exercises to help you create revision notes, to test your understanding and to prepare you for examinations.

Search and find

Write out the question and the answer by referring back through the text to form revision notes.

1. List five sources of information about job vacancies.
2. Why are job advertisements important to both the firm and the applicant?
3. List four specific pieces of information that the job applicant can obtain from the advertisement.
4. What does it mean when an advertisement states that applications must be in 'first hand'?
5. Make a list of six suggestions you would give someone to help him or her to write a letter of application for a job.
6. What is a curriculum vitae? What information does it contain?
7. In what way does an application form differ from a cv?
8. What is the function of 'referees' and 'testimonials' in relation to applications for employment?
9. Give a brief summary of the main functions of the personnel department of a firm.
10. What is a short list?
11. What is the main purpose of the interview?
12. Why might a job applicant be required to complete an aptitude test?
13. In what way can someone usefully prepare for a job interview?
14. List six points the candidate should observe during the interview.
15. Give four examples of questions that might be asked of an applicant at the interview.
16. Suggest four questions the job applicant could ask when invited to do so.
17. Why would a firm be interested in the welfare of its employees?
18. In what way might a firm show its care for the welfare of its employees?
19. How would the personnel department in particular be involved in the welfare of employees?
20. Briefly describe the kind of information likely to be found in personnel records. Why is the security and confidentiality of personnel records important?
21. What regulations exist to protect an employee from unfair dismissal?
22. Explain the purpose of redundancy payments.

What do you know?

Write out the complete sentence and insert the missing word, which can be chosen from the list at the end of the questions.

1. If job applicants are told to write in 'first hand', the letter should be . . . . .
2. A CV is a brief . . . . . of the applicant for a job.
3. The . . . . . department is concerned with finding the right person for a vacant job.
4. Short-listed applicants for employment are usually . . . . . before any job offer is made.
5. All new members of staff need to be . . . . . with other members of the firm.
6. A staff . . . . . programme introduces new employees to their workplace and colleagues.
7. Sometimes staff being transferred to other departments will require training in new . . . . .
8. A firm may have its own in-house . . . . . which is used to keep workers up to date with the company's activities.
9. Personnel records are kept . . . . . by the personnel department.
10. Today, workers are protected against . . . . . dismissal.

Choose the missing words from the following:

history	skills	personnel	unfair
handwritten	newspaper	acquainted	confidential
interviewed	orientation		

Multiple choice

Select the appropriate answer, a, b, c or d.

1. A short list of job applicants consists of those who:
   a) nearly got the job
   b) can begin work at short notice
   c) sent a letter that was too short
   d) are to be invited for an interview

RECRUITMENT, SELECTION AND TRAINING

2 The purpose of recruiting is to:
   a) select existing workers for promotion
   b) find the right person for a vacant job
   c) show people how to do their new job
   d) interview prospective employees

3 Which of the following is not a purpose of a job interview?
   a) to test the candidate's intelligence
   b) to assess the candidate's appearance
   c) to assess the candidate's suitability for the job
   d) to give the candidate the opportunity to ask questions

4 The purpose of an induction programme is to:
   a) help new employees become familiar with the firm
   b) introduce a new product to the public
   c) allow employees to choose their hours of work
   d) publicise job vacancies

5 Which of the following is not a normal function of a personnel department?
   a) dealing with resignations
   b) providing testimonials
   c) dismissing unsuitable workers
   d) payment of salaries

6 Which of the following is the least suitable method of applying for a job?
   a) by letter
   b) by completing an application form
   c) by telephone
   d) by sending a curriculum vitae

7 Testimonials are:
   a) examination results
   b) statements from reliable persons
   c) a brief history of job applicants
   d) people providing references

8 What is the name given to people who provide testimonials?
   a) referees
   b) directors
   c) applicants
   d) colleagues

9 The main purpose of an aptitude test is to:
   a) test someone's intelligence
   b) establish how truthful a person is
   c) assess a person's suitability for the job
   d) check how creative someone is

10 If an advertisement for a job says that applications should be in 'first hand', this means that applications should:
   a) be delivered by hand
   b) be typewritten
   c) be in a sealed envelope
   d) be handwritten

Key words

Find out the business-related meaning of each of the following words. Write a separate sentence for each word to show your understanding.

applicant   qualifications   references
induction   welfare   aptitude
notice   dismissal   redundancy
compensation

Structured questions

1 Refer to the advertisement for an office junior (figure 5.1), and answer these questions.
   a) Name the company that has advertised this vacant position. (1)
   b) To whom in particular should applications be sent? (1)
   c) What qualities are required of applicants for this job? (2)
   d) What will be the yearly salary to be paid and, assuming that wages are paid monthly, what would be the gross monthly income? (2)
   e) Why do you think that the job advertised requires an 'aptitude for figure work'? (2)
   f) Explain what the four 'fringe benefits' listed involve. (4)
   g) Write a suitable letter of application for this position using the correct method of letter layout. (8)

2 You have left school and are looking for employment.
   a) Give two reasons why you should read a job advertisement carefully. (2)
   b) List three tips that you would suggest people might take into account when writing letters of job application. (3)
   c) Advertisements for jobs frequently ask applicants to provide a curriculum vitae (cv). Give three examples of information that would be included in a cv. (3)
   d) Briefly describe four ways you and other school leavers could find employment, and list the various people who could help you. (4)
   e) Give an outline of the different sorts of induction and training you might receive, either within a business or through some organisation outside of your employment. (8)

3   Read again the letter of application in figure 5.2, and answer these questions.

   a) Name the person who is applying for employment and the name of the company they are approaching. (1)

   b) The job being applied for is that of General Sales Clerk. What kind of duties could this type of occupation include? (2)

   c) Why is a prospective employer interested in an applicant's personal interests? (3)

   d) If you were considering this application, what aspects of past experience would you consider important? Give reasons for your choice. (4)

   e) Letters of application are often used to form a 'short list'. What is the purpose of a short list and what factors influence its formulation? (4)

   f) List *three* questions that might be asked at an interview by the *interviewer*, and *three* that the *interviewee* might ask. (6)

4 a) State two of the main functions of a personnel department. (2)

   b) Briefly describe one form that staff training might take within a firm. (2)

   c) State two methods that a company could use to keep its employees informed of events that the business is involved in. (2)

   d) A firm received 40 letters of application in response to a job advertisement placed in the local press. List four points the firm might take into account to decide a short list of people to be invited for interview. (4)

   e) Why is the interview crucial for both the job applicant and the employer? (4)

   f) Most firms consider that staff welfare is important. Briefly describe three ways that a firm might be involved in the welfare of its employees. (6)

Research assignments

1   Your friend has been short-listed for a job that she has applied for. Explain the advice you would give your friend to help her to be successful at the interview. In what ways might your advice vary depending on the type of job involved?

2   Fizzy Pop Ltd. is a manufacturer of soft drinks, and you are employed in the public relations department. The company is to have a visit from a number of young people from the local school who are to do three weeks of work experience prior to leaving school. You have been asked to talk to them about various aspects of business work. Write notes for your talk about four different occupations in business, including an explanation of the qualities needed for each of the positions you have chosen.

3   Collect at least five advertisements for *varied* kinds of job in *different* types of business organisation. What differences do you think exist in the way each business recruits employees, and how far do you think these differences are reflected in the advertisements you have collected?

4   Give a detailed description of the various ways that businesses recruit employees. How do these differ in relation to the size of the firm? Include personally researched evidence to support your answer.

5 a) Describe what you would consider would be a suitable orientation programme for your school/college for:
       i) new students
       ii) new teaching staff.

   b) Present some evidence from new students and teaching staff showing how some of them view your ideas.

Chapter 6
MOTIVATION OF EMPLOYEES

6.1 Job satisfaction

People spend a large percentage of their life at work. Therefore, it is important that they get some satisfaction from their job. Not all jobs can give satisfaction, and people have different ideas of what constitutes a good job. For some people pay is the most important factor; others will have some other priority. Often it is a combination of many factors which makes a job satisfying. The following are just some of these factors. What others would you include? What would be your own order of priority?

- Pay and opportunity for wage increases
- Promotion prospects
- Working hours and times of attendance
- Holiday arrangements
- Job security
- Friendship and relationships between employees
- Conditions in which the work is carried out
- The nature of the duties to be performed.

Some of these factors are within the influence of the employee, but the employer has by far the greater effect on working conditions. However, there are laws which ensure that working conditions do not fall below an agreed minimum standard. Some of these laws are examined later in this chapter.

Abraham Maslow, a psychologist, formulated a '**hierarchy of needs**' in the 1940s which are still relevant today. A hierarchy means that the more important things are at the top, and less important things are at the bottom. Maslow identified the following five levels in the hierarchy of needs, with number five being the most important and ultimate goal:

1 **Basic** Physiological requirements for survival; in the work situation these include food, drink and a tolerable level of comfort, e.g. ventilation, rest, shelter and, of course, payment.

2 **Safety** A safe working environment incorporating protection against danger, including job security.

3 **Social** Friendship and companionship of fellow employees, a sense of belonging and being part of a team.

4 **Self-esteem** Recognition of a job well done; status and recognition of achievement, promotion and possibly independence.

5 **Self-fulfilment** Achieving personal ambitions; reaching full potential; complete job satisfaction.

At any given moment in time, one of these needs is dominant, and the needs in this group have to be met in order for the individual to be able to move onto the next level in the hierarchy. In the work environment, employees must be provided with the opportunity to fulfill these needs.

6.2 Wages

Wage differentials

Wages are the reward paid for labour. Not surprisingly, wages are considered more important to most people than many other things in life. This is because the level of earnings has such a considerable effect on the quality of life. The amount of income received influences the type of house and furnishings one can have, the quality of car owned, and where and for how long holidays are taken. The poorly paid person cannot hope to compete with the highly paid person with regard to standard of living and leisure facilities. But for a variety of reasons, some people are better paid than others, and it is important to understand why this is so.

The key to the reason for **wage differentials** is demand and supply. For the purpose of comparison, we can take the wages of doctors and bus drivers as examples of where differences in wage levels exist. Both of these occupations are important to the community, but the doctor's wage is considerably higher than that of a bus driver. In other words, the cost of the doctor's services is far higher than the cost of the bus driver's services. Alternatively, we could say that the supply of doctors is smaller than the supply of bus drivers, forcing up the price of the doctor's services.

The supply of doctors is smaller than that of bus drivers for the following reasons. These same reasons can also be applied to many other examples of occupations where wage differences exist.

- Being a doctor requires a high degree of skill and academic ability.
- The medical training period is too long for many people.
- There is a degree of risk involved in medicine (e.g. infection).
- Medical work requires a special aptitude.

What other reasons can you think of for wage differentials?

Rates of pay

There are several ways by which wages may be calculated, and sometimes a wage payment may combine more than one of these.

Flat rate
A set rate of pay per week or month based on a standard number of hours. Many workers are paid by this system, but it does not always provide incentive to give extra time or effort.

Time rate
The worker is paid a set amount for each hour worked. The worker is paid **overtime** at a higher rate of pay for additional hours worked.

Piece rate
This is not as common today as it was in manufacturing in the past. A payment is made for each good quality item produced to encourage the production worker to give maximum effort.

Bonus
Paid to employees as a share of additional profits gained by the employer due to increased effort or efficiency of the work group.

Commission
A payment made additional to a flat or time rate as a percentage of the value of sales or business promoted.

Deductions from pay

Gross pay is the total amount earned by the employee before any deductions have been made.

Net pay is the amount received by the employee after any deductions have been taken away. This figure is particularly important because it represents the actual income the worker receives.

Statutory deductions
These are compulsory deductions enforced by law:

- *Income tax*: deducted from each wage payment through the PAYE (Pay As You Earn) system.
- *National insurance*: weekly contributions to the state welfare scheme (for health services etc.), taken from each payment of wages.

What other types of statutory deductions are you aware of that you could add to this list?

Voluntary deductions
Wage earners can decide whether or not they want further deductions to be taken automatically from their wages. Examples of such voluntary deductions include the following.

- Union membership fees.
- Contribution to company social club fund.
- Payments to private pension schemes.
- Insurance premiums.
- Private medical scheme payments.
- Credit union savings payments.

Payment of wages/salaries

A payroll department is responsible for the payment of wages. People employed in this department need an aptitude for working with figures, and are often required to be familiar with the use of a computer.

When an employee is paid at a time rate, he or she will have a time card (clock card) which is kept in a rack near a time clock. As the employee arrives and leaves work he or she 'clocks' on and off by inserting the card into the time clock. The times printed on to the time card are used by the payroll department to establish how much the employee should be paid.

Whether payment of wages is made by cash, cheque or credit transfer, the employee receives a pay advice. This is usually a slip of paper that is filled in by the payroll department, often by computer, so that the employees can see how their net pay has been calculated. The pay advice will contain the following information:

- employee's name and work number
- tax code
- national insurance number
- gross pay

MOTIVATION OF EMPLOYEES

PAY ADVICE		
CHARTRITE LIMITED		— Employer
1 APR 99	167	— Works number (identification number allotted to each employee)
B STONE		— Employee
Tax	33⅓%	— Indicates level of tax-free allowances
Contribution letter	B	
N.I. No.	YK868347A	— National insurance number
Pay and allowances		
Basic Pay	420.94	
Total	**420.94**	— Earnings before deductions (A)
Deductions (R = Refund)		
Income Tax	83.40	— Tax on this instalment of wages
Nat. Insurance	11.58	— Contribution to state welfare scheme
PENSION	27.89	
UNION	3.20	— Voluntary deductions
Total	**126.07**	— Total deductions (B)
Balances and totals to date		— Total income tax paid in the current year on the PAYE system
Income Tax	166.80	
Nat. Insurance	23.16	— Total National Insurance contributions paid in the current year
Taxable Gross	786.10	— Total gross wages earned to date
Net Pay	**294.87**	— Actual amount received (C) A−B = C

Fig. 6.1 **Pay advice**

- bonus, commission, overtime
- compulsory deductions
- voluntary deductions
- net pay.

Much of the payroll department's work of calculating wages and producing pay advices can be assigned to computers. When the worker clocks in and out, the time data can be recorded on the time card by punched holes or magnetic ink characters. The data can be read by computer and used to calculate net pay automatically; then the pay advice is printed out.

Fringe benefits

Some firms offer 'invisible' additions to the wages of their employees. These are called **fringe benefits** or **perks**. The following are examples of the kinds of benefits given by employers in addition to wages.

- Free or subsidised meals
- Company car
- Free membership of private health schemes
- Low interest-rate loans for house or car purchase, etc
- Reduced prices for company products or services
- Assistance with expenses in removal to a new abode
- Help with payment of private education fees.

6.3 Working conditions

Although wages are important in motivating people to work hard and effectively, we have recognised in this chapter that other factors, such as job satisfaction, are also important. Obviously, what our job involves affects the way we respond to work, and the content of a job is summarised in a job description and a job specification. The number of hours that we are required to work and the times of the day we have to do the hours also influences how we feel about our job.

Most employers recognise that working conditions are important in motivating people to work hard, but there are certain laws and rules that have been established to ensure that minimum standards of comfort and safety are adhered to by employers.

```
JOB DESCRIPTION – Karl James

Clerk/Typist ──────────────── Job Title

Entry Grade I EL $20,000 p.a. ── Grade/Salary

8.00 am – 4.00 pm ──────────── Hours of Employment

Marketing ───────────────── Department To Work In

Sales Manager ───────────── Responsible To

1. Open, date stamp, and
   distribute incoming mail.
2. Prepare outgoing mail.
3. Copy-type letters,
   memoranda and other        Functions, Duties
   work as required.          and Responsibilities
4. Classify, file and
   retrieve documents.
5. Deal with telephone enquiries.
6. Act as relief receptionist.

Induction training under
supervison of personnel
department. Salary review    Supervision and
after 6 months. Review of job  Assessment
description after 12 months.   Procedures
```

Fig. 6.2 Job description

The nature of the job

Job description
This is a broad general statement which may include:

- job title
- details of duties and responsibilities
- place or department where work is to be carried out
- special features or skills and qualifications related to the job
- supervision and assessment arrangements.

Job specification
This is a detailed statement drawn up from the job description, and it contains references to the qualities required of candidates for the job. It includes:

- responsibilities involved
- qualifications and past experience needed
- skills of initiative or judgment necessary
- physical fitness required
- personal characteristics considered important.

Contract of Employment Act
This act requires employers to give employees particulars of their terms of employment in the form of a contract, which must either be given to the employee or kept where they have access to it. The contract includes:

- job title
- hours of work
- holiday arrangements
- rate of pay and how frequently paid
- period of notice to be given by either side
- person to contact in event of a grievance
- legal rights such as belonging (or not belonging) to a union.

Hours of employment

One of the most important terms of employment is the hours of work. This refers not only to the total number of hours to be worked, but also to what times of the day or night the hours have to be worked.

Although some people do 'shift work', most people work fixed hours. Consequently, most people are travelling to and from work at similar times. This results in traffic jams and congestion on public transport, and discomfort for travellers. It also means that public transport is not being used economically.

Not everyone finds it convenient to work the same hours as others. Workers sometimes need periods of time when they are not required to be at work. In addition, many businesses have periods of the day when not all members of staff are required to be present. At other busy 'core' times, everyone is needed at the same time.

Flexible working time (FWT)

Flexitime or **flexible working time** (FWT) is a system of arranging working hours so that at **peak** or **core** times all members of staff are at work, but their other hours are flexible, as long as they complete the required total number of hours per week.

The working day of the firm is defined in three ways:

1 *Band time*: this is the total period of time the business operates, for example, 8.00 am to 6.00 pm.

2 *Core time*: this is the period of time when all members of the firm are expected to be at work.

3 *Flexible time:* this is the period outside the core time when employees can choose whether they work or not, as long as they complete the total number of weekly hours they are paid for.

BAND TIME
8.30 am to 5.30 pm

Core time 11.00 am to 2.00 pm
Flexible time 8.30 am to 11.00 am
Flexible time 2.00 pm to 5.30 pm

Total hours to be worked by employee = 35 hours per week

Fig. 6.3 Flexible working time

To choose their working hours, employees first calculate core time. Core time in the above example is 5 days × 3 hours (11.00 am to 2.00 pm) = 15 hours. This leaves 20 hours (35 − 15 = 20) of working which can be chosen from FWT. Before choosing the hours of flexitime, employees will have to take into account the time they wish to use for lunch breaks. Most firms will insist that the employee takes at least a 30-minute lunch break.

Health and safety

The health and safety of employees is a major aspect of working conditions. Both the employer and the employee have responsibilities in this respect. These can be summarised as follows.

- The employer's duty can be summed up as the responsibility to provide a safe workplace, including arrangements for hazards such as fire, and the maintenance and safety of machinery and equipment.

- Employees have the duty to take reasonable care for the safety of themselves and other working colleagues at all times, and to co-operate with the employer on all matters of safety.

The duty of employers to provide safe working conditions is backed up by a range of laws, although most employers recognise that it is in their interests to secure the health and safety of their employees.

The Factories Acts

The various Factories Acts, such as those of Barbados and Trinidad and Tobago, deal with health and safety in the workplace. These Acts include the following rules.

- Workplaces must be properly lit and well ventilated.

- Sufficient toilet and washing facilities must be provided.

- Moving machinery must have a fence around it.

- Hoists, lifts, etc. must be properly constructed and maintained.

- Floors, passages and stairs must be kept unobstructed.

- Floors must not have slippery surfaces.

- Fire escapes must be provided and maintained.

- Rooms must not be overcrowded (a minimum of 8.5 cubic metres per person).

- Temperatures must not fall below 16°C (after the first hour of working).

- There must be adequate supplies of fresh or artificially purified air.

- There must be suitable natural or artificial lighting.

- Suitable and sufficient sanitary conveniences must be conveniently accessible and must be clean and properly maintained.

- Accessible washing facilities with running hot and cold water, soap and clean towels, must be provided.

- Accidents must be reported.

6.4 THINGS TO DO

This section contains a variety of exercises to help you create revision notes, to test your understanding and to prepare you for examinations.

Search and find

Write out the question and the answer by referring back through the text to form revision notes.

1. Why is it important that people gain satisfaction from their jobs?
2. Why are Maslow's 'hierarchy of needs' important in business?
3. Why are wage differentials often the source of envy and discontent between workers?
4. List five factors which influence the supply of people suitable for a particular form of employment.
5. Briefly describe each of the following ways of calculating wages: flat rate, time rate, piece rate, bonus, commission.
6. Explain the differences between gross pay and net pay.
7. If you have earned a gross wage of $110.28 and must pay deductions totalling $27.36, what will be your net pay?
8. Give examples, and explain the difference between statutory deductions and voluntary deductions.
9. Cash is one way of paying wages. Name two others.
10. What is the purpose of a time card system? How can this system be of help to the payroll department of a firm?
11. List at least six items of information likely to be found on a pay advice.
12. Briefly describe the way that a computer could be employed in the payroll department.
13. What are fringe benefits? Give six examples.
14. List the kind of information that is contained in the contract of employment.
15. How does a job description differ from a job specification?
16. Why are hours of employment important to the working conditions of an employee?
17. What is flexible working time? Why is it possible to operate this system for people working in a restaurant, but very difficult to adopt for a school?
18. 'Employees as well as employers have a responsibility for safety in the workplace.' Explain this statement.
19. What aspects of health and safety in the workplace are contained in the Factories Acts?

What do you know?

Write out the complete sentence and insert the missing word, which can be chosen from the list at the end of the questions.

1. It is important that people get some . . . . . from their job.
2. . . . . . are the reward paid for labour.
3. Some occupations command a high wage because they require a high degree of skill and . . . . . ability.
4. Sometimes a . . . . . is paid to workers as a share of additional profits achieved due to increased efficiency.
5. . . . . . pay is the total amount earned by the employee before deductions have been made.
6. The worker receives . . . . . pay after any deductions have been taken away.
7. A pay . . . . . is issued with a wage payment so that the employee can see how their net pay has been calculated.
8. Much of the work of a wages department can be assigned to . . . . .
9. A job . . . . . is a broad general statement about an area of work responsibility.
10. All employees should have access to their . . . . . of employment.

> Choose the missing words from the following:
>
> | net | computers | bonus | satisfaction |
> | gross | wages | advice | academic |
> | description | contract | | |

Multiple choice

Select the appropriate answer, a, b, c or d.

1. Which one of the following is a compulsory deduction from wages?
   a) union membership fees
   b) private medical fees
   c) income tax
   d) contribution to the company social club

2. Which one of the following would be considered a fringe benefit of a job?
   a) a bonus
   b) a company car
   c) commission
   d) yearly holiday leave

3   Which of the following statements is untrue in relation to flexible working hours?
    a) all workers have to be present at core times
    b) workers do not have complete choice of working hours
    c) all workers have to be present during band times
    d) flexible hours are chosen outside core times

4   Net pay is:
    a) gross pay minus all deductions
    b) total pay for the whole year
    c) gross pay minus compulsory deductions
    d) the amount of tax-free pay allowed

5   A worker earns a gross wage of $328.25 and pays $81.60 income tax and $36.40 national insurance. The worker's net pay will be:
    a) $118   c) $210.25
    b) $446.25   d) $246.65

6   Statutory deductions are those:
    a) required to be paid by law
    b) which the worker can choose to pay
    c) paid only by the unemployed
    d) which benefit the employer

7   Gross wages are:
    a) total earnings minus deductions
    b) extra wages earned as overtime
    c) earnings not including overtime
    d) the total amount earned

8   Which of the following rates of pay is least likely to act as an incentive to employees to work harder?
    a) bonus
    b) flat rate
    c) piece rate
    d) commission

9   A commission is related to:
    a) the number of hours worked
    b) the value of items sold
    c) how many faulty goods are produced
    d) how many hours overtime have been worked

10 With which of the following rates of pay would overtime be associated?
    a) time rate   c) bonus
    b) piece rate   d) commission

Key words

Find out the business-related meaning of each of the following words. Write a separate sentence for each word to show your understanding.

subsidised   differentials   statutory   bonus
flexitime   employee   employer   hazards
grievance   colleagues

Structured questions

1   The following questions are related to the time card shown in figure 6.4. Ronald Latter is paid at a time rate of $12 per hour. Overtime is paid at the rate of time-and-a-half and Saturday work is paid double-time. If employees are five minutes or more late for work, a 30-minute pay penalty is imposed. Pay is calculated to the nearest full 15 minutes.

TIME CARD								
Works No. 323	Department Sales	Employee's Name Ronald Latter			Week Commencing Mon. 5 May		
Day	Ordinary Time		Overtime		Hours		
	In	Out	In	Out	In	Out	Basic	Overtime	Saturday
Monday	0807	1201	1300	1700			7½		
Tuesday	0800	1202	1301	1701	1730	2030	8	3	
Wednesday	0759	1200	1259	1701	1731	1932	8	2	
Thursday	0801	1201	1301	1700			8		
Friday	0758	1200	1303	1701			8		
Saturday					0900	1201			3
					Total Hours				

............hours at £......... = ...

............hours at £......... = ...

............hours at £......... = ...

Total gross pay £

Fig. 6.4   Time card

a) Briefly explain the purpose of a time card. (1)

b) What is meant by the terms 'time-and-a-half' and 'double-time'? (2)

c) What is the firm hoping to achieve by imposing a '30-minute pay penalty'? Where can the penalty be seen imposed on this time card? (3)

d) How can the use of time cards help to make it possible to operate a 'flexitime' system? (4)

e) Calculate the following aspects of Ronald's pay:
   (i) flat rate earnings
   (ii) overtime pay
   (iii) Saturday pay
   (iv) total gross pay (4)

f) 'Although wages can motivate workers they do not necessarily give job satisfaction.' Discuss this statement. (6)

Table 6.1 *Sales record*

Name	Jan $	Feb $	Mar $	Apr $	May $	June $	Total sales	Commission due $
B Carter	11,500	12,500	14,000	11,000	13,000	15,000	77,000	7,700
J Brady	9,400	10,000	11,000	9,000	9,000	11,000	59,400	5,940
P Daly	12,500	12,000	13,000	11,000	12,000	13,000	73,500	7,350
P Chantrey	9,000	9,500	9,500	10,000	11,000	10,500		
M Perry	10,000	10,500	11,000	11,000	12,000	13,000	67,500	6,750
C Stone	9,600	9,500	11,500	11,000	11,000	11,500	64,100	6,410
Total $	62,000	64,000	70,000	63,000	68,000	74,000		

2   Refer to the job description in figure 6.2 and answer these questions.

   a) Why is it important for an employee to have a job description? (2)

   b) The job description refers to 'induction', which is sometimes called 'orientation'. Why is this important for new employees? (2)

   c) Why would existing employees possibly need training as well as new recruits? (3)

   d) List three functions of the personnel department other than induction and training. (3)

   e) How does a job specification differ from a job description? (4)

   f) Another document that is issued to all employees is the Contract of Employment. List six different items of information contained in this document. (6)

3   The following questions are all related to the pay advice in figure 6.1.

   a) What is the purpose of a pay advice? (1)

   b) Explain how this employee's net pay has been calculated. (2)

   c) This pay advice relates to just one calendar month of employment. Assuming that the employee's rate of pay and monthly deductions do not change, what would be the figure for gross pay and net pay for a 12-month period? (2)

   d) How can allocating an employee a works number assist computerised handling of payroll management? (2)

   e) State three functions the union is likely to carry out on this worker's behalf in return for the payment being made to it. (3)

   f) Identify the two compulsory and two voluntary deductions from pay shown on this pay advice. (4)

   g) Clearly explain the similarities and also the differences between income tax and national insurance. (6)

4   Table 6.1 shows the sales record of a team of sales representatives over a six-month period. Each representative is paid a basic wage, plus a commission of 10% which is paid at the end of each six-month period.

   a) On which month was the total sales of the six representatives highest? (1)

   b) Which salesperson has achieved the highest overall total sales? (1)

   c) What work does a sales representative do? (2)

   d) What is the total sales figure achieved by representative P. Chantrey for the six-month period, and how much commission will that person receive? (3)

   e) What do we mean when we say that 'each representative is paid a basic wage, plus a commission of 10%'? (3)

   f) What was the total sales of the whole sales team for the six-month period, and how much in total will be paid by the company in commission? Show all calculations. (4)

   g) Draw a line graph to plot the total combined sales of all the representatives month by month over the period covered by the record. Write a brief summary report of what your graph shows. (6)

5 a) Name two methods of wage payment other than by cash. (2)

   b) Why does the receipt of wages monthly make it more important to budget carefully than when payment is made weekly? (2)

   c) Norma Robinson receives a basic pay of $320.80 plus a bonus payment of $60.40, and she pays the following deductions:

Income tax	$74.60
National insurance	$14.50
Private medical scheme	$20.00

   (i) How much will Norma's gross pay be? (1)
   (ii) How much net pay will she receive? (2)
   (iii) How much will Norma pay in compulsory deductions and how much will she pay by voluntary payments? (3)

   d) Explain each of the following terms related to earnings:
   (i) overtime (2)
   (ii) commission (2)
   (iii) piece rate. (2)

   e) Give four reasons why there are differences between the rates of pay people receive. (4)

6 Although some people work shift work, most people work fixed hours. This question is about hours of employment.

   a) Some people have to work shift work. What is shift work? (1)

   b) State two problems that are caused by the majority of people working the same hours. (2)

   c) What is flexible working time (FWT)? (2)

   d) In what way can FWT help to reduce the problems caused by most people working similar hours? (3)

   e) In relation to FWT, explain each of the following terms:
   (i) band time
   (ii) core time
   (iii) flexible time. (6)

   f) 'Both a restaurant and a bus company may have two core times, but their core times will often be at different times of the day.' Explain this statement in relation to flexible working time. (6)

Research assignments

1 A top-class sportsman could well earn $500,000 in a year, while a truck driver might earn $20,000 a year. Give a detailed explanation of the reasons for wage differentials using examples to illustrate your answer. Present documented evidence of other examples of wage differentials.

2 Carry out a survey to establish what percentage of people in your sample have a job description. Ask four people in your sample to let you have a copy of their job description. What observations can you make about the information you have collected?

3 Collect a variety (at least five) of advertisements for contrasting occupations that include details of wages to be paid. With reference to specific advertisements in your samples explain the differences in wage levels that you can observe.

4 What evidence would you offer that supports the view that job satisfaction is just as important as wages?

Chapter 7
INDUSTRIAL RELATIONS

7.1 The importance of industrial relations

The employees of an organisation are the most important and also the most costly of its resources. They are important because they are so essential at all levels of business operations. But most people work for a livelihood, and the role they play in the organisation is of less importance to them. This can be a source of conflict between the employer and the employee.

Employees will want to obtain the highest wage they can, so that they can buy the material things they want. The employer, however, will want to keep the firm's wage bill as low as possible, and this can result in a kind of continual tug-of-war between the employer and employee.

The term '**industrial relations**' is generally used to refer to the degree of conflict or peace in industry and between employers and employees.

7.2 Trade unions

Trade unions are associations of workers in an industry or group of industries who join together in their common interest to regulate the relations between employees and employers. By cooperating together in this way, members of a union hope to win concessions from their employers, and this reflects the motto of the trade union movement: '*In unity is strength*'.

Trade unions are organised nationally with '**shop stewards**' located within the workplaces. These people provide the link between the members and the union committee, and they act as spokespersons between the workers and the firm's management.

Trade unionism developed in the Caribbean region after the First World War as a reaction against the owners of factories accompanying an upsurge in demand for improvement in the conditions of working class people. Today, it is generally agreed that trade unions play a controversial but important role in industry. They are important to employers because they enable them to negotiate with a small number of people rather than many.

There are different types of union, classified according to the types of worker they represent. In many countries, the trade unions have joined together to form congresses or councils. In the Caribbean, for example, the Caribbean Congress of Labour (CCL) is an example of this type of union of unions. It has affiliate members in most West Indian territories.

The Caribbean Congress of Labour (CCL)

The CCL is a regional body to which unions in the thirteen nations of CARICOM belong. It is the umbrella body of the labour movement in the English-speaking Caribbean.

The CCL is a member of the International Labour Organisation (ILO), the American Federation of Labour-Congress of Industrial Organisations (AFL-CIO), and the International Confederation of Free Trade Unions (ICFTU) among others.

Individual unions also have direct affiliations with some international unions. For example, those unions with a socialist philosophy tend to belong to international unions with similar ideologies. However, with the unification of Eastern Europe this situation may well change.

Trade union aims

Trade unions aim to secure for workers:

- participation in company decision-making processes
- improved wages and reduced working hours
- better working conditions
- full employment and national prosperity
- job security
- benefits for members who are sick, retired or on strike
- improved social security payments such as unemployment and sickness benefit and pensions

- an influence on government
- a reasonable share in the wealth of the country
- improved public and social services.

Fig. 7.1 A typical union structure

7.3 Collective bargaining

The main function of trade unions is to obtain improved wages and working conditions for their members. Sometimes the employer reaches a satisfactory wage agreement with individual employees, but wage settlements are often the result of **collective bargaining**. This refers to talks between representatives of employers and trade unions to decide pay rates and other terms and conditions of employment.

The union represents a group of workers and negotiates a settlement on their behalf with an employer or a group of employers. It is just as much in the interest of the unions as it is in the interest of the employer to reach a speedy settlement, because both sides can only benefit if there is continuity in working.

Although pay is one of the main subjects of collective bargaining, many others can be involved, including:

- hours of work
- holiday entitlement
- sick pay
- pensions
- maternity leave
- working conditions
- training
- promotion
- redundancies
- recruitment.

Although negotiations between employers and employees may not reach an agreement, there are other means of solving the deadlock.

- **Conciliation** is where a third party is appointed to try to help find a solution that is acceptable to both sides.
- **Arbitration** is where both sides of a dispute request that it goes before an arbiter, whose verdict both sides agree to accept. The Industrial Disputes Tribunal is the arbiter in most of these cases.

7.4 Industrial legislation

In the Caribbean region certain laws have been implemented which specify forms of behaviour considered reasonable for both the employers and the unions. Rules covering actions that should be avoided by management and the union are often set out in union brochures, and sometimes on membership cards. The following are typical of these rules.

The union must not:

- coerce anyone to join or not to join a union
- coerce employees in their choice of the parties to bargain on their behalf
- charge unfair membership fees
- refuse to bargain collectively with an employer
- cause the employer to pay for services not rendered
- influence an employer to discriminate against an employee.

The employer must not:

- interfere with or restrain employees who wish to join a union
- discriminate against people because of union membership
- refuse to bargain collectively with employees' representatives
- discriminate against employees who testify before tribunals.

7.5 Restrictive practices

Restrictive practices are the methods or pressures used by unions in an industrial dispute. The following are some of the most commonly used.

Strike

If wage negotiations break down completely, or some other dispute arises, workers may cease work (withdraw their labour). There are two main types of strike.

- **Official strike:** workers withdraw their labour on advice, in consultation, and with union approval and backing. Under these circumstances the union may provide strike pay from the funds contributed by members.
- **Unofficial strike:** sometimes called a 'wildcat' strike. The workers cease work without union backing.

Demarcation dispute

A demarcation dispute is one where *who does what* is in question; a dispute between unions may be involved. This is a situation where one group of workers objects to another group doing particular work. Often this kind of dispute is the result of differences in rates of pay between one group of workers and another. It may be that one group of workers is doing work that another group thinks 'belongs' to them.

Overtime ban

Overtime provides a convenient way for employers to get extra working hours from employees without having to take on extra workers. When an overtime ban is in force the workers refuse to work additional hours.

Work-to-rule

Work is carried out in accordance with every minor rule, with workers following all the rules and regulations of the company exactly. By sticking strictly to the rules in this way, work is slowed down and productivity is reduced.

Go slow

This has similarities to a work-to-rule. The workers do their job thoroughly, but at a slower pace than normal, thus causing a fall in output.

Closed shop

A closed shop means that all workers in a firm belong to one union, and they refuse to work with anyone who is not a member of that union.

Picketing

In order to ensure maximum effect from their industrial action, a group of workers on strike may stand outside the firm's entrance and try to persuade other workers not to 'cross the picket line', that is not to enter the premises.

Sit-in

Workers occupy the premises, ensuring that no goods enter or leave, and preventing the operation of the firm. Sometimes, such as when a factory is threatened with closure, the sit-in becomes a 'work-in'. Workers occupy the factory and keep it in operation without the presence of the management.

Union busting

Union members may refuse to work on or move certain machines or equipment, or refuse to work with other people or groups. Someone who goes against the union's wishes by working during a stoppage is sometimes called a **union buster**.

Fig. 7.2 **Pressure groups**

7.6 Pressure groups

Pressure groups are organisations (sometimes voluntary) which seek to persuade the government, local council, or some other organisation to recognise their views and respond to them. They try to influence the decision-making process by demonstrating the strength of their feelings.

The trade unions are an example of a pressure group. They not only try to influence employers on behalf of their members, but they also present the views of their members on 'social issues'.

Pressure groups are not all formal ones. Sometimes an informal group will develop spontaneously, perhaps due to a passing situation, for example the planned development of an industrial estate in a predominantly residential area.

Although pressure groups are often portrayed in the media as trying to influence the authorities, they do at times try to influence business also. Apart from workers trying to influence pay awards, the general public pressurise businesses by protesting about issues such as advertising techniques, sexual inequality and environmental conflicts.

Governments and businesses are subject to pressure from groups both within and outside the organisation. Inside the business, pressure may come from groups of shareholders trying to influence company policy. But the main pressure on firms tends to be external pressure, that is, consumer pressure.

The most obvious pressure that consumers can put on a firm is to take their business elsewhere, although if the firm is very powerful or has a monopoly this may be difficult. Consumers are also assisted in their attempts to put pressure on businesses by the various consumer protection facilities that are dealt with in detail in Chapter 10 of this book.

Some television and radio programmes act as watchdogs to expose firms who are guilty of malpractice, and many newspapers and magazines run 'consumer watchdog' articles which attempt to protect consumer interests.

7.7 THINGS TO DO

This section contains a variety of exercises to help you create revision notes, to test your understanding and to prepare you for examinations.

Search and find

Write out the question and the answer by referring back through the text to form revision notes.

1. What do you understand by the term 'industrial relations'?
2. Why would you say that employers and employees are bound to come into conflict?
3. What is a trade union?
4. Briefly describe the main specialist types of union that exist.
5. What are the aims of trade unions?
6. What do you understand by the term 'collective bargaining'?
7. List the kind of issues other than pay that a trade union might take up through collective bargaining.
8. Say what you understand by the terms 'conciliation' and 'arbitration'.
9. Briefly outline the basic rules which unions and employers must observe during negotiations.
10. What are restrictive practices? What do they aim to achieve?
11. Explain the difference between an 'official' strike and an 'unofficial' strike.
12. Trade unions use a variety of methods to try to persuade employers to agree to wage claims. Explain how each of the following methods operates:
    a) overtime ban
    b) work-to-rule
    c) go slow
13. In what way is a demarcation dispute one where 'who does what' is in question?
14. What are pressure groups?
15. In what way do pressure groups influence businesses?

INDUSTRIAL RELATIONS

What do you know?

Write out the complete sentence and insert the missing word, which can be chosen from the list at the end of the questions.

1. The . . . . . of an organisation are the most important and also the most costly of its resources.
2. The term 'industrial relations' refers to the extent to which peace or . . . . . exists between employers and employees.
3. Unions are important to . . . . . because they allow them to negotiate with a small number of people.
4. One of the aims of trade unions is to secure improved working . . . . . for workers.
5. Wage settlements are often the result of . . . . .
6. . . . . . is where a third party is appointed to try to find an acceptable solution to a dispute.
7. . . . . . is where both sides of a dispute request that it goes before an arbiter.
8. A . . . . . dispute is one about 'who does what'.
9. . . . . . groups are voluntary organisations which seek to persuade the authorities.
10. When workers . . . . . they withdraw their labour.

Choose the missing words from the following:

pressure   conditions   arbitration   employees
conciliation   employers   strike   negotiations
demarcation   conflict

Multiple choice

Select the appropriate answer, a, b, c or d.

1. The union representative in closest touch with members is the:
   a) executive
   b) shop steward
   c) local official
   d) employer

2. If you are an office worker, which type of union are you likely to belong to:
   a) craft
   b) industrial
   c) general
   d) white collar

3. Which of the following forms of industrial action would not have the official backing of the trade union?
   a) selective strike
   b) wildcat strike
   c) overtime ban
   d) token strike

4. A closed shop is where:
   a) all workers in a firm belong to one union
   b) shop workers close the firm down
   c) only some people are allowed to join the union
   d) a firm refuses to allow workers to join a union

5. The methods used by trade unions in an industrial dispute are called:
   a) disruptive actions
   b) negotiation methods
   c) restrictive practices
   d) trade disputes

6. In an industrial dispute a union might ask its members to take all but one of the following actions. Which is the odd one out?
   a) overtime ban
   b) picketing
   c) work-to-rule
   d) union busting

7. Which of the following circumstances is an example of a demarcation dispute?
   a) female workers complain of sexual harassment
   b) an electrician objects to a plumber connecting a shower to the electricity supply
   c) workers follow company instructions exactly
   d) workers on strike try to persuade other people not to enter their employer's premises

8. Collective bargaining means:
   a) union rules
   b) bargains agreed to by workers
   c) pay settlements
   d) groups of people negotiating

9. Industrial legislation refers to:
   a) laws deciding legislation
   b) management negotiating practices
   c) laws relating to industrial action
   d) industrialists' union rules

10. Trade unions must not:
    a) coerce someone to join a union
    b) bargain collectively
    c) charge people for being members
    d) go on strike

Key words

Find out the business-related meaning of each of the following words. Write a separate sentence for each word to show your understanding.

concessions   settlement   continuity   dispute
coerce   discriminate   overtime
               wildcat   picketing

CARTER STRIKE SOLUTION

It looks as if the long-running dispute at the Carter electronics plant may finally be coming to an end, with the unions and management yesterday agreeing upon a pay award of 12.5% linked to a productivity agreement worked out between the management and shop stewards.

Rose Webber, the union spokesperson, said, 'I am delighted at the agreement and will be putting it to our members in a ballot tomorrow with a recommendation for acceptance'. For the management, Peter Stewart commented that the productivity deal was vital to enable the company to fund the wage rise, which is twice the current rate of inflation, without any compulsory redundancies.

Provided the agreement is accepted by the workforce, the plant could be back in full production next week after six months of disruption. One picket said, 'I'll be glad to get back to work, but I won't work with any union busters'.

Fig. 7.3 Industrial dispute

Structured questions

1 Look at the newspaper article in figure 7.3.
   a) How long has the dispute referred to in this article been going on? (1)
   b) What information in this article indicates that the settlement that was reached was a result of negotiations? (2)
   c) What is the function of a shop steward? (2)
   d) What is a productivity deal? (3)
   e) Why might the negotiations have resulted in redundancies were it not for the productivity deal? (4)
   f) Explain each of the following terms used in this article:
      (i) picket
      (ii) union busters. (4)
   g) There is some evidence in the article of the kind of restrictive practices that have been used during the dispute.
      (i) List the methods used.
      (ii) Describe two other methods that the workers could have used. (4)

2 a) What is a trade union? (2)
   b) Explain the basic difference between a white collar union and other types of union. (4)
   c) Describe two functions of a trade union. (4)
   d) Explain three possible advantages of being a member of a trade union. (4)
   e) Describe two possible disadvantages of being a member of a trade union. (6)

3 a) What are restrictive practices? (2)
   b) One of the people who plays an important part in organising restrictive practices is the shop steward. What are shop stewards? (2)
   c) What is a 'closed shop'? (2)
   d) Describe two forms of restrictive practice. (4)
   e) Briefly explain the terms 'conciliation' and 'arbitration'. (4)
   f) In what way does collective bargaining benefit both the worker and the employer? (6)

4 a) What do you understand by the term 'industrial relations'? (2)
   b) Briefly describe one way in which trade unions can help to avoid industrial conflict. (2)
   c) In what ways can industrial unrest be seen to be damaging to both employees and employer? (3)
   d) Name three different types of union from the Caribbean region and explain the types of worker they represent. (3)
   e) Identify *two* advantages and *two* disadvantages of being a member of a trade union. (4)
   f) 'If the main aim of workers is to obtain the highest wage and best working conditions, and employers seek to keep costs down, conflict between the two is inevitable.' Discuss this statement. (6)

Research assignments

1 Your best friend has just started work in a local factory and has been asked by the shop steward if he would like to join the trade union. Some workers are members and others are not. Advise your friend of all the implications of taking up or turning down the offer. Back up your advice with information from reliable published sources.

2   Describe the work of trade unions. Considering that they all have similar aims, why are there sometimes disputes between unions? Obtain some information from major unions and the press to complement your answers.

3   Collect at least four newspaper articles containing reports of industrial problems. In each case describe the influence that trade unions might have on the event in question. Comment on whether their involvement is likely to improve or worsen the situation.

4   What contribution do you feel trade unions make to the economy of your country? What evidence can you present to support your answers?

5   You have been selected by your school to attend the Youth Congress on trade unionism in the English-speaking Caribbean. Apart from being in attendance you have been asked to give a 15 minute presentation on collective bargaining. Prepare the paper you will read at the meeting using the following guidelines:

a)   introduce the topic

b)   explain the broad meaning of collective bargaining

c)   describe collective bargaining objectively

d)   give any additional information you think important

e)   produce a collection of appropriate overhead projector transparencies and indicate where they should be included in your talk.

Chapter 8
MARKETS

8.1 What is a market?

Earlier in this book, we learnt that production is a very important activity. Production aims at satisfying human wants, and that is why firms need to find out what products and services consumers want before embarking on full-scale production. In other words, the producer must find out what is happening in the market-place if production is to be aligned with the needs of the consumer.

Although you might think of a market as a place, as where the farmers' and other producers' products are sold, it need not be a physical meeting place. A market can be defined as 'any situation which brings **buyers** and **sellers** into contact (perhaps through others) to transact business'. In other words, the seller might be located right here in the Caribbean, but the buyer might be in Europe or North America. Or, the seller might be located in one of the OECS (Organisation of Eastern Caribbean States) countries, and the buyer might be in Jamaica or Barbados or Trinidad and Tobago. Or, the buyer and seller might be in different parts of an island. Nevertheless, the exchange of goods and services can still take place. Letters and telecommunication methods would be used in such cases to bring the buyers and sellers into contact, or they may make contact through other people acting on their behalf.

A market consists of four important elements:

1 buyers
2 sellers
3 goods or services
4 price.

It is the interconnection of these elements that makes it possible for a market to operate. Take away any of these elements and it is difficult for the market to function effectively.

Markets play an important part in the sale and distribution of goods and services, and are therefore particularly important to a firm's marketing department, which is examined in Chapter 9.

It is important to realise that not all markets are concerned with the sale of goods. Some markets provide specialist services. For example, the stock market, which is dealt with in Chapter 20, makes it possible for investors to buy and sell securities.

Fig. 8.1 The market mechanism

8.2 Financial markets

Financial markets can be divided into two broad categories, the money market and the capital market.

The money market

This is not a market in the physical sense, but refers to a number of institutions which provide short-term loans. The market includes the following.

- *Commercial banks* provide loans and overdrafts to businesses and also to individuals.

- *Hire-purchase companies* allow individuals and businesses to borrow money and pay it back later in instalments while the goods purchased are used as security against the loan.

- *Credit unions*: members pool their savings into a common loan fund. These funds are then used to provide members with low-cost loans.

The capital market

This also is not a physical market, but a number of institutions providing long-term loans, almost entirely to business and industry. This market includes the following.

- *Insurance companies* loan out some of the money they collect as premiums in the form of long-term loans.

- *Building societies*: apart from loaning out money for house purchase, building societies invest some of the money deposited with them by providing loans for the capital market.

- *Investment trusts* buy shares of other companies using the money they get from the sale of shares in their own company.

- *Unit trusts* invite the public to buy 'units'. The money received from selling the units is then used to buy shares in many different companies.

- *Pension funds* collect regular contributions from members and provide them with pensions when they retire. The contributions are made to work by investing in low-risk securities.

- *Issuing houses* arrange long-term capital for businesses by selling shares of the company concerned to the public.

- *The Stock Exchange* provides a market-place for buyers and sellers of second-hand securities (the stock market).

- *Development banks*: these are special financial institutions that provide industrial finance to aid economic development. They play an important role in developing countries where there is a shortage of finance in both the short and long term.

8.3 Commodity markets

This type of market is found in major cities throughout the world. Goods are sold in these markets in very large quantities, often by grade or sample.

London is the main world centre for commodity markets. These markets provide facilities where large numbers of buyers and sellers of raw materials meet, set prices, and trade in a wide variety of commodities. Most of these commodity markets are over 100 years old.

The London commodity markets include cotton, wool, sugar, tea, coffee, cocoa, copra, vegetable oils, grains, furs, diamonds and many others. The London metal exchanges deal in silver, aluminium, lead, copper, zinc, tin and nickel. Some Caribbean-produced products, such as sugar, coffee and spices, are just a few of the commodities sold through these markets. In addition, Caribbean countries also make purchases in these markets.

Commodity market specialists

There are three main categories of specialists in these markets.

- *Merchant*: buys on his own behalf, pays promptly and may provide his own transport.

- *Broker*: buys and sells on behalf of others on a commission (brokerage) basis.

- *'Del credere' agent*: sells on behalf of others and also guarantees payments for goods in return for extra commission.

Methods of sale

Private treaty. Where a commodity can be graded (e.g. wheat and cotton), the seller and buyer come to a private agreement on the purchase price by negotiation.
Auction. Where goods vary in quality or grade (e.g. tea, coffee, tobacco and wool), a representative sample is offered, and buyers or their agents bid. Purchase goes to the highest bidder.
Spot and futures markets. Markets which deal in goods for immediate delivery are called **spot markets**, because goods and payments are available immediately ('on the spot'). **Futures markets** are those where goods are being sold for delivery and payment at some time in the future. It is only possible to sell as a 'future' if the commodity can be graded.

8.4 The consumer market

The consumer market is one in which everyone participates. We have wants and needs for a variety of products and services. Generally, when people purchase goods we say they are **customers** and when they receive a service or advice they are referred to as **clients**.

Many of the wants and needs of consumers are satisfied through the commercial activities of the channels of distribution such as retail, wholesale and foreign trade. We shall examine these in Chapters 11 and 12. Other social needs for specialist help or advice are satisfied by government services such as health, welfare and education. In addition to the social services provided by the government, there are many private sector organisations such as those engaged in banking and insurance which also provide services to meet consumer requirements. Some of these organisations are examined in other places in this book.

8.5 Channels of distribution

During the process of marketing and distribution, merchandise usually passes through the hands of one or more **intermediaries** between the producer and the consumer. Commerce provides the important links between the producer and consumer.

Commerce can be divided into two broad areas, **trade** and **services to trade**. Trade is the branch of commerce directly engaged in the change of ownership of goods and consists of the retailers, wholesalers and exporters and importers who are considered in later chapters. The services (aids) to trade are those businesses and organisations that assist trade in carrying out its functions, and these are examined in various places throughout this book. They include communications facilities.

Fig. 8.2 The structure of commerce

Trade (home and foreign)
Home trade refers to sales to the local market (domestic), and **foreign trade** refers to sales overseas. Several types of business people are involved in trade.

- The **wholesaler** is intermediary between producer and retailer, and sometimes sells direct to the consumer.
- The *retailer* buys commodities from a wholesaler or direct from the producer and sells in small quantities to consumers.
- The *importer* brings commodities into the country.
- The *exporter* sends commodities to another country.

Services (aids to trade)
- *Banking* provides short-term finance, and facilities for the easy transfer of payments.
- *Finance*: various institutions (e.g. the Stock Exchange) provide long-term finance for industry and commerce, and offer consumer credit.
- *Insurance* spreads the risks faced by industrial and commercial businesses.
- *Transport* moves commodities from one place to another.

Communications
- *Postal*: the transfer of written communications through mail services.
- *Telecommunications*: the immediate distance transfer of written, verbal or data communications by electronic devices.
- *Advertising* provides potential customers with information about available goods and services.

Direct services
This is the general name given to the many occupations that are not of a productive or commercial nature, but which are important to the well-being of the population. Examples of people offering these are doctors, nurses, teachers, policemen, entertainers and athletes.

8.6 A common market

In the foregoing section you will have seen that one of the channels of distribution, trade, links to the foreign market. An important feature of modern international trade is the concept of a **common market.**

The members of a common market (a group of countries) trade with each other, and make agreements binding on all of the trading countries. For instance, countries agree to charge each other the same rate of import duties or none at all.

Two well-known common markets are the European Union and the Caribbean Common Market. These are examined in more detail in Chapter 12.

8.7 THINGS TO DO

This section contains a variety of exercises to help you create revision notes, to test your understanding and to prepare you for examinations.

Search and find

Write out the question and the answer by referring back through the text to form revision notes.

1. Why do firms need to find out exactly what people in their market want?
2. Define the term 'market'.
3. Name the four elements of a market mechanism.
4. Briefly describe each of the institutions which make up the money market.
5. Which organisations constitute the capital market? How does the function of this market differ from that of the money market?
6. What is a commodity market? Why do you think commodity markets have an important influence outside the countries in which they are sited?
7. Briefly describe the work of the three main categories of commodity market specialists.
8. Make a comparison of the various methods of sale used in commodity markets.
9. Why is the consumer market the most important to many businesses?
10. What is meant by the term 'channels of distribution'?
11. What is commerce?
12. Why are the businesses that provide services to trade just as important as those that actually do the trading?
13. What is a 'common market'?

What do you know?

Write out the complete sentence and insert the missing word, which can be chosen from the list at the end of the questions.

1. ..... aims at satisfying human wants and needs.
2. The main function of a market is to provide facilities for buyers and sellers to .....
3. Markets play an important part in the sale and ..... of goods.
4. The ..... market is a source of short-term loans.
5. The ..... market consists of institutions that provide long-term loans.
6. Development banks are special financial institutions that provide finance to aid ..... development.
7. Goods are sold in very large quantities in ..... markets.
8. A broker buys and sells on behalf of others on a ..... basis.
9. The ..... market is one in which everyone participates.
10. ..... provides the important links between the producer and the consumer.

Choose the missing words from the following:

economic   commerce   money   consumer
commodity   trade   distribution   production
commission   capital

Multiple choice

Select the appropriate answer, a, b, c or d.

1. Which one of the following is essential for the existence of a market?
    a) all buyers and sellers are present at the same time
    b) sellers are in contact with buyers
    c) premises are provided for the holding of the market
    d) a committee is elected to control the market

2. In which of the following markets would a foreign tourist be able to convert his or her currency into Caribbean dollars?
    a) the insurance market
    b) the stock market
    c) the consumer market
    d) the money market

3. Which of the following is a member of the capital market?
    a) insurance companies
    b) finance companies
    c) hire-purchase companies
    d) merchant banks

4. Which of the following is a member of the money market?
    a) commercial banks
    b) pension funds
    c) a stock exchange
    d) investment trusts

5. Which one of the following is not a part of a market situation?
    a) a broker buying shares for a client
    b) a street trader selling ice cream
    c) a nurse caring for the elderly
    d) an auctioneer accepting bids

6 The market for 'second-hand' securities is known as:
   a) a commodity exchange
   b) a stock exchange
   c) the capital market
   d) the new issue market

7 All of the following are part of the channels of distribution except:
   a) producing
   b) importing
   c) exporting
   d) retailing

8 Which of the following commodity market traders guarantees payment to his client?
   a) broker
   b) merchant
   c) factor
   d) del credere agent

9 Which of the following terms refers to a market where goods are for immediate delivery?
   a) future
   b) spot
   c) static
   d) speculative

10 Which of the following conditions is necessary for 'futures' trading to take place?
   a) full payment must be made in advance of purchase
   b) the buyer and seller must actually meet
   c) there must be a guaranteed market for the commodity
   d) it must be possible to grade the commodity

Key words

Find out the business-related meaning of each of the following words. Write a separate sentence for each word to show your understanding.

specialist	overdrafts	merchant	auction
customer	client	consumer	target
intermediaries	trade		

Structured questions

1 a) Who is a consumer? (2)
   b) Name two middlemen between the producer and the consumer. (2)
   c) What do you understand by the term 'consumer market'? (4)
   d) Name the four elements of commerce that are directly involved in the marketing of a producer's goods. (4)
   e) Describe the importance to the marketing and distribution of goods of four aids to trade. (8)

Toucan Development Bank Ltd

Toucan Development Bank Ltd provides reliable advice and financial backing for a wide range of businesses from agriculture and manufacturing to catering and tourism.

If you want to invest in Trinidad, come and talk to the Toucan.

Fig. 8.3 A development bank

2 Look at the advertisement in figure 8.3.
   a) What is the function of a development bank? (2)
   b) What 'goals' might the bank help the businessman to realise? (2)
   c) What sort of 'technical assistance' might this specialist bank give to its customers? (3)
   d) How does the function of a development bank differ from that of a commercial bank? (4)
   e) Why might a business require a foreign exchange loan? (4)
   f) How are the services of this particular bank likely to enable a business to explore 'new markets'? (5)

3 a) Why is 'marketing' so important to a manufacturer? (5)
   b) Mr Whitely is planning to produce pottery for sale in the tourist resort area. However, being new to this business, he knows very little about the marketing of such products. Discuss the concept of marketing with Mr Whitely. (15)

Research assignments

1 You are a member of a group of students who have been asked to carry out research on the financial market. The group leader assigned you the topic: 'the capital market'. Detail the information you would include in your presentation to your entire class.

2 Collect as much information as you can on the Caribbean Common Market. Put this information in a scrapbook. Include pictures of some of the products traded on the Caribbean Common Market. Share the information with

your classmates through a carefully prepared illustrated talk.

3 Interview ten persons in your community in order to find out what influences their choice of one brand of a product over another brand of the same product. Share your findings with your classmates through a display presentation or illustrated lecture. *Note*: Write out your interview questions so that it will be easier for you to get through the interview.

Chapter 9
THE MARKETING DEPARTMENT

9.1 What is marketing?

In Chapter 8 we concentrated on learning what a market is and discovered the various types of markets that exist. Some of these types of market have a direct influence on the distribution of goods, that is, how the goods reach the consumer. The marketing department of a large organisation is concerned with this: getting the products to the consumer.

Marketing refers to all the processes involved in selling goods or services in the most profitable and efficient manner. It begins with an examination of what people want from a product or service (**market research**). This is followed by **product development**: an assessment of how to produce a product or service that will satisfy people's requirements, and at the same time make a profit. The next stage is to develop a **marketing strategy** that will get the product to the appropriate market at a competitive price. This will involve creating an **advertising campaign** that is backed by selling and distribution procedures.

The flowchart in figure 9.1 shows the way that the marketing process is developed.

Marketing in this sense is a two-way process. It connects those who produce goods and services with potential buyers. It also finds out what products and services consumers want and relays this information to the producers. This enables them to make the right things available.

Fig. 9.2 Marketing is a two-way process

Marketing concepts

A **marketing concept** refers to the typical business goal of satisfying customers' wants and trying to make a profit in the process.

We say that a business is pursuing a **sales concept** when it tries to sell something before learning what the customer wants. Sometimes it suits a producer to operate in this way. For example, if a manufacturer is well equipped to produce a particular product it might go ahead and manufacture, and rely on its sales force to persuade the consumer to buy.

In pursuing a marketing concept, however, a business will firstly find out what customers want and then try to meet this demand. What the customer wants is known as the **customer concept**, pursuing which, the business may well do what the customer wants despite, perhaps, preferring to do otherwise. For example, a store might stay open until late in the evening to please its customers, even though this adds considerably to its wage bill.

Fig. 9.1 Marketing flowchart

93

The way that a business finds out what the customer wants is by **market research**. This is the systematic and continuous evaluation of all the factors involved in the transfer of goods and services from the producer to the ultimate consumer. It is particularly concerned with the reactions of consumers. (Refer also to Chapter 10.)

Sales is a support system for marketing. In other words, sales is a marketing strategy which facilitates exchange. Therefore, a major part of the work of a marketeer is to choose the best possible methods of sales to match the products being marketed. For example, the sales strategies for a new flavour soft drink would differ from the sales strategies for a property. Market research plays an important role in the development of sales strategies.

9.2 The marketing department

A firm's marketing department is concerned with selling its products or services. This can mean disposing of products the firm has produced, but more often it is a case of identifying what customers want (customer concept) and then arranging to meet the need that exists, hopefully making a profit in the process.

There are many ways to organise a marketing department, and its structure will be influenced by the size of the firm. In a large company it would be possible to split the department into several sub-divisions, each with a specific marketing function. In a small organisation a few members of staff may have to incorporate several of these functions into their duties.

Fig. 9.3 Typical structure of a marketing department of a large company

The functions of a marketing department

The marketing department is controlled by the marketing director or a senior manager. This position entails carrying out sales policies decided by the board of directors, and supervising the work of all people employed in the department, including the company's **sales representatives**, whose job is to visit potential customers and obtain orders.

All documentation related to sales of the firm's products are dealt with either directly or indirectly by the marketing department. This includes sending out **mail shots** (sales leaflets), dealing with customers' enquiries and orders, arranging for the despatch of goods, and sending out invoices and statements of account (refer to Chapter 13).

A major part of the work of the marketing department is to choose the method of sales to be employed. This will vary according to the product or service being marketed. For example, the method of marketing a new chocolate bar will differ from that used to sell a valuable antique.

The way that products are to be distributed is given careful consideration. This involves decisions of which **channels of distribution** should be used, and whether trade will be directed through wholesalers, retailers, or by direct marketing. (Refer also to Chapter 11.)

The marketing department is obviously involved in advertising the firm's products. Where the firm is large, it may have a separate advertising department. This department will carry out the instructions of the marketing department, and will also offer advice on marketing strategies, including market research. These aspects of marketing are covered in more detail later in this book.

9.3 Marketing mix

Those directly involved in marketing generally follow the customer concept defined earlier; that is, they try to see things from their customers' point of view. Where a business wants to influence a specific group of customers (e.g. teenagers), then they are its **target market**. A business often has many target markets, perhaps one for each of its products or services, and it may well approach each target market in a different way.

Once a business has identified its target market it will select what it considers is the most appropriate **marketing mix**. The marketing mix is a collective term that is used to refer to the whole range of marketing activities, techniques and strategies that a firm uses to reach its target market. The variables of a marketing mix can easily be remembered by referring to the 'four P's': *product, price, place* and *promotion*.

Product
Clearly, the product, good or service (or even an idea to be sold) plays an important role in marketing. There is little point in trying to market something that the

Fig. 9.4 The 'four P's'; variables of the marketing mix enabling the seller to reach the target market

Fig. 9.5 A brand name has to be short, descriptive, and easy to pronounce, and it must appeal to the target consumers

consumer does not want. For this reason, the needs of the consumer must be focused on.

Packaging is linked with the product. Packaging is the outer wrapping or container for goods. Packaging not only presents the product in an attractive way but it also gives details about the contents, any potential hazards, correct usage, etc. In this respect packaging:

- protects the product
- promotes the product
- preserves the life of the product
- prevents health hazards that could result from use of the product
- makes it more convenient for the consumer to handle the product
- enhances the general appearance of the product.

An old-established product in a new and improved package usually enhances the marketing potential of the product.

Branding is another important aspect of the product. Branding refers to giving a product a distinctive name, term, symbol or even a design to enable it to be recognised easily.

A **brand name** (or **trade mark**) is that part of branding which represents the actual letter, letters, word or group of words which make up the name of the product. The brand name differentiates one product from another similar or dissimilar product. Trade marks can be registered so that they can only be used by one firm.

Price

No matter how attractive a product is, a crucial factor in the success of the marketing strategy will be the price. It is important to the seller because it incorporates profit, and it is important to the consumers because it affects their ability to purchase what they want. Price determination is examined later in this chapter.

Place

Those involved in marketing a product have to ensure that it reaches a place where consumers can conveniently make purchases. Getting the item to this convenient place is called **distribution**. This involves wholesalers, retailers, importers and exporters, which are dealt with in Chapters 11 and 12. Distribution also depends on transportation which is covered in Chapter 14.

Promotion

This refers to the ways in which consumers are made aware of the availability of the product or service and the qualities it has. Advertising is the most important aspect of product promotion, and this is dealt with in Chapter 10.

Sales promotion is any activity that supplements advertising and other aspects of visual promotion. The following are just a few of the strategies used in sales promotion. You should look for examples of them.

- Trading stamps
- Free gifts/gift tokens
- Loss leaders
- Competitions
- Product demonstrations
- Exhibitions
- Free samples.

Fig. 9.6 The strategies involved in the marketing mix are aimed at meeting the needs and desires of the consumer

From the foregoing you can see that the marketing mix aims to get the right product to the consumer at the right price, and to a convenient place where it can be bought. The consumer is made aware of what is available through product promotion. All the strategies involved in the marketing mix are aimed at meeting the needs and desires of the consumer.

9.4 Product life cycle

In addition to deciding on the marketing mix, a firm must consider how sales might develop. All products move through identifiable stages, which are referred to as the **product life cycle**. Understanding this 'cycle' assists in the preparation of a sound marketing plan.

Pre-launch

This stage consists of all the developmental work undertaken before the product is put on the market. During the pre-launch phase, the decision has to be taken as to whether it is worthwhile to pursue the new development. Once it has been decided to proceed, a considerable amount of capital is consumed with no income being earned for some time. The time between the design of a product and its production is known as the **lead time**.

Introduction

In the early stages of marketing, sales tend to be low, but large amounts of capital continue to be consumed. It is some time before the break-even stage (see Chapter 19) is reached and the product begins to show a profit.

Growth

If all goes well, sales and profits are steadily rising. Marketing becomes more economically viable as an increasing volume of cash comes in from customers. This is a time for vigorous advertising to promote maximum demand for the product.

Maturity

During this crucial period the rate of sales growth begins to slow down. The advent of maturity is often signalled by a falling off in profits. The product reaches its ceiling and begins to decline. This is a crucial period for the business because it is important to recognise the signal to improve the product or find a new one.

Decline

This is the period when sales volume shows a marked fall. Decline reveals that the product has lost its appeal or competitive edge. If steps have not already been taken to improve the product it will probably now have to be withdrawn in order to avoid making a loss.

Fig. 9.7 Product life cycle

Most products have a life cycle similar to that shown in the graph in figure 9.7, which plots a product from its introduction through to its decline. The production and marketing sections of the firm have to be aware of the position in their life cycle in order to maximise profits, and to plan the introduction of replacement products at the appropriate time.

Product range and product mix

From the foregoing examination of product life cycle you will realise that if a firm markets only a single product it faces a considerable risk. In fact, most products are not marketed on their own but are part of a **range** of products. For example, a firm might produce a range of cake mixes, etc. Many small firms commence their business in this way. A large firm will have a **product mix** which consists of several different products, each with its own range, e.g. cake mixes, biscuits, chips, instant sauces, dessert toppings, etc.

9.5 Merchandising

Merchandising is an important marketing technique. It refers to the **display** of goods so that potential customers can conveniently see them and be influenced to buy. The following are just some of the methods of merchandising used by sellers of goods.

- Eye-catching window displays, including special offers.
- Use of in-house displays to reduce the number of employees needed to sell the goods.
- Careful layout of premises, allowing customers to get near to goods and move into other parts of the store.
- Packaging design that presents goods attractively.
- Opportunities for customers to inspect goods closely and perhaps touch them.
- Clear labelling and price marking to reduce the need for customers to ask questions.
- Eye-level shelf displays for high priority goods.

Packaging and branding are important features of merchandising. Producers are required to comply with certain regulations related to the information that must be shown on their products (e.g. contents, weight, etc.), but they also want to put them in containers that will appeal to the customer.

Branding refers to giving a product a distinctive name that will be easily recognised and identified with the item in question. This is of considerable advantage in advertising a product, because if the brand name is easily recognised then less expense is involved in trying to make the public aware of the qualities of the product.

An example in which merchandising is particularly apparent is in self-service stores, but you should not think of merchandising as being confined to the retail trade. Merchandising is used by any business that displays goods rather than just keeping them inside their premises.

9.6 Price determination

All free markets involving many buyers and sellers operate according to the law of demand and supply. That is, if demand for goods and services increases faster than supply of them, then prices rise. If supply increases faster than demand, prices fall. In other words, the price of goods and services is determined by the interaction of the forces of demand and supply, and this of course has a direct influence on production.

Fig. 9.8 Interaction of demand and supply

Demand

The demand for any commodity is the amount that consumers are prepared to purchase at a given price in a given period of time. For each price the demand is different. Usually, the lower the price the higher the quantity demanded, and vice versa, although there are exceptions. **Giffen goods** is a name give to those essential and relatively cheap goods for which demand is likely to increase following a rise in price. The term 'Giffen' is from a nineteenth-century economist of that name who noticed that when the price of bread increased, consumers bought more of it, being unable to afford to buy other more expensive alternatives such as meat and fruit.

The table in figure 9.9 shows an individual's possible demand schedule for candy bars at various prices. A demand schedule can also be shown graphically by

Individual's demand schedule	
Price of each candy bar	Quantity demanded at each price
40c	1
35c	2
30c	3
25c	4
20c	5

Fig. 9.9 Demand schedule and demand graph

plotting the data on a demand curve: the point X indicates that at a price of 30c, the person would be likely to buy three bars.

This demand schedule and demand curve only refer to an individual consumer, but market demand is created by many people. A market demand curve is obtained by summing the demand curves of all individuals, so we can expect the market demand to behave in a similar way to individual demand.

Both the individual demand curve and the market demand curve express a relationship between the demand for a commodity and the price of it, but there are other determinants of demand.

Determinants of demand

- The price of the commodity
- The price of other commodities
- The income of the buyers
- Population or number of buyers
- The buyer's scale of preferences, i.e. how much the buyer values or prefers the items he or she wants in comparison with other commodities.

If one of the conditions of demand changes, the demand curve moves to a new position, as shown in figure 9.10.

For example, a rise in income or purchasing power could increase market demand and shift the demand curve to the right (D to D_1). On the other hand, if one of the determinants causes a fall in market demand, the curve moves to the left (D to D_2).

$D \rightarrow D_1$ = increase in demand
$D \rightarrow D_2$ = fall in demand

Fig. 9.10 Changes in demand

Supply

Supply is the amount of a commodity that producers are willing to put on to the market at various prices in a given period of time. For each price the amount supplied is different. Alternatively, we could say that the supply curve shows the price that is necessary to persuade the producer to provide output. Usually, the higher the price the more of the commodity the producer will want to supply and vice versa, but as is the case with demand, there are some exceptions to this.

A supply schedule and graph can be constructed in a similar way to a demand schedule and graph. Unlike the demand curve, the supply curve usually slopes upwards to the right.

Equilibrium price

Price is the charge assigned to something, or the **exchange value** for a product or service. The demand for a product or service will be influenced by the price of it.

From our examination of supply and demand so far, it should be clear to the reader that buyers want to buy at the lowest price they can, whilst sellers want to obtain the highest price they can for their goods. Whilst these may at first seem conflicting interests, closer examination shows that it is a combination of demand and supply that determines price.

THE MARKETING DEPARTMENT

Market supply schedule

Price	Quantity
10c	100
20c	200
30c	300
40c	400
50c	500

Price	Quantity demanded	Quantity supplied
$5	100	500
$4	200	400
$3	300	300
$2	400	200
$1	500	100

Fig. 9.11 Supply schedule and supply graph

Fig. 9.12 Market for teddy bears — amount demanded and supplied at various prices during one week

When any two forces balance each other they are said to be in **equilibrium**. Under the conditions of a perfect market, the price of a commodity is determined by the interaction of supply and demand. This can be made clearer by looking at a combined demand and supply schedule which is also expressed graphically for simple observation.

As shown in figure 9.12, it is only at the price of $3 that the number of teddy bears the consumers wish to buy is equal to the amount of teddy bears the producer is willing to supply. This is called the **equilibrium price**, which is the only price at which the amount willingly demanded and the amount willingly supplied are equal.

In the diagram it can be seen that the equilibrium price is at the intersection of the demand and supply curves. We can also see that if the price is above the equilibrium price, there is an excess of supply and insufficient demand. The result of this is that the price falls towards the equilibrium price. Alternatively, if the price is below the equilibrium price there is insufficient supply and excess demand. This results in the price rising towards the equilibrium price.

There are many other factors that a firm will take into account in its pricing strategy:

1 Provided they cover their costs, a firm may look at the prices charged by their competitors and make their own price more competitive accordingly. This is called **market-orientated pricing**.

2 Most products have a **price plateau** which represents the level of price that the consumer expects to pay for a particular service or product. If a firm's price is too much above the plateau price, the customer will not buy it. If the firm's price is too far below the plateau, the customer may think that the product is inferior and not buy it.

3 A firm may keep its initial **mark-up** low to enable a **penetration price** to be charged whilst a new product or service is established. It may then be possible to raise the price.

4 With **psychological pricing** firms will keep their prices just below certain levels so that they appear cheaper to the customer — e.g. charging 99c instead of $1, or $99.99 instead of $100.00. Sometimes, it is necessary to raise a 'low' price to avoid the customer forming the suspicion that there is something wrong with the product.

5 Some products may be sold at a loss so that they attract customers into a store, with the loss being recovered on other products sold at the same time. Products sold at a loss are known as **loss leaders**.

6 A firm may operate a **differential pricing policy**. This is where the same product is sold at different prices to different market segments. For example, many transport facilities will offer lower prices at off-peak times.

9.7 Competition

Competition enhances the efficiency of the economic system. It is a major factor in the determination of price.

There are two main types of competition: perfect, pure or free competition, and imperfect competition.

Perfect competition

Perfect competition results from a market situation in which the products of the market-place are of the same kind, are well known to the participators in the market, and where 'breaking into' the market on the part of both buyers and sellers poses little or no problem. In other words, no one buyer or seller dominates. The competitiveness of the market eventually forces costs and prices to settle at the lowest possible levels, whilst production climbs to its peak.

Imperfect competition

When there are very few producers of goods and services in the market-place there is **imperfect competition**. In other words, there is less evidence of rivalry and excessive exchange in the market-place. In this atmosphere there is a **monopoly** or an **oligopoly**.

Monopoly
A monopolistic situation results when a single organisation controls an entire line of products, and is therefore able to determine the selling price. However, the seller is unable to fix both the price and the quantity supplied; the seller fixes prices at the highest level that the market is likely to tolerate. Cement production in Jamaica is a good example of this monopolistic situation. The price of the product is set by a single firm.

Oligopoly
Oligopolistic situations result when a few large suppliers dominate the market-place. There are many examples of oligopolies in the Caribbean. The products being marketed are generally the same in kind, e.g. soap powder. Prices are usually tightly structured. The aim is to reduce or even prevent competition.

Cartels
Cartels are also members of the imperfect market. A cartel consists of a number of firms within a particular industry, such as the Organisation of Petroleum Exporting Countries (OPEC) in the petroleum industry. The firms agree on things such as pricing, production levels, sales and the division of the markets.

Government intervention
Governments are sometimes obliged to intervene and protect consumers from imperfections in the working of the price system. There are two basic methods of government intervention that are used.

- *The control of prices* through taxation or **subsidies**. Taxation increases production costs, whereas subsidies reduce them.
- *The control of demand* by **rationing**, which is an attempt to influence production and consumption by regulating effective demand.

Imperfect competition influences on market

It will have been obvious from the elements of imperfect competition we have looked at here, that they demonstrate how supply and price can be influenced by a powerful business or governments. They can set prices to whatever level they wish, even to the extent of charging unreasonably high prices. They can restrict output, which can ensure they will still sell their products, whatever price they charge. They can also influence what will exist within the market, e.g. fashion and other market trends.

Caribbean market structure

Monopolies in the Caribbean can be seen in the **public utilities** companies, where light, power and water supply are usually provided by a State Corporation or a nationalised industry. Telecommunications, telegraph and telephone services are provided by the Cable and Wireless Company.

Newspaper companies of Jamaica, Barbados, Trinidad and Tobago, among other nations, operate in an oligopolistic market structure. The oil companies operating within the region do so within an oligopoly market structure. However, oil prices are fairly stable throughout the region. This type of market structure is also seen in the electronic media whereby some media houses own television and radio stations. Radio Jamaica Limited is one such media house.

Multinational corporations control the production of bauxite and oil. These also operate within an oligopoly market structure. Their operations can be described in a global context rather than in a regional context.

The role of governments

From the foregoing it will be realised that governments have an important part to play in a free economy to ensure that, whilst imperfect competition may be impossible to avoid, it is not allowed to exploit the public. Governments attempt to restrict the development of non-competitive market structures such as those examined earlier. The major goal is to ensure consumers are protected from unfair practices. In some cases, because of the size of the countries involved, and the resources available, it is difficult to prevent monopolies from developing.

However, not all monopolies restrict the supply of essential products in order to gain the highest profits possible, or produce inferior goods. Some monopolies have been able to operate efficiently and thus produce large quantities of goods at reasonable cost to the consumer.

Governments, therefore, put policies in place by which such businesses are to be guided. They also intervene when situations arise that are untenable.

9.8 Public relations

All businesses care about what the public think of them, and they will use a variety of ways to try to influence the public to have a high regard for the firm and its employees. The extent to which the public have a good impression of a business is called **public relations**, or **goodwill**.

In a large company it is possible to employ a specialist called the **public relations officer** (PRO), who has the responsibility of promoting a good public image. In a smaller business this role has to be carried out by the owner or a responsible senior employee. But the promotion of public relations is really the responsibility of all employees.

Good public relations may be promoted in direct ways such as making donations to charities, giving away free samples and gifts, operating prize-giving competitions, using famous personalities to endorse the company's goods and so on. These and many other methods are deliberately used to encourage the public to look on the business in a favourable way.

It is not unusual for trade associations to sponsor research and technical information projects for the benefit of their members. In addition, the trade association may undertake publicity campaigns at home or abroad aimed at creating trade for all members.

There are also many indirect ways that companies use to promote their public image, and often these will draw on the help of all employees. For example, potential customers will be influenced by the manner in which employees talk to them on the telephone or at the shop counter. They will also be influenced by the way that their enquiries or complaints are dealt with.

Many companies take particular care with the way that they handle after-sales services, because they recognise that this is a vehicle for good public relations. They try to ensure that when a customer has a complaint about a purchase made, it is turned to the seller's advantage by showing courtesy and a willingness to put things right quickly.

9.9 Trade associations

Manufacturers' associations

A manufacturers' association has many similarities with a chamber of commerce, but in this case each association consists of people from a similar business. An example is the Citrus Growers Association. These organisations provide an ideal forum for the exchange of information between members, and on occasions a common body for carrying out wage negotiations with trade unions. Such associations have a number of aims, but an important one is to create **codes of practice** that are to be followed by their members. In this respect the trade association acts as a focal point for dealing with consumer complaints, as well as promoting goodwill for all its members.

Chambers of commerce

Chambers of commerce are voluntary associations of business people. They are sited in towns and cities where commerce is particularly active. Their members come from a wide range of businesses; for example, retailing, finance and transport. In other words, chambers of commerce consist of people from different types of business. They help to develop and expand business in their locality, and also help with foreign trade. They give their members advice on a wide range of matters including legislation, customs regulations, recovery of bad debts, and many other important aspects of trading practice.

Chambers of commerce exist in many overseas countries also. Through links with the chambers of commerce of other countries useful information and many contacts for businesses both at home and abroad can be provided — an increasingly important service.

Chambers of commerce also take an interest in education and training for employment. A difficulty faced by educationalists is identifying what skills commerce and industry want students to leave school or college with. The answer to this question can be obtained in part through chambers of commerce and manufacturers' associations.

9.10 THINGS TO DO

This section contains a variety of exercises to help you create revision notes, to test your understanding and to prepare you for examinations.

Search and find

Write out the question and the answer by referring back through the text to form revision notes.

1. You are employed by a major company that manufactures a range of soft drinks. Briefly describe the process the company would be likely to follow in marketing a new drink.
2. Why is marketing said to be a 'two-way process'?
3. Explain the difference between 'sales concept', 'marketing concept' and 'customer concept'.
4. Describe the functions of a marketing department.
5. What sort of things do you think help a business in identifying its 'target market'?
6. What is meant by 'marketing mix'?
7. Describe the stages involved in a product's life cycle.
8. How does 'product range' differ from 'product mix'?
9. What is merchandising?
10. List at least six merchandising techniques used by the seller of goods.
11. What are branded goods?
12. What do you understand by demand? What are the determinants of demand?
13. Use the information in the table to produce a demand graph.

Price per unit (cents)	Quantity demanded at each price (kilos)
45	1
40	2
35	3
30	4
25	5

14. With the aid of a simple diagram, explain the way a demand schedule can form a demand graph.
15. List the factors that determine demand.
16. Use simple diagrams to describe the effect of changes in demand on a demand curve.
17. What do we mean by the term 'supply'?
18. What do you understand by 'price'?
19. How does supply and demand help to identify 'equilibrium price'?
20. How does perfect competition differ from imperfect competition?
21. How does monopoly differ from oligopoly?
22. Give examples of monopolistic situations in the Caribbean region.
23. 'Not all monopolies are in conflict with public interest'. What is your view?
24. Briefly describe the work of a public relations officer.
25. Why are public relations an important aspect of a firm's operations?
26. What part do trade associations play in business?

THE MARKETING DEPARTMENT

What do you know?

Write out the complete sentence and insert the missing words, which can be chosen from the list at the end of the questions.

1. Marketing connects those who produce goods with potential . . . . . .

2. The . . . . . concept refers to the business goal of trying to satisfy customers and make a profit in doing so.

3. The way a business finds out what customers want is by market . . . . . .

4. A firm's marketing department is concerned with . . . . . its products.

5. In a large firm it is possible to . . . . . the marketing department into several sub-divisions.

6. Sales . . . . . visit potential customers and obtain orders.

7. A business will often have a number of . . . . . markets.

8. If supply increases faster than demand, prices . . . . . .

9. Usually, the lower the price the . . . . . the quantity demanded.

10. When any two forces balance each other they are said to be in . . . . . .

Choose the missing words from the following:

target	buyers	divide	fall
higher	marketing	selling	research
equilibrium	representatives		

Multiple choice

Select the appropriate answer, a, b, c or d.

1. A business finds out what people want by:
   a) product development
   b) advertising
   c) marketing strategy
   d) market research

2. A 'mail shot' involves:
   a) sending out leaflets
   b) identifying the target market
   c) receiving letters from customers
   d) despatching goods by post

3. The complete range of techniques used in selling a company's goods is called:
   a) sales representatives
   b) marketing mix
   c) advertising
   d) product range

4. In which of the following stages of a product life cycle do sales begin to decline?
   a) introduction
   b) growth
   c) maturity
   d) decline

5. The correct name for the collection of products a firm markets is called:
   a) product range
   b) product banding
   c) product development
   d) product research

6. A firm will introduce a new product at which of the following stages in the product life cycle?
   a) pre-launch
   b) growth
   c) decline
   d) maturity

7. When demand increases:
   a) price is likely to rise
   b) supply will increase
   c) price will fall
   d) supply will fall

8. Supply is best defined as:
   a) the amount of a product or service people are willing and able to buy at a given time and at a given price
   b) the quantity of a product or service that firms provide at a given time and at a given price
   c) products that many people want to purchase
   d) the amount that is added to a product's cost to decide the selling price

9. Which of the following definitions is most appropriate as the main function of merchandising?
   a) it brings buyers and sellers together
   b) it sells advertising space
   c) it is concerned with the display of goods
   d) it costs out the selling price of products

10. Public relations is best described as:
    a) the total process of building goodwill towards a business
    b) persuasive communication of products and services
    c) a combination of various methods of sales promotion
    d) direct contact between a seller and a buyer

Keywords

Find out the business-related meaning of each of the following words. Write a separate sentence for each word to show your understanding.

distribution	oligopoly	representatives	monopoly
design	research	costing	commodity
cartel	branding		

THE MARKETING DEPARTMENT

Structured questions

1. This question is related to the illustration of a product life cycle shown in figure 9.7.

   a) What is meant by 'product life cycle?' (2)

   b) At what stage in a product life cycle is marketing at its maximum level? (2)

   c) Why is it important for both the production and marketing departments to be aware of the position of their products in the life cycle? (4)

   d) Compare the functions of the production and marketing sections of a large organisation. (4)

   e) When is the most appropriate time in a product life cycle:
      (i) to begin new product development? (2)
      (ii) to introduce the new product? (2)

   f) Why is it important that the production and marketing departments should cooperate with each other? (4)

2. a) The advertisement in figure 9.13 refers to a 'product line' (i.e. product range). Name four different items that might be included in the range. (2)

   b) State four different appropriate places to sell this company's products. (2)

   c) How could branding assist the marketing of the product range? (3)

   d) Name three marketing occupations between completion of production and eventual purchase by the consumer. (3)

   e) Briefly describe four different ways in which the public might be made aware of this product range. (4)

   f) What factors would be likely to influence customers to purchase Lushlock's products? (6)

3. Juicyfruit Ltd. is a major producer and distributor of fresh fruit and fresh vegetables. Juicyfruit's own fleet of delivery vehicles plays an important part in distributing its products throughout the Caribbean region. The figure 9.14 shows how Juicyfruit can quickly distribute its products in the Caribbean to reach the final consumer within 24 hours.

Fig. 9.14 Juicyfruit Flowchart

a) Why is it important for Juicyfruit to distribute its products within 24 hours? (2)

b) Explain the difference between an 'imported product' and a 'home-grown product'. (2)

c) Why do Juicyfruit's own fleet of delivery vehicles play an important part in distributing its products? (4)

Do you want to improve the condition of your hair?

Do you suffer from hair loss or dandruff?

We have the answer

LUSHLOCKS

is a completely new hair care product line from Vincent & Son Martinique Ltd
PO Box 9 Bellefontaine

Fig. 9.13 Hair care advertisement

d) Why would a supermarket chain be able to sell Juicyfruit's products at a lower price than an independent retailer? (4)

e) Describe the difference in marketing techniques that a supermarket chain would be likely to employ in comparison with an independent retailer. (8)

4 Read the newspaper article in figure 9.16 and answer the questions that follow:

> **BUYING FROM YOUR OWN HOME**
>
> **Television shopping has just arrived in the Caribbean. For one hour, every Saturday morning, families will be able to shop from their TV screens.**
>
> **Each product will have a four minute slot. During this time viewers can telephone using one of 200 lines, free of charge. They will be able to order a product over the telephone and pay by quoting their credit card number.**
>
> **The 'Armchair Shopping Show' will follow the pattern of successful shopping shows running in the United States of America.**
>
> **In the Caribbean, mostly branded name products will be sold, with nothing costing below $200, and presented in an interesting and informative way. Typical items will include clothes, washing machines, cameras, and other goods.**
>
> **The idea began with the Homes Shopping Network, in the USA, a 24 hour show. The US show started from nothing in 1986 and by 1990 had a turnover of $4 billion a year.**

Fig. 9.15 Television shopping

a) What is meant by the following terms used in the newspaper article:
   (i) branded name products (2)
   (ii) turnover of $4 billion a year? (2)

b) In what way is television shopping likely to be convenient for consumers? (2)

c) What marketing techniques are likely to be used by the seller? (4)

d) How will the producers of goods advertised on the 'Armchair Shopping Show' benefit? (4)

e) What factors will determine whether or not the 'Armchair Shopping Show' is a success? (6)

Research assignments

1 Visit two different types of local business, such as a food store, clothing store, or furniture store. Compare the merchandising techniques that each uses, and comment on whether differences that exist arise from the nature of the products or from differences in techniques.

2 Choose a product or service that is of interest to you. Visit four different stores that sell the product or service. Make a comparison of the ways each store markets the product or service. What advice would you offer any of the stores?

3 Name a product or service that you purchased recently. Describe the marketing techniques that you know helped you to make your choice and purchase. Take three products you would not buy and frankly describe the marketing techniques that could help to change your attitude to these products.

4 Assume that a major company is planning to build a large sports complex and has asked for your help. You are required to identify different groups of people who would be likely to pay to use the complex, and indicate the features or facilities that should be included in the sports complex so that it will appeal in the fullest to each of these groups of people. Describe in detail how you would carry out this assignment.

5 Describe a promotional plan that could be used to market your school or college in order to make as many people as possible aware of the good features of it. How could you evaluate the effectiveness of your plan? In what ways would you motivate other students to participate in the plan.

6 Considering a particular product, such as a car, explain why deciding on the marketing price requires a knowledge of the product life cycle. What evidence can you present proving that product life cycles really exist?

7 What evidence can you find that monopolies exist in the Caribbean region? To what extent do you feel they operate adversely or otherwise to the best interests of the consumers?

Chapter 10
MARKET RESEARCH AND ADVERTISING

10.1 Aims of market research

In Chapter 9 we learnt that the marketing concept requires a firm to be aware of the customer's needs, to try to meet those needs, and to attempt to make a profit in the process. Market research assists the firm to meet the goal of the marketing concept by helping the process of finding out what the customer wants. In other words, market research identifies the marketing strategy that will reach the target audience.

Market research investigates what consumers are buying or are likely to buy in the future. The research is normally carried out before launching the advertising campaign. Thoroughly carried out, market research can help to direct advertisers to the most economic and effective way of running their campaign. Sometimes market research is carried out after the product is already well-established, in order to assess and improve advertising and evaluate product performance.

The aims of market research

Market research has three broad aims.

- *To find out what the public wants* so that the business does not waste resources producing goods or services that are not required.
- *To assess likely volume of demand* to ensure that over-producing does not occur.
- *To discover what will influence consumers* — product name, style and colour of packaging, best target audience, price range, effective hidden persuaders.

In order to achieve these aims the marketeer needs to be aware of the following factors that influence consumer behaviour.

Choice. Where there are several competitors in the market consumers will have several alternatives to choose from. For this reason the marketeer is forced to be competitive.

Taste. People differ in their preference for goods and services, and therefore the marketeer has to identify these preferences.

Tradition. In some circumstances there may be a longstanding tradition that influences consumer behaviour. For example, products such as scent have traditionally been associated with members of only one of the sexes.

Income. The amount of money a person earns clearly affects his or her ability to purchase. Consequently, some highly priced products and services will only be purchased by the higher-paid wage earner.

Brand loyalty. Marketeers often try to create loyalty for their products with consumers. The hope is that customers will stay with their existing product because it has satisfied them for some time. Conversely, brand loyalty also makes it difficult for the marketeer to woo consumers away from a product that they are satisfied with.

The importance of market research

Market research provides a marketeer with information which will help in making decisions about:

- where to sell a product or service
- how to sell it
- which customers need the product and exactly what they want
- how to price the product
- how to promote the product
- who are the competitors in the market-place
- what the size of the market is.

The person responsible for market research has to be able to answer a number of appropriate questions in order to come up with useful information which can aid marketing decision-making in the firm.

Those carrying out market research find out the information they seek by asking a cross-section of the public (from all age-groups and social backgrounds) a number of carefully designed questions. The questioning is carried out in a variety of places.

In the street, shop or home
The researcher has a set of prepared questions. The answers to many of these questions can be recorded quickly by ticks in boxes marked Yes or No. The telephone is increasingly being used for research in the home.

Questionnaires circulated in shops or homes
A carefully constructed questionnaire must be:

- easy to understand
- simple to answer, perhaps by ticks
- capable of useful analysis (frequently by computer).

Sampling
- Members of the public may be invited to try the product, or compare one or more samples and make constructive observations.
- Test marketing may be carried out by selling the product in a small sample area in order to assess likely demand prior to commencing full-scale production.

Fig. 10.1 A market research questionnaire can be used to collect information about potential markets for goods and services

10.2 Types of market research

The following are some of the market research strategies used by marketeers.

Experiments

A product may be developed and marketed in one or two limited geographical areas. During this process, data are collected, tabulated and analysed. The findings are then used in deciding whether the 'pilot' experiment suggests that it would be worthwhile embarking on large-scale production and distribution.

Observations

Observation is perhaps the most widely used form of market research. The observations may be **formal** or **informal**.

Using the observation approach, the researcher watches how people behave or respond to certain situations. For example, does a change in packaging design have the effect of improving sales?

Guidelines to be followed during the observations are set out by the researcher, and appropriate notes are made during the period. The information collected is passed on to the researcher's firm for analysis and decision-making.

Surveys

Sometimes we encounter market research personnel in supermarkets, our communities, in airport buildings and other places. These people use **questionnaires**, personal interviews or telephone interviews based on carefully constructed questions to establish the views of consumers.

It is impossible to survey every consumer, and therefore a sample is used. This sample has to be representative of the whole population. So, the **representative sample** includes both sexes, a variety of age groups, country and town dwellers, and people who are poor as well as those who are not.

The main ways of conducting surveys are as follows.

- *By post.* This is by far the easiest method but it has its disadvantages in that many people will not bother to complete and return the questionnaires.

- *By personal interview.* This is the most common method, but it can be expensive because it is very labour-intensive.

- *By telephone.* This approach is becoming increasingly common, although it sometimes has the counter-effect on consumers that they are put off the product because they object to being disturbed in their home.

10.3 Market research in action

The market research team

Market research is carried out by specialists called **market researchers**. In a large organisation several such specialists will be used to form a team.

The market research team must ensure that their research is relevant to the needs of the firm as well as to the needs of the consumer. Research must be accurate, and also timely if it is to achieve the desired result. For example, if an organisation that produces clothing for teenagers learns from its research findings that certain types of T-shirt are popular among teenagers during the summer months, then, to meet the demands of the teenagers, the T-shirts must be produced to the required specifications. Decisions must be made on the right:

- styles
- colours needed
- quantity required
- sales timing for the summer
- places where the buyers can access them.

If a business is not large enough to employ its own market researchers, it can hire the services of a **market research agency**, which is a firm that specialises in this work.

Sources of information

The sources of information from which a market researcher collects data can be classified as primary or secondary:

Primary data is usually drawn from original sources. In other words, none of the data has been collected previously by someone else. This type of data can be collected through experiments, observations and interviews, as described earlier.

Secondary data refers to information that is already in existence in a form different from the one the researcher intends to use, but which may be useful to managers in the decision-making process. In other words, secondary data has already been gathered previously by someone else, and the researcher's intention is to access the data and make use of it. Rich sources of secondary data for the market research team include a firm's files, annual reports, manuals and brochures.

Secondary data also includes items such as government statistics, reference books, newspaper articles and even the sales literature of competitors. Because the researcher does not actually have to go out into the field to collect this data first-hand, it is often referred to as **desk research**. The **internet** has become an important source of desk research.

Research procedures

The following are typical examples of procedures followed by professional researchers:

1. Identify the problem to be solved or the information to be obtained.
2. Set limits to the problem. Focus on one or a few manageable things.
3. Draw on current knowledge (of the product or of the market).
4. Seek out new knowledge (current knowledge might be inadequate, irrelevant, or just out of date).
5. Consider all possible solutions to the problem (careful examination of current and new knowledge).
6. Attempt to find alternative solutions to the problem.
7. Select the best solution to the problem. This should always be related to the target market.
8. Try out the identified solution, e.g. experiment with a sample or a trial run.
9. Evaluate, and adjust where necessary.

10.4 Functions of advertising

The main functions of advertising are as follows.

- To announce new products.
- To highlight the unique features of a product.
- To build a firm's image around its products.
- To highlight special events, such as concessions, sales and late openings.
- To increase market share by stimulating demand.
- To educate consumers about the products.

The purpose of advertising

It would be pointless for a business to develop a product or service if there were no way to tell consumers about it. Advertising is a means of communication: it is used to make consumers aware of the goods and services that producers and traders have to offer. An advertisement is a message that uses words, pictures or sound:

- to **inform** potential buyers of the availability of goods and services

- to **persuade** people to buy or to behave in a particular way.

Informative and persuasive advertising

Informative advertising gives detailed information about the goods or services available and leaves consumers to decide, without persuasion, whether or not they wish to purchase. An informative advertisement contains useful details such as specification, sizes, colour and material. This type of approach can also be employed in public relations and image creation.

Fig. 10.2 **Informative advertisements**

Persuasive advertising uses a variety of techniques to persuade people to buy a product or service, irrespective of whether they need it or not.

Fig. 10.3 **Persuasive advertising**

Advertising's 'hidden persuaders'

One of the ways an advertiser may use an advertisement to promote sales is to persuade the consumer that the advertiser's product will make the consumer better off in some way. Some of the motives to which this type of advertisement appeals are far from obvious and, therefore, they are sometimes called 'hidden persuaders'. Some of the motives to which persuasive advertisements appeal are the following.

- *Sex appeal*: the product is claimed to make the user attractive to the opposite sex.
- *Ambition*: the advertisement implies that those who use the product will be successful.
- *Personality appeal*: famous personalities are shown using the product to give it an acceptable image.
- *Social acceptability*: the advertisement implies that by using the product the consumer becomes more acceptable to others.
- *Work simplification*: the product is claimed to make a task easier to carry out.
- *Health*: the advertisement suggests that use of the product contributes to good health.

10.5 Forms of advertising

Advertising media

There are a wide variety of ways in which an advertisement may reach the public, but not all are suitable for every advertisement. There are many media through which advertising may take place, each of which has a varying degree of effectiveness and cost.

- *Television and radio*: very expensive, but it is the most effective method of reaching a large audience.
- *National press*: reaches a wide area, but is expensive and, therefore, mainly used by large companies.
- *Local newspapers*: offers cheaper advertising rates for cover of a limited area. Free local newspapers rely on advertising to meet costs.
- *Magazines or journals*: usually have a more limited circulation than newspapers, but reach a selected audience, offer greater scope for colour advertisements, and have a longer life.
- *Cinemas*: reach a relatively small audience but can be effective, particularly in advertising local shops, etc.
- *Posters and hoardings*: eye-catching, high impact signs, sited in public places or on public transport.
- *Point of sale*: use eye-catching shop counter or window displays to influence the consumer to buy on impulse.

- *Exhibitions*: attract large numbers of people who already have at least some interest in the product. Exhibitions also enable specialists in a field to meet and compare products and experience.
- *Circulation*: by leaflets can be an effective medium but if they are delivered by hand, it is very labour-intensive, and costly if they are posted (a 'mail shot').
- *Word of mouth* (by recommendation): sometimes encouraged by firms carrying out a 'whispering campaign' by giving away free samples which they hope the users will talk about favourably.

The marketeer has to decide which medium is most appropriate for the product or service he or she is trying to sell. Often, a combination of the forms of advertising listed above will be incorporated into the seller's advertising campaign.

10.6 The advertising campaign

An **advertising campaign** consists of all of the processes a firm uses to sell its goods or services. A campaign is based on a clearly defined plan, much of which is formed as a result of market research (described earlier).

Some firms are large enough to have their own advertising department, others may decide it is preferable to employ an advertising agency to carry out an advertising campaign on their behalf. Whichever is the case, the advertiser or agency will have to take many factors into account. The following questions must certainly be answered if the campaign is to be effective.

- Which groups of the public ('target audience') is the campaign intended to reach?
- How much money is available to be spent on the campaign?
- How extensive is the campaign intended to be — countywide, countrywide or worldwide?
- Which techniques will catch the attention of buyers?

Some of these questions, such as the amount of money to be put into the campaign, can only be answered by the advertiser. Others can be solved through market research.

Fig. 10.4 Forms of advertising

Advertising agencies

Advertising agencies are businesses which specialise in assisting others with their advertising needs, a service for which they are paid.

The extent of the work that the agency undertakes for their client depends on how much the client wishes to spend on advertising a product. The agency may work in conjunction with the client's own advertising department, advising them how they might conduct their campaign, or alternatively it may be employed to organise the complete advertising campaign.

It takes the work of many skilled people to formulate a single advertisement, and the formulation of a complete campaign for a large national company is a vast undertaking. An agency handling such a campaign employs people with specialist skills associated with marketing.

Apart from market research, an advertising department or an advertising agency is concerned with artwork and space-buying.

Artwork
This involves the formation of the pictorial display of the advertisement, and includes the creation of the wording to go with the advertisement. In these aspects of advertising **brainstorming** gets good results. The team creating the advertisement brainstorm by freely expressing ideas until the most suitable wording and visual display is found.

Space buying
This is the process of hiring the most appropriate space in which to display the advertisement: not only the most effective but also the most economically appropriate. For example, although television is one of the most effective forms of advertising, it is far too expensive for selling a few inexpensive items.

10.7 Is advertising wasteful?

There is no real answer to this question because it depends on one's personal point of view. Some people argue that advertising benefits the consumer in a variety of ways, whereas others suggest that it causes an added expense to be met by the consumer. What do you think?

Arguments for advertising

- Makes consumers aware of the range of choice available.
- Encourages healthy competition between suppliers.
- Promotes demand and makes mass production possible.
- Mass production provides employment and also keeps prices down.
- Helps to pay for sports events and concerts.
- Contributes towards the cost of newspapers and magazines.
- Brightens up town centres with colourful displays.

Criticisms of advertising

- The cost of advertising has to be incorporated into the price of goods or services.
- Most advertising aims to persuade people to buy whether they need the commodity or not.
- 'Hidden persuaders' appeal to emotions and prejudices.
- Some advertising encourages anti-social habits and behaviour.

Fig. 10.5 Key advertising agency personnel planning an advertising campaign

- Some advertising misleads by making exaggerated claims.
- It encourages people to be wasteful and discard products for new ones.

10.8 Consumer protection

The need for consumer protection

All people, businesses and even governments are consumers, although we usually refer particularly to individuals when talking about consumers. We have seen in Chapters 1 and 2 of this book that the aim of production is to make things that can be used by consumers. In fact it has been said that the sole end and purpose of all production is the consumer. We have also seen in this chapter that advertising aims not only to inform us about goods and services, but also to persuade us to buy them.

With the growth of large-scale production and the increased spending power of many people, the motivation for firms to obtain and maintain a larger share of the consumer market has risen considerably. This has been further encouraged by technological changes which have revolutionised not only products and the way they are manufactured, but also the manner in which they are marketed.

At one time, the attitude of the law in relation to the protection of consumers was **caveat emptor**, or 'let the buyer beware'. In other words, consumers were expected to protect themselves. Today, consumers are protected in a number of ways by legislation and government agencies, but it is still important for consumers to help protect themselves by shopping wisely.

Traders cannot go against consumers' rights without facing the risk of legal action. Traders need to know the rights of their customers and realise that they have a responsibility to treat them fairly in order to meet their legal obligations. In addition, traders have rights concerning their suppliers similar to those customers have against traders, so long as they have not agreed to give up those rights.

The Sale of Goods Act

This British law has been very influential in the Caribbean as a major legal standard for the protection of consumers. It has been amended several times since it was first established in 1893. Today, the act has several implications.

The act covers all goods (including food) bought from a trader through a shop, a doorstep seller, or sales by mail order. The seller has three main obligations.

- Goods must be of *merchantable quality*. This means that goods must be reasonably fit for their normal purpose, bearing in mind the price paid, the nature of the goods and how they were described. Thus a new item must not be damaged and must work properly.
- Goods must be *as described*. They must correspond with the description given by the seller, or with labels on the item or the packaging.
- Goods must be *fit for any particular purpose made known to the seller by the customer*. For example, if the customer asks for plates that are 'dishwasher safe', the seller has an obligation to ensure that the plates sold meet the requirement made known to him by the customer.

When things go wrong

Of course, things go wrong, and it may not always be the fault of the seller. Before you charge off to the shop to complain about faulty goods, ask yourself three simple questions:

- Was it a fault I should have noticed when buying?
- Was it something I was told about?
- Am I expecting too much from something cheap?

If the answer to all three questions is 'no', then go ahead and complain. Take along proof of purchase (e.g. the receipt), and remember to act in a reasonable manner. Most respectable traders will want to put things right.

If you have no success at the shop, write to the head office. Keep copies of all correspondence. Should you still not be satisfied you may well need support from some other agency, or you may decide to take legal action.

Supporting agencies

There are a variety of agencies that support the consumer; the following are just some of them.

The Metrication Board of Trinidad and Tobago
This board was established to plan, coordinate and supervise the change-over from imperial units to metric. But the board also provides consumer protection by raising consumer awareness through lectures, seminars, leaflets, handbills and advertising pertaining to metric equivalents of the imperial system.

The bureaux of standards
Bureaux of standards institutions are government agencies which try to help to protect consumers by ensuring that goods produced meet certain minimum requirements with regard to quality and basic raw materials. Sometimes a bureau will try to encourage a producer to manufacture in a particular way to meet the bureau's standards.

Ministry of Consumer Affairs

In nearly all the countries in the region, overall government responsibility for consumer protection is administered by this ministry. The brief of the ministry includes the following:

- giving advice to consumers
- control and supervision of prices
- promotion and implementation of food policy legislation
- control of quality and weights and measures
- enforcing fair trading practices
- supervision of hire purchase and credit control.

The ombudsman

An ombudsman is a government-appointed person who is charged with investigating malpractices, maladministration and injustices brought to his notice by the public. It is often the case that an ombudsman specialises in particular areas of public concern, but many governments have such a person to investigate consumers' complaints.

10.9 THINGS TO DO

This section contains a variety of exercises to help you create revision notes, to test your understanding and to prepare you for examinations.

Search and find

Write out the question and the answer by referring back through the text to form revision notes.

1. In what way does market research help a firm to achieve a marketing concept?
2. What kinds of decision do market researchers hope to be able to make from the data collected?
3. Briefly describe the factors that influence consumer behaviour.
4. Where is market research carried out?
5. Describe some of the strategies used by market researchers to gather information.
6. Why is it often important that a market researcher uses a 'representative sample'?
7. Explain the difference between 'primary data' and 'secondary data'.
8. What is the aim of advertising?
9. How does 'informative' advertising differ from 'persuasive' advertising?
10. What are 'hidden persuaders'?
11. Briefly describe the various advertising media.
12. What do we mean by the term 'advertising campaign'?
13. What is the function of an advertising agency?
14. List the arguments for and against advertising.
15. Why is there a need for consumers to be protected?
16. List the main forms of consumer protection that exist in your country.
17. In what way is self protection the best form of consumer protection?

What do you know?

Write out the complete sentence and insert the missing word, which can be chosen from the list at the end of the questions.

1. The marketing concept requires a firm to be aware of the customer's . . . . .
2. Market research provides a marketeer with information which helps to make . . . . . about marketing goods or services.
3. Those carrying out market research find out the information they seek by . . . . . a cross-section of the public.
4. A . . . . . sample includes people from a variety of backgrounds.
5. . . . . . data refers to information that is collected from original sources.
6. . . . . . data refers to information that is already in existence.
7. The main aim of advertising is to make consumers . . . . . of the availability of goods and services.
8. . . . . . advertising leaves consumers to decide, without persuasion, if they wish to purchase.
9. The . . . . . audience is the section of the public an advertising campaign is trying to reach.

10 Advertising ..... are businesses which specialise in assisting others with their advertising needs.

> Choose the missing words from the following:
>
> agencies   decisions   primary   target
> questioning   representative   aware   needs
> secondary   informative

Multiple choice

Select the appropriate answer, a, b, c or d.

1. Which of the following statements about advertising is false?
   a) it can be wasteful of resources
   b) it does not cost the consumer anything
   c) it informs the consumer what is available
   d) it encourages consumers to buy

2. The type of organisation that is set up to carry out market research on behalf of other businesses is:
   a) an agency
   b) a marketeer
   c) a broker
   d) an investigator

3. 'Hidden persuaders' are:
   a) prices not shown in advertisements
   b) products bought unseen
   c) goods delivered that were not ordered
   d) subtle advertising techniques

4. Which of the following forms of advertising media generally displays the largest size of advertisement?
   a) television
   b) poster
   c) hoarding
   d) newspaper

5. A market research questionnaire is used to:
   a) collect information about potential markets for goods
   b) compare one or more products
   c) tell people what a company is trying to sell
   d) identify areas that are most densely populated

6. Which of the following advertising media will reach the most people?
   a) television
   b) magazines
   c) newspapers
   d) posters

7. The advertising method most likely to be successful in catching the fleeting glimpses of passers-by would be:
   a) newspapers
   b) leaflets
   c) posters
   d) magazines

8. Which of the following words best describes the methods that companies use to send their advertising messages to potential buyers?
   a) questionnaires
   b) media
   c) promotion
   d) marketing

9. Which of the following statements is an example of wording that might be included in an informative advertisement?
   a) the route to good health
   b) to keep you young and attractive
   c) used by the 'Whatsit' pop group
   d) machine washable

10. Space buying refers to:
    a) renting office space
    b) hire of open spaces
    c) obtaining a place to display an advertisement
    d) purchase of building plots

> **Key words**
>
> Find out the business-related meaning of each of the following words. Write a separate sentence for each word to show your understanding.
>
> marketeer   surveys   interview   observations
> campaign   agency   advertisement   brainstorming
> brand   questionnaire

Structured questions

1. Refer to figure 10.6.
   a) Define the term 'prototype'. (2)
   b) What is the purpose of a prototype? (2)
   c) What is a 'brainstorming session'? (2)
   d) Describe the kind of market research that would be carried out:
      (i) before the cleaner goes onto the market (3)
      (ii) after the cleaner goes on sale to the public. (3)
   e) List four contrasting questions that could be included in a market research questionnaire to help the development of an advertising campaign for this new product. (4)
   f) If the market research clearly shows that there is a need for the planned cleaner, why will there still be a need for an advertising campaign? (4)

MARKET RESEARCH AND ADVERTISING

Idle Hands Ltd is a manufacturer of household electrical goods. They have decided to produce a new product aimed at the busy working housewife: a remote controlled vacuum cleaner. The head of the product development department has been instructed to produce a prototype with electronic sensors to prevent collisions with furniture, etc.

A name for the new cleaner has yet to be decided; this will be the subject of a brainstorming session. The advertising campaign will be decided following market research and pilot marketing.

Fig. 10.6 Remote controlled vacuum cleaner

2 a) State one of the main functions of advertising. (1)

    b) Briefly state two ways in which advertising benefits the community. (2)

    c) State three criticisms of advertising. (3)

    d) Explain the difference between informative advertising and persuasive advertising. Give descriptive examples to illustrate your explanation. (6)

    e) Describe four of the main methods of advertising, and give examples showing when it is appropriate to use each method you have chosen to describe. (8)

3 Refer to the illustration of part of a market research questionnaire in figure 10.1, and answer these questions.

    a) Who would you consider are the target audience of this questionnaire? Give a reason for your answer. (2)

    b) A result of information obtained in this way could be the implementation of 'test marketing'. What do you understand by this? (2)

    c) Give at least two reasons why the company that has paid for this survey to be carried out would be interested in the hobbies and interests of the people surveyed? (4)

    d) How could the information collected by this questionnaire assist product development? (4)

    e) Describe how information collected by market research could be used to conduct an advertising campaign. (8)

4 a) Advertising is often concerned with creating the right 'image' for products. What is meant by image in this context? (2)

    b) For what purpose might a manufacturer of a new soft drink use a hoarding for advertising? (2)

    c) How would the advertising methods of a small local business differ from those of a major manufacturer? (4)

    d) Explain, with an example, circumstances when it could be more appropriate to place an advertisement in a magazine rather than a newspaper. (6)

    e) Describe the work of an advertising agency. (6)

5 a) Give two contrasting reasons why firms advertise their goods or services. (2)

    b) Advertising is generally directed at consumers, but consumers themselves also advertise. State three *cheap* ways that consumers might advertise items they have for sale. (3)

    c) (i) Briefly state *three* marketing techniques that a business may use in the selling of any product. (3)
       (ii) Show how you could use two of these techniques in the selling of a new portable cassette player. (4)

    d) In what ways can it be said that advertising is not always in the best interest of the consumer? (4)

    e) State, with reasons, why there are less criticisms of informative advertising than there are of persuasive advertising. (4)

6 Read the information in figure 10.7 about marketing, and then answer the questions which ask you to relate market research to this information.

    a) What does market research tell a business? (1)

    b) In what way would you say that market research helps a firm to set an 'acceptable and profitable price level'? (2)

    c) How would market research help a producer to 'match physical requirements with visual image'? (3)

MARKET RESEARCH AND ADVERTISING

> ## WHAT IS MARKETING?
>
> 'Marketing is the management process responsible for identifying, anticipating and satisfying customer requirements profitably'
>
> Don't think–as many people do–that marketing is just the smart 'in' word for selling. Selling is a vital indispensable component of marketing, but only one of several other activities. Marketing, thinking and planning begins at or even before the drawing board and ends only when the company is really satisfied with the products or service provided. Because marketing affects so many of the company's resources and activities, it is essentially a team effort.
>
> Good marketing is the end product of a well-led management team fully embracing the marketing concept. The marketing manager is responsible for the marketing plan and the basic information and guidance about prospective markets, their behaviour, size and potential for each product or service supplied by the company.
>
> ### The Marketing Spectrum
>
> - RESEARCH: identifying, analysing and predicting customer needs.
> - PLANNING AND DEVELOPMENT: deciding on who, what, when and how to meet these needs via new or existing product or service development.
> - PRICING: setting an acceptable and profitable price level.
> - PACKAGING: matching physical requirements with visual image.
> - PROMOTION: generating product awareness and influencing customers' purchasing decisions, e.g. advertising, public relations.
> - SALES: choosing the most efficient and effective sales approach.
> - DISTRIBUTION: evaluating the most efficient way of getting the product to your customer, whether directly or indirectly.
> - AFTER SALES: providing a comprehensive customer care service.
>
> The Marketing Spectrum comprises a number of different functions, many of which are undertaken by specialists. It is the role of the Marketing Manager to co-ordinate the efforts and advice of these people and, based on a view of the situation overall, decide on future action.

Source: The Chartered Institute of Marketing (UK)

Fig. 10.7 What is marketing?

d) Describe two examples of ways that market research can help a business to choose 'the most efficient and effective sales approach'. (4)

e) 'Marketing thinking and planning begins at or even before the drawing board . . . . .' How does market research contribute at this early stage? (4)

f) 'Good marketing is the end product of a well-led management team fully embracing the marketing concept.'
   (i) What do you understand by 'the marketing concept' in the sense in which it is used here? (3)
   (ii) Give examples of other wording included in this document that can be directly related to the marketing concept. (3)

Research assignments

1. You are the advertising manager of a firm that is developing a new soft drink. Describe how you would formulate an advertising campaign to promote the launch of your product into a highly competitive market. Compare your planned campaign with the marketing strategies of an existing soft drink.

2. 'Advertising is wasteful of resources and causes an increase in the cost of goods.' Discuss this statement, using appropriate data to support your arguments.

3. Sometimes market research takes the form of 'desk research', that is finding out information about a potential market by referring to reference sources readily available to anyone. Describe the application of some specific reference sources available to market researchers.

4. Using specific examples of marketing techniques employed by companies with which you are familiar, explain why advertising is important to industry, commerce and the consumer.

5. Using a selection of advertisements to assist you, explain why you consider that there is a case for consumers having some protection against the claims of advertisers. Describe the main forms of consumer protection and explain why you find some more relevant to you than others.

Chapter 11
LOCAL TRADE

11.1 The chain of distribution

In Chapters 8 and 9, your attention was drawn to the need to distribute goods so that they reach the intended customer. We could divide the target market into two broad categories:

- **local trade**: sales to local markets
- **foreign trade**: sales to overseas markets

In this chapter we will concentrate on local trade, and we will turn our attention to foreign trade in Chapter 12.

The chain of distribution for home trade links the producer with the consumer through two main intermediaries: the wholesaler and the retailer. Both of these traders are part of tertiary production because they add to the value of goods.

Producer → Wholesaler → Retailer → Consumer

Fig. 11.1   Chain of distribution

The wholesaler buys goods in very large quantities from the producer, thus helping to make mass production possible. If retailers can order a great enough quantity, they may buy direct from the producer, bypassing the wholesaler.

Producer → Retailer

Fig. 11.2   Bypassing the wholesaler

11.2 Wholesale trade

Producers need to sell their products in large quantities to enable them to carry out mass production and enjoy economies of scale. But many retailers cannot buy the large quantities that the producers and manufacturers want to sell. Wholesalers bridge the gap between producers and retailers by buying in large quantities and selling in smaller, more convenient lots to the retailer. The retailer in turn sells individual items to the consumer.

The wholesaler's premises are usually a large **warehouse** divided into sections dealing with specific commodities, and organised like a large supermarket.

Retailers may visit the wholesaler to choose their purchases, or orders may be telephoned in or passed to the wholesaler's representative on his or her periodic visits to retailers, and delivered in due course by the wholesaler's own delivery vehicles.

Types of wholesaler

There are two basic forms of wholesaler.

1. **General wholesalers** operate from large warehouses sited for convenient access from many local towns. They allow retailers credit, and deliver goods to retail shops.

2. **Cash-and-carry wholesalers** do not allow credit and do not deliver goods. Retailers come to the warehouses, select goods, pay for them, and provide their own transport.

Sometimes wholesalers specialise in a particular aspect of trade. For example, one might specialise in supplies in hair care products, whilst another might specialise in clothing and footwear.

Fig. 11.3   A wholesale warehouse

11.3 Functions of wholesalers

Acting as an intermediary

The wholesaler is positioned between the producer and the retailer. For this reason the wholesaler is sometimes referred to as a 'middleman' or 'intermediary'.

Producer → Wholesaler (middleman) → Retailer

Fig. 11.4 Wholesaler as middleman

But there are exceptions where the producer will sell direct to the retailer, or even straight to the consumer, bypassing both the wholesaler and the retailer.

Breaking of bulk

The wholesaler buys in large quantities from the producer and sells in smaller lots, usually to the retailer.

Taking on risks

The wholesaler predicts market trends and buys ahead of demand.

Warehousing

By storing goods, the wholesaler saves space for both the producer and the retailer.

Offering credit

The wholesaler may supply goods and allow the retailer to pay at some later date (**trade credit**). This may give the retailer the opportunity to sell the goods before he or she has paid for them.

11.4 Services provided by wholesalers

For the producer

- Reduces transport costs.
- Advises the producer of current market trends.
- Finishes goods by grading, packing and branding.
- Makes mass production possible by ordering in large quantities and therefore reducing production costs.

For the retailer

- Offers choice of products from many producers.
- Supplies small quantities to suit retailers' needs.
- Locally situated, providing quick access to goods, and open until late in the evening.
- Advises on latest trends and 'best buys'.
- Pre-packs goods ready for the retailers' shelves (graded, labelled, priced and weighed).

11.5 Elimination of the wholesaler

Wholesalers are sometimes referred to as 'leeches' because they increase the price of goods. However, there are arguments against this view.

- The wholesaling function would have to be carried out by others if wholesalers were eliminated.
- Wholesalers help smaller retailers to exist and therefore encourage competition.
- Wholesalers make mass production possible and so reduce overall costs.

Nevertheless, there are many ways in which the wholesaler is being eliminated. Sometimes the producer

Producer (Mass Quantity) → Sells at factor price (say 20c each) → **Wholesaler** (Bulk Quantity) → Sells at wholesale price (say 25c each) → **Retailer** (Single Items) → Sells at retail price (say 30c each) → **Consumer**

Fig. 11.5 Wholesaler breaking bulk

Without a wholesaler

Producers

Retailers

How many journeys would the manufacturers make altogether?

Fig. 11.6 Wholesaler reducing transport costs

With a wholesaler

Producers

Retailers

Wholesaler

How many journeys now need to be made? Now imagine the saving if there were one hundred or more retailers.

will bypass the wholesaler and sell directly to the retailer, as in the following circumstances.

- If the retailer is part of a large multiple chain, the chain can buy in large quantities and deal directly with the producer.
- When after-sales service is particularly important, for example, selling washing machines, televisions and cookers.

The producer sometimes omits both the wholesaler and the retailer, as in the following examples.

- Products made to specific requirements, for example, fitted furniture.
- Products sold by mail-order firms direct by catalogue, through agents or by advertisements.
- Very large, expensive items such as machinery for industry, which are sent directly to the firms ordering them.

11.6 Retail trade

Retailers are traders providing goods and services directly to the consumer. They are positioned either between producers and consumers, or between wholesalers and consumers. In other words, the retailer is the last link in the chain between the producer and the consumer.

The retailer buys in large quantities from the wholesaler and sells in small, convenient quantities to the consumer. If the retailer can order a great enough quantity he or she may buy direct from the producer.

The functions of retail trade

Today we live in a society in which specialisation plays a major part. Most of us concentrate on carrying out our particular specialisation and rely on others to satisfy most of our needs. For each of us to be able to specialise in this way requires an intricate pattern of distribution between producers and consumers. This involves a whole range of intermediaries such as banking, insurance, transport, advertising and the many other commercial activities that are dealt with in other parts of this book. Here we shall concentrate on retail trade. As the last stage in the passage of goods from the producer to the consumer, the retailer performs a number of important functions.

1 *Outlet*: the retailer performs a valuable service to the producer by providing an outlet for his or her products, thus saving the producer from the need to market his or her own goods.
2 *Stocks*: the retailer holds stocks which the consumer can purchase locally in small, convenient quantities.
3 *Choice*: the consumer is able to choose from the variety of products from different producers offered by the retailer.
4 *Information and advice*: retailers' expert knowledge and experience enable them to advise and inform customers on the quality and suitability of products.
5 *Feedback*: the retailer provides a feedback of consumer responses to wholesalers and producers. This helps the producer to become aware of what the consumer market wants, and also helps to ensure that consumers' requirements are satisfied.

LOCAL TRADE

11.7 Types of retailer

Door-to-door

Door-to-door trades people generally deal in relatively minor goods and services.

a) *Pedlars* carry goods from door to door on foot.

b) *Hawkers* use some method of transport.

c) *Mobile shops* are vehicles adapted to serve as travelling shops, for example the ice cream truck and soft drink truck.

Fig. 11.7 Selling bananas

Market traders

These operate from stalls in open or covered areas, sometimes along streets and sometimes in areas specially kept for markets. Market traders can often keep prices very low because they avoid expenses (overheads) such as electricity, high rent, shop fittings, etc.

Fig. 11.8 Street market in Bridgetown, Barbados

Independent shops

This category of retailer is not attached to a large organisation, and for this reason is referred to by a variety of names, including 'sole trader', 'corner shop', 'unit shop', and 'convenience shop'.

An independent shop is owned by a sole trader or small partnership and is typically sited away from town centres. It often specialises in offering a single commodity or service, as does a baker, butcher or confectioner. There are advantages and disadvantages in this type of retailing.

Advantages
- Gives personal attention to customers.
- Saves customer from travelling into town.
- Owner has a thorough knowledge of the business.
- Sometimes allows customers credit.

Disadvantages
- Cannot buy in very large quantities.
- Prices often higher than larger shops.
- Carries a limited range of stock.
- Difficulties in running the shop if the owner is sick.

Small retailers such as the independent shop are facing considerable difficulties in larger towns where they have to face the competition of large organisations that tend to be more cost-effective.

Fig. 11.9 An independent retailer in Dominica

Multiples (chain stores)

Multiples are chains of shops trading under a single name and all owned by one company. They are generally controlled from a central headquarters and tend to be sited in town centres and shopping precincts. Examples of multiples are Bata, Woolworths and Kirpalani.

Multiples enjoy many advantages over smaller retailers.

- Their large size enables them to bypass wholesalers and buy in large quantities direct from the producer.
- A single national advertisement can cover all branches nationwide.
- They have the resources to rent or buy stores in prime central sites with large car-parking space.
- They can afford to attract customers with loss leaders (goods sold at below cost price).

Supermarkets

A supermarket is a large self-service store. A self-service store is defined as a supermarket when it has more than 200 square metres of shopping area and three or more checkout points. Such stores are often organised as multiples.

Supermarkets deal particularly in prepacked, priced products. Loss leaders are frequently used to attract custom, and customers serve themselves. The provision of shopping trolleys reduces customers' awareness of the weight of their purchases and encourages impulse buying (unplanned purchases).

Because supermarkets are often organised in multiples, they usually enjoy the advantages mentioned earlier. They also benefit from economies of scale. For example they are able to employ specialist staff such as butchers, bakers and fishmongers. In addition, they save on staff because the customers do much of the work by serving themselves.

Although this type of shop has many advantages over other retailers it faces some disadvantages.

- Large premises in prime areas are expensive.
- Pilferage (stealing) levels are high.
- Customers receive little personal contact.
- Shopping trolleys are stolen.

Department store

This type of shop is sometimes called a 'shop of shops' because it is divided into commodity departments. Each department is operated like a single shop, and so is responsible for its own profitability.

Department stores tend to be comfortably equipped with carpets, lifts and a restaurant. Merchandise is attractively displayed, and credit facilities (sometimes interest-free) are given to suitable customers. Some have introduced their own charge cards.

Advantages
- Customers can shop in comfort.
- A wide variety of goods is available under one roof.
- Shop assistants give personal service.
- Sited in towns and convenient for public transport and car parks.

Disadvantages
- Large central sites are expensive.
- Cannot compete with prices of multiples.
- Comfortable surroundings can be a drain on profits.
- Labour-intensive compared with some retailers.

Fig. 11.10 (a)   A multiple

Fig. 11.10 (b)   A supermarket

Hypermarkets

These are a very large form of supermarket with a shopping area in excess of 5,500 square metres. They offer a very wide range of goods in many specialist departments similar to the divisions in a department store. Alternatively, parts of the hypermarket complex may be rented out to other approved traders.

Hypermarkets are usually organised in chains, like multiples. They are frequently sited on the outskirts of towns where land is cheaper. Good parking facilities are provided and some late night trading.

Mail order

Products are sold in a variety of ways through the mail-order method.

- Advertising in the press, on radio or on television which invites potential customers to buy by post.
- Direct selling, with customers choosing articles from a catalogue at home.
- Part-time agents selling to friends from catalogues in return for a commission.

Advantages
- Interest-free credit often given.
- Buying in the comfort of one's home.
- Goods chosen at leisure.

Disadvantages
- Prices often higher than in shops.
- Difficult to assess quality from a catalogue.
- Can be inconvenient to return unsuitable goods.

Vending machines (automats)

These retail outlets are open twenty-four hours a day, and provide a wide variety of products such as hot and cold snacks, confectionery, drinks, petrol, etc. Vending machines are sited in busy public places and they are sometimes the target of vandalism.

Catalogue shops

A catalogue shop publishes a comprehensive catalogue (like a mail-order catalogue) detailing all the products it has for sale. Catalogues are given away free to prospective customers.

Customers who see an item they are interested in buying visit the shop to see a sample of the item. If they like the product, they can then make the purchase on the spot.

Telephone order trading

Sales persons use the telephone to contact potential customers to try to persuade them to buy their company's products.

Sometimes the telephone canvasser knows about the person's interest, perhaps because he or she has replied to an advertisement. But sometimes the canvasser just selects the customer at random from the telephone directory. This is sometimes referred to as 'cold selling'.

11.8 Patterns in retailing

The following are just some of the many growing trends in the retail trade.

Shopping precincts

Sometimes called malls or shopping centres, these are shopping areas shut off from traffic, well served by public transport, road links and car parks, and often with an information centre.

Loss leaders

A loss leader is a popular product being sold at below market price to encourage customers to enter the shop.

Branded goods

Producers and retail multiples use a distinctive trade or brand name to allow easy identification of their goods. Sometimes large retailers buy products from manufacturers and have their purchases 'branded' with their own names.

Free gifts

Items such as tumblers, ashtrays and pens are sometimes given away free with purchases.

Credit facilities

Many retailers offer suitable customers credit facilities, sometimes without charging interest. Some of the larger retailers have introduced their own charge cards, which allow customers to pay for purchases later in instalments.

Franchise shops

A franchise agreement is made between an entrepreneur (business person) and a franchise house. The agreement allows the entrepreneur to use the name of a well-known company and the exclusive right to market its products within a specified area. This form of business is particularly common in the fast food ('takeaway') trade.

Logos

Many large firms now use logos (symbols) with the company title on their products to assist recognition.

Competitions and Lotteries

Some traders give 'lucky' numbers or competition tokens with each purchase.

Bar codes

A bar code consists of a pattern of vertical lines that a computer can read. Producers and large retailers are increasingly giving a bar code to each item on the shelves. As customers leave through the checkout, the bar-coded items are automatically totalled by the point-of-sale terminal (POS) computer link to produce an itemised bill for the customer. The same data transfer method can also be used to automatically update stock records and to decide when the retailer needs to order more stock.

Fig. 11.11 Example of a bar code

Selling through the Internet

Shopping via the Internet is a relatively new but fast growing method of trading. Customers can access a shopping channel through their Internet **service provider**. This enables them to make purchases directly from companies participating and selling through the system. The potential customer can view data related to products sellers have on offer. Having compared the offers of competing sellers and made their choice of purchases, consumers can place their order and pay directly by credit or switch card.

11.9 Selling on credit

Selling on credit means allowing a buyer the use of goods which are paid for after the purchase, perhaps over a period of time by regular instalments. There are a variety of forms that selling on credit may take.

Trade credit

Trade credit occurs where the seller allows the buyer to have goods and pay for them after an agreed period of time. For example, a producer or wholesaler may allow the retailer to have supplies and pay for them at the end of the month. This allows the seller the opportunity to resell the goods before he or she has even paid for them, thus increasing the scope of his or her business.

Hire purchase agreement (HP)

This is a contract for hiring goods for a fixed period with an option to purchase them for a nominal sum (e.g. $1) at the end of the period.

An initial **deposit** is paid, a percentage of the purchase price, and a number of equal weekly or monthly **instalments** are repaid over a given period. Interest is charged for the credit given.

The goods purchased do not become the property of the buyer until the last instalment has been paid. The item purchased must not be sold until the last repayment has been made because the seller or finance company remains the legal owner until the last instalment has been paid.

The seller can repossess the item if the buyer defaults on repayments.

Credit sale agreement

This is a deposit, instalment and interest system similar to an HP agreement, but the buyer becomes the owner of the goods immediately the agreement has been made.

In the case of a credit sale agreement, if the buyer defaults on the repayments the seller or finance company does not repossess the goods but can sue for repayment of the debt.

Note that most retailers do not finance HP and credit sales agreements themselves, but use companies that specialise in this kind of finance.

Interest-free credit

The buyer is allowed to pay for purchases by regular instalments but is not charged any interest.

Credit cards

The holder of a credit card can use it to make purchases up to a set amount without paying cash. The trader claims the money due for the purchases from the company that has issued the credit card.

The card holder is presented with an account from the issuer of the credit card. Payment of the outstanding amount can be made at once in full, or at some later time. Interest is charged on the outstanding balance.

Examples of credit cards are American Express, Diners Club and Visa.

Charge cards

Some retailers have introduced their own form of credit card for use in their stores. These allow approved customers to make purchases and charge these to their personal account, the money to be repaid later. The system is frequently linked to an instalment payment system operated by the firm, sometimes providing interest-free credit.

11.10 Mark-up and profit margin

Both of these terms refer to ways of looking at the differences between a trader's cost price and his selling price.

- **Mark-up** refers to the percentage profit which is added to the cost price by a trader to establish the selling price. For example, if an article has a cost price of 80c and it is to be sold for $1, the mark-up is:

$$\frac{20}{80} \times 100\% = 25\%$$

- **Profit margin** is the percentage of the selling price which is the seller's profit. For example, on an article with a cost price of 80c which is sold for $1, the profit margin is:

$$\frac{20}{100} \times 100\% = 20\%$$

11.11 Setting up a retail business

The following factors need to be taken into account when setting up a retail business.

How will the capital required be raised?

- Savings of owners.
- Borrowing from a bank or other institution.
- Contribution from partners.
- Selling shares privately or publicly.

What type of business is to be established?

- *Sole trader*: one owner running the business with or without employees to assist.

- *Partnership*: with one or more partners, which enables responsibilities to be shared, but also means that ownership and profits are shared.

- *Limited company* (private or public): shareholders provide capital in return for a share of the profits and some say in the operation of the business.

Do the owners or assistants have the necessary skills?

- A thorough knowledge of the products to be sold.

- The ability to manage a business, looking after accounts, stock records, cash flow, profit margins, wages, advertising, taxation, etc.

- The personality and temperament necessary to deal with employees and customers.

Where will the shop be sited?

The cost of sites varies considerably. A central or busy site may be good for trade, but will also be expensive. The entrepreneur needs to be sure that there is sufficient demand (or not too much competition) to support the shop in a chosen position.

LOCAL TRADE

What safeguards have to be applied?

- *Insurance*: public liability, employer's liability, fire, theft, plate glass, vehicles, fidelity bonds, bad debts and business interruption.

- *Health and safety laws*: the entrepreneur needs to ensure that the business has complied with legal requirements to protect the health, safety and welfare of its employees and customers.

11.12 THINGS TO DO

This section contains a variety of exercises to help you create revision notes, to test your understanding and to prepare you for examinations.

Search and find

Write out the question and the answer by referring back through the text to form revision notes.

1. List the functions of wholesalers.
2. Why is the wholesaler sometimes referred to as an intermediary?
3. In what way can the wholesaler be said to 'break bulk'?
4. Why is trade credit useful to the retailer?
5. List the services that the wholesaler provides
    a) for the producer
    b) for the retailer.
6. How does the wholesaler reduce transport costs?
7. In what way does the wholesaler help to make mass production possible?
8. Why is the wholesaler sometimes called a 'leech'?
9. Give three reasons why wholesalers are important even if they do cause an increase in distribution costs.
10. Give an example of a product that the wholesaler might grade or pack on behalf of the retailer.
11. Describe two circumstances in which the producer might sell direct to the retailer.
12. Give three examples in which the producer might bypass both the retailer and the wholesaler.
13. What are the main ways in which general wholesalers and cash-and-carry wholesalers differ?
14. Describe the functions of the retail trade.
15. Explain the difference between a pedlar and a hawker.
16. What are 'overheads'?
17. List the advantages and disadvantages of being a sole trader.
18. What are chain stores, and how are they generally controlled?
19. Name four examples of multiples.
20. List the advantages the multiple store enjoys over smaller retailers.
21. 'All supermarkets are self-service stores, but not all self-service stores are supermarkets.' Explain this statement.
22. Give three examples of the economies of scale gained by operating as a multiple shop.
23. What are the main disadvantages faced by supermarkets?
24. Why is a department store sometimes called a 'shop of shops'?
25. List the advantages and disadvantages of department stores.
26. What is a hypermarket?
27. List three methods of mail-order selling.
28. What are the advantages and disadvantages of buying by mail order from the point of view of the customer?
29. Make a list of ten items you can think of that are sold through vending machines.
30. What is a catalogue shop?
31. Describe telephone-order selling.
32. Briefly describe the features of a shopping precinct.
33. What are 'branded' goods?
34. Describe two techniques used by shops to encourage people to enter their premises.
35. What are franchise shops?
36. How does trade credit benefit the retailer?
37. Explain a hire purchase agreement.
38. What is the advantage to a customer of buying on interest-free credit?

39 Briefly describe the use of the credit card system in the retail trade.

40 Give three examples of credit cards.

41 Explain the terms 'mark-up' and 'profit margin'.

42 Describe three factors it is necessary to take into account when setting up a retail business.

43 Why is the siting of a shop very important?

44 Describe two legal requirements that need to be observed by the shop owner.

What do you know?

Write out the complete sentence and insert the missing word, which can be chosen from the list at the end of the questions.

1 The wholesaler is sometimes referred to as a . . . . . .

2 One of the functions of a wholesaler is . . . . . bulk.

3 The wholesaler makes mass . . . . . possible by ordering in large quantities.

4 Cash-and-carry wholesalers do not allow . . . . . .

5 Sometimes producers . . . . . the wholesaler and sell direct to the retailer.

6 The retailer is the last . . . . . in the chain of distribution between the producer and the consumer.

7 . . . . . traders operate from stalls in streets or special areas.

8 A . . . . . is one of a chain of shops situated in several towns.

9 A . . . . . store is sometimes called a 'shop of shops'.

10 Producers and retail multiples use a distinctive trade or . . . . . name to allow easy identification of their goods.

Choose the missing words from the following:				
breaking	credit	brand	market	multiple
department	production	middleman	bypass	link

Multiple choice

Select the appropriate answer, a, b, c or d.

1 In which one of the following types of production would a wholesaler be engaged?
   a) primary
   b) secondary
   c) tertiary
   d) service

2 A retailer buys goods worth $200 from a wholesaler, and is entitled to a 25% trade discount. What will this discount be?
   a) $50
   b) $150
   c) $20
   d) $25

3 The practice of giving products a particular identifying name is called:
   a) marking
   b) advertising
   c) identity
   d) branding

4 A typical example of a product that might be sold direct to the consumer by a producer is:
   a) meat
   b) groceries
   c) fitted furniture
   d) tobacco

5 A 'loss leader' is:
   a) a product being sold at below cost price
   b) an advertisement
   c) a stock item that cannot be found
   d) a leading store worker

6 Which one of the following statements is untrue?
   a) a hypermarket is larger than a supermarket
   b) a shopping precinct is cut off from traffic
   c) retailers are a tertiary industry
   d) trade credit is given by a retailer to a producer

7 If a trader is selling an article for $10 which he or she purchased for $8, the mark-up is:
   a) 20%
   b) 25%
   c) 30%
   d) 35%

8 If a trader has bought an item for $8 and intends to sell it for $10, the profit margin is:
   a) 20%
   b) 25%
   c) 30%
   d) 35%

9 Selling by vending machines is different from other forms of retailing because:
   a) no credit is given
   b) the buyer and seller do not meet
   c) hot and cold food is sold
   d) no delivery charge is involved

10 Retailers can be considered as producers because they:
   a) sometimes own factories
   b) sometimes help manufacturers produce goods
   c) tell manufacturers what to produce
   d) add to the value of goods

Key words

Find out the business-related meaning of each of the following words. Write a separate sentence for each word to show your understanding.

intermediary	pedlar	hawker	overheads
precinct	supermarket	credit	logo
profitability	franchise		

Structured questions

1.
   a) Why are supermarkets sometimes referred to as self-service stores? (1)
   b) State one advantage that a supermarket has over a sole trader. (1)
   c) Why is a supermarket able to operate with fewer staff than many other forms of retail outlet? (2)
   d) Describe two ways in which goods are displayed in this type of shop. (2)
   e) Name three other forms of retailing. (3)
   f) Supermarkets are often part of a multiple chain. What is a multiple chain, and what economies of scale does it experience? (3)
   g) List four disadvantages supermarkets face. (4)
   h) Describe two specific ways in which supermarkets try to encourage 'impulse' buying. (4)

2.
   a) Why does a small retailer tend to deal with a wholesaler instead of dealing direct with producers? (2)
   b) Give two examples of items that a consumer might buy direct from a producer. (2)
   c) State four ways in which a wholesaler might contact potential customers. (4)
   d) Give a brief comparison of the methods of the wholesaler and the retailer in the purchase and selling of goods. (4)
   e) Explain the difference between the general and cash-and-carry wholesaler. (8)

3. This question is all about types of retailer.
   a) What is a mobile shop? (2)
   b) Why is a market trader often able to sell goods at a price lower than a conventional shop? (2)
   c) State two ways in which a hypermarket differs from a supermarket. (2)
   d) Why are the majority of greengrocers independently owned, whereas supermarkets are usually part of a multiple organisation? (3)
   e) 'All supermarkets are self-service stores, but not all self-service stores are supermarkets'. Explain this statement. (3)
   f) State four special features that might attract customers to a department store. (4)
   g) In view of the competition from the larger forms of retailer, how are smaller types of retailer still able to exist? (4)

4. The following questions are all related to the things that an entrepreneur needs to take into account when setting up a retail business.
   a) What is a retail business? (1)
   b) What is an entrepreneur? (1)
   c) Name the type of business organisation that would be appropriate for two people setting up a small corner shop together. (2)
   d) State two possible ways by which the necessary capital could be raised. (2)
   e) Give two examples of the knowledge or skills that the owner or manager of a shop must have. (2)
   f) What considerations would be taken into account when choosing a site for a shop? (6)
   g) Describe two safeguards that the owners of a shop must observe in the interests of the staff or customers. (6)

5. Look at the magazine advertisement in figure 11.12, and answer the questions which follow.

Fig. 11.12 Free personal stereo

a) Name the form of retailing this advertisement is related to. (1)

b) Name the company that is trying to influence the sale of goods through this advertisement. (1)

c) State two items of information likely to be contained within the catalogue mentioned. (2)

d) What must the consumer do before receiving the 'free' personal stereo offered? (2)

e) How can the seller afford to give away a personal stereo 'free'? (3)

f) This form of retailing is called 'direct selling' under certain circumstances. Why is it sometimes referred to in this way? (3)

g) The advertisement claims that the method of shopping being encouraged is 'better'. Give four advantages of this type of shopping. (8)

6 This question is related to computer-based equipment used in retail marketing.

a) What is the name given to the series of lines that many shop products have on their labels? (1)

b) Where would a point-of-sale terminal be found in a shop and why would it be placed in this position? (2)

c) How does the use of point-of-sale terminals help to reduce queues in supermarkets? (3)

d) How do computers help to reduce staffing levels in the retail trade? (3)

e) In spite of their many advantages, some shoppers are not happy about the introduction of point-of-sale terminals. Why do you think this is the case? (3)

Fig. 11.13 Point-of-sale terminal with bar code reader

f) Explain how point-of-sale terminals help shops to improve their efficiency. (4)

g) Although computerised stock records are automatically updated, periodic manual stocktaking is also necessary. Explain why manual stocktaking has to be done occasionally. (4)

7 a) What is the name given to the computer terminal at the checkout point of a supermarket? (1)

b) What advantages does an itemised till receipt have over conventional supermarket receipts? (1)

c) What is the purpose of a bar code? (2)

d) Why does a computerised checkout system result in fewer mistakes? (2)

e) Write out the following supermarket operations in the correct sequence:
 • stock record updated
 • itemised receipt produced
 • bar code read by reader device
 • products taken off shelf by customer. (2)

f) The photograph in figure 11.13 shows a scanner being used to read a bar code. State one other method of reading a bar code. (2)

g) Although point-of-sale terminals increase the efficiency of shops, many do not have this facility. Give two possible reasons why some shops do not have them. (2)

h) Briefly describe two jobs that supermarket personnel do not have to do if computers are used in the store. (4)

i) Details of a purchase can be input to the computer by keyboard or by a bar code reader. Briefly compare these two methods. (4)

Research assignments

1 Discuss the view that wholesalers should be eliminated because they cause an increase in the cost of goods. What evidence can you present that supports your discussion?

2 Take any local retail business with which you are familiar and explain the sort of factors that the owner would have needed to take into account in setting it up. Include evidence that proves you have carried out personal research.

3 To what extent would you say that there is genuine competition between retail outlets in your town?

4 Explain, with examples, how retailers are assisted by each of the following:

   a) advertising

   b) transport

   c) wholesaler

   d) insurance.

5 Give a detailed explanation of the various forms of credit available to the consumer. To what extent do you feel that credit is a good thing? Carry out a survey of a cross-section of adults to identify which forms of credit are most frequently used.

Chapter 12
THE OVERSEAS MARKET

12.1 The importance of international trade

The reasons countries trade

The overseas market is important to businesses and to countries as a whole. It is important to businesses because it provides potential additional income from the sale of goods and services. It is important to countries because it is by selling overseas that the home country can earn money to buy things from other countries. By doing this the quality of life of all the countries involved can be improved.

Because the trading referred to here takes place in an overseas market it is often called 'foreign trade'. Foreign trade is the buying and selling of goods and services between different countries of the world.

- **Imports** are bought from other countries and result in an outflow of funds.
- **Exports** are sold to other countries and result in an inflow of funds.
- **Visible trade** refers to the import and export of goods (e.g. food, machinery, vehicles).
- **Invisible trade** is the importing and exporting of services (e.g. tourism, transport, insurance and banking).

Fig. 12.1   Examples of imported foodstuffs

A country is in many ways like a big family or a household. Both have to earn money in order to purchase things they need (e.g. food, shelter and clothing) and things they want (luxuries). Countries earn money by selling their products and services overseas (exporting) and they spend their money buying from other countries (importing). The result of this can be a better way of life for the population.

If people in a household, or country, earn more than they spend, they can build up a surplus, become wealthy, and generally have a better standard of living. If people or countries spend more than they earn, they get into debt, and generally this leads to a poorer standard of living.

Differences between countries in climate or natural resources mean that they have to trade in order to obtain goods which they cannot produce themselves, or do not find it economic to produce. One country may have natural deposits of oil or gas while another may have metal deposits not found in many other countries. By each country concentrating on producing those goods for which it has the comparative advantage, greater output is achieved more cheaply, which is in the best interest of all people. This is an extension of specialisation or the division of labour, and economists refer to it as following the **principle of comparative costs**.

Comparative cost

The principle of **comparative-cost advantage**, simply put, states that when a country is able to produce a variety of products, it will concentrate on those with a lower comparative cost of production.

Table 12.1 *Comparative costs of two products (i)*

	Costs per unit	
	computers	sugar
Country A	600	80
Country B	500	100

Table 12.1 uses a hypothetical situation in which the two countries involved trade only in two goods, computers and sugar. Country A is more efficient at producing sugar than country B, because it can produce it more cheaply than country B. Country A is said to have an **absolute advantage** in sugar, and country B in computers. If the two countries trade freely with each other, country A will specialise in the production of sugar and export it. Country B will specialise in the production and export of computers. This is to the mutual advantage of both countries.

It can also be mutually advantageous to trade even if a country does not have an absolute advantage in any commodity. Table 12.2 helps to clarify this.

Table 12.2 *Comparative costs of two products (ii)*

	Costs per unit	
	computers	sugar
Country C	600	200
Country B	500	100

In this second table it can be seen that country B has an absolute advantage in the production of both computers and sugar. However, country B has a **comparative advantage** only in the production of sugar. A unit of sugar in country B costs one fifth of a computer. So, sugar is relatively cheaper in Country B. Country C, on the other hand, has a comparative advantage in the production of computers.

From the foregoing it can be seen that it is to the mutual advantage of countries to specialise in producing and exporting commodities where they have comparative advantage, and import commodities from other countries where production is comparatively cheaper.

Sometimes the comparative advantage one country has over another is not the result of natural resources, but of advantages that have been developed. For example, a country may have developed the expertise to produce a particular commodity that other countries require, such as micro-electronic components. Countries will participate in international trade in order to use the specialisation of others, and obtain a wider variety of goods. Thus, by participating in foreign trade, each country enhances the way of life of its people. For example, although wheat is not grown in the Caribbean region, there is a considerable demand for flour (a by-product of wheat) and so this has to be imported. Similarly, we also import many technical products (e.g. computers).

12.2 Balance of trade

In the same way that every family has to budget to ensure it spends only what it can afford, so every country must also keep its spending within the limits of its income.

The family may keep a record of its income and expenditure, and countries also record the difference in value between imports and exports. The difference between the value of goods a country imports and exports is recorded in the **balance of trade**. Because goods can be seen they are collectively called **visibles**.

When exports exceed imports, the balance, or **trade gap**, is said to be *favourable* because a *surplus* has been created which has resulted in a net flow of funds into the country.

When imports exceed exports, the balance is said to be *adverse* (unfavourable). A *deficit* (loss) has been created which has resulted in a net outflow of funds.

Table 12.3 *Examples of balance of trade figures*

	($ million)	
1. Visible exports	+48,440	
Visible imports	−47,322	
Balance of trade	+ 1,118	*surplus*
2. Visible exports	+47,322	
Visible imports	−48,440	
Balance of trade	− 1,118	*deficit*

12.3 Balance of payments

In their trade with other countries, Caribbean countries buy and sell a number of services. Because these services, unlike goods, cannot be 'seen', they are collectively called **invisibles**. For example, the Caribbean region earns considerable income from tourists visiting our islands.

The balance of payments is a statement of the difference in total value of all payments made to other countries and the total payments received from them. This balance includes both visible and invisible trade, and it shows whether the country is making a profit or a loss in its dealings with other countries.

- A *favourable* balance of payments exists when there is net inflow of capital. The country has earned more than it has spent.
- An *adverse* balance exists when there is a net currency outflow. The country has spent more than it has earned.

The balance of payments comprises the **current account** and the **capital account**. The current account records trade in goods and services. The capital account records flows for investment and saving purposes.

Table 12.4 shows three examples of imaginary balance of payments figures.

Table 12.4 *Balance of payments figures*

	($ million)	
1. Visible exports	+48,440	
Visible imports	−47,322	
Balance of trade		+1,118 surplus
Invisible exports	+25,650	
Invisible imports	−23,120	
		+2,530 surplus
Balance of payments on current account		+3,648
2. Visible exports	+47,322	
Visible imports	−48,440	
Balance of trade		−1,118 deficit
Invisible exports	+25,650	
Invisible imports	−23,120	
		+2,530 surplus
Balance of payments on current account		+1,412 surplus
3. Visible exports	+48,440	
Visible imports	−47,322	
Balance of trade		+1,118 surplus
Invisible exports	+23,120	
Invisible imports	−25,650	
		−2,530 deficit
Balance of payments on current account		−1,412 deficit

Destination of the exports of Caribbean countries

Region	%
Other	3.8%
Africa	0.9%
Asia	1.0%
Intra-Latin America	20.2%
Japan	4.6%
European Community	19.0%
Canada	8.9%
United States	41.6%

Fig. 12.2 Trading partners in the Caribbean

Correcting a balance of payments deficit

A recurring balance of payments deficit situation is worrying for any country because it means that there is a sustained outflow of funds — the country is spending more than it earns.

A current account deficit can only be tolerated in the short term. A persistent current account deficit must be dealt with eventually, because other countries are effectively having to lend to the deficit country; they will not permit this to continue indefinitely.

The following are *temporary measures* that a country can take to correct an adverse balance of payments problem, but these are not satisfactory in the long term because often they only delay tackling a more deep-seated problem.

- Borrowing from the International Monetary Fund.
- Obtaining loans from abroad.
- Drawing on gold and currency reserves.
- Selling off foreign assets.

The best way to solve a deficit problem is to increase exports. Governments can help to achieve this by offering incentives to firms involved in exporting goods. These incentives may take the form of tax relief and extended or special credit facilities, or subsidies on home produced goods to make them cheaper.

There are a variety of other strategies that a country may use in an attempt to combat a persistent balance of payments deficit. These include devaluation, deflation, exchange control and import control.

Devaluation
Devaluation means lowering the value of a currency in relation to other currencies. This makes imported goods more expensive and exports cheaper. For example, if your country's dollar is devalued by 10%, overseas buyers will now only have to pay 90 cents for items that previously cost them $1. Conversely, you will have to pay $1.10 for imported goods which prior to devaluation cost $1.

Deflation
If people's income (or its spending power) is reduced, this can lead to a reduction in imports because people will buy fewer goods, including imports. Deflation can be achieved by wage-rise controls, restricting credit and hire purchase, increasing interest rates and increasing taxes.

Exchange control
The central bank may take direct action to reduce outward flows of currency by **exchange control**: placing limits on the amount of foreign currency that can be bought. By refusing requests for foreign currency, the central bank reduces the supply of domestic currency on the market, thus raising the price of the currency.

Import control
The two main methods of restricting imports are by the use of **tariffs** and **quotas**. A tariff is a duty or tax imposed on imports to increase their cost and discourage purchase. A quota is a numerical limit put on the quantity of a commodity permitted to be imported. Both of these methods are dealt with later in this chapter.

12.4 Methods of selling abroad

The channels for selling abroad can be grouped into two broad categories: (1) selling from the home base, and (2) selling from an overseas base.

Selling from the home base

There are several ways in which an exporter can sell abroad without going overseas. Advertising in foreign journals or circulating catalogues, brochures and other sales literature can be effective, although some items are not easy to describe and more direct contact is necessary. This can be achieved through contact with the agents of overseas buyers visiting the home country.

Where a firm is not large enough to operate its own export department, it may use an **export house**, which is a firm that specialises in securing orders from abroad. The export house may act as a merchant or an agent.

- *Merchant*: the export house actually buys the goods from the producer and then markets the goods overseas, accepting the risk of loss.

- *Agent*: the export house may market the goods on behalf of the seller, from whom it receives a commission.

Selling from an overseas base

The firm may send its own representatives overseas to make direct contact with potential customers. Alternatively, the exporter might employ an agent already based overseas and willing to seek contracts for sales in return for a commission.

Whichever of the foregoing approaches is employed, the representative or agent is helped by trade fairs and exhibitions, which provide a useful meeting place for buyers and sellers involved in international trade.

12.5 Difficulties faced by exporters

We have already recognised that it is important for a country to export in order to pay for its imports; but companies that engage in foreign trade face a number of difficulties. Some of these are also experienced in home trade, others are particularly evident in overseas trade. The main problems can be summarised as follows.

- *Language*: the exporter needs to be conversant with the language of the country to which he or she intends to export.
- *Differences in measurements, weights and sizes* have to be taken into account by the exporter.
- *Suitability* of products needs to be considered due to differing regulations, safety standards, etc. in some foreign countries.
- *Import regulations*: the exporter must observe and be familiar with the import regulations of other countries.
- *Damage* to goods during their long journey to the customer.
- *Packaging* may need to be stronger than that used for home trade.
- *Transport* will be more difficult to organise than for home trade, and the method chosen must be efficient and economic.
- *Documentation* and payment arrangements can be complicated in overseas trading.
- *Agent*: it may be necessary to find a suitable agent to act on behalf of the exporters to make contracts for the sale of goods.
- *Payment defaults* by overseas customers are more difficult to sort out than those in home trade.
- *Exchange rate fluctuations* can adversely affect the market price of exports:

a) a *rise* in the value of the dollar results in a fall in the cost of imports, and a rise in the price of exports.
b) a *fall* in the value of the dollar results in a fall in the cost of exports and a rise in the price of imports.

12.6 Free trade restrictions

If every country specialised in the things it does best, and then its products were freely traded anywhere in the world, all countries would gain maximum benefit. In fact, free trade between countries is difficult to organise. Countries sometimes use a variety of techniques in order to restrict free trade, sometimes in an attempt to correct an adverse balance of payments.

Subsidies   A government may give finance — a subsidy — towards the cost of the home-produced product to enable it to be sold at a lower price abroad.

Tariffs   These are a tax or custom duty imposed on imported goods to raise the price of foreign goods to the home consumer and thus protect the home market. There are two methods of imposing tariffs, which are collected by the customs department.

- **Specific duties** are a set price for each item imported.
- **Ad valorem duties** are calculated as a percentage of the value of the imports.

Note The importer can place goods in a 'bonded warehouse' under customs supervision until they are able to pay the duty due, or until the goods are re-exported.

Fig. 12.3   Trade barriers in CARICOM

Quotas A **quota** is a limit on the quantity of a product allowed to enter the country during the year. An 'import licence' must be obtained before goods subject to quota restrictions can be imported.

Exchange controls Sometimes a country will restrict the availability to importers of foreign currency, thus restricting their ability to pay for imports.

Embargo This is a straightforward government ban on trading between one country and another.

Reasons countries have trade restrictions

There are four main reasons why a country may decide to impose trade restrictions.

1. *To protect home producers.* Infant (newly formed) industries may need protection until they have become sufficiently established to be able to compete fairly. Other industries may require protection because they are important to future national security.
2. *To resist dumping.* **Dumping** means selling goods at a loss abroad. Some countries dump goods abroad either to reduce supplies at home or to increase their share of the market overseas. This kind of action can be very damaging to some industries in the country where the goods are being dumped.
3. *To safeguard jobs.* Even when goods are brought into a country fairly and competitively, their import may threaten a particular industry. Under such circumstances the importing country may feel it necessary to introduce trade restrictions.
4. *To correct a balance of payments deficit.* A continuous balance of payments deficit cannot be ignored. One way in which a deficit can be rectified is by reducing imports by the imposition of import control.

12.7 Regional and foreign economic institutions

Regional cooperation

There is hardly a country on this planet, whether rich or poor, large or small, which does not need to co-operate with at least one other country in order to meet its needs. But why do countries need to co-operate? Countries need to co-operate because the world's resources are not evenly distributed. In other words, no one country has all the resources it needs. For example, the peoples of the Caribbean are heavy consumers of bread, but the region does not produce the wheat that is needed to make bread. Therefore, the region has to import wheat from wheat-producing countries that can supply the product in the quantities needed. Likewise, countries of the Caribbean produce sugar, spices, bauxite, rice, citrus, oil, timber and chicklet among other products, for regional as well as international trade. To facilitate the necessary trade agreements, countries need to agree on trade policies related to import and export quotas, financing, transportation, foreign exchange, terms of trade and so on. Therefore, co-operation is almost mandatory if nations are to survive.

Regional trade

Regional trade has been a major feature of the Caribbean and is being facilitated through **regional strategies**. One such strategy is the Caribbean Community or CARICOM. International trade has also been seen as important among Caribbean nations for centuries. Caribbean countries rely on other countries buying their products such as coffee, spices, banana, sugar, bauxite, oil, rubber and other products. It is by selling products such as these that Caribbean countries are able to buy the many other items they need.

Local and regional economic institutions

Chambers of commerce
Chambers of commerce are comprised of businesses involved in commercial activities. The major concerns of such businesses are addressed and are represented at the highest level possible.

Caribbean Association of Industry and Commerce (CAIC)
In this association, individual chambers of commerce are represented. Members focus on the problems of trade in the region, and how they can cooperate in fostering the growth and development of commerce. Issues of trade are addressed at their forum.

Manufacturers' associations
These are local associations of manufacturers. Their main concern is how to maximise manufacturing; a most important contributor to economic activity in a country. The concerns of manufacturing are also concerns of the

governments since production is at the heart of economic development.

The Caribbean Community (CARICOM)
CARICOM is the region's premier economic institution. CARICOM fosters economic cooperation in the region. Countries of the English-speaking Caribbean comprise its membership. Recently, other countries have been brought into the membership because they are neighbours, even though their language may be different. A major focus of CARICOM is the Caribbean Common Market (CCM). The CCM involves a 'group arrangement' whereby:

- member countries do not impose duties on goods traded among themselves
- members do not restrict the quantity of goods to be traded among themselves
- there is a common agreement among member states on the rate at which duty should be charged on goods imported from countries outside the Community.

The CCM is governed by the Common Market Council, which is made up of representatives drawn from the member countries. Members must abide by the rules of the council.

Other bodies in CARICOM include the Conference, which is made up of the various heads of government of the member countries, and the Secretariat, which consists of the technical and administrative staff. All the groups work together for the common good of the countries involved. The CARICOM Secretariat is located in Georgetown, Guyana. Meetings and summits are held in the various member states from time to time.

CARICOM has the following aims and objectives.

- The establishment of a regionally known market called the 'Caribbean Common Market', with the main aim of economic integration among all member countries.
- The strengthening of economic or international trading relations among the member states in order to enhance development in several sectors of their economies.
- The co-ordination of economic and social ties among member countries.
- The regulation of social, cultural and economic activities among member countries.
- The maintaining of economic ties and their expansion among members, especially among the Less Developed Countries (LDCs).
- The achievement of an enhanced economic independence for each member country and for the region as a whole.
- The co-ordination of the foreign policies of all the member countries.
- Co-operation in the operation of common services, for example tourism and transportation.
- The promotion of a greater understanding of the people of member countries, especially in the fields of social, cultural and technological development.
- Trade liberalisation, i.e. freeing of trade barriers among member countries, with special reference to the removal or lowering of customs duties and other obstacles to trade which prevail among member countries.
- To permit individuals and companies to invest capital in other member countries.
- To extend the rights of individuals engaging in self-employed activities.
- The harmonisation of policies such as fiscal policies, double taxation, regional trade, agricultural development, tourism and industrial programmes.
- Special development activities for the LDCs in order to reduce the differences between the LDCs and the larger member states.
- The establishment of the Caribbean Investment Corporation so as to help industries in the LDCs.
- Joint negotiation for various types of agreement with developing countries, metropolitan countries and trading-blocs such as the European Union (EU), the Organisation of Petroleum Exporting Countries (OPEC) and others.

CARICOM is governed by the **Heads of Government Conference** which is the body responsible for policy-making and general direction. The CARICOM **Secretariat** is responsible for the implementation of policies and decisions made at the heads of government conferences, the Council of Ministers, and other sub-groups. It is at this level that the operational activities are carried out.

The Caribbean Development Bank (CDB)
This is a financial institution that has been established by Caribbean nations. The major aim of the bank is to provide funding for economic activities in the region. Additionally, the bank administers loans programmes for funding agencies. The CDB loans assist member states with activities associated with tourism, health and education, and agriculture, among other areas. Interest rates are low compared with those charged by other financial institutions. Member states also enjoy a 'period of grace' on the loan repayment plans. This means that the loan repayments do not begin as the contract would

normally have dictated, but at a later date worked out between the member state and the bank, hence the loans are termed **soft loans**. The **International Bank for Reconstruction and Development (IBRD)** provides financial services to the CDB.

The International Monetary Fund (IMF)
The IMF was established in 1944 at a 'monetary conference' in Bretton Woods in the United States of America. Its major purpose is to provide short-term lending to countries that are experiencing balance of payments problems by providing foreign currency needed to pay for goods and services. Member countries contribute to the fund. Amounts contributed are set aside to be drawn upon in time of need. In this way, members have special **drawing rights**. Draw down from the IMF funds are based upon how much a country has contributed.

The IMF provision can be summarised as follows:

- It provides short-term loans or temporary loans to countries.
- It helps countries in need and sets economic targets for them.
- It sets tough or stringent guidelines for economic management.

Unfortunately, many countries experience social and political hardships and consequently they are often not able to meet the IMF targets.

The International Bank for Reconstruction and Development (IBRD)
The IBRD, now better known as **The World Bank**, provides aid to developing countries. Most of the funding which goes towards providing aid comes from contributions made by Canada, the United States of America and the United Kingdom. Funding is also obtained through agencies and other financial institutions.

IBRD funding can be used to provide infrastructure as well as to improve health and education. The Caribbean Development Bank obtains funds for Caribbean development purposes from the IBRD.

The Inter-American Development Bank
The services provided by this bank are similar to those provided by the IBRD. However, the beneficiaries of funding are the Latin American, Caribbean and North American countries. The major providers of funding are the United States of America and Canada.

The organisation of Eastern Caribbean States (OECS)
This body comprises of the *less developed* countries of CARICOM. These countries include Antigua and Barbuda, Dominica, Grenada, Montserrat, St Kitts and Nevis, St Lucia, St Vincent and the Grenadines, and Grenada. The OECS Treaty was signed in 1981, and the headquarters is located in St. Lucia.

The OECS aims to bring about:

- reasonable and workable trading arrangements among members, their CARICOM sister states and the international community
- economic and political integration
- common policies in areas such as agriculture and hospitality and tourism
- common practices and procedures in industrial policies to prevent unfair competition among countries
- establishment of a single Central Bank
- a single currency — the Eastern Caribbean dollar (EC dollar).

The Organisation of American States (OAS)
This organisation was established in 1948 and its major objective is to foster good relations among countries of the Americas. Membership of the OAS is drawn from North America, Latin America and the Caribbean. The body is governed by a Charter that sets out the general purposes and principles, the nature of the organisation, and the rights and obligations of members. The major concerns of the OAS are:

- the fostering of good relations among members
- settling disputes when they arise between members
- assisting with the maintenance of cultural heritage of the members
- assisting with obtaining and monitoring aid programmes
- providing training through scholarship programmes.

Major trade agreements

General Agreement on Tariffs and Trade (GATT)
GATT was implemented in 1948. The major aim of the agreement is to promote free trade among its members. GATT supports the principle that no discrimination in tariff agreements should be levied against any member state. Therefore, the agreement aims to achieve **free trade agreements** among members through the reduction of tariffs and quotas.

The Caribbean, as well as other developing countries, have been able to arrive at an agreement called the

Generalised Trade Preference. This permits developing countries to receive **duty-free concessions** on manufactured goods that they sell on the world market to developed countries.

World Trade Organisation (WTO)
The WTO is a body established to perform a similar role to the GATT. Its responsibility is for the administration of multilateral trade agreements that are negotiated by its members. It provides a forum through which rounds of negotiations can take place. It maintains a very tight dispute settlement procedure and a new trade policy review mechanism. In other words, members of trade agreements who believe strongly that unfair practices are being pursued by other members, can take their cases to the WTO.

The banana trade provides an example of the effect of the WTO. Banana is a major earner of foreign currency for the Caribbean. The banana industry also provides employment for a large number of persons. However, the 1990s have seen political changes in Europe leading to the establishment of a Single Market. The market adopted an open market system. This incorporates cooperation on economic and monetary policy, joint research and technological development, employment and environmental protection and a charter to promote social cohesion and thus reduction of regional disparities. This means the Caribbean banana industry can no longer continue to receive special treatment from the United Kingdom, which is a member of the European Union.

The United States, on behalf of one of its companies that are involved in the banana trade in Latin America, complained to the WTO about the preferential treatment of some countries in the banana trade — the Caribbean countries were the main targets. The USA argued and lobbied for the removal of the preferential treatment to allow for an open market. The WTO eventually accepted the USA proposal, and the result is that the Caribbean banana industry has come under severe economic pressure.

The Association of African, Caribbean and Pacific Countries (ACP–LOME)
The LOME Convention, established in 1975, is another international trade agreement designed to foster international trade. Over 60 former British and French colonies were signatories to the LOME agreement. The agreement has been reviewed a number of times since its inception with the aim of making it as reasonable as possible. It allows 94% of the agricultural products of ACP–LOME countries to enter the European Union duty-free. Countries are assigned quotas specifying the quantity they are allowed to trade in this manner. Caribbean countries trade mainly in sugar and banana.

The LOME agreement includes an aid programme administered by the European Development Fund. Countries can obtain funding for road construction, the building of schools and for training.

The agreement also provides an Export Earnings Stabilisation facility to aid countries that experience adverse effects on their products as a result of natural disasters.

As a result of the closer linking together of the countries in the European Union, a number of these arrangements have changed and, therefore, Caribbean countries have had to seek other ways and means of marketing their products competitively.

Organisation of Petroleum Exporting Countries (OPEC)
This organisation was founded in 1960 by a group of the world's oil exporting countries, particularly those in the Middle East. The member countries co-operate to fix oil prices and control competition with the aim of protecting their interests, although they have also from time to time provided financial assistance to developing countries that are not members of OPEC.

The European Union (EU)

A **common market** refers to an arrangement in which a group of countries co-operate to foster trade between them. An essential feature of a common market is **to reduce trade restrictions** between member countries, and to charge a **common tariff** to non-member countries. Sometimes such an arrangement is referred to as a 'Common Market'. The EU is one such market.

The EU was at one time referred to as the European Common Market. Later, as the links between member countries were strengthened, it became the European Community, and today it is known as the European Union. The movement towards free trade between member countries has largely been realised, and today the emphasis is towards political and monetary union.

As a result of the progression of the EU, Caribbean nations have had their specific trade agreements or arrangements removed. Caribbean countries no longer receive preferential treatment in the UK market-place, but must now negotiate, and face the competition in the same way as any other country.

Aims of the EU

- To raise the living standards of people in member countries.
- To promote freedom of movement of labour, capital and services between member countries.

- To encourage close co-operation between members in matters of commerce, farming, finance, social services and legal systems.
- To reduce trade restrictions between members, and establish a common tariff policy for trade with non-members.
- To work towards monetary union and a single currency.

The Eastern Caribbean Common Market (ECCM)
The ECCM is an outcome of the OECS Agreement. The establishment of the ECCM was a major objective of the OECS.

The Caribbean Canadian Agreement
This agreement exists between Canada and the English-speaking Caribbean. The initiative allows for 98% duty-free concession on non-traditional products from the Caribbean entering the Canadian market.

North American Free Trade Agreement (NAFTA)
This trade agreement came into effect in 1992. The agreement is between the United States of America, Canada and Mexico. The objectives are to:

- remove protectionist barriers that will allow the USA, Canada and Mexico easy access to goods and services in their respective countries.
- provide a common forum that will enhance the development of policies beneficial to the USA, Canada and Mexico.
- provide freer movement of professionals among member countries.

Other countries of the Americas, including Caribbean countries, have been seeking to become part of this important trade agreement.

12.8 THINGS TO DO

This section contains a variety of exercises to help you create revision notes, to test your understanding and to prepare you for examinations.

Search and find

Write out the question and the answer by referring back through the text to form revision notes.

1. Why do countries need to trade?
2. Define the terms 'imports' and 'exports'.
3. Explain the term 'principle of comparative costs'.
4. Give one result of following the above principle.
5. Why is foreign trade particularly important to the Caribbean region.
6. Define 'balance of trade'.
7. What are 'visibles'? Give three examples.
8. Explain each of the following terms:
   a) trade gap
   b) surplus
   c) deficit.
9. What are 'invisibles'? Give three examples.
10. Explain the following statement. 'Balance of trade is related to visible trade, but balance of payments includes both visible and invisible trade'.
11. Why is it important to try to achieve a favourable balance of payments?
12. Briefly describe ways in which an exporter can sell abroad without actually going overseas.
13. Explain the difference between the work of merchants and agents.
14. Briefly describe eight problems, other than fluctuation in exchange rates, that are faced by exporters.
15. Clearly explain how fluctuation in exchange rates can affect the price of both imports and exports.
16. What are tariffs? Describe the two ways by which tariffs are collected.
17. What is the function of a bonded warehouse?
18. What is a quota?
19. When is it necessary to obtain an import licence?
20. Why might a government subsidise home-produced goods?
21. What is an embargo?
22. Summarise the four main reasons countries impose trade restrictions.
23. Describe the functions of at least three regional economic institutions other than CARICOM.

24. What are the aims of CARICOM?
25. How does the Caribbean Development Bank differ from commercial banks?
26. What are the basic regulations governing the provision of loans from the IMF?
27. How do you think that the main aim of GATT helps to promote international trade?
28. 'The World Trade Organisation has both a beneficial and a detrimental effect on the Caribbean region'. Briefly discuss this statement.
29. In what ways does the LOME agreement benefit the Caribbean region?
30. What is the aim of OPEC?
31. 'Both CARICOM and the EU are referred to as "common" markets.' Explain this statement.

What do you know?

Write out the complete sentence and insert the missing word, which can be chosen from the list at the end of the questions.

1. The overseas market can provide additional . . . . . for a business.
2. . . . . . are goods brought into the country.
3. Goods sent out of a country are called . . . . . .
4. Every country must keep its . . . . . within the limits of its income.
5. When exports exceed imports, the balance of trade is said to be . . . . . .
6. If a country imports more than it exports, the balance of trade is said to be . . . . . .
7. An export . . . . . is a firm that specialises in securing orders from abroad.
8. A government might impose trade . . . . . to protect home producers.
9. Sometimes a country restricts the availability of foreign . . . . ., which makes it difficult to pay for imports.
10. The . . . . . Bank provides aid to developing countries.

Choose the missing words from the following:

adverse   World   income   currency
house   exports   favourable   restrictions
imports   spending

Multiple choice

Select the appropriate answer, a, b, c or d.

1. The balance of payments is:
   a) the same as the balance of trade
   b) the difference between the value of visible imports and visible exports
   c) a periodic statement of all payments made to and received from other countries
   d) the total value of payments made to other countries

2. An adverse balance of trade occurs when:
   a) the value of exports exceeds the value of imports
   b) the value of imports exceeds the value of exports
   c) the value of imports and exports are equal
   d) taxes are imposed on imported goods

3. When a government puts a straightforward ban on trading with another country, this is called:
   a) tariff
   b) quota
   c) embargo
   d) exchange control

4. In which year was there an adverse movement in the balance of trade?

	year	exports ($m)	imports ($m)
a)	1989	75	71
b)	1990	83	79
c)	1991	81	85
d)	1992	98	89

5. In a country's balance of payments accounts, which of the following items would you expect to be shown with a minus sign?
   a) money spent by Caribbean tourists abroad
   b) money spent by foreign tourists in the Caribbean
   c) Caribbean goods sold overseas
   d) money received by Caribbean investors from overseas companies

6. A tax placed on imports is called:
   a) a subsidy
   b) an embargo
   c) a quota
   d) a tariff

7. The function of a bonded warehouse is to:
   a) sell to wholesalers for immediate cash
   b) hold goods until customs duty has been paid
   c) act as a middleman between producers and retailers
   d) supply retailers at trade price

8. Which one of the following would create invisible income on the balance of payments of a country?

a) export of goods
b) investing money overseas
c) imports of cars
d) subsidies

9 Which of the following is not an invisible trade item?
a) machinery
b) insurance
c) transport
d) tourism

10 When the government gives finance towards the cost of a home-produced product this is called
a) dumping
b) duties
c) subsidies
d) quotas

Key words

Find out the business-related meaning of each of the following words. Write a separate sentence for each word to show your understanding.

deficit   merchant   agent   commission   quota
dumping   tariffs   subsidies embargo   deficit

Structured questions

1 Consider figure 12.4.

   a) What do the letters CARTIS and CEDP stand for? (1)
   b) What is a 'profile'? (2)
   c) Why might a business not involved in foreign trade be interested in obtaining 'profiles' of exporters, importers, manufacturers or producers? (3)
   d) What 'trade' opportunities might a business obtain through the services of CARTIS and CEDP? (4)
   e) What are 'non-tariff barriers'? (4)

NEED TRADE INFORMATION?
OUR TRADE INFORMATION NETWORK
CAN PROVIDE THE FOLLOWING SERVICES

- Profiles of exporters/importers/manufacturers/producers
- Trade opportunities
- Market research data, including import/export regulations, non-tariff barriers
- Trade statistics

Contact our head office in Barbados Tel: (809) 436-0578 Fax: (809) 436-9999/436-2820
Or your National Trade Promotion Office

CARTIS The Caribbean Trade Information Service
CEDP Caricom Export Development Project
CARICOM   A Project of the Caribbean Community Secretariat

Fig. 12.4   Trade information advertisement

---

f) Explain the sort of 'market research data' that a firm interested in breaking into overseas trade would find useful. (6)

Table 12.5 *Trade figures of three countries*

Balance of payments figures ($ million)		
Country 1		
Visible exports	+48,440	
Visible imports	−47,322	
Balance of trade		+1,118 surplus
Invisible exports	+25,650	
Invisible imports	−23,120	
		+2,530 surplus
Balance of payments on current account		+3,648 surplus
Country 2		
Visible exports	+40,288	
Visible imports	−42,366	
Balance of trade		−2,078 deficit
Invisible exports	+25,650	
Invisible imports	−20,972	
		+4,678 surplus
Balance of payments on current account		+2,600 surplus
Country 3		
Visible exports	+48,440	
Visible imports	−47,322	
Balance of trade		+1,118 surplus
Invisible exports	+23,120	
Invisible imports	−25,650	
		−2,530 deficit
Balance of payments on current account		−1,412 deficit

2 Look at the imaginary balance of payments figures for three countries in table 12.5, and answer the following questions.

   a) Which country has the poorest trade balance? (1)
   b) Which country has the most favourable balance of payments? (1)
   c) Explain clearly the difference between exports and imports. (2)
   d) Explain the terms 'visible' and 'invisible' and give three examples in each case. (4)
   e) Use examples from the figures shown in the table to assist you to explain the difference between the balance of trade and the balance of payments. (6)

f) Describe the likely effect on your country's balance of payments if there was:
   (i) a decline in the number of tourists visiting your country
   (ii) a devaluation of the dollar in relation to other countries.
   Give reasons for your answers. (6)

3 a) State two ways in which banks provide help for exporters. (2)

   b) Why is it important for all countries to try to sell overseas? (2)

   c) Describe briefly the likely effect on your country of each of the following:
      (i) increased expenditure by the residents of your country on holidays overseas
      (ii) a foreign country is 'dumping' goods on your market that are already being produced in factories in your country. (6)

   d) Explain the significance of each of the following to overseas trade:
      (i) tariff
      (ii) quota
      (iii) embargo
      (iv) exchange control
      (v) subsidies. (10)

4 Study the following information and answer the questions related to it.

THE BENEFITS OF FOREIGN TRADE

All countries gain advantages from trade with other countries. These advantages benefit both industry and consumers. Businesses can benefit from the opportunities they gain for increased specialisation and greater economies of scale. Another advantage of foreign trade is that the increased competition that comes from abroad encourages home-based producers to become more efficient. However, a major benefit for consumers is that they are able to choose from a wider range of goods and services.

---

a) Give two examples of specialisation that are evident in international trade. (2)

b) In what way can international trade provide opportunities for greater economies of scale? (2)

c) How does competition from abroad encourage home-based producers to become more efficient? (3)

d) List three items which consumers in your country could not buy without foreign trade. (3)

e) Why is it more difficult for businesses to trade overseas than at home? (4)

f) Suggest three ways that your country could encourage more overseas tourists to visit it. (6)

Research assignments

1 'It is possible for a country to have an adverse balance of trade but a favourable balance of payments.' Discuss this statement using imaginary data to illustrate your answer. What is the record of your country over the past 10 years?

2 Describe some of the difficulties faced by exporters and say how these problems may be overcome. What evidence can you provide that shows the problems do exist, and that they can be overcome?

3 Describe the various methods a manufacturer from your country might employ to sell his or her products overseas, including mention of the various agencies that can be used. To what extent do you feel your government helps exporters?

4 'Overseas trade is important to every member of our country.' Discuss this statement using specific examples to justify your answer.

5 'Imports threaten home producers and can ruin national prosperity.' Discuss this statement, incorporating the views of others obtained through your own first-hand research.

Chapter 13
BUSINESS DOCUMENTATION

13.1 Transactions

The complete process of supplying goods or services from the initial enquiry to eventual payment is called a **transaction**. At various stages in a transaction, documents are raised.

When trading, both the buyers and the sellers of goods need to use certain documents to make sure there is no confusion about what has taken place between them, and to provide a record or proof of activity at some later date. Within this chapter we shall study the style and the use of the main business documents.

In a similar way that each house owner decorates his or her house in the manner that appeals to him or her, so each business designs its documents in the manner that it feels is most attractive or most workable for its requirements. Therefore, you may find that the same document may have a different style of layout for different companies. We shall follow a typical business transaction from start to finish and study the documents that are used at each stage, in the order in which they appear in trading.

Fig. 13.1 Business letter headings

MS A. BUYER & CO. LTD.
11 PARMETER ROAD,
KINGSTON.
Tel: 93-694608

Mr. A. Seller & Co. Ltd,
64 Marcus Garvey Drive,
Kingston 11.
Tel: 93-694609

It will be of help to your study of this topic if you bear in mind that the documents are moving in two directions: to and from the buyers and sellers of goods or services. We shall assume that the buyer is female and the seller male.

Fig. 13.2 Documents move in two directions

13.2 Making enquiries

Letter of enquiry

A person wishing to buy goods will try to find out information about them. She will send a letter of enquiry to a seller (or many sellers), requesting information such as:

- specifications (details of the goods)
- prices
- delivery period
- primary procedures.

The enquiry may be a letter or it may be a standard printed form on which the information required is to be filled in.

Sometimes, rather than send enquiries direct to prospective suppliers, an intending buyer may invite, perhaps by advertisement, any number of people to make an offer (or tender) for supply of the goods or services required. A **tender** is a competitive quotation, one submitted in competition with other tenders.

The supplier who submits the tender which appeals most to the buyer will usually be sent a **contract** which states exactly what has been agreed. Contracts are dealt with later in this chapter.

```
MS A. BUYER & CO. LTD,
    11 PARMETER ROAD,
        KINGSTON.
     Tel: 93-694608


Mr A. Seller & Co. Ltd,              1 June 2000
64 Marcus Garvey Drive,
Kingston 11.

Dear Sirs,

We would be pleased to receive at your earliest
convenience your best quotation for the supply
of the following items.

Your quotation should indicate delivery period,
carriage terms, prices and cash discounts.

20 Reams     A4 Bond Typewriting Paper White
20 Reams     A4 Bank Typewriting Paper Yellow
10 Reams     A5 Bond Typewriting Paper White
10 Reams     A5 Bank Typewriting Paper Yellow

Yours faithfully,
for MS A. BUYER & CO. LTD.,

    S.Webber

S. Webber
Chief Buyer
```

Fig. 13.3 Letter of enquiry

Quotation

Having received the enquiry, the seller will send a quotation that says what he can offer. This can take many forms. He might send a price list which gives a description and price, or he might send an illustrated leaflet or catalogue with prices indicated.

The seller may send a letter which gives details of prices as well as descriptions of the items to which the enquiry relates. Again, such a letter may be a basic printed type of form which can be used for a whole range of products or quotations.

In the following example, note how the seller uses a separate catalogue reference number to identify each item he offers. This helps to avoid confusion where two particular descriptions are so similar that a mistake can be made.

Where the seller is unable to quote a precise price, he quotes an **estimated** or expected cost.

Apart from prices and specifications, the quotation also give details of discounts offered.

- *Trade discount*: given to people in the same trade as the seller to enable them to make a profit on resale.

- *Quantity discount*: given to encourage the buyer to place a large order.

- *Cash discount*: this is shown as 'terms' on many documents; it is given to encourage prompt payment.

The quotation also includes details of the arrangements for carriage (transport) of the goods. In other words it states who is required to pay for transport costs.

- *Carriage paid* (carriage outwards): The cost of transport of goods is included in the price, in other words the *seller* pays transport costs.

- *Carriage forward* (carriage inwards): The cost of transport is not included in the price and must be paid by the *buyer* of the goods.

```
              QUOTATION

          Mr A. Seller & Co. Ltd,
          64 Marcus Garvey Drive,
               Kingston 11.
              Tel: 93-694609


Ms A. Buyer & Co. Ltd.,              4 June 2000
11 Parmeter Road,
Kingston.

Dear Sirs,

We thank you for your letter of enquiry dated 1st June 2000
and we are pleased to offer the following quotation to
supply the mentioned items.

Please note that the prices, terms and delivery periods are
those current at the time of writing, and are only valid for
a period of three months from the date of this letter, after
which time a new quotation should be requested.

20 Reams    A4 Bond Typewriting Paper White.
Cat.No. 3498    $1.30 per ream

20 Reams    A4 Bank Typewriting Paper Yellow.
Cat.No. 3100    $0.90 per ream

10 Reams    A5 Bond Typewriting Paper White.
Cat.No. 3499    $0.85 per ream

10 Reams    A5 Bank Typewriting Paper Yellow.
Cat.No. 3101    $0.60 per ream

Delivery is carriage paid 6 weeks from receipt of order.

Terms: 5% 7 days, 2½% 28 days, otherwise net.

Yours faithfully,
for MR. A. SELLER & CO. LTD.

    B.Henry

B. Henry
Sales Manager
```

Fig. 13.4 Quotation

- *Ex works*: This is similar to carriage forward in that when a price is quoted 'ex works', the price refers to the goods at the factory, i.e. carriage is additional to the price.

The foregoing are the main terms that are used in quoting and trading, but there are some others that are used (usually in abbreviated form) that you should be aware of.

- *C/F (cost and freight)*: cost includes freight charges.

- *CIF (cost, insurance and freight)*: same as above, but also includes cost of insurance whilst goods are in transit.

- *FOB (free on board)*: cost includes freight charges, including loading on to a ship.

- *FOR (free on rail)*: as above, but includes loading on to a rail wagon.

13.3 Purchasing

Order

If the buyer finds the quotation satisfactory, she will send the seller an official order, which advises him of the:

- goods that are required
- place to be delivered
- date delivery is required
- agreed price.

In the example of an order in figure 13.5, you will note that the order has a number in the top right-hand corner. This makes it easy to refer to a particular order and also easier to find it in a filing system.

You will note that the delivery address is different from the address from which the order has come. This could

---

ORDER   No. 013448

MS A. BUYER & CO. LTD.
11 PARMETER ROAD,
KINGSTON.
Tel: 93-694608

Mr A. Seller & Co. Ltd,   10 June 2000
64 Marcus Garvey Drive,
Kingston 11.

Quantity	Description	Price
20 Reams	A4 Bond Typewriting Paper White. Cat.No. 3498	1.30 per ream
20 Reams	A4 Bank Typewriting Paper Yellow. Cat.No. 3100	0.90 per ream
10 Reams	A5 Bond Typewriting Paper White. Cat.No. 3499	0.85 per ream
10 Reams	A5 Bank Typewriting Paper Yellow. Cat.No. 3101	0.60 per ream

Deliver to Ms A. Buyer & Co. Ltd,
Shop 21,
Spanish Court,
New Kingston.

S.Webber
Signed Head Buyer

Delivery 6 weeks from date of order

Please note this company will only honour official orders signed by an authorised member of this company, and will only accept goods of the standard, style and price indicated on this order.

Fig. 13.5   Order

occur where a business has an office at one address, and a warehouse or factory at another.

Even when an order has been placed by telephone, it is customary to send a confirming order in writing, and in fact many sellers will not actually despatch goods by telephone request only. In such an event the word 'confirmation' will be typed in capitals on the order.

Stationery Requisition	
From	Marketing Dept.
To	Stationery Store

QUANTITY	DESCRIPTION
50	C6 Envelopes
2	A4 Lever Arch Files
1	Box A4 Carbon Paper
1	Box small paper clips
4	Reams A4 blank paper

Signed *Justin Time*   Date *24 June 2000*

Fig. 13.6   Stationery requisition

Sometimes there is a need to order items within an organisation as opposed to from an outside supplier. For example, the government may establish a 'department of supplies' from which other government departments or ministries purchase their supplies. In some business organisations departments and sections also have to obtain their stationery from some form of central supplies division.

To call the document requesting internal supplies an 'order' could be confusing, so to differentiate between an internal and an external order an internal request for supplies is called a **requisition**.

Acknowledgement of order

Having received the order from the customer, the seller sends an acknowledgement stating:

- that he has received the order
- that he is willing to supply the goods required
- when he expects to carry out delivery.

The acknowledgement may be in the form of a letter or a printed form. If looks similar to the order because it is sending back the same information as the order supplies.

When the buyer receives the acknowledgement, she will check it thoroughly to see that it agrees with the order.

13.4 Despatch

Advice note

The advice note is sent ahead of the goods to advise the buyer ('**consignee**') that the goods are on the way to her and that she should expect their arrival. If the goods do not arrive within a reasonable period of time (dependent upon how far the goods must travel), then the buyer will notify the seller ('**consignor**') so that he can make enquiries with the carrier of the goods.

The advice note is sent to the buyer's office and may show prices as well as details of the goods being sent.

Delivery note

The delivery note is usually packed in with the goods, and when the buyer unpacks the parcels she will check that she has received the items stated on the delivery note. Where a company uses its own vehicles to deliver goods the driver will be given a carbon copy of the delivery note which he will get the receiver of the goods to sign to confirm delivery. Note that the delivery note does not reveal the seller's prices.

If the goods are delivered by transport other than the seller's own, then a document, very much the same as the delivery note but called a **consignment note**, is given to the carrier to obtain a signature.

13.5 Charging

The invoice

This is one of the most important and probably the most well known of trading documents. It is sent from the seller to the buyer to advise her how much she owes the seller for a particular delivery of goods.

The invoice states:

- the quantity of goods supplied
- the individual prices
- the total amount owed.

BUSINESS DOCUMENTATION

```
                         ADVICE NOTE              No. AN.137892

                      Mr A. Seller & Co. Ltd,
                       64 Marcus Garvey Drive,
                           Kingston 11.
                          Tel: 93-694609
Ms A. Buyer & Co. Ltd.,                      Date    15 June 2000
11 Parmeter Road,
Kingston.                                    Dated   10 June 2000

              Order No.        O.13448
              Despatch details one carton - rail    Terms:
                               14/6/2000            5% 7 days
                                                    2½% 28 days
                                                    otherwise net
```

Quantity	Description	Amount	Price
20 Reams	A4 Bond Typewriting Paper White. Cat.No. 3498	1.30 per ream	26.00
20 Reams	A4 Bank Typewriting Paper Yellow. Cat.No. 3100	0.90 per ream	18.00
10 Reams	A5 Bond Typewriting Paper White. Cat.No. 3499	0.85 per ream	8.50
10 Reams	A5 Bank Typewriting Paper Yellow. Cat.No. 3101	0.60 per ream	6.00

Deliver to Ms A. Buyer & Co. Ltd,
Shop 21, Spanish Court,
New Kingston.

Fig. 13.7   Advice note

```
                        DELIVERY NOTE             No. DN.137892

                      Mr A. Seller & Co. Ltd,
                       64 Marcus Garvey Drive,
                           Kingston 11.
                          Tel: 93-694609
Ms A. Buyer & Co. Ltd.,                      Date    14 June 2000
11 Parmeter Road,
Kingston.                                    Dated   10 June 2000

              Order No.        O.13448
              Despatch details one carton - rail    Terms:
                               14/6/2000            5% 7 days
                                                    2½% 28 days
                                                    otherwise net
```

Quantity	Description	Amount	Price
20 Reams	A4 Bond Typewriting Paper White. Cat.No. 3498		
20 Reams	A4 Bank Typewriting Paper Yellow. Cat.No. 3100		
10 Reams	A5 Bond Typewriting Paper White. Cat.No. 3499		
10 Reams	A5 Bank Typewriting Paper Yellow. Cat.No. 3101		

Deliver to Ms A. Buyer & Co. Ltd,
Shop 21, Spanish Court,
New Kingston.   E & OE

Fig. 13.8   Delivery note

BUSINESS DOCUMENTATION

It need not necessarily be regarded as a demand for payment, because many invoices may be sent by a seller to a buyer, and it may be that the buyer will pay for all the invoices in one payment at the end of the month.

Where the buyer's office is separate from the warehouse or factory, the invoice is sent to the office.

Look at the invoice in figure 13.9 and you will see that it shows:

- the individual invoice number
- the buyer's order number.

The buyer then knows which order the invoice refers to.

Can you spot the following terms on the invoice? Take note of what each means.

- E & OE. You will see these letters in the bottom left-hand corner of the example invoice, and they stand for the words 'errors and omissions excepted'. By this the seller is telling the buyer that he reserves the right to correct any error made on the invoice at some later date. For example, our invoice reads $58.50, but had the person preparing the invoice keyed in $8.50 by mistake the seller has reserved the right to correct the error when he discovers it.

- Terms — 5% 7 days, 2½% 28 days, otherwise net. This wording on the invoice refers to a cash discount which the seller offers to encourage the buyer to pay the debt quickly. If the amount owed is paid within seven days, the seller will allow 5% off the invoice price. If the buyer takes more than seven days, but less than twenty-eight days to pay, the seller will allow 2½% off the invoice price. Where the buyer takes more than twenty-eight days to pay the terms are net, in other words no discount will be allowed.

INVOICE   No. I. 137892 — • Serial number of seller's invoice

Mr A. Seller & Co. Ltd,
64 Marcus Garvey Drive, — • Name and address of seller
Kingston 11.
Tel: 93-694609

Ms A. Buyer & Co. Ltd.,
11 Parmeter Road,
Kingston.

Date   16 June 2000 — • Date of invoice
Dated 10 June 2000 — • Details of Buyer's order

Order No.   013448
Despatch details one carton - rail — • Method of despatch
                 14/6/2000

Terms: — • Cash discounts offered for prompt payment
5% 7 days
2½% 28 days
otherwise net

Quantity	Description	Amount	Price
20 Reams	A4 Bond Typewriting Paper White. Cat.No. 3498	1.30 per ream	26.00
20 Reams	A4 Bank Typewriting Paper Yellow. Cat.No. 3100	0.90 per ream	18.00
10 Reams	A5 Bond Typewriting Paper White. Cat.No. 3499	0.85 per ream	8.50
10 Reams	A5 Bank Typewriting Paper Yellow. Cat.No. 3101	0.60 per ream	6.00

Gross invoice $ 58.50 — • Before deduction of discounts
Less 20% Trade discount 11.70 — • Discount given to other Traders
Net invoice $ 46.80 — • Amount to be paid by buyer

Deliver to Ms A. Buyer & Co. Ltd, — • Delivery address can be different from invoice address
Shop 21, Spanish Court,
New Kingston.

E & OE — • E & OE - Errors & omissions excepted - seller reserves the right to correct errors at later date

Fig. 13.9   Invoice

148

Pro forma invoice

In appearance this is exactly the same as the invoice except that it has 'pro forma invoice' as its title.

Where a seller does not know a buyer, he may be unsure whether he will receive payment in due course if he sends the goods, but at the same time will not want to miss the opportunity of supplying an order.

To get around this problem, before despatching the goods the seller will send the buyer a pro forma invoice which will charge for the goods in advance. When payment has been received he will then deliver the items ordered.

Credit note and debit note

It may arise that a customer is sent an invoice, and before the invoice is paid it is discovered that the customer is entitled to some reduction in the amount charged. The document which shows the reduction is called the **credit note**. It is sent by the seller to the buyer.

There are many reasons why the customer may be entitled to a reduction of the invoice value. For example:

- the price charged on the invoice may be too high
- some of the goods sent may be faulty or too few sent
- discounts omitted or too small
- errors in charging for transportation.

Whatever the reason, the credit note has the effect of reducing the debt that the buyer owes to the seller. The credit note is usually printed in red, and shows:

- the reason the credit note is issued
- the goods involved, their price and value
- reference numbers of documents involved in the sale and supply.

The **debit note** (sometimes called a supplementary invoice) has the reverse effect of the credit note, in that it makes an additional charge. For example:

- the original charge on the invoice was insufficient
- more goods were sent than invoiced and the buyer agrees to keep them.

Note. The debit note and credit note are both sent by the seller. They both have a similar appearance except for their colour and the word 'debit' or 'credit' as a title.

Tax on purchases

Jamaica has introduced a General Consumption Tax (GCT) whereby a percentage (currently 10%) tax is levied on a number of items and services. Other Caribbean islands have their own method of taxing goods and you should familiarise yourself with the system applied in your area, and the manner of calculating it into trading documents.

```
                        CREDIT NOTE                              CN3478

                     Mr A. Seller & Co. Ltd,
                      64 Marcus Garvey Drive,
                         Kingston 11.
                         Tel: 93-694609
                                                     21 June 2000
 Ms A. Buyer & Co. Ltd.,                     Date    16 June 2000
 11 Parmeter Road,
 Kingston.                                   Dated   10 June 2000


                      Credit against  013448
                      Order No.       ........................
                      Invoice No.     I137892
                                      ........................

 Quantity                                        Price    Amount

 20 Reams by allowance in respect of overcharge  0.10     $ 2.00
           on item A4 Bond Typewriting Paper
           Cat. No. 3498

           Charged @ $ 1.20 per ream
           Price     $ 1.20 per ream


 E & OE
```

Fig. 13.10   Credit note

Statement of account

Rather than expect a customer to pay for each individual invoice that has been sent, which could mean that she would have to write out several cheques during the month, the seller will send a statement of account at the end of the month to sum up all the business that has taken place during the month. Thus, the statement of account is used only for credit transactions. The statement of account shows:

- any amounts outstanding and unpaid from previous statements — shown by the words 'to account rendered'
- amounts which increase the debt the buyer owes to the seller (invoices and debit notes)
- amounts which decrease the debt (credit notes issued and payments made).

Look at the statement of account in figure 13.11. Note that it shows all business between a buyer and seller for a month. Where the debt is increased it is shown under 'debit'. Anything that reduces the figure in the amount column is shown under 'amount'.

Payment arrangements

The arrangement between the seller and the buyer for payment of goods and services supplied will depend on how well the seller knows the buyer. The following are the most common arrangements.

- *Payment in advance*: the seller may require payment prior to supply by cash with order (CWO) or in response to a pro forma invoice.
- *Cash on delivery* (COD): the buyer is required to pay the carrier the value of the goods on delivery.
- *On receipt of invoice*: to gain the benefit of cash discounts offered for prompt payment.
- *Against statement of account*: where the buyer has been granted trade credit, payment can be delayed until the end of the month.

Payment of debts

By cheque

There are many ways to pay a debt, but the most popular in business is for payment to be made by cheque. It is

---

STATEMENT OF ACCOUNT

Mr A. Seller & Co. Ltd,
64 Marcus Garvey Drive,
Kingston 11.
Tel: 93-694609

Ms A. Buyer & Co. Ltd.,
11 Parmeter Road,
Kingston.

Date 1 July 2000

Terms:
5% 7 days
2½% 28 days
otherwise net

Date	Details	Debit	Credit	Amount
1st June	To account Rendered May			120.30
3rd June	by Invoice I.137879	28.20		148.50
7th June	by Invoice I.137886	70.00		218.50
16th June	by Invoice I.137892	46.80		265.30
21st June	by Credit CN. 3478		2.00	263.30
23rd June	by Debit DN. 4166	3.50		266.80
27th June	by Cash Received		250.00	16.80

Amount outstanding $ 16.80

E & OE

- Amount Outstanding from previous statement
- All amounts which increase the buyer's debt are entered in the debits column and added to the cumulative amount. All amounts which reduce the customer's debt are listed in the credits column and taken away from the cumulative amount.
- Amount outstanding to be paid or carried forward to next account.

Fig. 13.11   Statement of account

possible to obtain a receipt stating that payment has been made, but usually this is unnecessary unless payment is made by cash.

Where the buyer sends a cheque covering only some of the invoices listed on the statement a **remittance advice note** will also be sent listing the invoices which the cheque is intended to pay.

By cash
For small amounts, cash in the form of coins and bank notes may be used. These are **legal tender**. This term refers to the universal acceptance of certain methods of payment where there is no doubt about their worth. In this respect a cheque is not legal tender, even though it is one of the frequently used methods of payment.

Banker's draft
This is a cheque drawn on a bank instead of a person's bank account. A banker's draft is guaranteed by the bank. This makes the draft as good as cash because the bank has guaranteed it for the customer, who has paid the value of the draft to the bank in advance. The bill of exchange discussed in the following section is another form of banker's draft.

13.6 Foreign trade documents

Most of the documents referred to so far in this chapter may also be used in foreign trade, but there are also some documents which apply particularly to that purpose. The following are the main documents used in foreign trade.

Payment documents

Bill of exchange
The bill of exchange is a document that is sometimes used in home trade, but it is most commonly used in foreign trade. It is particularly used in the settlement of international debts.

The bill of exchange is made out by the seller/exporter (the **creditor**) of goods requiring that the buyer/importer (the **debtor**) pays a sum of money on demand, or on an agreed future date (usually after three months).

Both the buyer and the seller benefit from the use of a bill of exchange. The buyer (importer) obtains **credit** on the transaction, and the seller benefits because instead of waiting for payment he can either sell the bill at a 'discount', or 'negotiate' it by using it to pay off his own debts, or use it as collateral against a bank loan.

Documentary bill
This is a bill of exchange with all related documents of title attached, including the invoice and insurance policy. This can be used to give a bank the right to take possession of the goods if the bill of exchange is not honoured when it **matures** (when payment is due).

Documentary credit
An exporter can request that a customer (the importer) makes payment for goods by 'documentary credit'. This enables the exporter to obtain payment before the documents of title/ownership are released to the importer. The importer arranges for her bank to guarantee that the payment will be made when the documents of title are handed over.

Letter of credit
A letter of credit is an assurance given by an importer's bank of the financial standing of the customer undertaking to make the payment required in due course. The letter of credit is in fact the letter sent from the importer's bank confirming this arrangement.

Other documents

Bill of lading
The bill of lading is used in the shipping of goods and it represents the title to ownership of goods. It shows details of the goods, their destination and the terms under which the shipping company agrees to carry the goods. Three copies of the bill of lading are raised:

1 one is retained by the exporter
2 one is given to the ship's captain
3 one is given to the importer who has to produce her copy to take possession of the goods on arrival.

Air waybill
This is used in connection with air transport and it serves as a receipt for goods carried by an airline. It is a kind of bill of lading for air transport. But it is not a document of title, and the sender of the goods does not have to be given a copy. In fact, because air transport is so fast, the goods could arrive before any documentation, so often documentation accompanies the goods.

Manifest
A summary of all the bills of lading and cargo a ship is carrying.

Freight note
The bill or charge for shipping goods; it is sent to the exporter by the shipping company.

Certificate of origin

This is a document certifying the country of origin of goods. It is sometimes required by the importing country if it has been agreed that the goods of a particular country will be allowed to enter the country at a more favourable tariff rate.

Import licence

This is issued by the importing government giving permission to bring certain commodities into the country. It can be used to enforce quotas (government limits on particular goods allowed to be imported).

Export licence

An export licence is sometimes needed before certain goods are allowed to leave a country (e.g. works of art of historical value).

13.7 Stock records

The importance of stock

Stock is the goods or materials held by a business. The stock can be for internal use (e.g. stationery), or for external use, such as to supply customers.

Stock is part of the capital or **assets** of a firm. It is important because it is used to support internal operations, as well as to meet orders from customers. For these reasons a business must hold adequate stocks in order to continue its operations. However, holding stock can also adversely affect **cash flow**. If a business holds too much stock, it can be a drain on its resources.

Stock levels

Minimum and maximum stock levels are often established to ensure that:

- sufficient stocks are available for internal operations
- stock is readily available to meet customers' orders
- too much stock is not held.

Minimum stock level
This is the lowest level to which stock is allowed to fall. It is used to safeguard against the possibility of running out of stock. When stock falls to the minimum level, further supplies are ordered to arrive before existing stock is completely used.

Maximum stock level
This is the greatest figure that the stock of a particular item will be allowed to rise to. It is used to ensure that stock does not rise above what is considered to be an economic level, and to avoid tying up capital unnecessarily.

INTERNAL STOCK
STATIONERY STOCK CARD

Item: A4 Headed Paper–981
Location: Store Cuppoard 5
Max. stock: 30 Reams
Min. stock: 15 Reams

Date 20 __	Receipts			Issues			Balance in stock
	Supplier	Order no.	Quantity	Department	Req. no.	Quantity	
7 Jun							20
8 Jun				Pool	208	2	18
9 Jun				Sales	239	2	16
12 Jun				Export	241	1	15
14 Jun	Printwell	SS.143	15				30
16 Jun				Transport	300	4	26
18 Jun				Admin	302	10	16
18 Jun	Printwell	SS.143	12				28

Fig. 13.12 This is a simple handwritten stock record.
1 Explain the purpose of the 'receipts' and the 'issues' sections.
2 How is the 'balance in stock' figure calculated?

STOCK RECORD CARD

Item: Desert Crisps – Cat. No. 37
Stock Price: $8.50 per carton
Location: Block 3 Room 35
Max. Stock: 7000
Min. Stock: 2000

Flavour	1	2	3	4	TOTAL
Stock carried forward	1500	2000	2000	1500	7000
Bastin 1/11/00	100 / 1400	100 / 1900	100 / 1900	100 / 1400	400 / 6600
Perry 17/11/00	300 / 1100	300 / 1600	250 / 1650	250 / 1150	1100 / 5500
Scattergood 4/12/00	800 / 300	800 / 800	800 / 850	800 / 350	3200 / 2300
New supplies 10/12/00	1200 / 1500	1200 / 2000	1150 / 2000	1150 / 1500	4700 / 7000

Fig. 13.13 A computerised stock record
1 What is the purpose of the minimum and maximum stock figures?
2 Why do you think a stock record may include a 'stock price'?

Stock records

The term 'stock records' refers to the ways in which additions and deductions from stock are recorded, together with the current overall balance. The basic principle of all stock recording systems involves *adding* new stock, *deducting* withdrawals, and maintaining a *cumulative balance*.

There are a variety of methods of recording stock movements and businesses will choose which method they feel suits them best. Two examples are given in figures 13.12 and 13.13, but there are many other ways of recording stock.

Computerised stock records

In the case of a small, simple stock record system, it may be maintained on cards and may be handwritten. Larger stock records may be **computerised**. For example, a stock record system can be incorporated into a computer **spreadsheet**. This computer program automatically carries out all the calculations necessary in response to stock increases or decreases, and instantly calculates a new balance. It can even be programmed to signal when the minimum stock level has been reached.

A **bar code** system extends the computerised stock record system further. All stock items are labelled with a unique bar code, which is a pattern of thick and thin lines (see figure 13.14). This bar code incorporates the **product code number** (stock identification number).

As items are taken out of the stockroom, or as a customer presents items being purchased at the cash-point (**point of sale** (**POS**)), the bar code on each item of good is 'read' by a scanning device connected to the main computer. This enables stock records to be instantly updated. The computer can even be programmed to order replacement stock automatically when the minimum stock level is reached.

13.8 Business Contracts

What is a contract?

One of the most important business documents is a contract. A contract is a legally binding agreement between two or more persons or parties whereby something is done or promised to be done, or given or promised to be given. It is more than just an agreement because it is enforceable by law. In other words, if any of the parties do not abide by the contract other parties can take legal action against them.

Although we have begun this section by referring to a contract as a document, this does not have to be the case. An agreement can be formed verbally in such a way that it constitutes a contract (see later).

A written contract takes a particular format. In other words, the wording, phraseology and terms used follow an accepted format that is recognised as legally

BUSINESS DOCUMENTATION

Fig. 13.14 A bar code is sometimes used to assist stock recording. (Courtesy of John West Foods Ltd.)

1 How is the information contained in a bar code passed to the main computer?
2 How do you think a 'product code' is used to update stock records?

significant. Such written contracts may be formalised by a seal or by a witnessed signature. An advantage of a signed contract is that the parties concerned cannot dispute the contents.

The parties of a contract

We have said that a contract is a legally binding agreement between parties. It is possible to have two or three parties, and these are:

- *the offeror* — the person who makes the offer
- *the offeree* — the person to whom the offer is made
- *the acceptor* — the offeree, having accepted the offer.

There can be a complication with regard to the foregoing relatively simple status. Sometimes the offeror could end up becoming the offeree and acceptor. For example, if A (offeror) offers to sell something to B (offeree) and B makes a counter-offer (such as 'You are asking me to pay too much, I offer to pay less'), then if A accepts the counter-offer, A now becomes the offeree and acceptor.

Consideration is the name given to the price or benefit which the parties to a contract get. Obviously, it is usual for both the offeror and the acceptor to benefit, and the consideration is the item of value (e.g. goods, services, money) that each gains.

From the foregoing you will realise that there are three elements or sides to an agreement: offer, consideration and acceptance.

Fig. 13.15 Negotiating a contract

The parties must *intend* to create a legal relationship, otherwise no legal liability exists. For example, an unscrupulous person might argue that a contract was verbally negotiated whereas the other party did not

154

Fig. 13.16 The contract process

intend this, or vice versa. But a court would consider the conduct and circumstances of the parties to decide whether or not there was an intention to create a contract.

Offer and acceptance

A contract comes into effect when a definite offer has been made and it has been unconditionally accepted, i.e. when all parties have agreed that something should take place.

Many such agreements are formally written down and signed by the parties concerned, but this does not always have to be the case. Spoken words can have the same legal effect as written agreements, so long as the parties involved agree that they are making a contract — a legally binding agreement.

Delivery of contracts

Obviously for someone to accept an offer it must be communicated to them; they must know what is being offered. Similarly, for a contract to be put into effect it must be **communicated**, it must be received by the parties. Therefore, delivery is an important aspect of contracts.

Delivery is the act of handing over the document. In the case of a speciality contract, which is discussed later, it does not become effective until the contract is actually delivered. A simple contract, on the other hand, becomes effective immediately the offer is accepted.

Where postal communication is used in the formation of contracts there are three clear rules which apply.

1 The offer must be communicated. In other words, the offeree must be made aware of the offer. For this reason a letter containing an offer must be received by the offeree.

2 **Acceptance** is considered complete once the letter of acceptance is put into the post. In other words, the time when the letter is posted completes the agreement, and not the time when the acceptance letter is received.

3 If the offeror wishes to **revoke** (cancel) the offer, this must be done before acceptance. In the case of post, this means before the time the acceptance is posted.

Invitation to treat

An **invitation to treat** is a rule that you need to be familiar with in relation to contracts. This is an expression of intent to negotiate; it is not itself an offer and does not compromise the parties. The basic rule is that an invitation to treat is not an offer which can bind the parties in legal relations. For example, a farmer places the advertisement in figure 13.17 outside his gate.

Fig. 13.17 Sign

This advertisement is an expression of an intention to negotiate. The farmer is not definitely saying the eggs will be available, or that he will sell them to you. Similarly, at an auction the auctioneer invites people to bid for what he has on offer. If the bid is insufficient he may decide not to sell.

An invitation to treat is a preliminary stage in the development of a contract, and places neither the seller nor the buyer under obligation; by attending an auction you are not obliged to buy and the auctioneer need not necessarily accept your offer.

The principles of invitation to treat can also be seen to be applicable in a shop situation. For example, if a shopkeeper displays an article with no visible price tag and you wish to buy the item, the shopkeeper has the right to say that the article is not for sale; perhaps it is only for display purposes. In this respect we can see that invitation to treat implies that there could be some reservations attached to the apparent offer to sell.

Discharge of contracts

There is a variety of ways in which contracts can be **discharged** (brought to an end); the following are some of these.

- *By completion*: the parties carry out what they have agreed.
- *By lapse of time*: by not meeting an agreed deadline.
- *By mutual agreement*: the parties agree to cancel the contract.
- *By notice*: where one party has the right to end the contract by warning in advance.
- *By legislature*: if the original contract was illegal.
- *By bankruptcy*: if one of the parties becomes bankrupt.
- *By breach*: when one or both parties make it impossible or impracticable to complete the action agreed.

Types of contract

There are three main types of contract: a simple contract, a speciality contract and a contract of record.

Simple contracts

A simple contract needs no special form; it may be conveyed in writing, orally or implied by the conduct of the parties involved.

These are the most basic of contracts and we are making these every day of our lives. For example, when you get on a bus, the driver has offered you a ride, you have accepted the offer and you are expected to pay for the journey. A contract has been carried through from start to finish.

Speciality contracts

A speciality contract is an agreement for a specific purpose and involves a written format. These are some of the important features of speciality contracts.

- They must be in written or printed form.
- The contract must be signed by the parties.
- It is customary (but not essential) for the contract to be 'witnessed'.
- Sometimes a seal is applied.
- The contract must be **delivered**. In other words, all parties involved must have a copy.

Examples of speciality contracts are dealt with in other parts of this book; speciality contracts include contracts of insurance, hire purchase or credit sale agreements, sale of goods agreements and property mortgages or leases.

A contract of record

These are obligations imposed upon someone by a court, often ordering someone to do or not to do something. For example, a court might instruct a business that it must cease trading.

1 PRE-CONTRACT
- Enquiry: e.g. potential buyer seeks information
- Invitation to Treat: e.g. auctioneer invites bids
- Statements of intent: e.g. declarations of intent

2 NEAR CONTRACT
- Offer made

3 CONTRACT STAGE

OFFER → AGREEMENT ← CONSIDERATION
↑
ACCEPTANCE

Fig. 13.18 Three stages in the development of a contract

Capacity

In the legal environment, the term '**capacity**' is used to identify who is eligible to enter into a contract. Generally speaking, all persons are eligible to enter into contracts. However, anyone who enters into a contract must, of necessity, be able to take responsibility for his/her actions associated with the contract. Therefore, to ensure that persons are not exploited or taken advantage of by virtue of their particular circumstances at any point in time, the law makes certain provisions. Thus, the following persons are not normally accorded full capacity.

Minors. Minors are persons under the legal age of 18 years of age. In the Caribbean, minors are not normally allowed to enter into contracts.

Drunks. Persons who are drunk are in a state which suggests temporary loss of consciousness and, thus, are unable to undertake any binding legal decision. If 'soberness' can be proven, though, then full capacity would be accorded to such persons.

Insane. Persons who are insane are not normally accorded full capacity. The argument is that if a person is insane, it is hardly likely that such a person would be able to make informed decisions and thus take responsibility for the outcomes of a contract entered into during that state of insanity. However, if it can be proven that such persons are, without a doubt, capable of entering into contracts, then they would be accorded full capacity.

Aliens. An alien would not be granted full capacity if his or her country is at war with the country in which he or she is domicile. An **alien** is a person who lives in a country other than his or her own and who is not a naturalised citizen of that country. When peace returns between the two countries, then the alien could be accorded capacity under the law.

Exceptions to the capacity law
- A minor could be permitted to enter into a contract if it can be proved that what is required by the minor is a necessity. According to the provisions of the law of capacity, a necessity is an article which is deemed 'reasonably necessary to the minor, having regard to the minor's station in life'. 'Having regard to the minor's station in life' is the operative phrase here. According to the law, the article must be deemed a necessity at the 'time of sale' and at the 'time of delivery'.
- Minors may also be permitted to enter into contracts of an educational value, for example, a contract for a student loan.

Legality

'Legality' means that all contracts must be drawn-up in accordance with the requirements of the legal framework of a country.

1 **Possibility**   This means that within the context of consideration, the parties to a contract must be in a position to deliver the requirements of the contract. However, from time to time 'impossibility' arises, and thus interferes with the possibility of meeting the obligations of the contract. For example, a contract may have been drawn-up between two parties to use a particular venue for an event. However, if the facility is destroyed by a freak storm just before the event, then the party responsible for that part of the contract can use the best possible method to carry out his/her side of the contract. For example, if the other party has another suitable venue, the party's side of the contract can be fulfilled.

Thus the freak storm introduced an impossibility into the arrangements, and so it was not possible to deliver the contract as was expected.

2 **Genuineness of parties to a contract (Good faith)**   In any contract, all parties must enter of their own free will. In other words, duress and coercion should never enter the picture. In the course of formulating a contract, a mistake of misrepresentation could occur. However, there are legal provisions to handle such situations.

3 **Termination of a contract**   All of the following are ways in which a contract may be terminated:

- *By performance.* This means that all the parties to the contract have carried out their part of the agreement.

- *By agreement.* The parties to the contract, in this case, may decide to cancel the contract before it comes to fruition.

- *By breach of contract.* This means that a party to a contract did not carry out his/her part of the agreement.

- *By renunciation.* This is a situation in which the contract is partially carried out by a party to the agreement.

- *By merger.* This comes about when parties to a contract find it necessary to substitute the current contract for a superior one.

- *By lapse of time.* This occurs when a party to the contract fails to meet his/her obligations to the contract before the stipulated time-frame. For example, if acceptance is not made within the stipulated time-frame, then the contract can be terminated. Sometimes, too, no exact time is stipulated for acceptance, but by virtue of the specific circumstances, the contract can be terminated.

- *By bankruptcy.* If a party to an agreement becomes bankrupt, then the contract can be terminated.

- *By death.* A contract may be terminated in the event that a party to it dies. However, the party's agent or beneficiaries may be required to continue with the terms of the contract.

Other contract terminology

Expressed rejection. This is a situation in which an offeree notifies the offerer of rejection of an offer.

Implied rejection. If the offeree makes a counter-offer, or a conditional acceptance, then, by law, this would be deemed 'implied rejection'. However, if the offeree requests additional information, thus averting any chance of error or misrepresentation, then this cannot be seen as 'implied rejection'.

Frustration. The provisions of the law may render a contract 'frustrated' if:

- the law governing the agreement changes, thus making its performance illegal.
- illness or death prevents a party to the contract from performing an action of a personal nature.
- an action to be taken in the performance of the contract is not taken.
- a necessary item or object which makes the contract a contract is partially or wholly destroyed.

Period of limitation This relates to the time-frame within which a party to a contract can take action against the other party for breach of contract. In the case of a simple contract, the time-frame is six years, and twelve years in the case of a speciality contract.

13.9 THINGS TO DO

This section contains a variety of exercises to help you create revision notes, to test your understanding and to prepare you for examinations.

Search and find

Write out the question and the answer by referring back through the text to form revision notes.

1. What is a transaction?
2. Why do businesses use trading documents?
3. What is the purpose of an enquiry?
4. Briefly describe the various forms that a quotation might take.
5. What is an estimate?
6. Describe the various discounts used in trading.
7. Why is it useful to use catalogue numbers as well as descriptions in price lists and other trading documents?
8. Explain the difference between an order and a requisition.
9. State four items of information contained in an order.
10. What is the purpose of an advice note?
11. How does the function of a delivery note differ from that of a consignment note?
12. State four items of information found on an invoice and explain the purpose of this document.
13. How does a pro forma invoice differ from the standard invoice?
14. What is the difference in function between a debit note and a credit note?
15. What is the function of a statement of account, and what is the purpose of the debits and credits columns?
16. Describe the various arrangements for the payment of debts between sellers and buyers of goods.
17. Explain how a bill of exchange assists a business involved in foreign trade.
18. What is documentary credit? Explain how this assists foreign trade.
19. Explain the similarities and the differences between a bill of lading and an air waybill.
20. What is the difference between an import licence and an export licence?
21. What is stock and why is it important to businesses?
22. How can stock levels affect the cash flow of a business?
23. Describe the basic principles of stock recording.
24. How can a computer spreadsheet be used to maintain stock records?
25. What is a bar code and what kind of information can it contain?
26. In what ways can a bar code system be said to be an 'extension' of a computerised stock record system?
27. 'A contract is more than an agreement.' Explain this statement.
28. Why are contracts important to business people?

29. Briefly explain each of the following parties of a contract and give examples of them in practice: offeror, offeree, acceptor.

30. 'An agreement is the result of an offer, a consideration and an acceptance.' Carefully explain this statement.

31. What is a 'counter offer'?

32. Why is the delivery of a contract just as important as its formation?

33. What do you understand by 'invitation to treat'?

34. How does a speciality contract differ from a simple contract?

35. What is a contract of record?

36. What does it mean when it is said that a contract has been 'signed, sealed and delivered'?

37. Give examples of legal 'capacity'.

38. What are the exceptions to capacity law?

39. In what ways might a contract be terminated?

40. How does 'expressed rejection' differ from 'implied rejection'?

What do you know?

Write out the complete sentence and insert the missing word, which can be chosen from the list at the end of the questions.

1. The ..... seeks out information about products a seller has to offer.

2. The ..... is a communication that says what a seller can offer.

3. To advise the seller what he wishes to buy the buyer will send an official ......

4. Where it is not possible to give a precise price the seller may give an ..... cost.

5. Firms may offer their customers a ..... to encourage prompt payment of debts.

6. The seller will ..... receipt of an order to confirm that he is willing to supply the goods or services requested.

7. An ..... note will be sent to tell the buyer when her goods have been despatched to her.

8. The ..... advises the buyer how much she is expected to pay for goods or services.

9. A statement of account ..... the trading position between the buyer and the seller.

10. A ..... note can be used to give a refund to the buyer.

Choose the missing words from the following:

summarises	order	discount	enquiry
credit	quotation	invoice	estimated
advice	acknowledge		

Multiple choice

Select the appropriate answer, a, b, c or d.

1. A statement of account is sent:
   a) at the end of the month
   b) when the goods have been paid for
   c) with the goods
   d) when the goods have been ordered

2. A trade discount would be shown on:
   a) a statement of account
   b) a remittance advice note
   c) an invoice
   d) a consignment note

3. Which of the following would be a likely reason for the issue of a debit note?
   a) too few goods were delivered
   b) a refund on returned packing material
   c) some goods were returned as faulty
   d) the invoice undercharged the buyer

4. Which of the following documents gives permission for certain goods to be brought into a country?
   a) import licence
   b) export licence
   c) bill of exchange
   d) letter of credit

5. Which of the following statements is false? The letters E & OE stand for:
   a) errors and omissions extra
   b) errors and omissions excepted
   c) extra and ordinary exceptions
   d) exports and orders excepted

6. The document that would be sent to a buyer to summarise a complete month of trading is:
   a) an advice note
   b) the invoice
   c) a remittance advice note
   d) a statement of account

7. An advice note is used to advise:
   a) the seller what the buyer requires
   b) the buyer that goods have been despatched
   c) the seller that some goods have been stolen
   d) the buyer how much they must pay

BUSINESS DOCUMENTATION

8   Which of the following is the bill or charge for shipping goods?
    a) a freight note
    b) a bill of lading
    c) a manifest
    d) a consignment note

9   Which of the following is the correct interpretation of the trading abbreviation COD?
    a) cargo on deck
    b) credit on demand
    c) cash on delivery
    d) charge on delivery

10 The word 'terms' refers to:
    a) the agreement between the buyer and seller
    b) the period during which delivery will be made
    c) cash discount given for prompt payment
    d) a charge made for delivery

Key words

Find out the business-related meaning of each of the following words. Write a separate sentence for each word to show your understanding.

transaction   specification   consignment   debts
overcharge   rendered   debits   debtor
credit   creditor

Structured questions

1   Refer to the invoice in figure 13.9 and answer the following questions related to it.
    a) Name the seller and the buyer involved in this transaction. (2)
    b) Most trading documents show a number similar to that shown in the top right-hand corner of this example. What is the purpose of this number? (2)
    c) On what date were the goods on this invoice ordered and on what date were they despatched? (2)
    d) The goods on this invoice were supplied 'carriage paid'. What does this mean? How does this differ from goods sold 'ex-works'? (4)
    e) How does the function of an invoice differ from that of a statement of account? (4)
    f) Explain the difference between a cash discount and a trade discount, using data from the invoice to illustrate your answer. (6)

2   All the following questions are related to the invoice in figure 13.9.
    a) Why do both the seller and the buyer need copies of this document? (1)
    b) Find the following numbers on this invoice and explain the purpose of each of them: 13448, 137892, 3498. (3)
    c) How does the function of a pro forma invoice differ from that of an invoice? (4)
    d) Under what circumstances might the information contained on this invoice result in the need to issue a credit note *and* a debit note. (4)
    e) Explain each of the following terms using data from this invoice to illustrate your answer:
        (i)   gross invoice amount
        (ii) net invoice amount
        (iii) trade discount
        (iv) E & OE. (8)

3   Refer to the statement of account in figure 13.11 and answer the following questions related to it.
    a) How frequently are statements such as this sent out? (1)
    b) What purpose does this document serve? (2)
    c) Name the creditor and the debtor involved in these transactions. (2)
    d) Why does this document show three months: May, June and July? (3)
    e) Give possible reasons for the entries 'by credit' and 'by debit'. (4)
    f) Clearly explain the meaning of the details, debit, credit and amount columns, using data from the document to clarify your explanation. (8)

4   All the following questions are related to the statement of account in figure 13.11.
    a) How much did the customer owe on the statement of account previous to the one illustrated? (1)
    b) What is the meaning of the wording 'to account rendered May'? (1)
    c) What will be the amount shown as 'to account rendered' on the next statement of account? (1)
    d) In what way is the creditor protected if he or she has made an error on this document? (2)

e) What was the total amount actually spent by the buyer during the period covered by the statement? (2)

f) The figure in the amount column is sometimes called the 'cumulative balance'. Why is it referred to in this way? Use examples from this statement to illustrate your answer. (4)

g) Draw a simple flowchart that includes at least *eight* stages and documents in a business transaction, correctly showing the position of the statement. (4)

h) Explain how all of the documents/stages listed in your answer to (g) would be used in the course of one transaction. (5)

5 All the following questions are related to the documents and stages shown in the flow chart in figure 13.19.

a) What is the name given to the complete chain of business shown in this illustration? (1)

b) At what point in this chain would the customer be asked to pay their outstanding account? (1)

c) Where in the chain would a debit note be most likely to appear? (1)

d) Give two reasons why a debit note might be issued. (2)

e) Under what circumstances would this diagram show the words 'consignment note', and where would this appear in the diagram? (3)

f) State three items of information likely to be found in a quotation. (3)

g) The flow chart shows that the remittance is being paid by cheque. Assuming that the transaction involves foreign trade, clearly describe the functions of *three* documents that are likely to be involved in payment arrangements. (9)

6 a) Polly Darton allowed Mary Banilow to keep her horse free of charge in the field Polly owns. What could be said to be the consideration involved here? (2)

b) Sally Burton placed an advertisement to sell her car for $3000. David Tew bought the car and paid the full price but he borrowed the money from Caribbean Bank Ltd. Name (i) the offeror, (ii) the offeree, and (iii) the acceptor in this situation. (3)

c) Ian Legon paid $100 deposit to Selene Robbins against purchase of her car on the understanding that Selene will keep the offer open for one month while Ian raises the rest of the money. Before the month is up Selene accepts an offer of more money for the car than she was originally asking. What is Ian's position? (4)

d) Sima Paxman offered to sell her house to James Roberts at a certain price. James said he would think it over and let Sima know. One month later James contacted Sima to say he had decided to buy the house, but Sima has now promised to sell it to someone else. Is Sima in breach of an agreement? Give reasons for your answer. (4)

e) Tim Osler owns a milk bar. He purchased a second-hand pinball machine from Future Technical Ltd. for $1000, for which he signed a sales contract. Later he discovered that some of the functions on the machine did not work properly. When Tim asked Future Technical for a refund of his money the company drew his attention to a clause in the sales contract

Fig. 13.19 Flowchart for question 5

that disclaimed any liability for defects. Clearly explain how you see Tim's position if he were to sue Future Technical in court, and advise him concerning future contract negotiations. (7)

7. The following questions are related to the section on business contracts.

   a) Define the term 'contract'. (1)

   b) Briefly describe three types of contract that are used in the business environment. (6)

   c) Mrs K. Williams agreed to sell A. Levy a motor car for $400,000. However, on the morning of the signing and handing over of the motor vehicle as well as all the relevant papers, Williams was still intoxicated from a drinking spree she engaged in the night before. Williams handed over the documents to Levy and informed her that the motor car was a gift, and so she need not pay for it. Levy drove the car to her home. Two days later Williams contacted Levy and asked her for the money ($400,000). Levy reminded Williams that she had given her (Levy) the car as a gift, and refused to give Williams the $400,000.

   Advise Williams, including clear reference to appropriate legal provisions. (5)

   d) (i) Draw a diagram depicting the stages of a contract and
      (ii) explain each stage of the development of the contract. (8)

Research assignments

1. You are the managing director of a medium-sized manufacturing company engaged in the production and sale of small items of farm equipment. Design five trading documents that you are likely to use in your business. For each document give a detailed explanation of the important functions of the various parts of it.

2. You work for a manufacturing company that is currently only engaged in home trade, but is considering expanding into overseas trade. Write a detailed report for your managing director explaining some of the ways in which documentation can support this development.

3. Visit local firms and collect samples of the documents used in *local trade* as well as *foreign trade*. Put the documents in a scrap book under the headings:

   a) documents used in local trade
   b) documents used in foreign trade.

   Display the documents collected on the bulletin board in your classroom or on a chart. Use appropriate headings.

4. Investigate a small and a medium-sized local business you have access to. Obtain permission to examine their stock record procedures. Formulate a few questions that will guide your search. Write a report on your findings, including examples of differences you have identified in the methods that each size of business employs.

Chapter 14
TRANSPORTATION

14.1 The importance of transportation

Transport is a form of **communication**, a means of making contact between two distant points. It provides services that enable workers to go to and from work, raw materials to reach the producer, and finished products to be distributed. An efficient transport system reduces the amount of capital tied up in stocks, because new supplies can be obtained quickly. It also makes international trade possible by providing a means of physical contact between trading countries. In fact, an efficient transport system saves a business time and money.

Transport plays an important part in the marketing of goods because without transport raw materials would not reach the producer, and the finished article would not be distributed.

For marketing to be effectively carried out there is a need for a sophisticated transport system which enables goods to reach the right place, at the right time and in the right condition.

The importance of transport can easily be understood if we examine the distribution of a single product. Consider the transportation involved in the movement of bananas from the Caribbean region to the European market. The fruit must be taken from the plantation to the port, where it is loaded on to a ship with a cooling system to preserve the bananas during the long Atlantic voyage. Upon arrival in Europe the cargo is transshipped on to road or rail transport for the journey to the wholesale produce markets. Many further journeys are then arranged by wholesalers and retailers before the fruit reaches the consumer. Timing is important at every stage of the journey to ensure that the bananas, which are harvested in a green condition, reach the consumer before the ripening process is complete.

In relation to transport, the **consignor** is the person sending cargo and the **consignee** is the person to whom it is being sent. The firm transporting the cargo is often called the **carrier** and cargo is sometimes referred to as **freight**.

14.2 Choice of transport

Each type of transport has its special uses. Some are more suitable for a particular task than others. Consequently, choosing an appropriate method of transport for particular circumstances is one of the skills essential for business success. Transport users will take the following factors into account when choosing the form of transport to use.

- The nature of the goods.
- How urgently the consignment is needed.
- The value of each item.
- The cost of the transport.
- The distance the consignment must be transported.
- The size and weight of the load.
- The convenient position of terminals, e.g. station, docks and airport.
- The possibility of combining loads to reduce costs.
- The reputation of the carrier.

14.3 Methods of transport

As in most other areas of the world, there are five methods of transportation in the Caribbean region: rail, road, water, air and pipelines.

Rail

Rail transport is generally a lot more widely used in overseas countries than it is in the Caribbean. However, we need to be aware not only of our own limited use of railways but also of the importance of rail in other countries. This is because it is used by some of our businesses, particularly those engaged in the overseas market.

Fig. 14.1 Methods of transport in the Caribbean

Advantages of rail transport
- More comfortable and easier for passenger travel than road transport.
- Faster than road on long distances.
- Less labour-intensive than road transport.
- Especially suited for container traffic.
- More economical in fuel-use than road transport.

Disadvantages of rail transport
- Routes determined by railway lines and stations.
- Equipment costs are very high.
- Relies on road transport for transshipment.
- Less economic than road movement for short journeys.

Road

One of the main reasons that rail transport has limited use in the Caribbean is that the length of journey is often not sufficient to offset the inconvenience of transporting cargo from road on to rail and later back on to road for local delivery. Conversely, road transport is by far the most important in the region because journeys between delivery points are relatively short.

Advantages of road transport
- Door-to-door service provides maximum flexibility.
- Fast over short distances.
- Risk of damage reduced by lack of need for transshipment.
- Can reach places inaccessible to other forms of transport.
- A good road network speeds up movement and reduces congestion.
- Less tied to a rigid timetable than railways.
- Suitable for speedy direct delivery of perishable goods.
- Other forms of transport rely on road transport to connect with terminals such as airport, station and docks.

Disadvantages of road transport
- Expensive to operate in large congested cities.
- Subject to mechanical breakdowns.
- Affected by adverse weather conditions (e.g. high winds, floods).
- Loads are limited in size and weight.
- Some roads are unsuitable for very large vehicles.
- Slower than railways over long distances.
- Wastes resources if truck returns empty.
- Tax on vehicles and fuel must be incorporated into costs.

Water

Water transport is important in the Caribbean not only because it helps in the transportation of goods and people between islands, but also because it provides an important link to other parts of the world. The majority of all our raw materials (e.g. bauxite and petroleum) sold to other countries are transported out of the region by water.

Two forms of water transportation are used in the region: river transport and sea transport.

River transport

Rivers provide a means of moving goods and people into inland areas, although they are only used to a limited extent in the region. For example, timber is floated down the Belize River, and in Guyana river transport is used for much heavy traffic. However, overall, river transport is not used to the extent that it is in many other parts of the world.

Sea transport

Sea transport is particularly important to the Caribbean region for the obvious reason that it is a group of islands surrounded by sea. The following are the main forms of sea transport used in the Caribbean.

Passenger liners
Passenger liners are built primarily for passenger travel, particularly cruising. They carry some cargo, and as they follow fixed routes and keep to a regular timetable, delivery dates can be guaranteed. However, high freight costs limit use to high-value cargoes.

Cargo liners
Cargo liners sometimes carry a few passengers, although their main purpose is to deliver cargo. They operate on fixed routes and to a regular timetable. A vessel always sails from a port on time, even if some of the scheduled cargo has not arrived.

Tramp ships
Tramps are ships that have no timetable or set route. They will carry any type of cargo to any part of the world. The vessels are chartered through a charter party agreement (see later).

Special freighters
For special cargoes there are a variety of purpose-built ships.
- *Container ships*: cellular design vessels for fast load/unload.
- *Bulk carriers*: for ore and grain.
- *Tankers*: for oil and other bulk liquids.
- *Ferries*: roll-on/roll-off ferries can carry vehicles. Hovercraft have proved particularly successful in this role in some parts of the world.

Advantages of sea transport
- The way is free and gives access to most parts of the world.
- A large ship can be propelled with a relatively small amount of power.
- The natural buoyancy of the water enables ships to carry very heavy loads, which gives economies of scale.

Disadvantages of sea transport
- The main disadvantages of sea transport is that it can only carry its cargo as far as the ports. Thereafter the cargo has to be transferred to some other form of transport to reach the final destination.
- Sea transport is a relatively slow method of moving freight.

Requirements of a sea port

Efficient sea transport operations require the provision of good terminal facilities which enables vessels to 'turn round' quickly. The following are the main requirements of a modern port.

- Clear access channel with deep water.
- Some protection from rough seas.
- Wharves with appropriate lifting gear and equipment such as that necessary for moving containers, etc.
- Warehouses, including specialist storage, such as refrigeration, bonded stores, hazardous cargo.
- Supplies of oil, water and other ship's requirements.
- Repair facilities such as dry docks.
- Customs and immigration facilities.
- Good links with road or rail network.
- Buildings for offices and commercial services such as banks and restaurants.

Fig. 14.2 The port of Kingstown, St Vincent

TRANSPORTATION

Fig. 14.3   Grantley Adams International Airport, Barbados

Air transport

This is the youngest but most highly technical form of transport. It is constantly expanding in the volume of passengers and freight it handles. It is by far the most important method of transportation of people, both within and to and from outside the region. Air transport makes a major contribution to the tourist industry, but it is becoming increasingly important also for carrying cargo.

Advantages of air transport
- It is the fastest form of transport.
- It operates to timetables, mostly on direct routes.
- It reduces the risk of damage or pilferage.
- Shorter transit time reduces insurance costs.
- Packaging costs reduced.
- Particularly effective over long distances.
- Containers are now being used to speed up cargo loading and unloading.

Disadvantages of air transport
- High operational costs result in high freight rates.
- Weight and size of cargo are limited.
- Sometimes affected by adverse weather conditions.
- Relies on other forms of transport to and from airport.
- Not suitable for short distances.
- Causes noise and pollution.
- Economic use is limited to certain cargoes, particularly light-weight, high value, urgently required commodities such as drugs, mail or high value perishable goods.

Requirements of an airport

In a similar way that a sea port demands facilities that enable it to operate efficiently, an airport also has requirements that must be met if it is to fulfil its functions.

Siting
The siting of an airport is very important. Whilst it would be convenient to site an airport in a country area where land costs are cheaper than in cities, most air travellers are heading for one of the world's major cities where they can link up with other forms of transport. For this reason, an airport has to be sited as near as possible to a major city, but avoiding high rise buildings and causing as little noise and pollution as possible.

Road and rail links
Road and rail links play an important part in providing easy access for travellers and freight. If the road and rail links are speedy and efficient, they can allow the airport to be sited further away from a city centre. The modern terminal also requires facilities for long- and short-term parking as well as freight storage areas such as a bonded warehouse.

Operational, repair and safety facilities
A wide range of equipment and repair services are necessary to keep aircraft flying. For example, sophisticated radio, radar, computer and other technical equipment (and the people to operate them) have become increasingly important at busy international

airports. In addition, aircraft use vast quantities of highly inflammable fuel. This must be stored safely, and a fleet of tankers and other vehicles is needed to load fuel, luggage and freight on to aircraft. In addition, safety and medical services such as fire engines and ambulances must be permanently ready for action.

Customs and immigration officials
These are needed to regulate the import of goods on which duty must be paid, as well as to check for prohibited items such as drugs and firearms. Immigration officials are also necessary to ensure that those who enter the country have the right to do so.

Terminal buildings and personnel
Terminal buildings containing baggage and freight-handling equipment are required to ensure speedy movement of passengers and cargo. Within these buildings there may be hotel accommodation and commercial services such as banks, a post office, a duty free shop, and bars and restaurants. Airports require a variety of personnel to operate the terminal buildings. Security staff have become increasingly important.

Pipelines

Pipelines allow the transport of commodities without using a vehicle. Examples are gas, oil and water.

14.4 Containerisation

A container is a large pressed steel box available in two International Standards Organisation (ISO) sizes, capable of carrying twenty or thirty tonnes of cargo. The container is packed at the factory or inland pooling depot and delivered to the container terminal by rail (freightliner) or road, and deposited in the container parking area in the dock container terminal.

The containers are moved around the terminal by straddle carriers. The container is loaded precisely into position in the ship's hold by special gantry cranes.

Containerisation is also increasingly being used in air transport, to help speed up 'turn round'.

Fig. 14.4 Containers on the dock at Fort de France, Martinique

Advantages of containerisation
- Reduced staffing requirements lowers transport costs.
- Damage and pilferage is reduced.
- Packaging and insurance costs are reduced.
- Ship/aircraft 'turn round' is speeded up considerably.

14.5 Transportation terminology

- *Air waybill*: used in air transport as a receipt given to the consignor by the aircraft captain.
- *Bill of lading*: a document used in shipping which includes:
  a) a description of the cargo and its destination
  b) title of ownership of goods in transit
  c) a receipt for goods aboard ship.
- *Charter party*: a contract made between a shipowner and a consignor for the transport of cargo.
- *Consignment note*: accompanies goods being transported by land and is signed by consignee on delivery.
- Delivery terms:
  a) *Carriage forward*: cost of transport to be paid by consignee.
  b) *Carriage paid*: cost of transport is paid by consignor.
  c) *Cost insurance, freight* (CIF): cost of goods includes freight and transit insurance.
  d) *Franco*: price of goods includes delivery to buyer.
  e) *Free alongside ship* (FAS): cost of goods includes delivery to side of ship.
  f) *Free on board* (FOB): cost includes freight as far as loading on to ship.
  g) *Free on rail* (FOR): transport costs are paid by the seller as far as railway.
- *Freight note*: a bill presented to the consignor by the shipping company for shipping goods.
- *Lloyd's List*: a daily newspaper published by Lloyd's of London listing ship movements.
- *Manifest*: a summary of all the bills of lading and cargo a ship is carrying.
- *Shipping agent* (freight forwarding agent): a company specialising in deciding the best form of transport and arranging necessary documentation.

14.6 THINGS TO DO

This section contains a variety of exercises to help you create notes, to test your understanding and to prepare you for examinations.

Search and find

Write out the question and the answer by referring back through the text to form revision notes.

1. Why can transport be said to be a form of communication?
2. Why is transportation particularly important to the Caribbean region?
3. List the factors that a business would take into account when deciding which form of transport to use.
4. List the advantages and the disadvantages of the railways as a means of carrying freight.
5. Give one reason why rail transport is not extensively used throughout the Caribbean region.
6. Give three advantages and three disadvantages of using road transport as part of the system of distribution of manufactured goods.
7. State one example where road transport would be preferable to rail transport.
8. Why is road transport important to both air and rail transport?
9. Why is sea transport particularly important to the Caribbean?
10. Briefly describe the four basic classes of ship, including mention of the circumstances or cargo for which each is particularly suited.
11. List the advantages and the disadvantages of sea transport.
12. List the requirements of a modern port.
13. What are the advantages and the disadvantages of air transport?
14. List three examples of cargo for which you think air transport is particularly suited.
15. Give a detailed description of the facilities needed for an airport to function efficiently and safely.

16 Name the form of transport that does not need a vehicle.
17 What is containerisation and what are the benefits gained from this method of freight handling?
18 Explain the purpose of at least four documents used in transportation.
19 Describe four delivery terms related to transportation.
20 What is a shipping agent?

What do you know?

Write out the complete sentence and insert the missing word, which can be chosen from the list at the end of the questions.

1 An efficient transport system reduces the amount of ..... needed to be tied up in stocks.
2 Some forms of transport are more suitable for a particular ..... than others.
3 The ..... of an item will have some influence on the form of transport that can be used.
4 ..... transport is less labour intensive than road transport.
5 A major advantage of ..... transport is that it provides a door-to-door service.
6 ..... transport is particularly important to the Caribbean because the region consists of so many islands.
7 Passenger liners follow ..... routes.
8 A ..... ship has no timetable or set route.
9 A main advantage of sea transport is that the ..... is free and gives access to most parts of the world.
10 ..... transport is the youngest but most highly technical form of transport.

Choose the missing words from the following:

| sea | tasks | fixed | capital | road |
| air | tramp | rail | way | value |

Multiple choice

Select the appropriate answer, a, b, c or d.

1 Bananas are transported out of the Caribbean by sea rather than air because:
a) sea transport is the quickest method available
b) speed is the most important factor
c) bananas are a relatively low-value product
d) only ships provide a container service

2 A large truck would be transported into the Caribbean from Europe by:
a) road
b) rail
c) air
d) sea

3 Transportation is important to businesses because:
a) it makes it possible to explore new markets
b) an efficient transport system saves time and money
c) it provides employment for people
d) it enables workers to reach their place of employment

4 Which of the following goods is air transport the least suitable for?
a) fuel
b) mail
c) medicines
d) jewellery

5 State which of the following is not a true advantage of sea transport.
a) does not rely on other forms of transport
b) carries large loads economically
c) the 'way' is free
d) has access to most parts of the world

6 A ship that carries general freight on a scheduled route is called a:
a) tramp
b) cargo liner
c) bulk carrier
d) tanker

7 An air waybill is:
a) a route schedule for aircraft
b) an instruction given to an aircraft captain
c) the invoice for air freight
d) a receipt given to air cargo consignors

8 Which of the following types of ship is based on a cellular design to allow for fast loading and unloading?
a) an oil tanker
b) a cargo ship
c) a container ship
d) a tramp

9 Which of the following refers to the person to whom goods are being sent?
a) consignee
b) consignor
c) carrier
d) charterer

10 The main advantage of road transport is:
    a) the large loads it can carry
    b) the employment prospects it provides
    c) the fact that it is not labour intensive
    d) the flexibility it offers

> **Key words**
>
> Find out the business-related meaning of each of the following words. Write a separate sentence for each word to show your understanding.
>
> consignor   consignee   carrier   terminal
> freight   consignment timetable schedule
> perishable   dock

Structured questions

Table 14.1 *Transport use data for Noland*

Passenger transport in Noland: Estimated passenger kilometres (thousand million kilometres)				
	1989		1999	
		%		%
Air	2	0.50	3	0.60
Rail	36	9.11	35	6.97
Road				
Public service vehicles	54	13.68	42	8.37
Cars and taxis	297	75.19	410	81.67
Motorcycles	3	0.76	7	1.39
Pedal cycles	3	0.76	5	1.00
Total	395	100	502	100

1   The data in table 14.1 shows the volume of inland passenger transport for the imaginary country of Noland. Answer the questions related to the data.

   a) Which type of inland transport, air, rail or road, carries the greatest volume of passenger transport? (1)

   b) The data shown here relates to domestic passenger traffic. What is meant by 'domestic' in this respect? (2)

   c) State the total percentage of passenger traffic carried by road in 1989 and in 1999. (2)

   d) Draw an appropriate graph to show a comparison between air, rail and road as a percentage of the volume of domestic passenger traffic carried in both 1989 and 1999. (3)

   e) Briefly state the general trend that can be seen between 1989 and 1999 in relation to each of the three categories of transport shown. (3)

   f) What trend can be observed if public transport is compared with private transport? (3)

   g) Explain some of the possible reasons for the trends that can be observed in this data. (6)

2   The graph in figure 14.5 shows the cost per kilometre of transporting bulky and heavy loads for various journeys up to 350 kilometres.

Fig. 14.5 Transporting bulky and heavy loads

   a) (i) Which is the cheapest method of transport for a journey of 100 kilometres? (1)
      (ii) Which is the cheapest method of journeys exceeding 300 kilometres? (1)
      (iii) At what distance does it cost the same to transport goods by road as it does by rail? (1)

   b) Complete table 14.2 which aims to show the difference in total costs between road and rail transport for various journeys. (3)

Table 14.2

Miles	Road	Rail
125		
200		
300		

c) Why does road transport have an advantage over rail transport for shorter journeys, but is at a disadvantage for longer journeys? (4)

d) Why does rail transport depend heavily on road transport? (4)

e) Other than distance, what other factors will influence a business's choice between road and rail transport for delivering goods? (6)

3 a) State two major factors that need to be taken into account when choosing a site for an airport. (2)

b) Why do airports rely on other forms of transport? (2)

c) What is the function of an air waybill? (2)

d) What part does a freight forwarding agent play in the transportation of goods? (3)

e) Describe examples of goods and circumstances for which air transport would be appropriate, and others for which air freight is impracticable. (5)

f) What are the requirements for an efficient and safe airport? (6)

4 a) Briefly explain each of the following delivery terms related to the carriage of goods:
   (i) carriage forward (1)
   (ii) carriage paid (1)
   (iii) franco (1)
   (iv) CIF (1)
   (v) FOB. (1)

b) The following are documents used in freight transport. Explain the purpose of each of them:
   (i) consignment note (2)
   (ii) bill of lading (2)
   (iii) freight note. (2)

c) Describe the function of each of the following people involved in the movement of goods:
   (i) consignee (3)
   (ii) consignor (3)
   (iii) shipping agent. (3)

5 The graph in figure 14.6 shows the cost of various means of transport.

Fig. 14.6 Cost of means of transport

a) Why is the line for water transport a relatively level line? (2)

b) List the cheapest methods of transport at each of the distances shown as A, B, C and D. (4)

c) Which of the points X, Y and Z would you consider to be related to air transport? Give reasons for your answer. (6)

d) List the factors a business would take into account in deciding which method of transport to use. (8)

6 The data in figure 14.7 refers to the domestic transport of the imaginary country of Noland in 1989 and 1999.

	1989		1999	
		%		%
Road	1537	84.54	1444	86.21
Rail	176	9.68	79	4.72
Water: seagoing	44	2.42	57	3.40
Water: internal	11	.61	7	.42
Pipelines	50	2.75	88	5.25
Total	1818	100	1675	100

Fig. 14.7 Domestic goods transport of Noland

a) Which method of transport generally carries the greatest volume of goods? (1)

b) Name two forms of goods that would be likely to be transported by pipelines. (2)

c) The data shown here refers to the 'domestic' transport of goods but it includes seagoing water transport. Why is it possible to include seagoing transport in domestic data? (2)

d) Use an appropriate form of graph to compare the volume of freight carried by each of the categories of transport in 1989 and 1999. (3)

e) Which category shows the greatest percentage increase in transported goods 1989 — 1999, and which shows the greatest percentage decline? (4)

f) How important are the methods of transport shown in this data in the Caribbean region? (8)

Research assignments

1 Describe the features of four contrasting forms of sea transport, including an explanation of the types of freight for which each would be used. Obtain examples of four documents used in transport of freight by sea and clearly explain the function of each.

2 Discuss the importance of transportation to the CARICOM economy. Use examples from current newspapers to support your discussion.

3 Compare road, rail, water and air vehicles as means of transport for freight and passengers. What evidence exists to show that some of these are more important than the others to your country?

4 Carry out a survey of at least ten local businesses to establish the methods of transportation they use. Give reasons for any differences identified.

5 Study any firm which you know sends its goods to a number of different markets. Comment on the various delivery methods the firm uses.

6 If a new factory were established in your locality producing household utensils for sale throughout the Caribbean and overseas, what transport facilities would be likely to be used? Present evidence to support your research?

Chapter 15
COMMUNICATIONS

15.1 The importance of business communication

Communication is the process of making contact between two points. The contact can be achieved by the actual physical movement of items or people. It can also be the transfer of information or messages from one person or one place to another.

Communication is particularly important for businesses because it is through communication that a firm makes contact with its customers and suppliers and between the various internal parts of its organisation.

There are four elements of all communication: the *transmitter*, the *message*, the *medium* of transmission and the *receiver*. The transmitter is the person or the organisation that is sending the message or package. The message is the information or item that is to be communicated. The medium is the method being used to send the message or item, such as letter, telephone or transport, and the receiver is the person or organisation for whom the message is intended.

For communication to be carried out effectively, all of the elements involved have to be clear and effective. Take, for example, two people talking on the telephone. The person speaking must use clear speech (transmission), the words they say must be carefully chosen (message), the telephone system (medium) must not be faulty, and the person receiving the call (receiver) must listen carefully.

Apart from the need of businesses to send and receive messages, effective communication is also important because it helps them to operate efficiently and also helps them to create a good public image.

Communication is an expensive aspect of a firm's operations, so the method to be used has to be given careful consideration. Having decided what is the most appropriate method to be employed, it is important that it is used in the most economical manner. For example, being precise when using the telephone, or ensuring that employees do not use the firm's telephone for personal calls.

Fig. 15.1 What aspects of telephone use illustrate the four elements of communication?

External communications

Communications between a firm and other organisations take two main forms: postal communication and telecommunication. These will be examined later in this chapter. But advertising and transport, which are dealt with in Chapters 10 and 14, are also aspects of communication.

Advertising is the method of communication by which a business makes potential customers aware of the products or services it offers. In advertising the transmitter is the seller, the receiver is the potential customer, the message is the information contained in the advertisement and the medium is the poster, television, or some other method used to communicate the message.

Transport is also a form of communication. It is a means of making physical contact between two distant points. It also provides facilities which enable workers to

173

go to and from work, and which enable raw materials and finished products to be moved.

Internal communications

The systems of communication within an organisation are also vital because they play an important part in enabling the firm to operate smoothly and effectively. The purpose of internal business communication is to inform, organise, direct, motivate and negotiate.

The various parts of the organisation have to be kept informed of the activities of other sections so that they can make a useful contribution to achieving the firm's aims.

The different internal sections of the firm have to be kept informed of the activities of other parts of the business and organised and **co-ordinated** so that they carry out the part that they play in the control and operation of the organisation's activities.

Communication is important in directing people or parts of the organisation in specific tasks so that they contribute to the achievement of the firm's **aims**. Communication also plays an important part in the management function of **motivating** employees or departments to work hard and enthusiastically so that the firm gets maximum benefit from their efforts.

Policies have to be formulated and decisions have to be taken and communicated between the members of the organisation. At times there will be conflicts of views which have to be resolved. This may be achieved by informal discussions and interviews, but often through formal business meetings.

15.2 Internal methods of communication

The methods of internal business communication can be divided into three broad categories: written, oral and visual.

Written

- *Suggestion schemes* allow employees to communicate ideas to the management for improvements in the organisation's practices.
- *Manuals*: instruction booklets dealing with equipment use or business procedures make employees aware of company requirements and safety measures.
- *Letters*: although letters are a common method of communication, they are only used occasionally internally: for notices of appointment, promotion or dismissal, and also sometimes between sections of the organisation which are at different sites.
- *Memorandums*: these are the most common method of internal written communication used. Memorandums, (memos) are brief notes, without formal opening or closing, typed or written on a standard form.
- *Minutes*: these are a summary of what has taken place at a meeting. They keep those who were unable to attend a meeting informed of what has taken place, as well as acting as a reminder to those who were present.
- *Notices*: display of information on notice-boards is another way that employees can be kept informed about the firm's activities, jobs being advertised internally, safety, etc.
- *House magazines and journals*: these are another way in which the activities of a firm or organisation are communicated to employees or members.

MEMORANDUM

TO: Olivia Carter, Ian Smith, Jill Jones
FROM: Gordon Massey
DATE: 22nd March
RE: Trade Discount

As from 1st April the trade discount to be given to 'higher category' customers is to be increased from 20% to 25%. This will apply to all customers with an annual trade account with us in excess of $500,000 p.a.

Please arrange for all computer records to incorporate this new arrangement.

It might be a good idea to formulate a list of 'higher category' customers (similar to our 'bad debtors' list) to be held by all sales personnel. This will be on the agenda for the next Heads of Department meeting.

Fig. 15.2   A memo

Oral

It is through oral communication that most internal consultation takes place. This takes many forms.

- *Speech*: everyday speech is the most common and the most direct form of oral communication, usually in face-to-face contact, e.g. instructions from a superior to a subordinate.
- *Interviews*: these are a direct form of oral communication that allows individual discussion, as when selecting people for employment or promotion.
- *Meetings*: or discussions among a group of people. Meetings are examined in more detail later in this chapter.

- *Telephone, intercom and paging*: these internal systems of telecommunication make it possible to make contact between members and sections of the organisation when face-to-face contact is not convenient.

Visual

One of the most effective ways to communicate information is by using a picture, a diagram or symbols. This can make the presentation of statistics more interesting. **Charts** and **graphs** can be used in this manner, and these can be made even more effective by the use of colour or shading.

The following are the main methods used in business and they can be displayed using a variety of media from leaflets to notice-board posters, or on computer screens:

- pie chart
- bar chart
- line graph
- flowchart.

Fig. 15.3 **Methods of communicating information visually**

15.3 Business meetings

Meetings are a useful form of internal communication when it is necessary to have discussions within or between groups of people. They give the opportunity for an exchange of ideas and for **collective efforts** to solve problems and formulate policies.

Most organisations have specific **rules** for conducting meetings. Apart from observing conventional rules related to the manner of behaving at a meeting (e.g. addressing the chair), the firm may incorporate other regulations such as the frequency of the meeting, or the minimum number of people (a **quorum**) required to be present before a decision can be taken.

Principal officers

The principal officers of a meeting are a chairperson and a secretary. A treasurer is also often involved. Each of these officers has a specific role to play.

The **chairperson** is responsible for the correct conduct of the meeting, and for summing up the consensus of opinion expressed by those at the meeting. If at a time of voting the members are equally divided, the chairperson has the '**casting vote**' to arrive at a final decision.

The **secretary** is responsible for sending out notices giving the date, time and place of a meeting, and for preparing the agenda which shows the items to be covered during the meeting. The secretary is also responsible for producing the minutes, a summary of what has taken place at a meeting, and for ensuring that decisions taken at a meeting are carried out.

The **treasurer** is responsible for all the financial matters of the organisation associated with the meeting. This involves ensuring that payments due are received and that those owed are paid on time, maintaining adequate cash flow, and preparing balance sheets and financial reports.

Agenda

The agenda is a summary of the items of business to be discussed at a meeting. The agenda follows an accepted order of presentation. See the example in figure 15.4.

Types of meeting

General meetings are open to all members of the organisation and they are held monthly, quarterly or annually. This last is the Annual General Meeting (AGM).

Extraordinary meetings are additional general meetings called to discuss some special business or unexpected event.

Committee meetings: Sometimes it is not necessary for all members to be present at a meeting. Under such circumstances a variety of smaller committees may be formed, each of which has a specific function.

- *Standing committee*: this is a permanent group elected to carry out specific regular duties such as deciding marketing policies.

- *Ad hoc or sub-committee*: this type of committee is set up to deal with a particular matter over a short period of time, for instance planning to participate in a trade exhibition, or investigating a disciplinary matter.

```
                         AGENDA
1.   Apologies -- received (usually in writing) from
     those unable to be at the meeting.

2.   Minutes -- the minutes or notes made from the last
     meeting are read.

3.   Matters arising (out of the minutes) -- discussion
     and follow-up of matters or decisions taken at the
     last meeting.

4.   Correspondence -- discussion of important letters
     received since the last meeting.

5.   Reports -- may be made by people who have special
     information to give to the meeting, for example,
     reporting back from the work of a committee.

6.   Special matters -- here will be discussed the
     purpose of the present meeting; decisions which
     have to be made; proposals to be discussed and
     noted on; action to be followed before the next
     meeting.

7.   Next meeting -- date, time and place of next
     meeting.

8.   Any other business (AOB) -- at this point members
     bring up matters or questions not included in the
     agenda.
```

Fig. 15.4 What's on the agenda?

15.4 Business correspondence

The most basic way that a firm communicates with others outside the organisation is through correspondence (letters). Letters provide a printed, permanent record of what is being communicated.

Business letters generally have a printed **letterhead** and they tend to conform to accepted conventions. Look at the sample business letter shown in figure 15.5 and see what aspects of it you are familiar with.

15.5 Postal communication

The post offices in the Caribbean provide a variety of communication services, particularly for the delivery of letters and parcels. Many of the facilities allow air or surface delivery, and there are provisions for insurance with some of the services. The most important of these services are summarised here.

Letter post

In the Caribbean we have a two-tier postal service in that for many of the postal facilities a first-class or a second-class service is available. First-class mail is faster but also dearer than the second-class service.

Business reply service

This is a service mainly used by business people to encourage people to write to them. The idea is that the person sending the letter does not have to pay any postage because the envelope or postcard has a licence number on it. The number refers to the person the communication is being sent to and he or she will eventually be charged the **postage**.

This service is used, for example, when a company sends out leaflets or brochures showing products they wish to sell, and enclosing a printed business reply card which those interested in the products can just fill in and put in the post.

Freepost

This service is in some ways similar to the business reply service in that the person sending the communication does not have to pay postage so long as they address the communication in the correct manner, which means including the word Freepost in the address.

Poste restante

A letter or package may be sent to a post office in a particular town marked 'Poste restante' or 'To be called for'. The post office will keep the package until the person to whom it is addressed calls for it, giving proof of identity.

BARBADOS SUPPLIES
Barbados House, President Street, Bridgetown, Barbados
Telephone: 234 234567   Telex: 76543 Barbados   Fax: 0987
Directors: E. Wilson A. Nelson M. Winston

Your Ref: EM/JW

Our Ref: EC/OP/7

20th March 2000

Grant Ventures Ltd
12 The Quay
Bridgetown

Attn. Mrs M Grant

Dear Madam

Order Number BS 0654

We are in receipt of your letter dated 16th March and we regret to note that the consignment delivered against the above order contained three items which were not as specified in your order, but were included in the items contained in our invoice number 098761.

We have made arrangements for delivery of the correct items by our own transport. They should be with you by Thursday. We would be grateful if you will hand the incorrect goods to our driver on arrival.

Apologies for any inconvenience caused by this error and thank you for your co-operation in this matter. We look forward to supplying you with our goods in the future and take this opportunity of enclosing our latest sales brochure.

Yours faithfully
BARBADOS SUPPLIES

P. Otello

Mr P Otello
Sales Manager

enc

the parts of a letter
a Letterhead
b Reference number
c Date of letter
d Name and address of addressee
e Salutation
f Subject
g Body of letter
h Complimentary close
i Signature
j Enclosures

Fig. 15.5 Business letter

Registered post

Valuable items sent through the post should be sent using this service, which provides a form of **insurance cover** for the items being sent. The more valuable the item the greater the charge. Special registered envelopes can be purchased for use with this service, although they are not necessary.

The registered letter is not put into the normal post box but is passed over the post office counter and a receipt is issued by the counter clerk. Should the package be lost, the sender can claim against the post office for compensation.

Recorded delivery

For a small fee the sender of a letter can arrange for the post office to obtain a signature when they deliver the letter. For a further charge the post office will advise the sender that they have obtained a signature.

This service is taken up by merely filling in a form with the name and address of the person to whom the letter is addressed.

When the sender passes the packet over the post office counter, the clerk stamps the certificate which is now proof of postage. It does not of course prove that delivery has been carried out.

This service is suitable where the sender wants to have proof that he sent something through the post, for example proof of despatch of important documents, but would not be suitable for sending valuables because the maximum compensation available is limited when compared with the registered service. Recorded delivery is cheaper than registered post.

15.6 Telecommunication

Telecommunication has become increasingly important as a means of contact both within and between businesses. Initially, this was due to the speed of contact which telecommunications made possible. More recently, the increasingly wide range of facilities, coupled with costs falling in real terms, has made very extensive use of telecommunications more practicable, even for small businesses.

Telephone

The telephone is an important aspect of business communication because it allows immediate one-to-one contact, both within the organisation and with outside bodies. Apart from the basic telephone call system there are sub-systems such as telephone answering machines, paging devices, and intercom facilities. Other services include conference facilities where several callers can be contacted simultaneously allowing them all to speak as if they were present at one place in a meeting.

Telex

The main disadvantage of the use of the telephone in business is that the communications are not in printed form, and there are times when it is essential that a message is delivered immediately and also in printed form. The telex services makes this possible.

Subscribers to the telex service rent a machine called a teleprinter and have their telex call number listed in the telex directory. Subscribers can directly call up other subscribers at home and overseas twenty-four hours a day, and on a worldwide basis.

Charges for telex calls are based on:

- distance between telex subscribers
- length of message.

The telex service is being rapidly replaced by the facsimile transmission service.

Facsimile transmission (Fax)

This service provides facilities for the transmission of black and white documents, letters, photos, etc.

The prepared A4 size document is fed into a machine and a copy of it is immediately transmitted to another machine sited elsewhere at home or abroad. The facilities can be used as an electronic mailing service, reducing the need to use conventional postal services.

The Internet

The Internet (Net) is a world-wide interconnected group of over one million computers that is continually developing. Each of the computers that form the Internet is connected to its own local network. The result of this is that whenever a user accesses the Internet, they are in fact linking into another computer, and that computer will link to another. These links go on almost unending. Through the Internet information is drawn from other computers via a telephone line or a cable, and the source computer could be situated anywhere in the world.

The Internet makes it possible for users to research data from anywhere else in the world, and to find out immediately what is happening somewhere else. Libraries, newspapers, universities, museums and stock markets are just a few examples of sources of data that can be accessed around the world through the Internet. It makes it possible to converse with experts around the world from your own computer.

The process of accessing the Internet is through an **Internet service provider**. This provider connects others (called '*users*') to the Net by using a variety of tools and protocols. They charge the user for this service and this is how the Internet service provider makes a living. In order to become an **Internet user** it is necessary to pay a connection fee and then a monthly fee on top of this; also the cost of a telephone call while connected to the Internet. The cost of the call depends upon where the service provider is situated. This is important because it means that whilst a user may be accessing a computer in a foreign country the cost of the call will only be that to their local 'provider'. This is why it is important for a user to find a provider that will have a local **POP (Point of presence)**, as this will reduce the cost of their calls.

The following are just a few examples of uses of the Internet:

Electronic mail: The Internet allows users to send E-mail to anyone connected to the Net, as well as to non-Net users who are connected to commercial on-line and mail services. The process of communication is instantaneous. E-mail messages can be left for people to collect when they next connect to the system, and they can even be notified that a message awaits them if required.

Search for information: Whatever information the user is searching for can be found through the millions of computers connected to the Net. This information can include not only data banks and text but also graphics, sound and video.

Download files: When a user has located the information that they have been searching for, it is a simple process to download the files directly to the user's terminal, or disk.

15.7 THINGS TO DO

This section contains a variety of exercises to help you create notes, to test your understanding and to prepare you for examinations.

Search and find

Write out the question and the answer by referring back through the text to form revision notes.

1 Why is communication important to business?
2 Why is it important that each of the four elements of communication are clear?
3 How do internal and external communications differ?
4 Give examples of ways in which communication helps the internal organisation of a business.
5 What are the similarities and the differences between a letter and a memorandum?
6 Briefly describe some of the oral forms of communication used within a business.
7 It has been said that 'one picture is worth a thousand words'. How can this statement be applied to business communication?
8 How can meetings contribute to good internal communications?
9 Describe the functions of the principal officers of a meeting.
10 What is an agenda?
11 Give a brief description of the various types of meeting.
12 'Business letters generally follow a standard format.' Explain this statement.
13 What do we mean when we say that the Caribbean has a two-tier postal service?
14 How does the business reply service help a firm to attract customers?
15 Why should valuables always be sent by registered post?
16 Why have telecommunications become increasingly important to businesses?
17 What advantages does the telephone have over the postal services? In what way is it at a disadvantage when compared with the post?
18 'The telex service combines the speed of telecommunication with the written record of a letter.' Explain this statement.
19 Why can facsimile transmissions be said to be a form of electronic mail?
20 In what ways does the Internet have considerable advantages over the telex and facsimile services?

What do you know?

Write out the complete sentence and insert the missing word which can be chosen from the list at the end of the test.

1 Communication is the process of making . . . . . between two points.
2 . . . . . is the method of communication by which a business makes potential customers aware of the products or services it offers.
3 . . . . . is a means of making physical contact between two distant points.
4 The various internal sections of a firm have to be kept . . . . . of the activities of other parts of the organisation.
5 . . . . . is the most common and the most direct form of oral communication.
6 A . . . . . chart is like a cake divided into sectors.
7 . . . . . are useful for discussions between groups of people.
8 The . . . . . is responsible for the correct conduct of a meeting.
9 The business . . . . . service encourages people to write to a firm because they do not have to pay for postage.

10 The fax machine provides immediate transmission of ..... text.

> Choose the missing words from the following:
>
> printed   pie   contact   chairperson
> informed   meetings   reply   speech
> advertising transport

Multiple choice

Choose the appropriate answers, a, b, c or d.

1. Which of the following does not include verbal communication?
   - a) interview
   - b) intercom
   - c) memorandum
   - d) telephone

2. Which of the following is not a form of visual communication?
   - a) notices
   - b) maps
   - c) pie charts
   - d) meetings

3. The person who has the casting vote at a meeting is the:
   - a) recorder
   - b) chairperson
   - c) secretary
   - d) treasurer

4. Which one of the following is a physical form of communication?
   - a) post
   - b) telecommunication
   - c) advertising
   - d) transport

5. The minutes of a meeting are:
   - a) the timing of a meeting
   - b) the feedback from a sub-committee
   - c) a summary of meeting discussions
   - d) the order of items to be discussed

6. An AGM is:
   - a) a list of items to be discussed at a meeting
   - b) a meeting open to all members
   - c) a method of voting at a meeting
   - d) a piece of computer equipment

7. Which one of the following postal services provides compensation for damage or loss of a packet?
   - a) first-class post
   - b) second-class post
   - c) registered post
   - d) business reply service

8. Which one of the following postal services provides proof of posting?
   - a) registered post
   - b) first-class post
   - c) second-class post
   - d) business reply service

9. The name of the machine used to send a telex message is a:
   - a) teleprinter
   - b) facsimile
   - c) pager
   - d) computer

10. Which one of the following communication facilities is the least likely to be used internally in a business?
    - a) memorandum
    - b) intercom
    - c) facsimile
    - d) telephone

> **Key words**
>
> Find out the business-related meaning of each of the following words. Write out a separate sentence for each word to show your understanding.
>
> precise   transmitter   receiver   motivate
> negotiate   policies   quorum   exhibition
> subscribers transmitted

Structured questions

1. Refer to the illustrations in figure 15.3 and answer the following questions related to graphs and charts.

   a) Use very simple diagrams and brief but clear explanations to describe each of the following ways of presenting statistics in graphic form:
      - (i) pie chart   (2)
      - (ii) flowchart   (2)
      - (iii) bar graph   (2)
      - (iv) line graph.   (2)

   b) Explain when it would be more appropriate to use a pie chart than a line graph to display data.   (3)

   c) A company's overseas trade for last year was as follows:
      USA   52%
      EU   41%
      CANADA   7%
      Display this data in the form of a pie chart with an appropriate key.   (3)

   d) The following data refers to a company's sales over a 12-month period:

Month	Sales $000s
January	240
February	200
March	300
April	170
May	180
June	280

July	190
August	220
September	310
October	220
November	300
December	250
Total	2,860

Illustrate this data in a bar chart in vertical or horizontal format. (6)

2. Look at figure 15.6, a magazine article about using computers whilst travelling, and then answer these questions.

   a) How does a 'laptop' differ from a portable computer? (2)

   b) In what way can a laptop computer reduce time wastage for a busy executive? (2)

   c) State four items that a business person would be likely to produce using a laptop computer whilst travelling. (2)

   d) What sort of information would a business executive be likely to want to receive from his or her base whilst travelling? (4)

   e) Why has the development and wider use of portable telephones made the application of laptop computers more practicable? (4)

   f) Why is the use of a laptop computer limited by its power, memory store and storage capacity? (6)

3. The six months' sales record in table 15.1 was circulated to all of a company's sale representatives to show how successful or otherwise each had been in comparison with the others in the team.

   a) What information is this data communicating and for whom is the information intended? (2)

   b) State two other appropriate ways (other than by line graph) that the information in the above table could be presented. (2)

Computing on the move

Laptop computers provide tremendous benefits for those who need computing power while on the move. And when used in conjunction with the telephone network, laptops become the business traveller's lifeline for essential and complicated messages to and from base.

The computer industry differentiates between what it calls a portable and a laptop. Portables are full-sized, mains-driven desktop micros that can be carried, e.g. to a car boot, and then set up at home.

Laptops are light, slim machines that can literally sit on your lap while you are in a car, train or aircraft seat. They are often battery-powered, and to minimise power loss the screens are usually liquid crystal displays (LCDs) – the same technology used on calculator screens. Depending on the machine's power, memory size and storage capacity, laptops can be used for all the jobs that are normally done on desktop micros, i.e. wordprocessing, communicating with electronic mail services, data storage, production of spreadsheets, keeping diaries, calculating figures, etc.

Both types are useful because they enable constructive use to be made of time often wasted while travelling or in hotels rooms. Memos, telexes, letters and reports can be written on the move and either printed on an office or portable printer, or sent to another computer over the telephone. Up-to-date price lists and quotations can be printed on demand for customers.

Fig. 15.6 Computing on the move

Table 15.1 *Sales data*

Name	Jan $	Feb $	March $	April $	May $	June $	Total $
N Jones	1,200	1,250	1,200	1,300	1,300	1,350	7,600
K Tew	900	950	1,000	1,050	1,100	1,150	6,150
J Gourly	1,000	1,000	950	950	900	1,000	5,800
J Wilson	1,100	1,100	1,200	1,200	1,300	1,250	7,150
S Warren	950	900	900	950	950	1,000	5,650
D Page	850	1,050	900	950	950	1,000	5,700
Total $	6,000	6,250	6,150	6,400	6,500	6,750	38,050

c) From the table state:
   (i) the name of the sales representative with the lowest overall sales
   (ii) the name of the representative with the highest sales for any one month
   (iii) the month which showed the highest total sales for the company
   (iv) the total overall sales for the company over the whole six-month period (4)

d) Draw a simple line graph to show the company's total sales month by month. (4)

e) Communicating information by circulating a sales table can be used to motivate employees, but it can also have the opposite effect on some. Discuss both sides of this statement, giving examples to support your arguments. (8)

4 Read the article in figure 15.7, and then answer the following questions.

a) What do the letters MD stand for? (1)

b) What is the function of an MD? (2)

c) In what ways can Selene's firm's problem be seen to be one of communication? (3)

d) Imagine that you are Selene's personal assistant. Compose a brief memo to all senior staff requesting that they attend a meeting next Wednesday at 5.00 pm to discuss the problem. Include an indication of what the meeting will be about. (4)

e) Selene has asked you to open the meeting by giving a brief summary of the reasons why the firm has been losing orders. Write out your notes for this introduction to the meeting. (4)

f) Assuming that you were given sole charge of improving the company's image, explain the steps you would take in an attempt to solve the current problem. (6)

5 a) State two items of information that can be found in a telex directory. (2)

b) Telex messages can be sent in code. Why might a firm want to send a coded message? (2)

c) Give a description of the method involved in sending a telex message. (4)

d) Clearly explain the difference between telex and facsimile as methods of communication. (4)

e) 'The internet is rapidly replacing both telex and facsimile transmission.' Why do you think this is happening? (8)

6 Look at the advertisement in figure 15.8.

a) Through which medium is this communication likely to reach its intended audience? (1)

b) Briefly state, in no more than ten words, the main message being given here. (1)

c) Name the transmitter and the intended receiver of this communication. (2)

A question of communication

Selene Roberts is the Managing Director (MD) of a medium-sized company in the Caribbean. Her firm manufactures a range of cardboard boxes. In the years since the firm was established in 1980, Selene's company has steadily increased its sales until about six months ago. Then Selene noticed a distinct fall in orders received, even though the firm's prices still compared favourably with those of competitors. One of the regular customers who had ceased to place orders was AJ Products. Selene arranged to visit Mr. Shah the MD of AJ Products, in an attempt to find out why his company had not placed an order with her firm for some time.

'Your sales staff could do with a bit of a shake up' said Mr. Shah, 'Whenever my people 'phone your firm the person they want to speak to is not there, and it seems that the people in the office never know where they are or when they are likely to return. We have requested that someone 'phones us back, but this doesn't happen. And another thing, the people you have answering the 'phone are not particularly helpful, in fact some of them could be said to be down-right rude. Quite frankly, until your staff learn to be a bit more helpful and efficient I can't see any prospect of further trade between our companies.'

Fig. 15.7 **Communication problems**

School Leaver Required

for busy estate agent's main office
Hours 08.45 to 18.00 + alternate Saturdays
Experience not necessary as training will be given - but applicant must have:
* Good standard of English
* Pleasant telephone manner
Write to: Barbara Bowen
Homewise Estates, 79 Tolcharde Avenue,
Basseterre, St Kitts

Fig. 15.8 **Job advertisement**

d) Name the two forms of communication medium through which applicants are advised to reply to this advertisement. (2)

e) This advertisement is not a particularly good example of communication because it leaves too many questions unanswered. For example, how much does the job pay? Give two other questions that the advertisement leaves unanswered in your opinion. (4)

f) Write out the advertisement again in a manner that you feel is a better example of communication. (4)

g) The job advertised demands two communication skills. Name these two skills and say why you think they are important for this particular type of business. (6)

7 Look at the copy of the minutes of a meeting in figure 15.9 and answer these questions.

   a) Briefly say what minutes are. (2)

   b) List the names of all the people who would receive a copy of these minutes. (2)

   c) These minutes say that the meeting was held at 1700 hrs, which is 5.00 pm. What are each of the following times?
   1300   1600   1830   2100 (2)

   d) The principal officers of a meeting sometimes include a treasurer, but no such position is shown in these minutes. Why do you think this officer was not represented at this meeting? (2)

   e) Draw up an agenda which could have been used for this particular meeting. (3)

   f) There were no 'matters arising' in these minutes. Give a brief description of an item that could have been included at this point in the meeting. (3)

   g) Compare the functions of the secretary and the chairperson at a meeting. (6)

8 Refer to the memorandum in figure 15.2 and answer the following questions.

   a) State two ways in which the function of a memo differs from that of a letter. (2)

   b) Why do you think that the trade discount is only being increased for some customers and not all of them? (2)

   c) What is meant by a 'higher category' customer? (2)

   d) What do you think a 'bad debtor list' is? (3)

MINUTES OF MEETING

A meeting of the Safety Committee of Daly Designs Ltd. held in the Conference Room on Monday 14th July 2000 at 1700 hrs.

PRESENT
Mr. P. Mahoney (Chairman)
Miss J. Shaw   Mr. T. Cryer (Security)
Mrs. J. Jones   Miss E. Ginger (Secretary)

1. APOLOGIES FOR ABSENCE
The Secretary reported that Mr. Flowers was unable to attend due to illness.

2. MINUTES OF THE LAST MEETING
The minutes of the last meeting had been circulated previously. They were approved, and signed by the Chairman.

3. MATTERS ARISING FROM THE MINUTES
There were no matters arising.

4. CORRESPONDENCE
The Secretary read a letter from Five Star Insurance who advised that the Company's buildings insurance cover be increased by 8%. It was agreed that this recommendation should be put into immediate effect.

5. SECRETARY'S REPORT
This had been circulated prior to the meeting and was accepted.

6. SECURITY OFFICER'S REPORT
The Security Officer reported that the recent fire drill was very successful and appeared to have been taken seriously by employees.

7. SAFETY NOTICES
Concern was expressed that many safety notices were now old and damaged and it was agreed that the Secretary would purchase replacements urgently.

8. ANY OTHER BUSINESS
There was no other business.

9. DATE AND TIME OF NEXT MEETING
This was fixed for Monday 16th October, 2000 at 1700 hrs. in the Conference Room.

P. MAHONEY
Chairman
21st July 2000

Fig. 15.9 Minutes of a meeting

e) Translate the following abbreviations included in this memo:
RE:,   p.a.,   % (3)

f) This memo has to be seen by three people. Suggest two different ways in which it could be arranged so that they all receive the information. (4)

g) What do you consider are problems that could arise from circulating lists of 'higher category' customers and 'bad debtors'? (4)

Research assignments

1. 'Effective communication is essential to business success.' Discuss this statement using examples of both internal and external communication which you have personally researched.

2. An important aspect of business communication is its application to the motivation of employees by management. Explain how communication can be effective in this way. What personally researched evidence can you provide to support your explanation?

3. Give a brief description of four internal and four external forms of communication used by businesses. Include identification of whom each element of communication is intended for. To what extent are your chosen examples influenced by the size and structure of a business organisation?

4. 'Telecommunications have become an essential feature of business communication, but postal services still play an important part.' Discuss this statement using specific examples to illustrate circumstances where postal services would still take preference over telecommunication services. How do you see the long-term future of these aspects of communication?

5. A newly formed Caribbean mail-order company is about to begin trading.

    a) Explain two different methods that the company might use to contact potential customers using postal services.

    b) Describe four different ways that the firm might use postal services to deliver goods.

    c) Collect four advertisements for items that will probably be delivered by different methods. Explain why the different methods would be appropriate.

6. Why have telecommunications become increasingly important to businesses? Describe four telecommunication services and give examples of their use in particular business situations that you can prove you have researched.

7. Why has speed become an important feature of business communication? Describe at least four telecommunication services that meet this need. Use examples from current literature to support your discussion.

8. 'The cost of telecommunications equipment has fallen in real terms and is therefore now being increasingly used by small businesses.' What evidence can you give to prove or disprove this statement?

9. Take one large and one small business in your area. Compare the communication methods they use and comment on any differences found.

10. Choose any firm in your area. Explain why telecommunications are an important aspect of the firm's operations.

11. Research the ways in which businesses in your locality are using the Internet. How extensive do you think the trend is?

Chapter 16
THE STRUCTURE OF THE BANKING SYSTEM

16.1 Caribbean banking

Banking activities in the Caribbean are similar to those carried out in other parts of the world. Immigrants from the Caribbean who reside in the United Kingdom, the United States of America and Canada, for example, can transfer money to and from their relatives quite easily by utilising an appropriate banking service. In fact, **telegraphic money transfer**, a modern banking service made possible through the integration of telecommunications technology and computer technology, is very popular in the Caribbean today. Funds transferred from one location to another can reach the recipient less than half an hour after transmission. Naturally, businesses benefit from this service too.

Caribbean banking has a long history. The first commercial bank to operate in Jamaica was established in 1836 by merchants based in the United Kingdom who had business connections in the island. The Central Bank of Jamaica records reveal that by 1846 the bank had six agencies in operation throughout the island. The bank was named the *Bank of Jamaica* (no relation to the now existing Bank of Jamaica).

The *Colonial Bank* opened its doors in Jamaica in 1837. Later on, branches were established in other West Indian islands and in British Guyana. Services in 'trade and travel' were the major concern of the Colonial Bank. Later on, planters found it necessary to open the *Planters Bank*, mainly because the banks which were then in existence were not in a position to meet their need for 'easy credit'.

Today, a variety of banks can be found in the Caribbean islands. These include regular commercial banks, specialised banks such as merchant banks, agricultural credit banks, development banks, investment banks, other financial institutions which offer banking services, and central banks.

Many of the banks which operate in the Caribbean are branches of banks located in North America and the United Kingdom. A few **national** banks are also in operation.

16.2 The central bank

Caribbean central banks are relatively new when compared to the central bank of the United Kingdom, for example. The first central bank in the Caribbean was put into full operation in the island of Jamaica in 1962, the year of the island's independence. Guyana and Trinidad and Tobago followed in 1966. The central bank is often referred to as **the bank** in its home country.

The functions of the central bank

A central bank, such as the Bank of Jamaica, has certain basic functions. These are summarised below.

It is the government's bank
Serving as the government's bank is a major function of a central bank. It manages the government's bank accounts, that is, the bank accounts of the various government departments.

The central bank also handles arrangements for government borrowing.

- *Short-term borrowing*: principally through the sale of treasury bills.
- *Long-term borrowing*: management of government stocks, which form the bulk of the national debt.

Management of the exchange equalisation account is carried out by the bank, and it is through this activity that the bank can influence the value of the dollar. It does so by selling or buying dollars to affect the foreign exchange market prices.

It acts as adviser to the government
The central bank advises the government on the formulation of monetary policy. Since regulations related to money and credit change from time to time as a result of a country's economic situation, the central bank ensures that the monetary policies adopted by government are in harmony with the real needs of the economy.

It executes the government's monetary policy

The central bank is responsible for carrying out the monetary policy of the government. This particularly involves the bank in exercising control of the money supply and the lending activities of the banks. It does this in a number of ways.

- *Open market operations.* The central bank can intervene in the financial market as both buyer and seller of bills, securities and certain other forms of credit instruments. The purpose of doing this is to influence the levels of money supply.

- *Bank rate.* This is the interest rate the central bank charges on its loans to the commercial bank as 'lender of last resort'. The bank can use this regulatory tool to influence the cost of borrowing.

- *Reserve and liquid asset requirements.* Commercial banks are required to place a percentage of the money they hold with the central bank, theoretically to ensure that they always have access to sufficient funds should there be a 'run of withdrawal requests'. In effect these deposits can be used as an instrument of monetary control when the central bank:
  - raises the percentage of deposits required
  - refuses to release the deposits to the commercial banks.

It is the 'lender of last resort'

If the commercial banks run short of cash they firstly recall deposits they have in the money market, thus reducing money in the market. If they still have insufficient funds, the commercial banks are forced to borrow. Where they cannot obtain sufficient funds from normal sources they are obliged to go to the central bank as a last resort.

It controls the issue of currency

The bank has the sole responsibility for the physical operations relating to the issue of currency.

It manages government borrowing

The central bank handles the arrangements for government borrowing. Here the bank issues 'treasury bills' which are used in short-term borrowing situations. From time to time, announcements inviting members of the public to invest in government treasury bills for a fixed period of time and at attractive rates are published in newspapers.

It is the bankers' bank

Each of the clearing banks has an account with the bank, and during the process of cheque clearing, debits and credits are made to these accounts as a means of inter-bank settlement.

The clearing banks keep about a half of their liquid reserves (short-call money) deposited at the bank and use these for settling debts among themselves (e.g. in cheque clearing activities).

The commercial banks rely on the bank if they run short of money or require loans.

```
  BANK A                    BANK B
┌─────────────────┐    ┌─────────────────┐
│ Cheques against │    │ Cheques against │
│    Bank B       │    │    Bank A       │
│   $50,000       │    │   $70,000       │
└─────────────────┘    └─────────────────┘
```

Bank A will settle the difference of $20,000 by transfer of funds within the clearing house system.

Fig. 16.1 Cheque clearing

16.3 Commercial banks

The commercial banks offer banking facilities to individuals and businesses. They are sometimes referred to as 'clearing banks' because they handle the exchange and settlement of cheques through the clearing house system described above.

The functions of clearing banks are dealt with in detail in the next two chapters, but they can be summarised as follows:

- acceptance of deposits of money
- provision of a system of payments mechanism
- supply of finance
- provision of a wide range of services.

16.4 Merchant banks

These are not banks in the commonly understood sense, but are private firms that offer highly specialised services almost exclusively for business customers. The main activities of merchant banks can be divided into accepting house activities, issuing house activities and capital market activities.

Acceptance house activities

The traditional activity of merchant banks is **accepting** (i.e. lending their name to) a **bill of exchange** issued by a less well-known trader, so that it becomes more acceptable because of the bank's good reputation in the financial world. By endorsing the bill, the accepting house guarantees payment of the bill should the drawer default (see Chapter 13 for application of bills of exchange in finance of international trade).

Issuing house activities

Merchant banks play a major role in assisting in raising company finance by sponsoring first issues of company shares on behalf of their clients, or acting as intermediaries between companies seeking capital and those willing to provide it. It should be noted that not all issuing houses are merchant banks (see Chapter 20 for notes on share issue).

Capital market activities

In addition to raising capital for companies by their issuing house activities, merchant banks are also involved in a wide range of other capital market operations, some of which are as follows:

- operating some current account services for businesses
- accepting larger deposits, generally for one year or more
- offering consultancy services to businesses wishing to become limited liability companies
- advising on company problems such as capital reorganisations, dividend policy, mergers and takeover bids
- providing finance for hire purchase to businesses
- assisting in the investment of trustee funds for large institutions
- acting as agents to companies establishing branches overseas
- dealing in the precious metals market.

Merchant banks are required to submit monthly returns to the central bank for scrutiny.

16.5 Other specialist banks

Agricultural credit banks

These are specialist banks which provide services to the agricultural sector. Small farmers who would not necessarily qualify for loans on the open market can be assisted through these financial institutions.

Development banks

As the name implies, development is the major concern of these banks. The Caribbean Development Bank (CDB), which has its headquarters in Barbados, is a prime example. The bank's aim is to provide financing to aid economic development, and to 'promote economic co-operation and integration' among its members (the English-speaking Caribbean). Other development banks exist. Their objectives are similar: to provide financing, technical assistance and management advice to support the productive sector.

Investment banks

These specialist banks deal mainly in investments. Their aim is to attract investors through the provision of attractive investment packages. The money is then re-invested in different types of securities, and interest is paid on investments.

Other non-banking financial intermediaries which contribute significantly to the economic development of a country are trust companies, credit unions and building societies.

16.6 THINGS TO DO

This section contains a variety of exercises to help you create revision notes, to test your understanding and to prepare you for examinations.

Search and find

Write out the question and the answer by referring back through the text to form revision notes.

1. How does a central bank differ from a commercial bank?
2. A central bank is sometimes called the 'bankers' bank'. Why is it referred to in this way?

3 Why are commercial banks sometimes referred to as 'clearing banks'?

4 What are the main functions of the commercial banks?

5 Why are merchant banks sometimes referred to as 'acceptance houses'?

6 In what way does a merchant bank help in raising capital for businesses?

7 List six other services which are provided by merchant banks for businesses.

8 Why are agricultural credit banks particularly important to the small farmer?

9 In what ways do development banks aid economic development?

What do you know?

Write out the complete sentence and insert the missing word, which can be chosen from the list at the end of the questions.

1 A central bank advises the ..... on the formulation of monetary policy.

2 ..... bills are issued by the central bank to provide short-term borrowing.

3 ..... in the form of notes and coins is issued through the central banks.

4 As the ..... bank, the central bank provides banking services for the commercial banks.

5 The ..... house system enables indebtedness between banks to be settled.

6 The ..... banks are those found in the high streets, providing banking facilities for individuals and businesses.

7 ..... banks provide highly specialised services for business clients rather than for the general public.

8 By accepting a bill of exchange, a merchant bank backs it with its .....

9 Merchant banks act as ..... between companies seeking capital and those willing to provide it.

10 Development banks are primarily concerned with aiding ..... development.

Choose the missing word from the following:

merchant	currency	reputation	bankers'
economic	clearing	government	commercial
intermediaries	treasury		

Multiple choice

Select the appropriate answer, a, b, c or d.

1 Which of the following is not a central bank?
 a) Bank of Jamaica
 b) Bank of England
 c) Barclays Bank
 d) Federal Reserve Bank of the USA

2 If the central bank sells more treasury bills than is necessary for short-term government finance, it will:
 a) increase the supply of credit
 b) have no effect on the supply of credit
 c) reduce the supply of credit
 d) force down interest rates

3 If a bill of exchange with a true value of $12,000 is bought one month before maturity for $11,900, the discount rate is:
 a) 2½% pa   c) 10% pa
 b) 5% pa   d) 20% pa

4 A central bank acts on behalf of the government to implement its:
 a) fiscal policy
 b) monetary policy
 c) banking policy
 d) foreign policy

5 In 'accepting' bills of exchange, merchant banks agree to:
 a) hold the bill until it is paid
 b) act as a guarantor for the bill
 c) ensure that it is written out properly
 d) pay the bill immediately

6 Notes and coins issued by a central bank are:
 a) government securities
 b) backed by foreign currency
 c) treasury bills
 d) legal tender

7 The main function of a central bank is to:
 a) regulate the economy
 b) give advice to big businesses
 c) accept deposits from the public
 d) offer loans and overdrafts

8 Which of the following types of bank is concerned with raising money for businesses through share issue?
 a) central bank
 b) agricultural credit bank
 c) commercial bank
 d) merchant bank

9 The majority of commercial banks in the Caribbean region are:
   a) subsidiaries of the central bank
   b) privately owned companies
   c) partnerships
   d) franchises

10 Which of the following functions is not performed by a central bank?
   a) issue of shares
   b) managing the government's bank accounts
   c) financial adviser to the government
   d) banker to the commercial banks

Key words

Find out the business-related meaning of each of the following words. Write a separate sentence for each word to show your understanding.

currency   credit   policies   endorsing
investment reinvestment shares   subsidiaries
treasury   intermediaries

Structured questions

1 Look at the cycle of credit in figure 16.2.
   a) How much cash is there circulating in the system? (1)
   b) How much money have the banks created? (2)
   c) State two methods which Mr B could use to borrow the $800 from the bank. (2)
   d) (i) State two functions of commercial banks illustrated in the diagram.
      (ii) State one function of commercial banks not illustrated in the diagram. (3)
   e) Briefly describe what the bank would do with the remaining $200 of Mr A's deposit that was not advanced to Mr B. Give reasons for your answer. (4)
   f) If the government wished to reduce the amount of credit in the economy, how could the central bank implement this policy? (8)

2 Consider the two bills in figure 16.3.
   a) What is the maturity value of the treasury bill shown? (1)
   b) Name (i) the drawer and (ii) the drawee of the bill of exchange. (2)
   c) Assuming interest rates of 10%, what would be the appropriate market value of the bill of exchange immediately after it had been issued? (2)

Fig. 16.2 Credit creation cycle

Fig. 16.3 Bill of exchange and treasury bill

d) Explain how the drawer of a bill of exchange may make use of a merchant bank and why he would be inclined to do so. (4)

e) Explain the difference in functions between a treasury bill and a bill of exchange (4)

f) Describe some of the ways that a central bank can influence the economy, including reference to the use of treasury bills (7)

3 a) What is a treasury bill? (1)

b) Who sells treasury bills on behalf of the government? (1)

c) State two factors that would influence the price that someone would be prepared to pay for a treasury bill. (2)

d) When a central bank acts as 'lender of last resort' (i) who is it lending to and (ii) why is it a 'last resort'? (3)

e) Exporters who receive bills of exchange as a method of payment may get them 'accepted' by a merchant bank. Explain what this means and how it helps the exporter. (5)

f) Apart from 'accepting' bills of exchange, describe the other work of a merchant bank. (8)

Research assignments

1 How do the functions of a central bank differ from those of other banks?

2 Private institutions in the money market both lend and borrow money, making a profit in the process. Choose two institutions from the money market and show how this happens.

3 Explain why bank deposits must be included in calculations of the money supply. Show how the central bank tries to regulate the money supply.

4 'Today there is no difference between the facilities provided by the various commercial banks.' Discuss this statement using examples from bank literature to support your discussion.

Chapter 17
BUDGETING AND BANK ACCOUNTS

17.1 Budgeting

The need to budget

Budgeting means having a plan for systematic saving and spending. This involves making sure that, over a given period of time, spending (expenditure) does not exceed income.

All people and organisations have to budget and to make sure that they do not spend more than they earn. Governments have to make sure that they strike a balance between what they collect through taxation and what they spend on the services they provide. And companies face the risk of bankruptcy if they allow their expenses continually to be higher than what the firm earns from its customers. Similarly, families and individuals have to budget to make sure that what they spend does not exceed what they earn.

Personal budgeting

We all differ in what we choose to do with the money we earn because we have different tastes. But we all face similar basic problems in making sure that we can meet bills when they come in and ensuring that we do not spend more than we can afford. This is why we need to budget.

Fig. 17.1   Personal income and expenditure

Look at the graph in figure 17.1. This shows the monthly income and expenditure of one person over a period of one year. The pattern is typical of most working adults. Notice how generally speaking what the person earns does not alter very much. There may be occasions when they earn a little extra in the form of a bonus, commission or overtime (April, June, July, August, October), and they might get an annual rise (June), but overall their **income** does not change very much from one month to another. But when we look at **expenditure**, this varies considerably. Perhaps sometimes several bills come in together, or there is a holiday to pay for, or maybe there is just a need to buy a present for someone special.

The main problem is how to meet bills when they total more than has been earned in a particular month. The answer is to plan ahead, preferably for twelve months, to form a personal budget. This is done by working out your total expected annual expenses on things such as rent or mortgage, electricity, telephone, insurance, etc., and dividing the total by twelve. This amount must then be saved each month so that you can meet the cost of each bill when it arrives. The part of your wages that is left over after saving towards your budget can first be used for daily expenses such as food and travel. Any remainder can be used for luxuries or investment.

Budget accounts

Banks operate this type of account to help people who find it difficult to organise or stick to a budget. The account operates on a similar principle to the personal budget described earlier and it aims to help to even out annual household expenses.

The account holder pays an agreed weekly or monthly amount to the bank, and the bank agrees to meet the costs of any bill up to an agreed credit limit. Whilst the account is in credit it earns interest, and interest is charged when the account is overdrawn. There is also a charge for each cheque or other withdrawal (such as a standing order).

17.2 Bank accounts

Deposit accounts

This type of account is used by individuals, businesses and associations wishing to keep in a safe place money not required for immediate use. With a deposit account:

- credit slips are used to pay money into the account
- withdrawal slips are used to take money out of the account.

No cheques are issued with this type of account, and therefore any transfer of money to another person can only be done by the use of cash.

The bank may require seven or more days' notice for the withdrawal of money from a deposit account, because they lend the money to others. Where small amounts are concerned this rule may not apply.

As a reward for lending their money to the banks, depositors are paid **interest**, which is a percentage of the money in the account.

The depositor cannot draw out of his or her deposit account more money than he or she has in the account.

The banks lend the money deposited with them to borrowers, and charge them interest. This is one of the main ways in which banks earn money.

Current accounts

The bank current account makes the transfer of money from one person to another very simple. You can open a current account by paying in a nominal amount at a bank. You will be issued with the following.

- *A credit or paying-in book* to pay money into your account.
- *A cheque book* to enable you to transfer money from your account to someone else.

The current account (also called the cheque book account or checking account) is meant to provide a place for keeping money that needs to be available for immediate use.

The bank will send you a **statement of account** (also called a **bank statement**) from time to time to tell you how much you have paid out, how much you have put into the account, what charges the bank has deducted from your account, and what is the balance in your account.

Banks have sometimes experimented with paying interest on money left in the current account. When interest is paid, it is usually at a lower rate than the interest on a deposit account.

By agreement with the bank it is possible to **overdraw** on a current account, that is, to draw out more money than you have in the account. Interest is charged to the customer on the overdrawn balance.

A **joint account** may be shared by two or more persons. In the case of a joint account (a 'business account' is similar), the account holders can make a variety of arrangements for signing of cheques. For example, cheques can be signed by any one, or any two of a number of authorised signatories.

17.3 Cheques

A **cheque** is a written instruction to the bank (the **drawee**) to pay money to the account holder (the **drawer**) or to another person (the **payee**). Most cheques are **order** cheques, which means they must be signed (endorsed) on the reverse by the named payee if he or she wishes to pass them on to someone else. So the three parties to a cheque are the drawee, the drawer and the payee.

There are five entries written on a cheque by the drawer:

1 the date on which the cheque is written
2 the name of the payee
3 the amount to be paid, in words
4 the amount to be paid, in figures
5 the signature of the drawer.

Written entries on a cheque should be made in such a way that they cannot easily be altered. For this reason they should not be written in pencil or with a pen whose ink can be easily erased. Care should be taken to avoid leaving spaces where someone could write in something extra.

If a mistake is made when writing a cheque, the error should be neatly crossed through, and the correct entry written in and signed by the drawer to show that it is his/her alteration and not a forgery.

Cheques may be **open** or **crossed**.

Open cheque

An open cheque does not have two parallel lines drawn across it. It is 'uncrossed'. The payee can do three things with the cheque:

- pay the cheque into his or her own bank
- exchange it for cash at the bank on which it was drawn
- pass it to someone else by signing the back of the cheque (endorsing it).

BUDGETING AND BANK ACCOUNTS

Fig. 17.2 A cheque

Although an open cheque can be useful, it does have drawbacks because if the cheque were to fall into the hands of someone dishonest they would also be able to cash it at the bank on which it is drawn. For this reason, banks prefer their customers to use crossed cheques.

Crossed cheques

Crossed cheques are safer than open cheques because they must be put through a bank account. In other words they cannot be exchanged for cash, unless the drawer is obtaining cash for himself or herself as will be explained later.

Open cheques can be crossed by drawing two parallel lines vertically across them, but banks provide cheques with the crossing already printed.

The crossing on a cheque is called a **general crossing** if nothing is written between the lines. But wording can be written between the lines of the crossing to make it a **special crossing**.

Post-dated cheques

An occasion could arise when you need to give someone a cheque that is dated sometime in the future, and this is called **post dating** the cheque. The bank will not pass the cheque for payment until the date you have written on the cheque arrives.

Dishonoured cheques

Cheques which are not passed for payment by the drawer's bank are said to have been dishonoured or to have 'bounced'. The drawee bank will write 'Refer to Drawer' or R/D on the cheque and send it to the collecting bank, who will in turn send it back to their customer (the payee). It is then the payee's responsibility to find out from the drawer why the cheque has not been honoured.

Refer to figure 16.1 in Chapter 16 for how banks clear cheques for payment.

A/C Payee only

This means that the cheque can only be paid into the account of the payee, but he can pay it into his account via any bank he wishes.

A/C Payee only.
Happy Bank
Roseau

This means the same as the above, but further instructs that the cheque can only be paid in at a certain bank.

Not Negotiable

The crossing 'not negotiable' acts as a protection against loss or theft and is a warning to anyone receiving such a cheque that they should be careful when accepting it. The reason for the warning is that if someone accepts a cheque crossed 'Not Negotiable' and it has been stolen, then the person accepting it is liable to refund the rightful owner with the amount shown on the cheque.

Fig. 17.3 Special cheque crossings

BUDGETING AND BANK ACCOUNTS

Reasons a cheque might 'bounce'
- The drawer may not have enough money in their account to cover the amount on the cheque.
- The cheque may be incorrectly completed, e.g. unsigned, or the figures and words differ.
- The cheque may be out of date ('stale'). The life of a cheque is six months.
- The signature of the drawer may differ from the example held by the bank.
- The cheque may have been altered and the alteration not signed.
- The cheque is post-dated.
- The cheque has been 'stopped' by the drawer, that is, the drawer has instructed the bank not to make the payment.

Cheque guarantee card

Cheque cards are issued by banks to trusted customers. The branch bank which has issued a cheque card to a customer undertakes to pay cheques supported by the card up to an amount which is displayed on the card.

The cheque card is mainly used to obtain cash from a bank other than that at which the customer's account is held, or to support a cheque offered to a trader in payment for goods or services. Having issued a cheque and used the cheque guarantee card it is not possible to stop payment of the cheque.

17.4 The bank statement

At regular intervals, or on request, the bank will send to a customer a bank statement which provides a record of all transactions that have taken place between the customer's account and the bank.

Amounts which reduce the balance in the account are shown in the payments column, and amounts which increase the balance are shown in the receipts column. As each payment or receipt is recorded a new balance figure is shown in a third column.

SPECIMEN ONLY issued by Bank Education Service

TITLE OF ACCOUNT T. D. ILETT

ACCOUNT NUMBER 8793132

IN ACCOUNT WITH
BANK OF EDUCATION
HOMETOWN

STATEMENT NUMBER 3

DATE	PARTICULARS		PAYMENTS	RECEIPTS	BALANCE
	Balance Forward				250.55
21 May		99681	123.72		126.83
		99682	53.80		73.03
27 May		BGC		512.32	585.35
1 June	Trusty Ins.	DD	15.00		570.35
3 June	Newtown Bld. Soc.	DD	202.00		368.35
5 June		99683	14.98		353.37
8 June		99684	123.42		229.95
15 June		99685	31.25		198.70
16 June	Sundry Credit			25.38	224.08
18 June	S.A.Y.E.	SO	35.00		189.08

ABBREVIATIONS

BGC Bank Giro Credit   DIV Dividend   O/D or DR Overdrawn Balance
DD   Direct Debit   CHS Charges   SO Standing Order
CD   Cash Dispenser   ADV Separately Advised   TFR Inter-Account Transfer

Fig. 17.4 Bank statement

17.5 THINGS TO DO

This section contains a variety of exercises to help you create revision notes, to test your understanding and to prepare you for examinations.

Search and find

Write out the question and the answer by referring back through the text to form revision notes.

1. What is budgeting?
2. Why do organisations and governments have to budget just as carefully as individuals?
3. Describe the way that someone might organise a personal budget.
4. How can a bank budget account help someone to manage their personal finances?
5. Briefly describe the use of a deposit account.
6. How does the function of a current account differ from that of a deposit account?
7. What is a cheque? List the five things written on a cheque by the drawer.
8. Explain who are the drawer, the drawee and the payee of a cheque.
9. How does a crossed cheque differ from an open cheque?
10. Describe some of the precautions that one can take to make a cheque safer.
11. What is a dishonoured cheque and why might it have been dishonoured?
12. What is the purpose of a cheque guarantee card?
13. What are the functions of a bank statement of account?
14. The balance column of a bank statement is sometimes said to show the 'cumulative balance'. Explain this term.

What do you know?

Write out the complete sentence and insert the missing word, which can be chosen from the list at the end of the questions.

1. All people and organisations have to ..... and ensure that they do not spend more than they earn.
2. We all differ in what we choose to do with the money we earn because we have different .....
3. We should only spend money on ..... after we have saved money for our budget.
4. A budget account helps to ..... out annual household expenses.
5. A ..... account is used for the safekeeping of money not required for immediate use.
6. The ..... account makes transferring money from one person to another very simple.
7. By agreement with the bank, it is possible to be ..... on a current account.
8. A ..... is a written instruction to a bank telling them to do something with the account holder's money.
9. A crossed cheque is ..... than an open cheque.
10. A cheque that has been dishonoured is said to have .....

> Choose the missing words from the following:
>
> safer   tastes   budget   cheque   overdrawn
> luxuries   current   bounced   even   deposit

Multiple choice

Select the appropriate answer, a, b, c or d.

1. A cheque dated seven months ago is:
   a) an endorsed cheque
   b) a dishonoured cheque
   c) a stale cheque
   d) a post-dated cheque

2. The person who is intended to benefit from a cheque is:
   a) the payee
   b) the drawer
   c) the drawee
   d) the endorser

3. Cheques can be drawn on:
   a) all bank accounts
   b) a savings account
   c) a deposit account
   d) a current account

4. A cheque dated three months ahead from today is:
   a) a dishonoured cheque
   b) a post-dated cheque
   c) a stale cheque
   d) an endorsed cheque

5. A crossed cheque is one which:
   a) must be paid into a bank account
   b) has been endorsed
   c) has not been passed for payment
   d) can be cashed anywhere

6   The reward for leaving money in a bank account is called:
    a)   return
    b)   percentage
    c)   credit
    d)   interest

7   A summary of all the transactions of a bank account is given on:
    a)   a bank draft
    b)   a bank overdraft
    c)   a bank statement
    d)   a bank cheque

8   When a cheque is not passed for payment, the drawer's bank will return it to:
    a)   the payee
    b)   the drawer
    c)   the drawee
    d)   the endorser

9   Endorsing a cheque is done by:
    a)   the payee signing the reverse of it
    b)   the bank stamping it
    c)   dishonouring it
    d)   the drawer signing the face of it

10 The correct name for the bank on which a cheque is drawn is:
    a)   the endorser
    b)   the drawer
    c)   the payee
    d)   the drawee

Key words

Find out the business-related meaning of each of the following words. Write a separate sentence for each word to show your understanding.

expenditure   bankruptcy   commission   investment
overtime   endorsed   forgery   overdrawn
interest   income

Structured questions

1   Refer to the bank statement in figure 17.4 and answer the following related questions.

    a)   Name the account holder.   (1)
    b)   What is the purpose of this document?   (2)
    c)   How much was brought forward from the previous statement, and how much will be taken forward to the next statement?   (2)
    d)   Why is it important for customers to receive bank statements regularly?   (2)
    e)   Explain the meaning of the following abbreviations shown on this statement:
         BGC,   DD,   SO.   (3)
    f)   Since this statement was issued, T. Ilett has written three cheques, for $133.66, $12.50, $7.80. In addition an inpayment has been made of $389.23. 'Reconcile' the bank statement to find out the present balance at the bank.   (4)
    g)   Give a clear explanation of the purpose of the payments, receipts and balance columns.   (6)

2   Your friend, Sybile, has regular employment and she earns $2,000 net basic wage each month. Sometimes she also earns $250 a month from overtime, although there are times when no overtime is available.
    Sybile faced the following basic expenses during her last twelve months of employment:

    | Rent | $640 | per month |
    | Fuel bills | $240 | per year |
    | Insurances | $240 | per year |
    | Fares | $240 | per month |
    | Food etc. | $320 | per month |
    | Holidays | $100 | per month |
    | Clothes | $ 80 | per month |
    | Telephone | $240 | per year |

    a)   What does the word 'net' mean in relation to Sybile's earnings? How much can Sybile expect to earn as her basic net wage for a complete year?   (2)
    b)   What was the total cost of all Sybile's basic expenses for the last year?   (3)
    c)   What is 'overtime'? Why is it best not to rely on overtime when making a personal budget?   (3)
    d)   What is a personal budget and why is it important to be able to operate one?   (4)
    e)   Sybile found that when her last telephone bill arrived she did not have enough money to pay it. But now Sybile says she will buy a new hi-fi system on credit. Explain how you would advise Sybile to handle her personal finances more sensibly, including mention of the ways in which a bank could assist her.   (8)

3   Look at the cheque in figure 17.5.
    a)   There are two reasons, other than the date, why the bank will refuse to pass this cheque for payment. What are these reasons?   (2)
    b)   The bank will write R/D on this cheque and return it to the payee. What do the letters R/D stand for,

Fig. 17.5 A refused cheque

and what must the payee do when the cheque is given back to her? (3)

c) Name the following parties to this cheque: the drawer, the payee, the drawee. (3)

d) The above cheque has a 'general' crossing. What is the effect of this? Describe and explain two other forms of cheque crossing. (6)

e) Why do banks offer more than one type of account to their customers? (6)

4 a) Give two examples of the information requested from someone opening a bank account. (2)

b) State two factors to consider when deciding whether to place your money in a current account or a deposit account. (2)

c) Explain how a person whose salary is paid straight into their bank account can obtain cash from their account. (2)

d) Clearly state three advantages of saving with a commercial bank from the point of view of a private individual. (6)

e) Give a clear explanation of the differences between a bank deposit account and a current account. Why might a business operate both of these types of account? (8)

5 a) What main advantage does a crossed cheque have over an open cheque? (2)

b) If the named payee of a cheque wants to pass the cheque to someone else, what must they do? Why might someone want to do this? (3)

c) Briefly state four reasons why cheques are sometimes dishonoured. (4)

d) List the five entries that the account holder must write on a cheque. (5)

e) Explain the importance of a bank current account to a trader, giving specific examples to illustrate your answer. (6)

Research assignments

1 Describe the process that a cheque goes through from the time it is written out to the time when the payment is actually credited to the payee's account. Design a collection of simple diagrams that illustrates the process involved.

2 The cheque system makes it both safe and easy for a trader to receive payments from customers, pay debts owed to suppliers and pay the wages of employees. Discuss this statement using illustrations and bank literature to support your discussions.

3 Assume the role of one of the commercial banks in your town. Explain to the owner of a local shop the advantages of having both a current account and a deposit account at your branch. What other banking facilities do you feel would benefit the shop owner?

4 Carry out a survey of services, other than bank accounts, that are provided by banks to assist the entrepreneur. Describe the services you have researched within a report, including relevant literature you have collected.

5 How can a bank assist local businesses, and how might the bank be influenced by the local economy?

Chapter 18
BANKING SERVICES

18.1 Standing order

Imagine that a business has purchased a piece of machinery on credit (i.e. paying for it by monthly instalments). This could mean that every month a member of the firm will have to remember to:

- write out a cheque
- produce a covering letter of explanation
- address an envelope and post it.

This obviously takes time and it is inconvenient. But more importantly, there is the danger that the payment may be forgotten. This can be damaging to the reputation of the company owing the money (the debtor). The commercial banks help businesses to avoid this problem by offering the **standing order** (SO) service.

The customer fills out a standing order form which instructs the bank to make regular payments on their behalf on a specific date of each month (or some other regular period of time), until further notice in writing is given. The bank will then make regular payments on behalf of their customer and will ensure that the payments arrive on time.

The standing order service is available to both business and private current account holders, but it can only be used if the regular amount to be paid does not vary. Where the amount to be paid varies a different service has to be used.

18.2 Direct debit

This is a variation of the standing order service. Instead of customers instructing the bank (the drawee) to make regular payments on their behalf, they complete and sign a form which gives permission for someone else (the payee) to withdraw amounts from their account at regular intervals. The amount withdrawn can be varied by the payee and the variations notified to the account holder (the drawer) at some later time.

This service is suitable for repayments of credit where the repayment amount varies. For example, with some forms of credit the repayment amount will change as the interest rate changes. Under these circumstances the standing order system would not be suitable but the direct debit method is.

Both the standing order and the direct debit systems have dual benefits for businesses. They not only make it easier for the business to make regular payments, but also help the business to receive payments from its customers.

18.3 Credit transfer

This is a means of transferring money from one bank to another without the use of cheques. There are two basic methods of credit transfer that are generally used, the single transfer and the multiple transfer.

Single transfer method

A form is filled out with the details of the person to whom the payment is to be made and their bank. The bank where the money is paid in (or where the drawer's account is held) will then transfer the payment to the bank where the account to be credited is held.

Multiple transfer method

Using this method, a bank customer writes out a single cheque, or gives the bank permission to withdraw a single amount from his or her account, and then use this to make several payments. For example, a private individual might want to pay several bills, or a firm may want to pay the wages of each of its employees.

A list or schedule is passed to the bank by the account holder showing details of a number of different accounts to be credited by direct transfer. The bank uses the drawer's cheque made out in favour of the bank or withdraws the total amount from the account. The bank

BANKING SERVICES

STANDING ORDER MANDATE

To: Any Bank

Address: High Street, Nassau, New Providence Island

Please Pay

Bank	Branch Title (not address)	Code Number
Other Bank	Hamilton	01-22-03

for the credit of

Beneficiary	Account Number
Highlife Finance Co. Ltd	3 2 3 1 1 5 6

†the sum of

Amount in figures	Amount in words
$25.37	Twenty five dollars and 37 cents

commencing

Date and amount of 1st payment		and thereafter every	Date and frequency
1 May 2000	$25.37		1st Monthly
*now			

*until

Date and amount of last payment	
1 April 2007	$25.37

quoting the reference

HP	2238	and debit my/our account accordingly

*This instruction cancels any previous order in favour of the beneficiary named above, under this reference
†If the amount of the periodic payments vary they should be incorporated in a schedule overleaf

Special instructions: None

Signature(s): A. Moment   Date: 10/4/2000

Title and number of account to be debited: A. Moment   0 1 2 3 7 3 5 4

Fig. 18.1 A standing order instructs a bank to make regular payments on the customer's behalf

Fig. 18.2 The credit transfer system saves the inconvenience of sending a cheque and a covering letter

Any Bank plc
Date 20. 9. 2000
Credit K. M. Hill
$50 notes
$20 notes
$10 notes
$5 notes
$1 notes
S. & I. notes
50c
20c
Silver
Bronze
Total Cash
Cheques. 50
P.O.'s etc.
see over
675-5 $ 50
Counterfoil

Date 20. 9. 2000 **bank giro credit**
Cashier's stamp & initials
Code No. 21 – 83 – 57
Bank Coral
Branch Scarborough, Tobago
Credit K. M. Hill
Fee | Number of cheques 1
675-5
Account No. 06230589
Paid in by C. S. Riley
Address 14 Island Road, Charlotteville   Ref. No.

$50 notes
$20 notes
$10 notes
$5 notes
$1 notes
S. & I. notes
50c
20c
Silver
Bronze
Total Cash
Cheques. 50
P.O.'s etc.
see over
$ 50

199

then credits each of the accounts listed in the schedule, thus saving the account holder the necessity of writing out many cheques.

18.4 Bank cards, credit cards and money cards

It has been said that we are moving towards a 'cashless society', and in many ways this is true. For example, in Chapter 17 we examined cheques, which are a means of making book transfers of wealth. In this chapter we have already examined the standing order, direct debit and credit transfer. These are all banking systems that make the use of cash less necessary.

There are various cards issued by banks and other organisations that also reduce the need to use cash. You should bear in mind that although we are going to be concerned with bank cards here, there are card systems in existence outside banking. For example, there are retailers' charge cards, telephone credit cards and others that are discussed elsewhere in this book. Together they all contribute to the view that we are developing a cashless society.

Credit card/money card

This card enables the holder to buy goods or services from a trader without using cash or a cheque.

The purchaser presents the card and signs a voucher when making a purchase and the trader claims the money from the issuers of the credit card and has the money credited to his or her account.

Eventually the holder of the credit card will receive an account from the issuers which he or she can settle by one payment, or alternatively pay monthly interest on any outstanding balance.

A bank customer might use a credit card to make many purchases in a month, and then settle the total debt by writing out one cheque or credit transfer, thus reducing both the number of entries on his or her account and his or her bank charges.

There are companies that specialise in credit cards, such as Access, American Express and Diners Club. Local banks also have their own credit card services.

Cash dispenser card

The bank customer is issued with a cash dispenser card when opening a current account. This usually allows the customer to withdraw money from his or her account at

Fig. 18.3 The credit card is presented and a voucher is signed by the card holder.

Fig. 18.4 Using a cash dispenser

any time of the day or night, seven days a week. This withdrawal is made from a cash dispenser (or cashpoint) in the outside wall of the bank.

The card holder is given a PIN (Personal Identity Number) for use with the card. Keying in this number on the key pad at the cash dispenser gives the card holder access to his or her account; therefore it is important to keep the PIN a secret. It is best to memorise the number rather than write it down where it might be seen by others.

To operate the cash dispenser, the card holder inserts the card into the machine. The card shows the holder's account number, and this can be 'read' by the machine and relayed to the bank computer. When the customer keys in his or her PIN, the bank computer checks that it is correct for the account to which the card corresponds. If the entered PIN is correct, then the dispenser will issue the money requested (up to a daily individual limit). The customer's account is immediately automatically debited with the amount withdrawn. The machine will also provide information such as the current account balance.

18.5 Electronic funds transfer

An important recent banking development is the movement towards an electronic payment system. This is known as EFT (Electronic Funds Transfer) and EPOS (Electronic Point of Sale). These are computer-controlled payment systems, and represent a special form of co-operation between retailers and banks.

While a checkout till operator in a shop is totalling up the customer's purchases using a computer (EPOS), the customer inserts a bank card into a machine linked to his or her bank, building society or credit card company. The customer then keys in his or her PIN and this is verified by the bank's computer. The computer authorises the payment immediately (by EFT) and debits the customer's account, assuming sufficient funds are available. The transaction may be rejected if sufficient funds are not available.

18.6 Borrowing from a bank

There are three main methods of borrowing from a bank: overdraft, loan and bridging loan. Banks often require some form of security (called '**collateral**') to safeguard against possible non-repayment of the amount owed. Collateral can take a variety of forms, e.g. property deeds, stocks and shares, etc. The items of collateral are sold by the bank in the event of the debt not being repaid.

Bank overdraft

With the permission of the bank, customers may write out cheques for more money than they have in their current account up to an agreed amount, which is the value of the overdraft. In such a case we say that the customer's account is '**overdrawn**' or 'in the red'.

The overdraft is particularly useful where a customer does not know exactly how much they need to borrow, or how long they will need it for. The amount of **interest** charged is calculated daily on the actual amount overdrawn. So if any deposit is paid into the account it has the effect of reducing the overdraft and the charge involved, whilst any cheques paid out increase it.

Bank loan

In the case of a bank loan the bank transfers the total value of the loan to the borrower's account, and repayment, including interest, is made in set amounts at regular intervals over the period the loan is to run. The bank will only make a loan available to applicants whom it feels are suitable borrowers.

The bank loan is a more suitable method of borrowing money when the required amount and length of time for repayment is known, because the annual rate of **interest** on a loan is likely to be lower than on an overdraft.

Bridging loan

A bridging loan is provided by a bank (or some other financial institution) as a temporary measure for a relatively short period of time (e.g. a few weeks) until other expected funds become available.

18.7 Miscellaneous bank services

Although the main business of banks is holding money on behalf of customers and granting loans and overdrafts to individuals and businesses, they also provide a wide range of other services.

Financial advice: banks employ specialist personnel who are available to give advice to both private and business customers on a wide range of financial problems, including investment and taxation.

Purchase and sale of stocks and shares: banks have their own brokers to buy and sell stocks and shares on behalf of their customers. They will also give advice and information related to company performance.

Dividends and returns: if investors wish, they can arrange for dividends and other returns on their investments to be paid directly into their bank account.

Executor and trustee services: banks can use their legal department facilities to carry out the terms of a will or administer an estate on behalf of the beneficiaries of a will.

Night safe: this facility is provided by banks to enable customers to deposit money when the bank is closed. Cash for depositing is placed in a special cash wallet together with a credit or paying-in slip. The wallet is dropped into the bank through a trap in the wall, and the amount enclosed is credited to the customer's account on the morning of the next working day. This service is particularly used by traders wishing to make deposits at the end of a day's trading.

Safe deposit box: this is a secure box kept in the bank's vault for the safe keeping of customers' valuables, important documents, etc.

Foreign currency: banks provide facilities for the purchase and sale of foreign currency. They can also arrange for foreign currency to be made available to a business person wishing to negotiate a deal overseas.

Traveller's cheques: these are special cheques charged against a bank and therefore guaranteed by the bank. This makes them acceptable throughout the world and useful to the business person or the individual when travelling. Travellers' cheques can be purchased at the local bank for use abroad. The cheques are 'safe' because if they are lost or stolen abroad they can immediately be cancelled and the bank will replace them. A further safeguard requires those encashing the cheques to sign in front of those cashing them, having first produced proof of identity such as a passport.

Limited company formation: banks will assist business people with the financial and legal difficulties involved in the formation of a limited company.

Bank draft: this is a cheque drawn on a bank instead of on a person's account. A bank draft is guaranteed by the bank (which makes it as good as cash) because the customer pays the value of the draft in advance.

Bill of exchange: this is a method of payment whereby the seller draws up a document and the buyer signs it (the opposite of the normal cheque transaction) agreeing to pay at some future date. The bill of exchange can be kept until payment is made, sold to someone else at a discount ('**discounted**'), or used as collateral against a loan ('**negotiated**'). These bills are particularly evident in international trade where exporters use them to guarantee payment for goods prior to despatch.

Bank references: a bank will act as a referee on behalf of suitable customers. This facility is useful when a firm wishes to buy on credit from another business, which requires some assurance that the firm making the purchases is trustworthy. When a firm makes a request for a reference in this way it is sometimes called a 'status enquiry'.

Banks also render a wide variety of other services, too numerous to deal with fully here. These include:

- investment advice
- wills and trustee advice
- taxation guidance.

18.8 THINGS TO DO

This section contains a variety of exercises to help you create revision notes, to test your understanding and to prepare you for examinations.

Search and find

Write out the question and the answer by referring back through the text to form revision notes.

1. Explain the similarities and the differences between the standing order and direct debit services.
2. Describe both the single and the multiple transfer system of credit transfer, including examples or when each might be used in preference to the other.
3. Why is it sometimes said that we are moving towards a 'cashless society'?
4. What is the function of a cheque guarantee card?
5. Describe the process of using a credit card.
6. How does the cash dispenser system work? What safeguards are there against possible fraud?
7. Explain the terms EFT and EPOS.
8. How does a bank loan differ from an overdraft?

9 What is a bridging loan?

10 In what ways will a bank assist people requiring financial and investment advice?

11 In what ways might a business be likely to use both the night safe and the safe deposit box facilities of a bank?

12 In what ways can a bank assist someone intending to travel overseas?

13 Why is a bank draft 'as good as cash'?

14 In what ways can a bank assist an exporter?

15 Under what circumstances might a business want a bank reference?

What do you know?

Write out the complete sentence and insert the missing word, which can be chosen from the list at the end of the questions.

1 The standing order service is useful if the ..... amount is to be paid on each instalment.

2 The direct debit service is useful if the amount of a credit repayment .....

3 Credit transfer is a system for transferring money ..... from one account to another.

4 The ..... credit transfer can be used by a firm to pay the wages of many employees.

5 A cheque card ..... payment of a cheque up to a maximum amount shown on the card.

6 A ..... card enables the holder to buy goods or services without using cash or cheque.

7 A cash ..... card allows a bank customer to withdraw money from his or her account outside banking hours.

8 With an ..... the customer is allowed to draw more out of his or her account than he or she has paid in.

9 A bank ..... is repaid in set amounts at regular intervals.

10 The bank ..... safe service allows a trader to deposit money outside banking hours.

Choose the missing words from the following:

| night | credit | dispenser | multiple | same |
| varies | overdraft | loan | directly | guarantees |

Multiple choice

Select the appropriate answer, a, b, c or d.

1 When a bank is asked for information related to the credit-worthiness of a customer, this is called a:
   a) credit reference
   b) worthiness assessment
   c) status enquiry
   d) credit information

2 If a firm wishes to pay the wages of all its employees using just one transfer from their account they will use the following service:
   a) credit transfer   c) standing order
   b) direct debit   d) account transfer

3 With a bank overdraft, interest is calculated:
   a) daily   c) monthly
   b) weekly   d) half-yearly

4 If a bank customer wants to pay a fixed amount to someone else every month, the service they will use is called:
   a) fixed order   c) direct debit
   b) credit transfer   d) standing order

5 The difference between the amount borrowed from a bank and the amount repaid is known as:
   a) debit   c) interest
   b) credit   d) overcharge

6 Which of the following does a standing order *not* save the payer?
   a) writing out a cheque
   b) legal liability for debts
   c) writing out an envelope
   d) remembering to make payments

7 When a bill of exchange is negotiated it is:
   a) sold at a higher price
   b) sold at a discount
   c) no longer of value
   d) used as collateral

8 A bank loan:
   a) does not include an interest payment
   b) is a fixed amount for a set period
   c) is a varying amount for a fixed period
   d) is available with a deposit account.

9 Cash dispenser machines and cards are used at:
   a) a bank   c) a night safe
   b) a supermarket   d) a travel agent

10 Which of the following does *not* contribute directly to the concept of a 'cashless' society?
   a) retailer's charge cards   c) cash dispensers
   b) cheques   d) credit cards

BANKING SERVICES

Key words

Find out the business-related meaning of each of the following words. Write a separate sentence for each word to show your understanding.

reputation   collateral   deeds   overdraft   dividends
executor   trustee   schedule   brokers   negotiate

Structured questions

1. Refer to the standing order mandate in figure 18.5 and answer the following questions related to it.

   a) What is the name of the person who has initiated this order, and who benefits from it? (2)

   b) Name the bank of
      (i) the drawer   (ii) the payee.   (2)

STANDING ORDER MANDATE

To: Any Bank PLC
Address: Enterprise, Barbados

Please Pay

Bank	Branch Title (not address)	Code Number
Other Bank	Westmoreland, Barbados	01-66-77

for the credit of

Beneficiary	Account Number
Goodtime Co. Ltd	6 6 6 7 7 4 2 1

†the sum of

Amount in figures	Amount in words
$60.77	Sixty dollars seventy seven cents

commencing

Date and amount of 1st payment		and thereafter every	Date and frequency
6 May 2000 *now	$60.77		6th Monthly

*until

Date and amount of last payment	
6 May 2017	$60.77

quoting the reference: HP 6600   and debit my/our account accordingly

*This instruction cancels any previous order in favour of the beneficiary named above, under this reference
†If the amount of the periodic payments vary they should be incorporated in a schedule overleaf

Special instructions: None

Signature(s): *Constance Credit*   Date: 10/4/2000

Title and number of account to be debited: C. Credit   0 1 2 3 4 3 2 1

*Delete if not applicable

Fig. 18.5 Standing order mandate

c) Why do you think that the amount to be paid is written in both words and figures? (2)

d) How many months is this order intended to operate for, and for how many payments in total? (4)

e) This order refers to hire purchase repayments. What will be the total amount paid at the end of the order period? (4)

f) Explain clearly the advantages that the standing order service has for both the individual initiating it and also for the beneficiary of it. (6)

2 The statement of account in figure 18.6 refers to the use of an Any Bank credit card by the account holder.

a) Who is the holder of the Any Bank credit card to which this statement refers and what is their account number? (2)

b) Why do you think that the use of a credit card is generally restricted to persons over the age of 18? (3)

c) What is meant by the entry 'previous balance $165.27'? (3)

d) Explain each of the following terms shown on this account:
   (i) new balance (2)
   (ii) credit limit (2)
   (iii) minimum payment. (2)

Any Bank Credit

STATEMENT OF ACCOUNT

Any Bank PLC (Plastics Department)
Westwood House
Manzanilla
Trinidad
PO13269

Enquiries: Trinidad 7634
To report card lost/stolen 7635

Please quote your account number
5334 003062545318
in all correspondence

MR MICHAEL DAVIS
6 FERNANDO ROAD
SANGRE GRANDE
TRINIDAD

Statement Date
14/02/99

12345
A minus sign indicates a credit

Date	Reference Number	Description	Previous Balance 165.27
17/01/99	HDY5XG	GOODBUY, GUANAPO	41.83
18/01/99	HDY6LJ	HERON SERVICE STATION, MANZANILLA	15.83
25/01/99	HDV623	BEST ELECTRICS, SANGRE GRANDE	27.99
01/02/99	HEP32X	PAYMENT THANKYOU	65.27-
05/02/99	HFNP37	HAPPY INN, CUMUTO	25.86
11/02/99	JKP83L	GOODBUY, GUANAPO	19.98
13/02/99	JL3SP9	HERON CAR REPAIRS, MANZANILLA	61.55
		INTEREST	2.00

New Balance
294.64

Your Credit Limit
$700.00

Minimum Payment
14.00

MINIMUM PAYMENT SHOULD REACH US BY 12/03/2000

DETACH HERE AND KEEP STATEMENT

Fig. 18.6 Credit card statement

BANKING SERVICES

Table 18.1 *Bank loan table for annual percentage rate 22.8%*

Period		$	$	$	$	$	$
Period of loan	Amount of loan	300.00	400.00	500.00	600.00	700.00	800.00
of loan	Total amount payable	351.63	468.84	586.05	703.26	820.47	937.68
18 months	Monthly repayments	19.54	26.05	32.56	39.07	45.59	48.84

Information required from borrower to support application for a personal bank loan: monthly income; monthly expenditure; total disposable income; details of employment; residential status (e.g. owner or tenant).

e) Clearly explain the difference in function of a credit card when compared with a cheque card. (6)

3 Consider the bank loan data in table 18.1.

a) What is meant by 'annual percentage rate 22.8%'? (2)

b) If someone wanted to borrow $400 to be repaid over a period of 18 months, how much would have to be repaid per month, and what would be the total interest over the period of the repayment? (2)

c) A bank may require some form of 'collateral' against a major loan. What do you understand by 'collateral'? (2)

d) Briefly explain the reasons for *two* of the items of information that the bank seeks before granting a bank loan. (4)

e) Describe fully the differences between a bank overdraft and a bank loan. (10)

4 a) What is a bridging loan? (2)

b) You go to purchase a second-hand car, and the seller says they would prefer a bank draft rather than a cheque. Explain why they would say this. (4)

c) In each of the following cases, explain clearly the circumstances in which it would be more appropriate to use the former rather than the latter:
 (i) direct debit, standing order (4)
 (ii) bank overdraft, bank loan. (4)

d) Describe the function of the bill of exchange as a means of payment in international trade, including an explanation of discounting and negotiating. (6)

5 a) Give a brief account of how the bank night safe facility operates. (2)

b) State two advantages of using a bank's night safe from the point of view of a business. (2)

c) List four types of business that earn much of their income outside of normal banking hours. (4)

d) Explain how cash dispenser machines benefit traders as well as private bank customers. (4)

e) Describe how the direct debit system operates, and explain how it benefits both bank customers and also the people to whom they must make payments. (8)

6 a) Give two examples of items that might be kept in a safe deposit box. (2)

b) Give two examples of circumstances where someone might approach a bank for a bridging loan. (2)

c) List four questions a bank manager might ask a customer before granting a bank loan. (4)

d) Explain the method of operation of the cash dispenser card system. Include a brief description of the way in which the bank computer checks that the correct person is receiving the payment requested. (4)

e) Describe the procedure involved in using a credit card, including an explanation of the precautions which exist to limit fraudulent use. (4)

f) Show how bank credit transfer facilities benefit the business person. (4)

Research assignments

1 a) Make a comparison between the use of credit cards and other forms of consumer credit such as retailers' charge cards and hire purchase systems.

b) Carry out a survey of a cross section of adults and present data that shows which of these facilities is most frequently used by the public.

2 To what extent would you consider that we have a 'cashless society' today? Support your views with data you have researched.

3. 'The services offered by the commercial banks are essential to the efficient operation of both industry and commerce.' Discuss this statement, including reference to at least five banking services.

4. Make a comparison of any two major banks and compare the services they offer.

5. So, who needs banks?

6. You are a bank employee and a potential new customer asks the following questions. Answer them fully, supporting your answers with appropriate literature:

   a) 'How can the bank help me in making regular mortgage payments?'

   b) 'How can I deposit or withdraw money outside of normal banking hours?'

   c) 'What is the procedure involved if I want to borrow money from the bank?'

   d) 'What facilities does the bank provide that I can use when I go abroad on holiday?'

Chapter 19
BUSINESS FINANCE

19.1 The balance sheet

We said in Chapter 2 that capital is one of the four factors of production. **Capital** is important because without it production would not take place.

The **initial capital** of a business comes from **investors** and **entrepreneurs**. The only reason that they take the risk of putting their money into a business is that they hope to make a **profit**. Achieving this profit is the aim of all business activity. Whether the business makes a profit, and the size of the profit, will depend on how efficiently the capital, or **assets** (things owned), of the business are used.

By looking at the financial facts and figures of a firm it is possible to get an idea of how 'healthy' it is, and what might be done if it is 'sick'. In other words, the facts and figures tell us how efficiently the assets are being used. A balance sheet provides a basis for understanding the financial position of a firm, but it is not the whole story.

A balance sheet is like a snapshot — it assumes that the firm has been 'frozen' at that time, showing the financial position of the business at a particular moment in time. A firm's balance sheet is a summary of two things:

- liabilities/debts (things owed)
- assets (things owned).

If you look at the example of a balance sheet in figure 19.1, you will see that it basically consists of two lists.

- The list on the left shows who the business is responsible to for various debts (**liabilities**).
- The list on the right shows all sorts of property the business owns (**assets**).

The items in both lists are placed in order of **liquidity**, i.e. how readily they can be converted into cash. The most liquid items (those easiest to turn into cash) are shown at the bottom of the list. The balance sheet shown here gives the financial position of the Florida Trading Company at a given time: 30 June.

There are other methods of presenting a balance sheet. For example, liabilities and assets can be shown vertically. The balance sheet for most banks shows the more liquid items at the top, the reverse of the balance sheet shown here.

```
       Balance Sheet FLORIDA TRADING COMPANY LTD.
                    as at 30 June 2000

   Liabilities           $           Assets                   $
   Capital         100,000.
                                     Fixed assets
                                     Land & Buildings    80,000.
   Long-term liabilities             Equipment/Fittings  20,000.
   Mortgage         44,000.          Vehicles            10,000.

                                     Current assets
   Current liabilities               Stock*              32,000.
   Tax to be paid    2,400.          Debtors             12,000.
   Bank overdraft    5,600.          Bank balance         5,400.
   Creditors         8,000.          Cash float             600.

                  $ 160,000.                          $ 160,000.

                                     * at cost price
```

Fig. 19.1 **Balance sheet**

BUSINESS FINANCE

Cash flow forecast FLORIDA TRADING COMPANY LTD.

Week	11	12	13	14	15
Cash at bank	$5000	$3500	$3000	$1500	?
Order received	$5000	$5000	$5000	$5000	?
Cost of production	$2500	$2500	$2500	$2500	?
Cash receipt	$1000	$2000	$1000	Nil	?

Fig. 19.2 Cash flow forecast

From the 'lists' shown on a balance sheet we can classify the capital used by the firm in various ways. This helps us to understand how effectively the business is using its assets.

19.2 Cash flow

The flow of money into and out of a business is called **cash flow**. It is the difference between the receipts from sales and the amount spent on expenses such as raw materials, interest paid on loans, dividends paid to shareholders, etc. Money received into the firm adds to its capital reserves, money paid out reduces them.

If income from sales is equal to expenditure, the business can possibly survive. If income from sales is greater than expenses the business makes a **profit**. If income is less than expenses it makes a **loss**, and unless something is done to correct this the firm will eventually go bankrupt.

The foregoing is a relatively simple way of looking at cash flow. In reality it is more complex. We can understand this complexity if we look at a simple imaginary **cash flow forecast**, a statement or estimate of cash receipts and payments over a given period.

The Florida Trading Company produces ornamental pots for the tourist industry. Whatever it sells, fifty per cent of the income goes in expenses. Most customers take at least four weeks to pay for the goods supplied. Today, in the fourteenth week of this year's trading, Florida has received an order for $5,000 worth of pots. Should it accept the order? At first sight the answer to this might seem to be obviously 'Yes'. But look at the simple cash flow forecast in figure 19.2 and then see what you think.

From the cash flow forecast you can see that at the start of week 11 of this year's trading, Florida had $5,000 at the bank. It then received an order worth $5,000 which cost $2,500 to produce. In that same week one of its customers paid Florida $1,000. On this basis Florida started Week 12 with a cash balance of $3,500 ($5,000 minus $2,500 plus $1,000 = $3,500). Now follow this process through to weeks 14 and 15: you will see that Florida has a cash flow problem. This is sometimes called a '**liquidity problem**'.

The difficulty described here does not mean that Florida should not accept the new order, but it does mean that they have to decide how they will finance the cost of production if they do accept it. Should they borrow from the bank, which will take some of their profit? Should they pressurise some of their customers to pay outstanding debts, which may cause them to lose customers?

To achieve even cash flow is far from simple. It is important to recognise that payment for goods or services

Fig. 19.3 **It is important that money going out of a business does not exceed the money it receives.**

209

supplied will often not be received until some future date. This means that the business must budget with this possibility in mind. If the company's budgeting is unsound, the firm will have to request extended credit from its own suppliers, seek financial support from a bank or some other financial institution, or obtain capital from another source. These considerations have to be taken into account before Florida Trading accepts their most recently received order.

One way of solving a cash flow problem is by using a **factor**. A firm that is owed money can 'sell' its debts to a type of business called a factor. The factor collects all the payments due and pays the firm the amount owed, less the charges for the factoring service. A major part of the payments due may even be paid by the factor before they have been collected. Charges for a factoring service can be very high, but it can solve a cash flow problem and can also save a business the cost of employing its own staff for debt collection.

Many businesses enter their cash flow forecast into a computer **spreadsheet**. This allows the firm to see instantaneously how various changes might affect the business. The different situations presented to the computer are sometimes called '*what if*' scenarios.

A cash flow forecast can be used by a firm to measure its progress against expectations. However, a forecast is no more than an estimate made at a given time, and there may be many reasons why actual cash flow differs from the forecast. For example, actual sales might be higher or lower than anticipated, or the cost of materials may have changed.

19.3 Costs and revenues

A business can be seen as a simple system: it buys things (**inputs**), it does something (**a process**) to the inputs and then sells the results of that process (**outputs**). The outputs could be goods or services (the enterprise's **product**). The product(s) could be made by the business, or they could be items bought for resale. The money that a business uses to pay for its inputs is called its **costs**. These costs can be divided into *fixed costs* and *variable costs*.

Fixed costs are those that have to be paid and do not alter (hence the term *fixed*), irrespective of what the level of output is. Examples are; rent on premises, insurance premiums, local government taxes and rates, office salaries and interest on loans.

Variable costs are related to output, and vary (go up and down) in line with the level of output, e.g. the amount of business done. Examples are raw materials and other stocks used, wages and electricity related to producing and selling, and transport.

It is useful to bear in mind that even fixed costs can change in the long term because, if output increases sufficiently, these may have to increase. For example, increased shop, office or factory space may be needed. By adding together fixed costs and variable costs, we arrive at the **total costs** of the business. The enterprise must cover these costs in order to make a **profit**. It is important that a business keeps control over its costs in order to **maximise** its profits (achieve the best possible return). For example, a producer will want to ensure it keeps raw materials wastage as low as possible, and a retailer will want to deter shoplifting.

The money a business receives from selling its products or services is its income or **revenue**. The revenue of a business is linked to the price and volume of its outputs. The greater the volume, the greater will be the revenue (but not necessarily a greater profitability). A business will want to sell each unit of output at a price greater than the total cost of the unit. This additional sum is called the **profit** or **mark-up**. (See also Chapter 11.)

19.4 Break-even

Provided the revenue received from each unit of output is greater than the unit's variable cost, each unit sold will cover part of the business's fixed costs. At some stage, as revenue rises, the total of the fixed costs will be covered. This is called **break-even point** — where total revenue equals total costs (i.e. both fixed and variable). At the break-even point, the business is making neither a profit nor a loss. This is shown in figure 19.4.

Fig. 19.4 Break-even chart

If a business does not sell the volume of output required to break-even, it will make a **loss** because it is not covering its total costs (also shown in figure 19.4). In such circumstances the business will eventually be forced to cease trading. The same situation will occur if a business does not sell its products at a price higher than the variable costs of those products.

A business has to calculate the break-even point for *each* of its products in order to:

- identify the level of sales required for total revenue to match total costs
- help set the selling price for the product
- show the effect of profit or loss at different levels of sales.

As with cash flow forecasts, computer **spreadsheets** enable businesses to see almost instantaneously how different selling prices or levels of output might affect the business.

19.5 Capital

Some people find the term 'capital' difficult to understand because it has so many meanings. In respect of business accounts **capital** refers to the value of the things owned by a business.

If you refer again to the balance sheet for Florida Trading in figure 19.1 you might be puzzled why capital is listed as a liability, when you perhaps would have considered it an asset. Capital is listed as a liability because it represents the money that the business owes to the owners or shareholders. It is the amount they might receive if the business were sold.

We said earlier that capital is the money, or the assets bought with money, used to run a business. The owner(s) of a business can use their own money, or somebody else's. In using their own money they will be limited in scope and rarely have enough. In using someone else's money they will either have to pay **interest**, or give up some part of the **ownership** of the business (e.g. to partners or shareholders). There are three main sources of capital.

Sources of capital

1 *Share capital (equity)*: money subscribed to the company by shareholders in return for a share of the company's profits ('dividend'). Share capital is not repayable.
2 *Loan capital* (loan, debt or debenture): usually a long-term loan which must be repaid at some time.
3 *Reserves* (retained earnings, undistributed profits, reinvestment): a percentage of gross profits being put back into the business.

You will observe that *share capital* involves giving up some of the ownership of the business. Obtaining capital from *reserves* results in less reward being given to the owner(s)/shareholders. *Loan capital* incurs a charge called **interest**, and is, therefore, a drain on the profits of the business.

There are many sources of loan capital, e.g. hire purchase, bank loans and overdrafts, trade credit (suppliers agreeing to wait for payment) and debentures. It is usual for those providing loan capital to insist on **collateral** being provided. This refers to the assets of the business that the lender will be able to take if the loan is not repaid. For example, a debenture is a special kind of loan to a business. It is often linked to specific assets (known as collateral) owned by the firm, such as particular items of machinery. Other forms of collateral include items such as deeds of property, insurance or endowment policies, land titles, etc.

Categories of capital

It is often useful to divide capital into categories, and use these in calculations to analyse and interpret a balance sheet. The following are typical of the categories and calculations commonly used.

Fixed capital + Circulating capital = Employed capital

Employed capital − Current liabilities = Capital owned

Circulating capital − Current liabilities = Net working capital

Fig. 19.5 Categories of capital

Fixed capital/assets. These are the durable (long-term) assets of a business which are used over a long period of time and are tied up in permanent use. Examples: land, buildings, machinery, furniture, vehicles, etc.

Circulating capital/current assets (working capital) is capital which is continually changing in quantity, total value or nature. Examples include stocks, cash, bank balance and the amount of money owed to a firm by its customers (debtors).

Employed capital. This is obtained by adding together the fixed and current assets of the firm. In other words, it is the total of all the assets being used by the business.

Current liabilities are debts which will have to be repaid in the near future. Examples include bank overdraft, debts owed to suppliers (creditors) and taxes payable to the government.

Capital owned is the net value of the assets owned by a business. In other words, it is employed capital minus current liabilities.

Liquid capital consists of that part of the current assets which are cash or are easily changeable into cash without delay, for example bank balance, cash in tills and debts owed by others (debtors). Liquid capital is important because it can be used to pay creditors immediately, and therefore it should always be above the current liabilities figure.

Net working capital is the current assets minus the current liabilities. Net working capital is particularly important because it takes into account the possibility of all the creditors to the business calling for payment. Therefore, it is important for a business to have sufficient working capital to exist as far as possible without borrowing from a bank.

Example
(CA − CL = NWC)
Current Assets = 50,000 −
Current Liabilities = 16,000
Working Capital = 34,000

19.6 Turnover

Turnover refers to the total sales of the business over the previous year and can indicate how busy the firm has been. Generally, the greater the turnover the more business the firm is doing. (However, this is not always the case. For example, if the firm has increased its prices it might be that increased turnover in reality does not indicate a greater volume of sales.)

Net turnover

This is found by taking the value of total sales and deducting the value of goods returned or credits issued. For example, if a firm has total sales of $100,000 but has given refunds of $25,000 to customers, net turnover would be $75,000.

Rate of turnover

This is sometimes called 'rate of stock turn'. It is the figure which gives the number of times the average stock held has been sold during the year. It shows how many times the stock has been turned over. There are two methods of calculating the rate of stock turnover.

1. $\dfrac{\text{Cost of stock sold}}{\text{Average stock at cost price}}$ = Rate of stock turnover

2. $\dfrac{\text{Net turnover}}{\text{Average stock at selling price}}$ = Rate of stock turnover

The 'value of average stock' in the above calculations is worked out by taking the stock value at the beginning and at the end of the trading period, adding them and dividing by two.

Example $
Stock at the beginning of the year   4,000
Stock at the end of the year   6,000
Average stock $\dfrac{\$10,000}{2}$ = $5,000

Using method 2: if we assume that the average stock at selling price is $5,000 and the net turnover is $50,000, the calculation is as follows:

$\dfrac{\$50,000}{\$5,000}$ = 10 = Rate of stock turnover

This means that the stock is turned over ten times in a year. Whether this is good or not would depend on the type of business the figure refers to. For a confectioner to turn over the stock only ten times a year would be acceptable, but for a greengrocer to do likewise would be unsatisfactory because it would mean that his or her stock would perish.

So the rate of stock turnover can also be seen as an indicator of how old the goods in stock are.

In making the calculations it is important to remember that the figures used must either both be at selling price or both at cost price.

Importance of rate of turnover

The rate of turnover indicates how busy a business is, and this is obviously a valuable indicator when a business is being bought, sold or valued because it allows comparison with other similar businesses.

- A low rate of turnover is associated with sellers of highly valued goods or consumer durables (long-lasting goods).

Examples:

	Normal rate of turnover
Jewellers	3
Electrical goods	6
Furniture and books	6
Confectioners	12

- A high rate of turnover is associated with businesses selling perishable goods.

Examples:

	Normal rate of turnover
Butchers	78
Dairies	67
Greengrocers	53
Bakers	42

- If the rate of turnover is increasing it would indicate that the firm is doing more and more business in real terms; it is selling more goods so profits should be increasing.

19.7 Profit

Profit is the **reward** the business person receives for taking the risk involved in business and for being able to combine all the factors required to produce and sell goods or services. In order to make a profit, the firm's turnover must be bigger than its operating expenses (the day-to-day costs of running the business).

The profitability of a business can be looked at from the point of view of either gross profit or net profit.

Gross profit

This is the revenue obtained from the sale of goods or services, minus their cost price. For example:

Sales − Cost of goods = Gross profit
($40,000)   ($30,000)   ($10,000)

Gross profit can be expressed as a percentage of the cost or of the selling price.

Example

	$
Selling price	1.00
Cost price	0.75
Gross profit	0.25

Mark-up (on cost price) = $\frac{25}{75} \times 100 = 33\frac{1}{3}\%$

Profit margin (on selling price) = $\frac{25}{100} \times 100 = 25\%$

Gross profit takes no account of the **overheads** the business has to meet, for example, wages, advertising, lighting, etc.

As a plain monetary figure, gross profit tells us little about a firm, but if we turn it into a percentage it can be compared with previous years' figures and with the gross profit figures of other similar businesses, indicating how competitive the business is. The method for calculating the gross profit percentage is as follows.

$$\frac{\text{Gross profit}}{\text{Turnover}} \times 100 = \text{Gross profit percentage}$$

Example

	$
Turnover	80,000
Cost of goods	60,000
Gross profit	20,000

As a percentage $\frac{20,000}{80,000} \times 100 = 25\%$

Most businesses require a gross profit of between 20% and 40% to ensure that they are covering their overheads (expenses) easily, and to reward the owners sufficiently. Over the years, the gross profit percentage should remain relatively stable, since if it drops too much the business may fail to cover its overheads and start to make an overall loss. There are a number of reasons for a falling gross profit percentage.

- Possibly the staff of the business are stealing stock or takings.
- Stock may be getting damaged or allowed to perish.
- New stock may have been bought in at higher cost price and the increases may not have been passed on to customers.
- The business may be employing more staff than is necessary for the volume of business (overstaffing).
- Expenses are rising (e.g. wages, heating, lighting, etc.) and this is not being incorporated into prices.

Net profit

This is the real profit made by the business after having taken into account the expenses incurred in carrying on the business, such as wages, rent, rates, advertising and bills of all kinds.

Net profit = Gross profit minus all expenses

Example
   Gross profit = $20,000, Expenses = $5,000
   Net profit = $20,000 − $5,000 = $15,000

Again this figure is better expressed as a percentage so that it can be used in comparison.

$$\text{Net profit percentage} = \frac{\text{Net profit}}{\text{Turnover}} \times 100$$

$$= \frac{15,000}{80,000} \times 100 = 18.75\%$$

19.8 Return on capital invested

This is the figure that matters most to the owners of a business. It is a figure that shows how much profit has been made as a percentage of all the capital employed in the business. The return on investment must be sufficient to make it worthwhile for the owners of the business to face the risks involved in enterprise. If the return on the investment is not sufficient, the owner(s) may be tempted to place their money in other less risky forms of investment. The risks in business are high, therefore the return on capital invested must be higher than the return from a no-risk investment.

$$\frac{\text{Net profit}}{\text{Capital employed}} \times 100 = \text{Return on capital invested}$$

19.9 THINGS TO DO

This section contains a variety of exercises to help you form revision notes, to test your understanding and to prepare you for examinations.

Search and find

Write out the question and the answer by referring back through the text to form revision notes.

1. What is the main aim of all businesses?
2. What is a balance sheet?
3. Explain the difference between assets and liabilities.
4. What is the meaning of the term 'cash flow'? Why is cash flow important to a business?
5. How can factoring help solve a cash flow problem? What other alternatives are there?
6. Explain the difference between fixed costs and variable costs.
7. Give three examples of 'overheads'.
8. Why does a business need to control its costs?
9. What do you understand by the term 'break-even'? How is break-even calculated?
10. Explain why the unit cost per item decreases when output increases.
11. Why would a business want to prepare a break-even forecast?
12. What is business capital and from where is it obtained?
13. Briefly describe each of the categories that capital can be divided into. Why is it useful to categorise capital in this way?
14. Why is it important that liquid capital should not fall below current liabilities?
15. A firm has fixed capital of $60,000, circulating capital of $6,000, and $7,000 current liabilities. What is its capital owned and its net working capital?
16. Define turnover. Explain the difference between gross turnover and net turnover.
17. What is rate of turnover, and why is this important to a firm?
18. The following figures relate to Florida Trading Company Ltd:

Jan. 1	$ 6,000
Dec. 31	$ 9,000
Net turnover	$60,000

    Calculate the rate of stock turnover and comment whether the rate would be good for a butcher's shop. Give reasons for your answer.

19. Explain the relevance to the business person of 'high', 'low' and 'increasing' rates of turnover.
20. Explain the difference between mark-up and profit margin.

21 Define profit and explain the difference between gross profit and net profit.

22 Florida Trading Company Ltd. is experiencing falling gross profit. List some reasons why this might be happening.

23 Why is the figure referred to as 'return on capital invested' the most important figure to the owners of a business?

What do you know?

Write out the complete sentence and insert the missing word, which can be chosen from the list at the end of the questions.

1 The initial capital of a business comes from investors and . . . . .

2 A balance sheet is like a . . . . . of the financial position of a business at a particular moment in time.

3 Money received into a business adds to its . . . . . reserves and money paid out reduces them.

4 It is important to recognise that . . . . . for goods and services supplied may not be received until some later date.

5 If a company does not have enough . . . . . capital, it is said to have cash flow problems.

6 . . . . . refers to the total sales of a business the previous year.

7 Rate of stock turnover can be seen as an indicator of how . . . . . goods in stock are.

8 . . . . . is the reward the business person receives for taking the risk involved in business.

9 . . . . . costs are relatively constant figures.

10 . . . . . costs change with increases and decreases in output.

Choose the missing words from the following:				
variable	snapshot	turnover	profit	working
entrepreneurs	payment	capital	old	fixed

Multiple choice

Select the appropriate answer, a, b, c or d.

1 Which of the following would be considered an asset of a business?
   a) tax owed to the government
   b) two jars of coffee
   c) the wage bill
   d) a delivery truck being bought on credit

2 Which of the following would be the likely rate of stock turnover for a butcher?
   a) 3   c) 12
   b) 6   d) 78

3 Sima's Shoe Shop buys shoes for $40 and sells them for $50. The mark-up is:
   a) 15%
   b) 20%
   c) 25%
   d) 30%

4 Which of the following equations would enable you to calculate the fixed capital of a business?
   a) employed capital – circulating capital
   b) employed capital + circulating capital
   c) employed capital + current liabilities
   d) employed capital – current liabilities

5 On a balance sheet, petty cash would be included under:
   a) fixed assets
   b) liquid assets
   c) current liabilities
   d) net working capital

6 Net working capital is found from which of the following equations?
   a) current assets – current liabilities
   b) current liabilities – liquid capital
   c) liquid capital + circulating assets
   d) circulating assets + current assets

7 The capital of a business can be defined as:
   a) the total value of the fixed assets of the business
   b) the gross profit of the business
   c) the money that is used to start the business
   d) the value of the stock the company holds

8 Capital that is used to purchase stock and raw materials is called:
   a) working capital
   b) employed capital
   c) capital owned
   d) fixed capital

9 Which of the following is an example of fixed capital?
   a) raw materials for processing
   b) stock for resale
   c) money owed by debtors
   d) computers for accounting

10 The term 'rate of turnover' is best defined as the:
    a) total sales over a given period
    b) gross profit minus the cost of the goods
    c) rate of loss of stock through stealing
    d) number of times the average stock is sold in a given period

BUSINESS FINANCE

Key words

Find out the business-related meaning of each of the following words. Write a separate sentence for each word to show your understanding.

liquidity   receipts   factor   bankrupt
factoring   debt   liability   asset
overstaffing   expenditure

Structured questions

1. This question is related to the balance sheet shown in figure 19.1.

   a) What is a balance sheet? (1)

   b) Why is a balance sheet sometimes referred to as a 'snapshot'? (2)

   c) If a competitor were considering making a take-over bid for Florida Trading Company, why would the contents of the balance sheet be important to them? (3)

   d) Why is a balance sheet important to both the owners and the workforce of the business? (4)

   e) Refer to the balance sheet in figure 19.1 and complete the analysis in table 19.1 of the trading figures of the Florida Trading Company Ltd. (10)

Table 19.1 *Florida Trading Company trading figures*

	$	$	$	$	$
1 Fixed capital	80,000 +	?	+ 10,000		= 110,000
2 Circulating capital	?	+ 12,000 +	?	+ 600 =	?
3 Employed capital	110,000 +	?			= ?
4 Current liabilities	?	?	?		= 16,000
5 Capital owned	?	−	?		= 144,000
6 Liquid capital	12,000 +	?	+ ?		= 18,000
7 Net working capital	?	− 16,000			= ?

2. Look at figure 19.6, and answer the following questions.

   a) List four examples of sources of business capital. (2)

   b) Briefly explain the difference between fixed assets and current assets. (2)

Fig. 19.6 Business finance flowchart

   c) Explain the difference between gross profit and net profit. Why do you think it is important to distinguish between these two aspects of profit? (4)

   d) The illustration shows that the net profit might be used in three ways: for repayments, dividends and reinvestment. Briefly explain each of these. (6)

   e) A shop's capital is $50,000. It has stock which cost $30,000 that is turned over three times a year, making 20 per cent gross profit on sales. Expenses are $7,000 for the year. Find the percentage of the net profit to the capital. (6)

3. Two stores have recorded the trading figures in table 19.2.

Table 19.2 *Trading figures*

	Store A $	Store B $
Sales	100,000	16,000
Average stock at cost	5,000	4,000
Profit margin	8%	30%
Expenses	4,000	800
Net profit	4,000	4,000

   a) Which store has the greatest sales? (1)

b) Name two expenses that both stores are likely to incur. (2)

c) What is meant by profit margin? (3)

d) What sort of goods in Store B are likely to be selling? Give reasons for your answer. (4)

e) Explain the fact that both stores have a net profit of $4,000. (4)

f) If you had $80,000 invested in Store A what would be your return on the capital invested? What could be done to increase your return? (6)

4 Table 19.3 shows various assets and liabilities of the Akela Trading Company Ltd.

Table 19.3 *Assets and liabilities of Akela Trading Co. Ltd.*

Assets	$	Liabilities	$
Factory	300,000	Trade debtors	10,000
Creditors	10,000	Reserves	100,000
Petty cash	500	Finished goods	18,000
Share capital	209,000	Tax due	4,000
Office typewriters	10,000	Overdraft	18,000
Typing paper	500	Machinery	100,000
Cash at bank	6,000	Raw materials	11,000
Debentures	87,000	Loans	105,000
Computer	10,000	Factory fittings	20,000
Unfinished goods	16,000	Trucks	40,000

a) Name the company to which this data refers. (1)

b) What are assets? (1)

c) Write one sentence to define the following terms and calculate their values from the above figures:
   (i) fixed capital (2)
   (ii) circulating capital (2)
   (iii) liquid capital (2)
   (iv) current assets (2)
   (v) net working capital. (2)

d) Draw up a balance sheet for the Akela Trading Company Ltd. using the data shown in the table. (8)

5 a) Using the information in table 19.4, and clearly showing all working, calculate for each store:
   (i) gross profit (3)
   (ii) net profit (3)
   (iii) rate of turnover. (3)

b) Write a report comparing the finances and trading strategies of each store. Explain the differences and account for the similarities. (11)

Table 19.4 *Comparison of two stores*

	Store A $	Store B $
Sales	100,000	16,000
Average stock at cost	5,000	4,000
Profit margin	8%	30%
Expenses	4,000	800

Research assignments

1 Make a comparison between the final accounts of two firms of similar size and comment upon the differences between them.

2 Explain the various ways by which a business might raise capital (a) for short-term and (b) for long-term use. Why does a firm need to make this distinction between sources of capital?

3 Why is cash flow forecasting important to all types of business? Use simple data to illustrate your answer using a small local manufacturing company as an example.

4 'Break-even charts do not give a precise picture of when a business will begin to make a profit, but they do provide a useful guide.' Explain this statement including a simple but clearly labelled break-even chart to illustrate your answer.

5 Write to a major public company in your region and ask for a copy of its most recent annual report and accounts. From the accounts explain the following in your own words.

a) How the net profit (or loss) figure is arrived at.

b) What percentage of the company's profit is paid to the shareholders and what percentage is retained.

c) Give your personal view of the prospects you see for the business and its shareholders in the year ahead.

6 a) Describe how a limited company may increase its capital employed:
   (i) temporarily
   (ii) permanently.

b) What evidence can you obtain that shows how a business you have access to has taken these steps.

7 What is meant by a company's capital? How is it that a business might only have $1,000 in petty cash and at the bank, and yet have capital of $50,000? Use specimen figures to illustrate your answer.

8 A large public company needs further capital for expansion. Describe three different ways in which it might try to raise this money, and give your views on what factors are likely to influence the method chosen.

9 Table 19.5 shows the balance sheet of a retailer. Obtain similar data from a retailer you have access to.

Table 19.5 *Balance sheet*

	$		$
Owner's savings	850	Fixed assets	8,225
Mortgage	8,000	Current assets	625
	8,850		8,850

(a) What is meant by each of the following:
  (i) Mortgage
  (ii) Fixed assets
  (iii) Current assets.

b) Why distinguish between these different aspects of a balance sheet?

10 a) Ask a local retail trader to allow you to produce a specimen balance sheet which shows the value of its 'fixed' and its 'working' capital.

b) Explain what is meant by 'fixed' and 'working' capital using data from your balance sheet to clarify your explanation.

11 Make a study of one local private and one public company. Write a report on the finance-related differences you can observe between them.

12 Take two local businesses that you have access to. One should be a private limited company and the other a public limited company. Find out their sources of capital (a) in the shorter, and (b) in the long term. What similarities and differences exist? Give possible interpretations of your findings.

13 Obtain examples of a variety of financial documents used by companies. Explain why it is important for a company to maintain proper financial records, using examples from the data you have collected to illustrate your explanation.

Chapter 20
STOCK EXCHANGES

20.1 Selling new shares

If a company wishes to raise capital, the methods it uses are the same whether it is a new company or an established one attempting to increase its capital. There are two broad choices. A company may either:

1. raise the capital privately, or
2. invite the public to subscribe to a share issue.

The sale of shares is an attractive option to a company because money raised in this way does not have to be repaid, whereas almost all other methods do involve repayment.

A new issue of shares may be made by:

- a new company forming
- a private company turning into a public company
- an existing public company trying to raise more capital.

The selling of new shares may be offered to the public in three main ways.

1. *The company may issue a* **Prospectus**. This is a leaflet or advertisement giving details of:

    - the history of the company
    - its plans for the future
    - the amount of capital it requires to raise
    - an invitation to the public to buy shares.

    A closing date for applications to buy is set, and after that date the shares are allotted to those who have applied to buy.
    If the issue is **over-subscribed**, in other words people wish to buy more shares than are available, the applicants receive a percentage of the shares they requested.
    If the issue is **under-subscribed** the company could end up in the position of not raising all the capital it needs. This is where it is an advantage to use an **issuing house** to sell shares on behalf of the company because they will often **underwrite** the complete issue. This means that if all the shares are not sold, the issuing house undertakes to buy all the remaining shares, thus guaranteeing that the company will raise the total capital it requires.

2. *The company may offer the shares for sale*: that is, sell the shares outright to an issuing house who then dispose of them as best they can, ensuring that the company will receive all the capital it wishes to raise.

3. *The company may 'place' the shares* with Stock Exchange brokers, who offer them to their clients, and to other brokers.

20.2 Selling second-hand shares

Once a company has raised capital by the sale of shares it has given up part of the ownership of the business to shareholders, and at the same time it puts this capital to use and the shareholders cannot change their minds and take the money back. However, if a shareholder was expected to invest his or her money with no opportunity to sell his or her shareholding, few people would be willing to take the risk of investing in business. In this respect the Stock Exchange plays a vital role.

The **Stock Exchange** provides a market-place where buyers and sellers of **securities** (the name given to describe all stocks, shares, etc.) can meet to buy and sell. As the shares they deal with have already been sold once, to the first owner, we say that the Stock Exchange is a market-place for 'second-hand' securities. The wider market of share dealing, including deals outside of the Stock Exchange, is called the '**Stock Market**'. 'Bidding' is the basis for carrying out deals. A sale is made when someone purchases a security at a price offered or as a result of their bid.

The Stock Exchange is responsible for making arrangements for the trading of shares and other securities. The Exchange sets the rules of operation in the Stock Market and ensures that members adhere to the rules at all times.

The Caribbean Stock Exchange

The Caribbean Stock Exchange, also referred to as the CARICOM Stock Exchange, is a relatively recent phenomenon. The idea of establishing a regional stock exchange was first proposed in 1988 by Michael Manley, the then leader of the opposition in Jamaica.

However, the CARICOM Heads of Government found the idea of a single regional stock market difficult to handle, and agreed to 'cross-border' trading on the markets of three CARICOM member countries — Barbados, Jamaica, and Trinidad and Tobago — which already had established stock markets.

The broad purpose of the CARICOM Exchange is to encourage Caribbean economic integration. 'Exchange controls' have been relaxed to permit cross-border trading in CARICOM shares. This will give rise to the 'free movement' of capital within CARICOM. Useful mergers resulting in larger companies will emerge eventually, and it is hoped that the Caribbean people will benefit greatly.

20.3 Securities traded

Ordinary shares

Ordinary shares are sometimes referred to as **equities** because each share has a claim to an equal division of the profit of the business. Equities carry the right to vote at shareholders' meetings, with each share carrying one vote. Therefore, the more shares held, the greater the voting power of the holder.

Each ordinary share is entitled to an equal share ('**dividend**') of the company's profit (if a profit has been made); the more shares that are held the greater will be the shareholder's dividend. The return that investors receive on their investment is dependent on the performance of the business over the period (six months or one year) since the last dividend was distributed. If the company has done well the reward for the shareholder will be good. If the company has not done well, the shares will be less profitable, and may even pay no dividend at all.

The general trend of ordinary share prices can be an indicator of the prosperity of the country in general and of industry in particular. The general trends (growth or contraction) are reflected all round the world in the stock exchange 'indices' — in the UK there is the Financial Times Index, in the US the trend is shown in the Dow Jones Index, and in the Caribbean the trend is reflected in daily newspapers and financial publications.

Fig. 20.1 Equities and voting power

Ordinary shares and debenture stocks (see later notes) illustrate the extremes of risk undertaken by investors in public companies. The ordinary shareholder takes the greatest risk and therefore reaps the greatest reward if the firm is prosperous, whereas the debenture holder takes little risk and therefore tends to receive less return on his or her investment.

There is, however, a type of holding which to some extent combines the speculative nature of ordinary shares with the security of debentures, and this is the **preference share**.

Preference shares

There are three classes of preference shares.

1 *Ordinary preference shares* carry a fixed rate of dividend which is payable (if sufficient profit is available) before any dividends are paid to ordinary shareholders, but after payment of interest to debenture holders.

As their name suggests, preference shares receive preferential treatment over ordinary shares in the payment of dividends and in a share of the assets in the event of the business going bankrupt.

Whilst preference shares are safer than ordinary shares, if the company is particularly profitable they are also less rewarding because of the fixed dividend. Normally preference shares do not carry any voting rights unless dividend payments by the company are in arrears.

2 *Cumulative preference shares* are similar to ordinary preference shares except that if the business does not make enough profit to allow payment of the dividend due one year, the amount outstanding is carried forward and held outstanding until payment can be met. The outstanding amount is allowed to accumulate until payment is eventually made.

3 *Participating preference shares.* It can be seen that, because of the relatively safe nature of preference shares and the fact that they pay a fixed rate of dividend, the preference shareholder does not reap any additional reward when the company's profits are good.

To overcome this situation some companies create shares called 'participating preference shares'. These are the same as other preference shares but they award the normal fixed dividend, and if there is still any profit remaining after payment of other dividends, the participating preference shareholder may receive a further dividend additional to the fixed rate already paid.

Debenture stocks

Strictly speaking, debentures are not shares but long-term loans to a company, which are usually to be repaid at some future date. They carry a fixed rate of interest which is payable every year whether the company makes a profit or not.

Debenture holders:

- do not share in the ownership of the company
- have no voting rights
- have no say in the running of the business.

However, debentures are transferable and, therefore, the holders can sell them via the Stock Exchange for the highest price they are able to obtain.

Debentures are secured against specific fixed assets owned by the business or generally against all the assets of the business. If the debentures are secured against specific fixed assets, they are called **mortgage debentures**. If a company goes bankrupt, debenture holders have a right to repayment before any funds are distributed to shareholders.

Investment trusts and unit trusts

Investment trusts and unit trusts have become increasingly popular, especially with the small saver. These trusts invest the capital they receive over a wide range of securities, thus spreading the risk involved. After paying administrative expenses, the net yield from the various investments is distributed as a dividend.

20.4 The return on shares

The return, or reward, given to shareholders is called a **dividend**, because it is a division of the profit available for distribution. The dividend is usually expressed as a percentage of the nominal or **par value** of the share, that is, the issue price (the price the share was originally sold for), normally in units of one dollar.

If the dividend is said to be 8% then for every $1 share the shareholder owns, he or she will get 8c (8% of $1). However, the shareholder may have bought the share for a price above its par value. If this is the case he or she is really interested in the actual return on the money paid for the share. This is called the **yield**.

The yield on a share is worked out as follows:

$$\frac{\text{Par value of share}}{\text{Market value of share}} \times \text{Rate of dividend} = \text{Yield}$$

The market value of the share is the price paid for it on the Stock Exchange. In our example, if the shareholder had paid $2 for the share, the yield would have been 4%.

$$\frac{\$1}{\$2} \times 8\% = 4\%$$

When the par value and the market value are the same, the dividend and the yield are the same. If the market value is below the par value, the yield will be greater than the dividend.

20.5 Factors affecting share prices

If speculators could accurately predict share price movement they could guarantee to make a fortune several times in one week. However, investment in shares remains speculative because there are numerous factors that influence the rise or fall in share prices.

Some of these factors can be summarised as follows:

- supply and demand for the shares
- recent performance of the company (good or poor profits)
- political changes affecting the company, for example change of government
- changes in interest rates or taxation
- popularity or otherwise of the company's products
- changes in market trends
- takeover or merger being considered
- general national prosperity
- industrial disputes, or settlements of disputes.

20.6 Speculation

There is an important distinction between an investor and a speculator. An *investor* buys shares in order to receive a share of the company's profits. A *speculator* on the other hand hopes to make a quick profit by anticipating changes in share prices. There are three types of speculator, and they are known by the colourful names of **bulls**, **bears** and **stags**.

- **Bulls** buy or hold shares anticipating a price rise, and make a profit by selling at a higher price. In a '*bullish*' market prices are generally rising.

- **Bears** sell shares anticipating a fall in market prices, perhaps buying them back later at a lower price, for example if they need to fulfil a contract to supply the shares. In a *bearish* market, prices are generally falling.

- **Stags** buy new issues of shares expecting to resell them at a profit when second-hand dealing starts on the Stock Exchange.

It should be noted that when referring to bulls, bears and stags, we are talking about the way someone is behaving and not three different people. An individual may be a bull at one time or bear at another. The terms may be used to describe someone even if he or she is not a member of the Stock Exchange.

20.7 How a stock exchange works

A free market

A stock exchange is a 'free' market in that prices are allowed to rise and fall in accordance with supply and demand. Such freedom and variations can only exist if buyers and sellers are able to trade, and this could create a problem. If all the people who wanted to sell or buy shares want to meet at the same market-place the result would be chaos. For this reason, only Members of the Stock Exchange are allowed to trade in the market. Those who are not Members have to buy and sell through the Members.

It is the Members of the Stock Exchange who take the part of the buyers and sellers of securities and thereby maintain a free market. There are two classes of Members of the Stock Exchange, **brokers** and **jobbers**.

Stockbrokers (brokers)

It is the brokers' business to buy and sell shares on behalf of their clients, obtaining the best deal they can for them, for which service they are paid a fixed rate of commission.

The brokers come into the Stock Exchange and visit several jobbers, checking prices before buying to ensure that they obtain the best price for their clients, who cannot approach the jobbers directly themselves. They will also offer advice to their clients, and such advice will be based on their knowledge and experience of the operations of the market.

Stockjobbers (jobbers)

Whereas brokers deal directly with people outside the Stock Exchange and bring their business into the market, jobbers stay in the Stock Exchange and only deal with brokers and other jobbers. Therefore they do not come into contact with the real sellers and buyers. Jobbers are in fact wholesalers of stocks and shares, hoping to make a profit (called the jobber's 'turn' or 'margin') by buying shares from brokers or other jobbers at one price and selling them for a higher one.

Jobbers tend to specialise in a particular range of securities. For example, some may specialise in government stocks whilst others specialise in oil or industrial shares. Other typical markets in which jobbers specialise are motors, aircraft, shipping, chemicals, rubber and mining property.

20.8 Striking a bargain

When you go shopping you will look around various shops trying to find the lowest price you can, and perhaps hoping to come across a bargain. If you discover your particular brand of chocolate is cheaper in one place than another, then you will buy in the cheaper shop. Brokers will also shop around different jobbers when buying or selling shares to try to obtain the best deal they can for their clients.

Eventually the shareholder will receive a '**contract**' giving the details of their deal(s), and in due course they will receive a '**share certificate**' signifying how many shares they own in a particular company.

Fig. 20.2 How the Stock Exchange works

20.9 The importance of stock exchanges

Many large businesses need to appeal to the public for the vast sums of money they require to finance the purchase of new premises or new machinery, or to expand the business. People are not willing to invest money to finance this sort of development unless they can be sure that they can get the money back again. But, as we have observed earlier in this chapter, the business uses the money invested with it and it cannot be returned.

When an investor needs his or her money back he or she does not need to go to the company with whom it was originally invested. Instead, the investor sells his or her shares to some other investor through the Stock Exchange. In other words, although the Stock Exchange does not directly raise new capital for business, it encourages people to invest in companies because it provides facilities for the sale of second-hand securities.

The government also needs to borrow money from the public to help finance the many industries and services it provides through central or local government. These require a continuous supply of new capital to fund new equipment and development research. Local and central governments rely on the Stock Exchange to help raise the capital they need.

All stock exchanges have an international importance because they provide a market for the shares of foreign countries. For example, Caribbean-based investors can easily buy shares in companies in other countries, and investors in foreign countries can similarly easily put money into businesses in the Caribbean region.

20.10 THINGS TO DO

This section contains a variety of exercises to help you create revision notes, to test your understanding and to prepare you for examinations.

Search and find

Write out the question and the answer by referring back through the text to form revision notes.

1. What are the two main choices open to a company wishing to raise capital?
2. Why is the sale of shares an attractive option for companies raising capital?
3. Briefly describe the three main ways a company might sell shares.
4. 'The term "stock market" has a wider meaning than "stock exchange".' Explain this statement.
5. What is the main function of a stock exchange?
6. A stock exchange is a market for 'second-hand' securities. Why is it described in this way?
7. In what ways are ordinary shares 'speculative'?
8. What is 'preferential' about preference shares?
9. Briefly describe each of the three categories of preference shares.
10. 'Debentures are not really shares.' Explain this statement.
11. In what way do unit trusts and investment trusts spread the risks faced by investors?
12. How do you work out the yield on a share? Why is yield the most important figure for an investor?
13. Clearly describe the activities of stock market speculators, including use of the terms 'bulls', 'bears' and 'stags'.
14. List the factors that influence share prices.
15. In what way can the Stock Exchange be said to be a 'free' market?
16. Explain the difference in function between a stockbroker and a stockjobber.
17. Why are stock exchanges important?

What do you know?

Write out the complete sentence and insert the missing word, which can be chosen from the list at the end of the questions.

1. The Stock Exchange is a . . . . . place for the buyers and sellers of all kinds of second-hand securities.
2. Ordinary shares are sometimes called . . . . . because they are entitled to an equal share of profits.
3. General market trends in share prices can provide an indicator of the . . . . . of industry.
4. . . . . . are not shares as such but are long-term loans to a company by investors.
5. Investment trusts and unit trusts spread the . . . . . of investing.
6. A stock exchange is a . . . . . market in that prices are allowed to rise and fall in accordance with supply and demand.
7. Only . . . . . of the Stock Exchange are allowed to trade in the market.
8. A . . . . . buys and sells shares on behalf of clients.
9. . . . . . are rather like wholesalers of shares.
10. The jobber's . . . . . is a name sometimes given to the profit he or she makes.

> Choose the missing words from the following:
>
> jobbers   members   market   turn   debentures
> free   equities   broker   risk   prosperity

Multiple choice

Select the appropriate answer, a, b, c or d.

1. The proportion of profits given to ordinary shareholders is called:
   a) interest
   b) dividend
   c) yield
   d) equity

2. A person who has bought some shares:
   a) will always make a profit when reselling them
   b) is known as a speculator
   c) can only sell them again at a loss
   d) receives a share of the company's profits

3. A person who has bought ordinary shares in a public company:
   a) has limited liability
   b) is lending money to the company
   c) receives a good rate of interest
   d) automatically becomes a director

4   The profit a jobber makes on trading shares is called:
    a) turn
    b) return
    c) interest
    d) dividend

5   The following name is given to someone who buys new shares in the hope of reselling them at a profit:
    a) bull
    b) bear
    c) stag
    d) buyer

6   A unit trust spreads the risk associated with investment in securities by:
    a) only investing in major companies
    b) investing in many different companies
    c) only accepting trustworthy investors
    d) investing only in government bonds

7   The most risky of the following forms of investment is:
    a) preference shares
    b) ordinary shares
    c) debenture
    d) unit trusts

8   Which one of the following best describe the method of trading on a stock exchange?
    a) auction
    b) barter
    c) spot dealing
    d) wholesaling

9   Which one of the following types of business is allowed to have its shares listed on the Stock Exchange?
    a) public limited company
    b) private limited company
    c) partnership
    d) sole trader

10 A stock exchange is referred to as a 'free' market because:
    a) companies can pay whatever return they wish
    b) jobbers and brokers compete freely with each other
    c) share prices fluctuate with supply and demand
    d) there is no charge made on share sales

Key words

Find out the business-related meaning of each of the following words. Write a separate sentence for each word to show your understanding:

capital   prospectus   speculator   yield
bullish   bearish   investor   profit
share   shareholder

Structured questions

1   This question is related to figure 20.2.
    a) State two ways in which an individual could reap a reward through owning shares. (2)
    b) Name two different forms of *organisations* that might want to buy or sell shares. (2)
    c) In what way does the illustration show that the Stock Exchange is a 'market'? (4)
    d) Clearly explain the difference in function between a jobber and a broker. (6)
    e) 'A stock exchange performs an important function not only for individuals but also for businesses and the economy in general.' Discuss this statement. (6)

2   Jim Gray inherited $3,000 which he decided to divide into three equal parts for investment purposes. $1,000 was placed with a unit trust. Another $1,000 was invested in the ordinary shares of Company A, and the remaining $1,000 was invested in the ordinary shares of Company B. Jim recorded the current value of his three investments once a week over a six-month period. His records are reproduced in the graph in figure 20.3.

Fig. 20.3 Jim Gray's investments

    a) Which of Jim's investments had the highest value at the end of the second month of the investment period? (1)

b) Which one of the investments reached the highest value over the six-month period? (1)

c) The firm that purchased Jim's investments for him charged him 'commission'. What is commission in this respect? (2)

d) Company A is a company whose shares are consistently high in value. Give two reasons that could influence this high value. (2)

e) State two ways that Jim could profit from his investment in ordinary shares. (2)

f) What are unit trusts and how do they reduce the risk associated with investment? (3)

g) Give a brief description of the process that would be followed if Jim wished to sell his shares. (4)

h) Jim's investment record shows widely differing rates of success and failure. Explain some of the possible reasons for this. (6)

3 a) Why is a stock exchange an important feature of a *laissez-faire* economy? (2)

b) Explain how both public limited companies and 'institutional investors', such as pension funds, benefit from the existence of stock exchanges. (3)

c) What do we mean when we say the Stock Market is 'bearish'? Who benefits from this sort of situation? (3)

d) Discuss the view that speculation is not in the best interest of the investor. (6)

e) 'When we talk about "bulls", "bears" and "stags", we are not talking about three individual types of person but about the way people are behaving.' Explain this statement, including a description of the function of these specialisations in the Stock Exchange. (6)

4 a) With regard to the Stock Exchange, explain what is meant by 'equities'. (2)

b) Why is the return on a debenture generally lower than that of an ordinary share? (3)

c) Why is investing in unit trusts generally less risky than investing in ordinary shares? (3)

d) Explain the difference between the dividend and the yield of a share. (4)

e) Explain the way the Stock Exchange encourages investors to help finance industry. (8)

Research assignments

1 Sophie Carter has inherited $10,000 which she has decided to invest in the ordinary shares of a major public limited company whose shares are listed on the Stock Exchange. Describe the process which would be followed in the purchase of these shares, and discuss the ways in which Sophie could profit from her investment.

2 Discuss the view that a stock exchange is only a place where speculators gamble. Present evidence to support your discussion.

3 Take any five companies of your choice that are listed on the Stock Exchange. Invest an imaginary $5,000, approximately $1,000 in each company. Record the weekly change in value of each of your holdings over a six-week period. At the end of the six weeks compare the total current value of your five holdings with the original amount invested.

4 Congratulations! You have won $60,000. Invest this money in three contrasting ways, including at least one non-stock exchange method. Record the progress of each $20,000 over a six-month period. Give reasons for any differences in return achieved for each of the chosen investments.

5 Why is it possible for $1,000 invested in government bonds to become worth, say, $1,500, whereas the same amount invested in a portfolio of ordinary shares could realise a market value of twice the original investment in just one year?

Chapter 21
INSURANCE

21.1 The insurance industry

The Superintendent of Insurance — Jamaica

The office of the Superintendent of Insurance was established by the Insurance Act of 1971 and pertinent regulations of 1972. Through these the Superintendent of Insurance is given the power to:

1 supervise the operations of the insurance industry
2 make decisions about the continuation or discontinuation of an insurance enterprise based on its operations as revealed in its annual report.

The aim is to protect consumers of insurance, who, prior to 1971, experienced difficulties as a result of the unscrupulous operations of some insurance businesses.

Insurance laws established prior to 1971 were included in the Companies Act and the Motor Vehicle Insurance (Third Party Risks) Act, which assisted in regulating some aspects of the insurance industry. These legal provisions were inadequate, and left insurance companies to operate largely as they wished, sometimes to the detriment of the consumer. Hence the regulatory laws and the accompanying government office were set up to ensure that procedures in the insurance industry are kept under surveillance.

Each Caribbean island has a regulatory authority with similar aims and objectives.

Insurance companies belong to various associations:

- Life Underwriters Association of Jamaica (LUAJ)
- Life Insurance Companies Association (LICA)
- Jamaica Insurance Advisory Council (JIAC)
- Brokers Association and General Agents Association.

Jamaican companies such as

- Life of Jamaica
- Mutual Life
- Insurance Company of the West Indies (ICWI)

have established offices in other Caribbean islands. Similarly, other Caribbean islands such as Trinidad and Tobago have established insurance businesses in neighbouring territories:

- Guyana and Trinidad Mutual Fire Insurance Co. Ltd.
- The Barbados Mutual Life Assurance Society.

21.2 The purpose of insurance

All individuals and organisations face a wide variety of risks, but only some of them actually suffer a loss during the course of a year. Insurance provides a system of providing compensation to those who suffer a loss.

Simply put, insurance is an agreement between an insurance company (the insurer) and someone who wants financial protection (the insured) that compensation (indemnity) will be paid if a particular loss occurs. Insurance companies are businesses, and therefore they charge for their services. The charge they make is called a **premium** and the contract drawn up between the insurer and the insured is known as the **policy**.

The purpose of insurance is to uphold the principle of indemnity, that is, to put someone who has suffered a loss back into the position they would have been in had the loss not been suffered.

Insurance companies are able to **compensate** people and organisations in this way in return for a relatively small charge. This is because insurance 'pools risks'.

Insurance is vital not only to individuals, but to all forms of business and the economy as a whole. If as individuals we had to face all the risks of life ourselves there are many things that we would not do, and at times we would even hesitate about leaving the safety of our homes. Similarly, many businesses would not be formed if individual entrepreneurs and their backers had to face all the risks of enterprise themselves. Insurance relieves individuals and business people from some of the risk they face. In this way it can be seen that insurance helps to promote trade.

Pooling of risks

To offset the possible effect of a loss, all those at risk can contribute a relatively small sum of money (called a

INSURANCE

Fig. 21.1 Pooling risks

- Many businesses at risk contribute money to a pool
- When one of the businesses suffers a loss
- The insurance company will help with finance for repairs

premium) to a fund ('pool') operated by an insurance company. The many small sums of money people pay in premiums form a large pool of money. When a contributor to the pool suffers a loss there is enough money in the pool to compensate ('indemnify') them.

The result of co-operating with others in this way is that risks are 'spread' or 'shared' between the many people and organisations that have contributed to the insurance pool. For this reason insurance is sometimes said to be the 'pooling of risks'.

For example, if a trader owns a shop worth $100,000 and it burns down, it would cause considerable hardship to replace it and it could in fact be impossible to replace it if the owner could not raise the money.

However, if many shop owners agree to pay a regular, relatively small amount of money into a pool, then when one of the shops is burnt down, there will be enough money in the pool to compensate for the loss. What has happened in this example is that the risk has been spread between the many shop owners.

21.3 Uninsurable risks

The success of insurance is dependent upon the ability of insurance companies to meet a loss if it occurs. The companies are able to ensure that they can meet any claims that arise by using statistical analysis.

The people within insurance companies who accept the risks of insurance (**underwriters**) use their records of past claims to calculate the probability of the risk involved occurring.

If it can calculate the probability of an event taking place, an insurance company will be willing to take on the risk involved, and it will be able to calculate how much to charge the customer (the premium). But not all events are insurable. The following are typical examples of uninsurable risks:

- when the loss is inevitable
- where there is insufficient past experience to assess risk
- if the proposer does not have insurable interest

You cannot insure against wear and tear on equipment and property

You cannot insure that you will do well in exams

Fig. 21.2 Uninsurable risks

- against fair wear and tear such as rust and corrosion
- that a business will be successful.

21.4 The principles of insurance

Insurance is successful and trusted because the parties to insurance honour four basic principles. They are the principles of:

- insurable interest
- utmost good faith
- indemnity
- proximate cause.

Insurable interest

With the exception of life assurance (where a husband and wife can insure the life of each other) it is not possible to insure against a risk unless you have an 'insurable interest'. In other words, the insured must be the one that would suffer financially if an event occurred. You can insure the house or car you own, but you cannot insure the car or house of your neighbour. If your neighbour's house burns down you have lost nothing (unless you have some property there, in which case you *would* have insurable interest).

Utmost good faith

This aspect of insurance means that the parties to an insurance contract must be truthful in the declaration they make. Obviously, this ruling affects the proposer more than it does the insurer, because it is the proposer who provides the information upon which the insurer decides the premium and issues a policy.

Indemnity

This is the insurance principle by which a policy-holder is compensated for the loss incurred. There are several important aspects to this principle.

- *No profiteering.* Although we take out insurance to receive some money in compensation should we experience a loss, we are not supposed to make a profit from our claim for compensation. The idea is that the insurance policy should indemnify the insured, in other words return him or her to the financial position before the event took place.

- *Overinsurance.* If the insured overinsures an item (more than its true value), in the event of a loss he or she will only be compensated for the true value.

- *Underinsurance.* If a loss occurs where the item is underinsured, the policy-holder will only receive a proportion of the loss.

  e.g. Shop value　　　$100,000
  　　　Insurance for　　$ 80,000
  　　　Damage by fire　$ 20,000 (i.e. one-fifth)
  　　　Compensation
  　　　(one-fifth)　　　$ 16,000

- *Contribution.* It would be easy for a situation to arise in which a claim could occur where two insurance companies are liable to indemnify the insured for the same event, for example, where two policies overlap. In such a case, both insurance companies will contribute towards payment of the claim.

  The proportion that each insurance company pays will depend upon the amount of insurance placed with each company in relation to the cover. For example, if a building valued at $16,000 (insured with A for $10,000 and with B for $6,000) is burnt down, A will pay 10/16ths and B 6/16ths of the loss.

- *Subrogation.* To subrogate means 'to take the place of'. When an insurance company pays out compensation on a claim, the money they pay out takes the place of the article damaged. For instance, if my car is 'written off' (too badly damaged to be repaired), the insurance company will indemnify me for the value of the car. The money they pay me takes the place of the car and the damaged vehicle now becomes the property of the insurance company, who will sell it and retain the scrap value.

- *Proximate cause.* When an insurance policy covers a particular risk, it is quite possible that damage may be incurred which is not directly related to the terms of the policy, but which still may be indemnified by the insurance company. For example, your house may be covered by fire insurance and, of course, the insurance company would be expected to pay out compensation as a result of a fire; but they will also pay for damage to doors caused by the firemen having to break into the house to fight the fire. However, such a claim will only be allowed if the loss incurred is closely related to the original event. For example, if your car is damaged in an accident and you leave it unattended for a long period of time the insurance company would be expected to pay for repairs to the car, but would not necessarily be expected to pay for a travel rug stolen from the back seat.

Fig. 21.3 Contribution to insurance

21.5 Types of insurance

There are four broad types of insurance: life, marine, fire and accident.

Fig. 21.4 Limitations of insurance

Life assurance

This type of cover is often referred to as 'assurance' rather than 'insurance'. At one time 'insurance' and 'assurance' had different meanings. Insurance was against a risk which might or might not happen, whilst assurance concerned an event which was inevitable (death or reaching a particular age). Today this difference is less important, but the word 'assurance' is still often used in relation to life policies.

There are two main types of life assurance: whole life and endowment.

1 *Whole life* policies provide for a payment after the death of the insured. Premiums are usually paid quarterly or annually by the person whose life is insured or by their spouse. The idea is that when the insured dies, someone will benefit from the policy, e.g. a spouse or dependent.

2 *Endowment* policies provide for a payment of a basic sum at a certain age or on the death of the insured, whichever occurs first. This provides not only for the dependents, but also a useful sum of money for the insured if he or she survives the period covered by the policy. A variation of this type of policy is one 'with profits' which, for a higher premium, entitles the insured to a share in the profits of the insurance company.

Marine insurance

This covers loss and damage to ships and their cargoes. Today, aircraft insurance also falls within this category. There are four broad categories of marine insurance.

1 *Hull insurance* covers damage to the vessel itself and all its machinery and fixtures.

2 *Cargo insurance* covers the cargo the ship is carrying.

3 *Freight insurance*: it is customary for an insurance policy to be taken out to cover the possibility that for some reason the shipper does not pay the transport (freight) charges to the shipowner.

4 *Shipowner's liability*: the owner of a vessel has to insure himself or herself against a wide variety of events, for example collision with other vessels or a dock, injury to crew members or passengers, and pollution of beaches.

Fire insurance

Fire insurance, as the name suggests, primarily covers fire risks. But many policies combine cover with other risks such as theft, storm, flood and lightning.

This form of insurance can include cover for loss of earnings (e.g. by a business) or for rental of alternative property whilst a building damaged by fire is being repaired.

Fire policies exclude certain special conditions such as fire resulting from earthquake or riots. In addition, items of high value (paintings, jewellery, antiques, etc.) must be insured separately.

Accident insurance

All insurance not contained within the foregoing categories is included under accident insurance. This type of insurance covers a wide range of policies. The following are the main examples.

Motor
Any vehicle taken on public roads is required to have a certain minimum level (third party) of insurance to ensure that drivers can meet their liability for injury to others. The two commonest types of motor insurance are as follows.

1 *Third party, fire and theft*: the motorist insures the liability for damage to other people and their property, plus the loss of damage to his or her own car through fire or theft.

2 *Comprehensive* policies not only give the above third party, fire and theft cover, but also provide compensation for accidental damage to the vehicle of the insured.

Personal accident and sickness
These are policies which can be taken out against death or disability in special circumstances, for example during holidays, flights, etc.

Liability
This type of policy covers the risk of liability for the injury or death of someone else. There are two main forms.

1 *Employer's liability* covers the employer's legal liability for the safety of each employee.

2 *Public liability* covers the liability of individuals and businesses for members of the public visiting their premises.

Property
Property insurance covers a wide variety of items from goods in transit or in store to buildings or contents. Applies to both the business person and the private householder.

Credit
This covers against losses resulting from bad debts, for example the failure of customers to pay for goods obtained on credit.

Fidelity
Fidelity insurance is used particularly by businesses to protect against loss by fraud and stealing by employees.

Insurance for business
The types of insurance cover business people might consider taking out would be as follows:

- employer's liability
- public liability
- damage to premises
- stock damage
- consequential loss (earnings)
- theft, burglary
- motor fleet
- bad debts
- product liability.

Business interruption
This is sometimes called '**consequential loss**' insurance. It provides insurance covering the loss of earnings of a business following a fire or some other specified damage. Business may have to be suspended for a time, resulting in a loss of earnings for both the owners of the firm and

the employees. This insurance cover is available for such losses, and the cover can include loss of wages, rent and the cost of temporary alternative accommodation.

21.6 The insurance contract

Insurance is provided by insurance companies, friendly societies, underwriters and the government (national insurance). Non-government insurance may be taken out through agents working for a particular company or through brokers selling insurance for a number of different companies. Whichever approach is used a similar basic procedure is followed.

The prospectus

If you visit the offices of an insurance company to find out what insurance policies they have to sell, it would take them too long to explain all the different forms of cover they have available. To save time, the insurance companies produce a leaflet, called the prospectus, which explains each type of policy that can be taken out with them.

The proposal

To formulate an agreement between the **insured** (the person buying insurance) and the **insurer** (the person selling insurance), it must be made clear what is being insured, in other words what risk is being covered, and how much the cover is going to cost. The precise details of what is required are given initially by filling out a proposal form.

As its name suggests, the proposal form tells the insurance company what risk the person buying insurance proposes to insure against. In other words it is a suggestion by the insured that he or she would like the insurance company to agree with.

It is essential that the proposer (the one who wants to buy insurance) gives every detail which applies to the risk, and conceals nothing. If what insurers call a 'material fact' is concealed, the policy will be ineffective.

The premium

When the insurance company has received the proposal form from the person wishing to take out insurance, the underwriters of the insurance company will work out how much they will charge to cover the risk being insured. This charge is called the **premium**, and to put insurance cover into effect, the person buying insurance cover pays the premium.

In calculating the premium for the cover, there are many points to take into consideration, and one of them is obviously the value of the item being insured. Another is the risk: an insurance company might charge 10% for one risk (say the stock of a factory) and 5% for another risk (say the buildings of the factory) to the same customer, because one risk is greater than the other. In such a case the premium on a $20,000 risk at 10% would be $2,000 and the premium on a $100,000 risk at 5% would be $5,000.

The insurance specialist statistician who calculates the premium based on the degree of risk is called an **actuary**.

The policy

This is a document sent by the insurer to the insured which states what has been agreed between the two parties. It is like a contract agreement. Many people find policies confusing because of the 'small print', which refers to the 'rules', clauses and 'exceptions' to the agreement, but in spite of the confusion it is important that you read this part of the policy and question the person selling the insurance about any point you do not understand. Failure to read policies, or ask for explanations, is the biggest cause of misunderstanding about insurance.

The following documents may also be issued in association with the insurance policy.

- *Certificate of insurance*: for employer's liability and for motor insurance, the law requires evidence that the insurance has been put into effect. A certificate issued by the insurer acts as evidence.

- *Cover note*: this is a temporary document provided whilst the certificate of insurance is being prepared.

- *Endorsement*: this is a notice of an amendment to the policy, usually by the insurer. The endorsement is attached to the policy and from then on becomes a part of the policy.

- *Renewal notice*: this is issued by the insurer prior to the expiry date of the insurance cover, inviting the insured to renew the cover and advising of the renewal premium and the date on which it is due.

The claim

If the risk insured against takes place, the insured completes a claim form and submits this to the insurer for consideration. **Loss adjusters** are frequently engaged by insurers to ensure that claims are settled fairly from the point of view of both the insured and the insurer.

The insurance company will only compensate the insured if the loss has been truly accidental; for example one cannot expect an insurance company to pay out on a claim for damage to a car through accident if the accident occurred because the vehicle was not kept in good order.

In making a payment against a claim the insurance company will only compensate for the **current value** of the item which has been lost or damaged. For example, if a housewife claims for the replacement of a carpet purchased five years ago and now damaged by fire, she will receive the current replacement price less an amount calculated to represent the five years' use she has had of the carpet. A modern development is 'new for old' policies, which give the claimants the value of the goods as new. These policies do of course cost more in premiums.

21.7 THINGS TO DO

This section contains a variety of exercises to help you create revision notes, to test your understanding and to prepare you for examinations.

Search and find

Write out the question and the answer by referring back through the text to form revision notes.

1 What is the purpose of insurance?
2 Explain how insurance encourages business activity.
3 In what way does insurance 'pool risks'?
4 Why are some risks uninsurable? Give four examples.
5 In what way can insurance be said to have a statistical basis?
6 Explain, giving an example, the meaning of 'insurable interest'.
7 Why does the insurance principle 'utmost good faith' affect the insured more than the insurer?
8 Insurance is said to be a contract of indemnity. What does this mean?
9 What do the terms 'contribution' and 'subrogation' mean in relation to insurance?
10 Giving an example, explain the insurance principle of proximate cause.
11 Why is life insurance often referred to as 'assurance'?
12 Name the four broad categories of insurance.
13 In relation to insurance, explain the terms 'whole life', 'endowment', and 'with profits'.
14 The word 'freight' is often used to refer to the cargo a ship is carrying. So, what is the difference between freight insurance and cargo insurance?
15 What sort of special conditions are excluded from fire insurance?
16 Define accident insurance.
17 Briefly explain the differences between third party; third party, fire and theft; and comprehensive motor insurance.
18 Why would the owner of a shop be likely to take out both employer's liability and public liability insurance?
19 Briefly describe four types of insurance not dealt with so far that you feel would be essential to a business. Give reasons for each of your choices.
20 Describe the process of putting an insurance contract into effect, including mention of the documents and any payments involved.

What do you know?

Write out the complete sentence and insert the missing word, which can be chosen from the list at the end of the questions.

1 Cover for ships and their cargoes falls under the category of . . . . . insurance.
2 Insurance that covers against loss of life is sometimes referred to as . . . . . .
3 Motor vehicle insurance comes under the category of . . . . . insurance.
4 The purpose of insurance is to provide monetary . . . . . to someone who has suffered a loss.
5 Those that take out insurance cover contribute money to a . . . . . .
6 An insurance company will only agree to provide cover if it can . . . . . the frequency with which an event could occur.
7 You cannot insure against a risk unless you have an insurable . . . . . .
8 In the event of a loss, the insured will fill out a . . . . . form.

9 Before they pay out a against a claim the insurance company may send a ..... to verify that the amount claimed is fair.

10 When two insurance companies are liable to indemnify against the same claim they each ..... towards the payment.

> Choose the missing words from the following:
>
> interest   contribute   pool   claim
> marine   assurance   loss adjuster   accident
> predict   compensation

Multiple choice

Select the appropriate answer, a, b, c or d.

1 The sum of money paid regularly to an insurance company by the policy-holder is called:
   a) a premium
   b) a claim
   c) a proposal
   d) a policy

2 Insurance protection against loss caused by fraud is called:
   a) national insurance
   b) burglary insurance
   c) accident insurance
   d) fidelity insurance

3 The principle of insurance that requires all information to be truthfully given is known as:
   a) subrogation
   b) proximate cause
   c) utmost good faith
   d) insurable interest

4 The temporary document issued whilst the policy is being prepared is called:
   a) proposal
   b) cover note
   c) claim
   d) renewal notice

5 Which one of the following terms represents the person engaged by insurance companies to ensure claims are settled fairly?
   a) broker
   b) agent
   c) underwriter
   d) loss adjuster

6 Which of the following statements is untrue?
   a) a business can insure against making a loss
   b) a broker sells the policies of many companies
   c) an agent works for a single company
   d) a business can insure against a flood

7 A man insured his shop for $60,000 but its true value was $80,000. A fire has caused $8,000 of damage. The insurance company will pay out:
   a) $6,000
   b) $3,750
   c) $5,000
   d) $4,200

8 In which of the following types of production would an insurance broker be engaged?
   a) primary
   b) secondary
   c) tertiary
   d) market

9 'Pooling of risks' means that:
   a) insurance companies share each other's risks
   b) money paid in premiums provides compensation
   c) all claims are collected together
   d) there must be insurable interest

10 Which of the following forms of insurance is compulsory?
   a) fidelity insurance
   b) business interruption insurance
   c) property insurance
   d) motor vehicle insurance

> **Key words**
>
> Find out the business-related meaning of each of the following words. Write a separate sentence for each word to show your understanding.
>
> insurance   proposal   prospectus   policy
> indemnify   subrogation   insurer   insured
>   compensation   liability

Structured questions

1 Figure 21.5 shows typical questions that are asked when someone is completing a proposal for car insurance.

> 1. What is your age?
> 2. Address where your car is kept.
> 3. What make and model of car?
> 4. What is the size of the car engine?
> 5. Has the engine been altered to increase its performance?
> 6. What is the year of registration?
> 7. Is the car normally kept in a garage?
> 8. How long have you been a qualified driver?
> 9. Is your car used for business purposes?
> 10. Will the vehicle be driven by any driver who is under 25?
> 11. Has any proposed driver of the car had any driving convictions in the last ten years?
> 12. What sort of cover do you want for your car?

Fig. 21.5   Proposal form questions

a) Why is the insurance company interested in the age of the proposer for motor insurance? (2)

b) Explain the relevance of Questions 4 and 5 to the premium that will be charged. (4)

c) Describe three types of motor insurance cover that it is possible to obtain. (6)

d) Take any four questions from the list not considered so far, and explain the purpose of including them on a motor insurance proposal form. Try to choose questions that deal with different factors that influence the amount of premium to be charged. (8)

2 Look at the newspaper article in figure 21.6, and answer the questions that follow.

FACTORY BLAZE

Fire has wiped out the factory of Tower Toys Ltd. on the Barn Mills Industrial Estate just weeks before the Christmas rush. The Chief Fire Officer said that the fire was caused by an electrical fault in a storeroom and quickly spread throughout the factory.

A spokesman for Tower Toys said that extensive damage to buildings, machinery and stock means that production will be suspended for at least two months. No one was hurt in the fire.

Fig. 21.6 News of a factory fire

a) Give an example of how the insurance principle of 'proximate cause' might apply in relation to the above event. (2)

b) Explain the effect on the insured's claim:
  (i) if the building was overinsured
  (ii) if the building was underinsured. (4)

c) The manufacturer referred to in the newspaper article was covered by both fire insurance and business interruption insurance. Describe the kind of things the manufacturer might claim for against each of these forms of insurance cover. (6)

d) The owner of this business would be required by law to have employers' liability insurance and he may also have public liability insurance. Give a brief description of each of these types of cover. (8)

BUSINESS NEWS

THE DANGER OF BEING UNDERINSURED

In a recent case two workmen employed by a firm were removing a large boiler from a cheese-processing plant. The workmen secured a rope around one of the pillars supporting the factory. As a result the building collapsed causing $500,000 of damage, and the manufacturer had to close down the plant for several weeks.

The company presented a claim to its insurers for the repairs to the plant, and for the cost of the loss of business. But the insurers would only meet 80% of the value of the claim because the firm were underinsured. Although the firm took a variety of measures to find the shortfall, they could not make the balance from their resources. And financial institutions were unwilling to lend money to a business that was in fact standing idle.

Within three months the firm was forced into bankruptcy, and what had been a thriving business employing 15 workers ceased to exist.

Fig. 21.7 Danger of underinsurance

3 Look at the article in figure 12.7, taken from the business section of a newspaper, and answer these questions.

a) What is the purpose of insurance? (2)

b) What is meant by underinsurance? (2)

c) Why is insurance unable to fulfil its main purpose in the example in this article? (3)

d) State at least three different categories of insurance which a business will generally need but which a private individual will not require. (3)

e) Briefly describe how the insurance company will have decided that it can only meet 80% of the cost of the claim of the dairy producer. Why not 85%? (4)

f) What led to the failure of the firm? How could this have been avoided? (6)

4 a) Explain what is meant by saying that insurance is based on 'pooling' of risks. (2)

b) Name two types of insurance which are compulsory by law. Name two types of insurance which are voluntary. (4)

c) Certain principles apply to all insurance contracts. Name three of these principles and explain fully what they mean for a person seeking insurance. Give an example in each case to show how these principles work. (6)

d) Explain fully four of the following terms associated with obtaining insurance: proposal, premium, policy, cover note, agents, brokers. (8)

5 a) In relation to insurance, briefly describe the meaning of the following terms:
   (i) indemnity (2)
   (ii) utmost good faith (2)
   (iii) insurable interest (2)
   (iv) premium. (2)

b) State one type of insurance which you would particularly recommend for each of the following. Give a different example in each case and explain the reason for your choice.
   (i) A factory engaged in manufacturing a highly inflammable product. (3)
   (ii) A firm employing six sales representatives each of whom drives a company car. (3)
   (iii) A shop employing people handling large amounts of cash. (3)
   (iv) A partner in a firm of solicitors. (3)

6 Table 21.1 is a simplified version of the type of table that an insurance company would issue to its agents to help them quote a premium for life assurance cover. The table shows that at 30 years of age a man is expected to live another 44.9 years, i.e. to 74.9 years of age.

a) What is the term for the insurance worker who calculates the statistics in a table such as this? (1)

b) If a man has reached forty years of age, what is his expectation of further life and to what age can he expect to live? (2)

c) To take out life assurance you are charged a premium. What factors other than age are considered in the calculation of this premium? (3)

d) Explain the differences the table shows between male and female life expectancy, and say why you think this difference exists. (6)

e) Give a clear explanation of the difference between insurance and assurance using examples to illustrate your explanation. (8)

Table 21.1 *Expectation of life table*

Years of age	Further expectation of life	
NOW	MALE	FEMALE
20	54.6	58.3
25	49.9	53.6
30	44.9	48.8
35	40.1	44.0
40	35.3	39.1
45	30.6	34.3
50	26.1	29.7
55	21.9	25.3

Research assignments

1 'Insurance is based on statistics.' Explain this statement, giving specific examples of the kind of information insurance companies use in calculating premiums.

2 How important is insurance to economies in the Caribbean region?

3 a) On the news the weather forecasters stated that recently installed computerised forecasting equipment will enable them to give reliable 24 hours' notice of weather conditions. In what ways could this help to reduce insurance claims?

b) What evidence can you find of other specific factors that influence the number of insurance claims?

Chapter 22
NATIONAL ACCOUNTS

22.1 The standard of living

What is the standard of living?

The term **standard of living** refers to the quality of life that the people of a country have: the types of house they live in, the quality of food they eat, the clothes they wear and so on. Obviously, standard of living is dependent upon the work people do and the wages they receive. Even the methods that workers use to travel are seen as contributing to the standard of living, as are methods of communication used and the entertainment that they have ready access to. The level of education the population receives is also seen as important.

The standard of living is often reflected in the average lifespan of the people of a country. It is likely that people who live where there is a high standard of living will generally live longer than those who have a poor standard of living.

Look at the table 22.1, which contains data relating to the average life expectancy of people in a number of countries. What reasons can you give to explain the differences that exist between countries and between the sexes?

Table 22.1 *Average life expectancy*

Country	Male	Female
Afghanistan	43	42
Barbados	73	77
Great Britain	72	78
Grenada	69	74
Jamaica	75	78
Libya	64	69
Madagascar	50	53
Nigeria	47	49

It is generally the case that countries with a poorer standard of living are located in the tropics, whilst countries which have higher living standards are found in the colder areas. This does not mean that standard of living is a result of temperature: it is very much to do with the stage of development that the country has reached, and the resources it has available. And, of course, the way that these resources are developed affects the standard of living.

Cost of living

As you can imagine, measuring the standard of living is a formidable task because there are so many factors involved, and some of these are difficult to quantify. Some of the main methods of measuring national prosperity will be examined shortly, but the **cost of living** gives some indication of the quality of life of people, and how it is changing from one year to another.

The cost of living refers to how much can be bought with a person's net income (after deduction of income tax). Measuring the cost of living is important because it is continually changing, and therefore it shows whether 'real' income is changing. In other words, are people better or worse off, taking into consideration rising costs and income increases? Measurement of the cost of living is achieved by constructing a 'price index'. There is more than one type of price index, but the most popular and more generally well known is the 'consumer price index' (CPI).

The CPI is made up of the prices of goods and services purchased by consumers. It is often used in the Caribbean and other parts of the world as a basis for negotiating wage increases. The object of this is to ensure that workers' wages maintain a constant or increasing value in 'real' terms.

A 'cost of living index' is constructed by taking the total value of a collection of items purchased by consumers in a particular year, which is referred to as the 'base year'. We say that the index figure for that year, say 1995, is 100. The same items are subsequently valued periodically (usually annually) and general price movements can be plotted on a graph similar to the imaginary one shown in figure 22.1.

Depending upon whether each new plotted position is above or below the base line, it is possible not only to know whether prices have generally risen or fallen, but

Fig. 22.1 Cost of living index

also to establish an approximation of the percentage change. The change can then be checked against wage rises, in order to establish whether workers end up better off in real terms.

Useful though it is, a cost of living index gives only a limited indication of the state of the economy of a country. Statistics included in the national accounts are a more revealing indication of the state of the economy.

22.2 National income

Economic growth refers to an increase in the output of all things we consume, use, invest in or otherwise produce. Economic growth is important because it usually means that the country is increasing its wealth, and probably improving its living standards. One way to assess economic growth is through measurement of the national income.

What is national income?

Imagine you were asked to calculate the total income of your family for the year: how would you go about doing so? You would probably add together the total yearly income of each member of the household, including any return received from savings or investments. But there are other ways of reaching the same figure. For example, it can also be obtained by adding together the total amount spent and the total amount saved by each member of the family in the year. You should understand that both methods reach the same answer because both look at the same amount of money, but in a different way. The national income of a country can also be assessed in a similar way.

If you were asked to assess your income, you would refer to wages and other returns which add to your wealth. You would not count money you invested in the building society last year, but you would include the interest you received this year. Income is a *flow*, and not a stock of money or equipment. National income is concerned with new additions to the wealth of the country for a specific period (normally a year).

Fig. 22.2 Circular flow of income

There are three approaches that can be used to measure the national income, and all the methods should reach the same answer because (in a way) they are all measuring the same thing.

1 *Income method*: the aggregate value of all forms of income, including personal incomes, profits of firms, rents, etc.

2 *Output method*: the total net output of every form of production, taking care not to count any output twice. 'Net' in this case implies subtracting an allowance for capital consumption (depreciation — fall in value due to wear and tear) on all buildings and machinery.

3 *Expenditure method*: the total value of all expenditure by consumers, firms and the government.

National income accounting problems

Quite apart from the obvious difficulty of data collection, there are a variety of problems associated with the foregoing methods of national income measurement. The following are some of these problems.

Money terms
It is not possible to add together things such as tons of fish, bottles of wine and thousands of tractors. To evaluate items such as these we have to express them in money terms. But the value of money is constantly changing, and inflation can cause it incorrectly to appear that national income is increasing. What is important is the real increase in national income, and to establish this requires allowances to be made for the changing value of money.

Double-counting
Double-counting can occur when output is considered. If timber is included in output measurement, should furniture made from timber also be included? The answer to this difficulty is that each firm should only count the value added to products by its activities. Theoretically this avoids counting output more than once, but in effect the result is still not a very precise measurement.

The 'informal' economy
Babysitting, bartending, taxi driving and car repairs are typical examples of jobs that are sometimes being done 'on the side', that is, without the Inland Revenue knowing about them, because the income is not declared for tax purposes. The work is usually done for cash rather than cheque payment, and for a charge lower than for 'official' work. Activities such as these are sometimes called the 'hidden' or 'underground' economy, but most commonly they are referred to as part of the informal economy.

Probably every developed country has its own informal economy, and in some countries it is so substantial that it props up the official economy. It has been estimated that the informal economy adds almost a third to the gross national product.

The informal economy is to be condemned because tax evasion by some in this way increases the tax burden of others. However, more important here is the fact that the informal economy creates a problem for recording domestic statistics. The main source of information for the income method is the Inland Revenue, but we have seen that the informal economy means that a large proportion of income is not recorded.

Uses of national income statistics

The final national income figure is only an estimate, because of the foregoing and other accounting difficulties which result in discrepancies. However, in spite of all the difficulties in measuring national income, the figures have several uses.

1 *Change in living standards.* Most governments use national income statistics to indicate changes in living standards.

2 *Comparison with other countries.* National income figures enable comparisons to be made between one country and another.

3 *Economic growth.* A comparison can be made between one year and another in respect of economic growth.

4 *Instrument of economic planning.* The figures provide the government with information which can be used to assess the effectiveness or otherwise of its past policies. This information can then be used in the planning of the economy, and implementation of the redistribution of wealth.

National income and standard of living

In order to get a general idea of the standard of living of a country, we divide the national income by the population, and the resulting figure is called **per capita income**. This figure allows us to make comparisons, for example, between the standard of living of one country and that of another. But such comparisons must be treated with caution.

Whilst national income is of vital importance in determining our standard of living, a high national income does not necessarily mean a high standard of living exists generally. It does not show how the income is distributed.

To illustrate this point, let us imagine that there is a Middle Eastern country called Hullabahoo, and that that country has experienced dramatic economic growth because of the discovery of vast deposits of oil five years ago. If Sheik Shinpad, ruler of the state of Hullabahoo, receives the vast majority of the national income, the country may be earning more, but its people will see little improvement in their living standards. Therefore, the way that the wealth is **distributed** is just as important to the population as the national income.

Although per capita income provides a useful indicator of the standard of living of a country, apart from ignoring the distribution of income, it has the following shortcomings. These have to be taken into account when making comparisons using per capita income.

1. There are variances in prices from one year to another, and between one country and another.
2. It does not take into account the effect government spending (e.g. on defence) has on national income.
3. It is possible that increased national income has resulted from increased working hours.

Factors influencing national income

Economic growth is important for increased national prosperity, but this is influenced by many factors, the following of which are particularly crucial.

1. *National resources*: the availability of resources such as fertile land and good climate, and how effectively these are used.
2. *Industrial development*: how well-equipped and technically advanced industry and commerce is.
3. *Quality of the labour force*: the size and health of the working population and the skills it has.
4. *Economic stability*: the extent to which economic activity is spread over a wide range of industries.
5. *Political stability*: political unrest will adversely affect investment and the achievement of economic objectives.

22.3 Gross national product (GNP)

When we looked at the output method of measuring national income earlier, we said that an allowance was made for 'capital consumption' or loss in value (depreciation) of buildings and machinery. In other words, in the case of national income measurement we only know the total production output after taking away that allowance. But in national accounting, it is useful to be able to measure the total value of all things actually produced in a country, that is, a figure which does not include a reduction for capital consumption.

In most countries, the principle measure of the total output of the country is called **gross national product** (GNP). The word 'gross' indicates that no deduction has been made for capital consumption.

The word 'national' in this instance does not imply that GNP is the total output produced within the borders of a particular country. The GNP measure includes some output taking place and produced by resources owned by people from other countries. Clearly, this outflow cannot be counted as part of our national income. At the same time, some sources of output are situated in other countries but owned by the citizens of the country in question. Therefore, the GNP can be defined as the total output of all the resources owned by residents of the country, wherever the resources themselves are situated.

The total output actually produced within the borders of a country is called the **gross domestic product** (GDP). GDP can be defined as the output of all resources located within the country, wherever the owners of the resources happen to live. In a similar manner to GNP, the GDP becomes *net* domestic product when an allowance for depreciation is deducted from it. In many ways, GDP is the more important measure.

National income of Noland
Simple imaginary analysis by expenditure method

	$ billions
Consumer expenditure	168.2
Public authorities expenditure	60.1
Gross domestic fixed capital investment	43.5
Value of physical increase in stocks	2.1
Exports of goods and services	73.3
Total final expenditure	347.2
less imports of goods and services	– 67.1
less taxes	– 38.3
plus subsidies	+ 4.1
Gross domestic product	245.9
Net property income from abroad	+ 2.2
Gross national product	248.1
less capital consumption	– 36.9
National income	211.2

The national cake

The amount of wealth or gross national product a country generates each year is sometimes referred to as

Fig. 22.3 Where the national wealth comes from

the **national cake**. The national wealth 'cake' is made up of contributions from various parts of the economy, including commercial activities such as services, distributive trades and transport, together with important contributions from industrial production and agriculture, fishing, etc.

Wealth in this sense is more than a stock of money and possessions. Wealth is the total of what the economy produces each year in the form of goods such as clothing and food, and services such as those of doctors or teachers. We normally find it convenient to measure wealth in money terms, but this can create problems, because not all wealth can be counted in money terms. For example, how do we put a precise value on the quality of education, medical care or environment? And yet sometimes the effect of things such as these can be greater and more important than the production of goods, to which we normally attribute wealth.

The well-known saying 'you cannot have your cake and eat it' is undoubtedly true, and yet many people want to do just this. As a country we cannot have what we have not earned; we cannot eat more cake than we have. Consequently, the bigger the slice of the cake one person or group takes, the less there is left to distribute to others. Clearly, we must make a bigger cake before we can distribute bigger slices from it. This is often the source of a continual wrangle between governments, employers and workers over demands for wage increases.

22.4 National expenditure

Whilst the gross national product tells us what was produced in a country, national expenditure tells us who bought what was produced. We can say that national expenditure is the sum of the following.

1. *Private expenditure*: this includes every kind of consumption spending by the population, from food and clothing to cars and entertainment (but excluding the purchase of homes).
2. *Public expenditure*: central and local government spending on goods and services, for example salaries of teachers and soldiers, provision of pensions and family benefits, etc., (but excluding capital expenditure on durable assets such as buildings).
3. *Gross domestic capital formation* (GDCF): this refers to the total investment by business firms, public enterprises and public authorities in new fixed capital such as new plant and equipment, buildings, ships and other durable means of production. The purchase of new dwelling houses is also included in GDCF.
4. *Overseas trading*: the effect of the net differences between the value of a country's exports and imports of goods and services (balance of payments).

From the foregoing it can be seen that national expenditure is necessarily identical in value with the national product, because it is merely another way of classifying the same information.

Public expenditure

This term refers to government spending. Some of this spending is carried out by local government, but by far the greatest expenditure is carried out by central government. In fact, so great is government expenditure that any cutbacks it implements can have a serious effect on employment statistics.

The following are typical of just some of the needs of a country that are met from public expenditure.

- *Defence*: maintenance of defence systems, army, navy and airforce.
- *Medical care*: provision of hospitals, doctors, dentists, etc.
- *Education*: the provision of basic, primary, secondary and further education.
- *Law, order and protective services*: the courts, police and fire services are the major items.
- *Environmental services*: water, sanitation etc.
- *Roads and transport*: government is almost the sole provider of roads and makes contributions to other transport facilities.
- *Grants and subsidies*: given to help develop or support key sectors of the economy.
- *Social services*: provision of many facilities such as benefits for the elderly, unemployed, sick etc.
- *Debt interest*: when the government spends more than it obtains through taxation it has to borrow. The total amount owed is known as the **national debt**. The government has to pay interest on this debt.

22.5 National debt

If you spend more than you earn you will end up in debt. There are two ways you can put the matter right. You can earn more, or you can borrow to pay off the debt. In the latter case you are creating another debt, but delaying ultimate payment. The government faces a similar problem.

Each year the government prepares the **budget**, in which it plans the next year's government revenue and expenditure. If expenditure equals revenue the budget is in **balance**. When income exceeds expenditure a **surplus** has been created, and a **deficit** results when expenditure exceeds income.

The **public sector borrowing requirement** (PSBR) indicates the extent to which the government borrows from other sectors of the economy and from overseas to balance its deficit on the expenditure and revenue accounts. The PSBR is an important indicator of how the government's policies are affecting the economy.

In many countries, the PSBR is partly satisfied through public sale of government stocks (see Chapter 16) at home and overseas, but much has to come from other sources. The national debt is the total amount owed by the government to people both in the home country and in other countries.

Wherever there is a budget deficit, the PSBR bridges the gap and results in an increase in the national debt. For most countries the national debt has accumulated over many years and today the total is so huge that it is no longer possible for it to be repaid, although it is important to restrict growth of the debt as far as possible.

22.6 Growth and development

Growth refers to an all-round expansion of the economy. It is concerned with the *quantitative* increases in the country's output. It is concerned with the *rate* of economic change, e.g. increase in tourism, increase in sugar production, increased construction of roads, building of more schools, etc.

Growth can be measured by changes in GNP, which reflects general increases in total net output. **Negative growth** means that the country is doing less well than in the previous year, **zero growth** indicates that there has been no change when compared with previous years. All governments are keen to see their countries achieve growth, because it generally results in an improved standard of living and greater economic and political stability.

Development is not the same as growth. It is a qualitative concept and is more concerned with the *pattern* of economic change. Development refers to the provision of facilities that enable growth to take place, for instance the availability of resources such as machinery and of a workforce with appropriate education and skills. Often development takes place in just some sectors of the economy, but provides thrust for other sectors. In order to have development, there must be growth. However, there may be growth but no development. Highly developed countries are better able to exploit their natural resources than underdeveloped countries, and consequently more advanced economies have a better standard of living.

An underdeveloped country tends to have the following features:

1. Poor economic performance.
2. High rate of population growth.
3. Low standard of living.
4. Relatively short life expectancy.
5. High unemployment.
6. Considerable dependency upon agricultural employment.
7. Poor educational opportunities.

Many (but not all) European countries, the United States, Japan and Australia are examples of highly developed economies. By contrast, most underdeveloped countries are situated in Asia and Africa. The Caribbean countries are part way between the two extremes. They are sometimes referred to as 'developing countries'.

Economic growth

Economic growth is the goal of all governments, and it is affected by the following factors.

- *Investment.* Capital accumulation and the use of capital to create further wealth through the provision of capital or equipment is essential to economic growth. For this reason, the government is keen to encourage saving and investment, and will also allocate a large share of its resources to development.

- *Technical progress.* Economic growth is promoted by the exploitation of technical development so that increased productivity can be achieved with the same resources. For this to take place the workforce must have the skills to take full advantage of new technology. Consequently, there must be adequate investment in education as well as technology.

- *Balance of payments.* A persistent adverse balance of payments will hinder growth and development. A continued unfavourable balance will 'bleed' the country of the capital that it needs to direct towards development and growth. It will also have the effect of discouraging capital inflows from overseas investors, who will be more interested in investing in more stable economies with healthy balance of payments positions.

- *Government expenditure.* Government spending is so extensive that it has the power to stimulate particular sectors of the economy when carefully directed. Public expenditure should be used, at least in part, to stimulate those sectors of the economy that will assist future output.

Development in the Caribbean

Caribbean economies are developing at a slow and uneven pace. This is due to problems of **economic dualism** referred to earlier in this book (see Chapter 2). Economic dualism results from a situation in which the economy is divided into two distinct sectors — one that can be said to be *advanced*, and one that is *backward*.

The **advanced sector** usually employs modern technological means, concepts, methods and procedures. This is seen in areas such as mining, manufacturing, hospitality and tourism, the financial sector including insurance and building societies, among other areas; while the **backward sector** continues to use old or outdated technology and other modes of operation that give rise to inefficiency. Backwardness in terms of productive activity can be seen in small farming and the craft industry, among other areas. Yet, these sectors coexist and somehow need each other.

The hospitality and tourism sector and the agricultural sector are two examples of this idea of economic dualism. The hospitality and tourism sector boasts modern methods of operation and thus produces a high quality product and service. The agricultural sector, on the other hand, especially in the area of small farming, does not enjoy the quality of technology and services employed by the hospitality and tourism sector. As a result, the needs of the hospitality and tourism sector are not adequately addressed by the agricultural sector, and this causes the sector to rely on businesses outside the region to provide the goods and services it needs. Where this happens, the small farmers and eventually the agricultural sector as a whole suffer, and economic dualism, which is undesirable, will continue to exist.

Therefore, clear linkage between the hospitality and tourism sector and the agricultural sector as a whole should be established. These sectors should be appropriately linked so that they each depend on the other for economic support.

The characteristics of underdevelopment in the Caribbean

1 Rapid population growth and high levels of unemployment due to the inability of countries to provide jobs in the quantity needed at any one time.

2 Low rates of income as a result of poor economic returns.

3 Low standards of living.

4 Inadequate educational facilities to provide people with the skills and competencies needed to support modern economic activities.

5 Worsening terms of trade in traditional agricultural areas such as banana and sugar in which large numbers of persons have invested, and areas on which many persons depend for employment, whether seasonal or not.

22.7 THINGS TO DO

This section contains a variety of exercises to help you create revision notes, to test your understanding and to prepare you for examinations.

Search and find

Write out the question and the answer by referring back through the text to form revision notes.

1 'The cost of living is just one aspect of the standard of living.' Explain this statement.

2 What is the consumer price index?

3 How is a consumer price index constructed?

4 Define national income.

5 What do we mean when we say that income is a 'flow' and not a 'stock' of wealth?

6 Describe the three methods of measuring national income.

7 What are the problems of measuring national income?

8 What useful purpose is there in measuring national income?

9 Define the term 'per capita' income.

10 'Rising national income does not necessarily imply a rising standard of living.' Discuss this statement.

11 List the factors that influence national income.

12 Define gross national product and say how this figure differs from national income.

13 The gross national product is sometimes referred to as the national 'cake'. What makes up the national cake?

Why is it true to say that we cannot 'have our cake and eat it'?

14 What is 'national expenditure'?

15 What is the national debt and why does it exist? To whom is the debt owed?

16 In what way is growth different from development?

17 How does 'zero' growth differ from 'negative' growth?

18 Give simple definitions to show the difference between an underdeveloped country, a developing country and a highly developed country.

19 Why are all governments keen to see economic growth?

20 Simply state the main factors that affect economic growth.

21 What do you understand by the term *economic dualism* in respect of the Caribbean region?

What do you know?

Write out the complete sentence and insert the missing words, which can be chosen from the list at the end of the questions.

1 The standard of living refers to the ..... of life that the people of a country have.

2 The cost of living refers to how much can be bought with a person's net ......

3 Economic growth is important because it usually means that the country is increasing its .....

4 Work that is done unofficially is sometimes referred to as part of the ..... economy.

5 Whilst national income is important, it does not necessarily mean a high standard of ..... exists.

6 Gross national product is the total ..... of all the resources owned by the residents of a country.

7 The total amount a government owes is known as the national .....

8 The public sector borrowing requirement indicates the extent to which the ..... borrows from other sources.

9 More ..... economies tend to have a good standard of living.

10 Economic growth is promoted by the exploitation of ..... developments to increase productivity.

Choose the missing words from the following:

| technical | quality | output | informal | debt |
| advanced | living | government | income | wealth |

Multiple choice

Select the appropriate answer, a, b, c or d.

1 The government achieves a budget surplus when it:
   a) spends more than it receives in revenue
   b) spends less than it receives in revenue
   c) reduces spending but increases revenue
   d) reduces revenue but increases spending

2 A consumer price index 'base' year is:
   a) the year when the index was lowest
   b) the year when the index was highest
   c) another term for standard of living
   d) indicated by the figure 100

3 In national accounting, GNP shows:
   a) how much the government owes
   b) what the government is spending revenue on
   c) the total output of the country
   d) the total revenue the government receives

4 Economic growth is important because it usually means that the country is increasing its:
   a) output   c) exports
   b) expenditure   d) consumption

5 Which of the following is the most appropriate definition of the cost of living?
   a) the quality of life of people
   b) changes in real income
   c) what can be bought with one's income
   d) variation in prices

6 The 'informal economy' refers to:
   a) tax evasion by some people
   b) a poor balance of trade situation
   c) a favourable balance of payments
   d) the extent of government borrowing

7 A company making 'Whatsits' spends $500,000 on labour and $500,000 on materials, and sells the 'Whatsits' produced for $2,000,000 in the year. What is the net output for national income accounting purposes?
   a) $2,000,000   c) $1,000,000
   b) $1,500,000   d) $500,000

8 The national income of a country cannot be calculated by:
   a) aggregate of all types of income
   b) aggregate of all types of saving
   c) aggregate of all types of expenditure
   d) aggregate of all types of net output

9 Which of the following would not be considered as income for national income statistics purposes?
   a) distributed company profits
   b) teachers' salaries
   c) interest paid on bank account savings
   d) money invested in savings accounts

NATIONAL ACCOUNTS

10 Which of the following would not be considered as expenditure for national income purposes?
   a) giving $5 to an official charity
   b) unemployment benefits paid by the government
   c) a new truck purchased by a local business
   d) stationery purchased by a school

> **Key words**
> Find out the business-related meaning of each of the following words. Write a separate sentence for each word to show your understanding.
>
> budget   depreciation   expenditure   index
> growth   development   output   income
> technology   resources

Structured questions

1 Refer to the data in table 22.2 showing the national income accounts of the country Noland for last year.
   a) What was the value of public expenditure last year? (1)
   b) Name two goods which would be considered part of consumer expenditure. (1)
   c) Calculate the value of 'taxes on expenditure' which are marked '?' in the accounts. (1)
   d) Refer to the data 'Total final expenditure'. Why is it necessary to *add* subsidies in the calculation? (2)
   e) Calculate Noland's balance of payments on current account from the data given. (2)

Table 22.2 *National income of Noland*

Analysis by expenditure method	$ billions
Consumer expenditure	137.0
Public authorities expenditure	48.9
Gross domestic fixed capital investment	41.6
Value of physical increase in stocks	– 2.9
Exports of goods and services	63.1
Total final expenditure	**287.7**
less imports of goods and services	– 57.8
less taxes on expenditure	– ?
plus subsidies	5.6
Gross Domestic Product	**199.2**
Net property income from abroad	0.2
Gross National Product	**199.4**
less capital consumption	– 27.9
National Income	**171.5**

   f) State another method, besides aggregate expenditure, which can be used to assess the national income. What problems are encountered using this method? (3)
   g) Explain the difference between GNP and national income. Why is the distinction between them important? (4)
   h) 'During the last five years, the national income of Noland doubled from $84.9 billion to $171.1 billion, but the standard of living in Noland did not double over this period.' Discuss this statement giving reasons to support your observations. (6)

2 a) Define national income. (1)
   b) Explain the difference between consumption and investment. Why is investment necessary to an economy? (4)
   c) With the use of examples, explain what 'injections' and 'withdrawals' are with reference to the circular flow of income. State how each affects the level of national income. (6)
   d) Show with the aid of a simple diagram that national income = national expenditure = national output. (9)

3 a) What is meant by the 'standard of living' of a country? (2)
   b) Why do some countries have a higher standard of living than others? (3)
   c) Describe four factors that influence the standard of living. (4)
   d) What is 'per capita income'? To what extent would you say that this can be seen as an indication of the standard of living of a country? (5)
   e) In what way could we measure the standard of living of any Caribbean country? (6)

4 a) What is economic growth? (2)
   b) Explain the difference between a 'boom' and a 'recession' in the economy. (4)
   c) Describe four factors that may lead to economic growth. (6)
   d) Economic growth does not always mean a better standard of living. Why is this? (8)

5 a) What is the purpose of a government's budget? (2)
   b) Explain the difference between a budget surplus and a budget deficit. (2)

NATIONAL ACCOUNTS

```
                                    $ millions
                        Interest on loans        $13
                        Replacement of
                        worn out machinery       $7
                        National Insurances      $5
Basic materials    Net  Corporation tax          $4
Energy            Profit Dividends               $6
Services                Reinvestment             $8
Taxes
$300 m

                        Labour                   $49
```

Fig. 22.4 Florida trading expenditure

c) State three services that governments provide which private enterprise would be unwilling to supply at an economic price. (3)

d) List three methods governments use to influence business activities. (3)

e) To what extent would you argue that governments interfere too much in business activities. (4)

f) One type of business that all governments try to influence is importing and exporting.
  (i) Why is this of such importance?
  (ii) How do governments try to influence this aspect of business? (6)

6 Study the chart in figure 22.4, which shows a breakdown of Florida Trading's expenditure, and answer the questions that follow.

  a) By the efficient use of the factors of production, businesses are able to create wealth. Name two such factors of production which are included in the data shown here. (1)

  b) What was the total output of Florida Trading Ltd.? (1)

  c) What was this company's net output? (2)

  d) Explain why net output and not total output is used in the compilation of national income accounts. (3)

  e) Explain the difference between depreciation and reinvestment. How much does Florida Trading spend on each. (4)

  f) By making a net profit, Florida Trading created $18 million of wealth. If all other companies in the economy did the same, the result would be economic growth for the country. By analysis of the breakdown of Florida Trading's net profit, show that economic growth may not always lead to a general rise in living standards. (9)

Research assignments

1 Find out the amounts your government spends on each of the main components of its expenditure. Present the data researched in some appropriate graphical form. Write a summary report which includes explanation of the ways your government raises the revenue it needs.

2 a) Give a detailed description of five contrasting services provided by the government of your country.

   b) In what ways would you say that there is a need for your government to improve the social services it provides? Give reasons for your answer.

3 a) Why is it difficult to use national income statistics to compare the standard of living in different countries? What other statistics might you consider using in order to make a realistic comparison?

   b) Make a comparison between the standard of living of your country and one other outside the Caribbean region.

4 Using real data, explain the way that your government attempts to redistribute incomes. Quote the source of your data.

5 a) A major priority of most governments is the provision of welfare for their citizens. To what extent would you say that this is dependent upon growth and development?

   b) In what ways would you consider your country is restricted in the welfare provisions it makes available to the population?

6 a) By examination of your household or a local firm, show that national income can be measured in terms of output, income or expenditure.

   b) Present data to show how your country's national income can be measured in these three ways.

Chapter 23
TAXATION AND INFLATION

We all pay tax in some form or other, either directly or indirectly. The government does not take this money from us without reason. The money taken is used to control and direct the economy as well as to fund government expenditure and redistribute wealth.

23.1 Principles of taxation

A tax is a compulsory money payment to the state by businesses and individuals levied on property, income and the use of goods and services.

The following four principles of taxation were stated by an economist, Adam Smith, over 200 years ago, but they are still sound concepts that are applied in economies around the world today.

1 *Equality*   Taxes should be based on the ability to pay. Those with higher incomes should pay a higher proportion of their income in tax than those with low incomes. In this way people bear a fair burden rather than all paying the same amount.

2 *Certainty*   The easier it is to understand a tax system, the less incentive there is to evade paying the amount levied. The form and manner of payment and the quantity to be paid should be clear and unambiguous to the contributor and to everyone else. In other words, the tax system should be clear enough so that those liable for tax are certain of what is expected of them.

3 *Convenience*   A tax should be convenient for the taxpayer to pay and for the tax collector to collect. The pay as you earn (PAYE) method of payment and collection of income tax is convenient because it is collected by employers before the employees receive their pay. PAYE is also a convenient system because it fits in with the normal activity of regular payment of wages.

4 *Economic*   Taxes should be collected as economically as possible because there is little to be gained if the cost of collection is more than the money received.

A tax may take one of three forms.

1 *Proportional*   Every taxpayer pays the same proportion of his or her income in tax.

2 *Progressive*   A taxpayer with a higher income not only pays a larger amount of taxes but also a larger proportion. Income tax takes this form in Caribbean countries.

3 *Regressive*   This refers to a situation where the tax represents a smaller proportion of a wealthier person's income than that of a poorer person as with a purchase tax.

23.2 Functions of taxation

There are five functions of taxation: to raise revenue, to maintain economic stability, to influence expenditure, to redistribute income, and to satisfy specific objectives.

To raise revenue

The main function of taxation is to raise **revenue** (money raised by taxation) to pay for things provided by the state which private enterprise would be unable or unwilling to provide at prices the majority of the population are generally able to pay. Police, medical care, education and roads are examples of where provision is largely met through taxation.

To maintain economic stability

Governments use taxation to exercise overall control of the economy in a manner that attempts to level out the 'highs' and 'lows' in economic activity, to promote economic growth and to try to achieve full employment. A major factor involved here is the control of inflation.

To influence expenditure

Taxation can be used to influence the level of total expenditure. The higher the level of taxation the lower the level of real expenditure is likely to be, and vice versa. This principle can be used to deflate or reflate the economy. Inflation is examined later in this chapter.

To redistribute income

Taxation can be used to effectively redistribute income and capital ownership in the community, by taxing some members of the community more than others, for example redistributing in favour of poorer members of the community. Redistribution of income will, in the long term, influence the distribution of wealth.

To satisfy specific objectives

Taxation can be used to achieve specific objectives such as the following.

- Discouraging habits like smoking, drinking and gambling.
- Encouraging activities such as healthy eating and safe driving.
- Stimulating production, exporting and the improvement of the balance of payments.
- Encouraging movement of industry into depressed areas.
- Promoting mobility of labour.
- Protecting particular industries, e.g. from foreign competition.
- Helping to re-organise, re-equip and expand key sectors of the economy.

23.3 Methods of taxation

No single method of taxation is ideal, and consequently governments use a variety of methods, which spread the burden over the population in what the government thinks is a fair way.

Generally there are two classes of taxes — **direct** and **indirect**.

Direct taxation

A direct tax is one that is levied directly on individuals or on companies. They are taxed 'at source'. Income tax, corporation tax, capital gains tax and capital transfer tax are examples of direct taxes.

Income tax

Income tax is both a direct tax and a progressive tax, and it is the most important and largest source of revenue for most governments. It is a tax on personal earned income. Wage earners are allowed a certain amount in tax-free allowances, and the rest of their income is taxed. It is normally collected by a system called 'pay as you earn' (PAYE). Through the PAYE system, the tax is deducted by the employer before wages are given to the employee.

Corporation tax

Corporation tax is levied on the profit of companies. As with individuals and income tax, companies are allowed to deduct certain expenditures as tax-free allowances from their gross profit. The remaining net profit is liable for tax.

Capital gains tax

Capital gains are the profits obtained from the sale of capital items such as business enterprises, property, land, machines, etc. A percentage of the profits from these sales has to be paid to the government as capital gains tax.

Capital transfer tax

Capital transfer tax is a tax on gifts or gratuitous transfers of personal wealth from one person to another, whether they take place during a person's lifetime, or at death.

Indirect taxation

An indirect tax is paid by the taxpayer indirectly to the tax authority. It is levied on one person but is collected and ultimately paid by someone else such as a retailer. Indirect taxes can either be **specific** or **ad valorem**.

- *Specific* This means that a specific sum of money will be levied irrespective of the value of the product — a set amount per item.
- *Ad valorem* In this case the amount of tax levied is a percentage of the value of the product. The higher the product value, the higher will be the amount of the tax paid.

Purchase tax, customs and excise duties, stamp duties, rates and property taxes are examples of indirect taxation.

Purchase tax

This is a tax applied to a wide range of consumer goods, and the tax rate varies depending on the type of goods in question. The tax is paid by the original seller (e.g. the manufacturer) and passed on to the consumer in the form of higher prices.

General consumption tax (GCT)
This is a variation of the purchase tax that has been adopted by some Caribbean countries. A percentage (currently 10%) tax is levied on many items and services. Such a tax has the effect of raising prices and bringing in revenue for the government.

Customs and excise duties
These taxes are charged in addition to purchase tax or GCT — on a variety of important goods such as motor vehicles, alcohol and tobacco. Customs duties are taxes levied on imports; excise duties are levied on home-produced goods. These taxes are intended to raise revenue for the government, but are also used to protect home industries from foreign competition.

Stamp duties
This method of taxation is payable on certain monetary instruments such as cheques, commercial documents and contracts.

Rates and property taxes
These taxes are usually raised by local government authorities, and the revenue is used to help provide localised services.

23.4 Economic effects of taxation

Effective taxation should achieve the functions stated earlier, but at the same time meet the longstanding principles of taxation (equality, certainty, convenience, economic). No single tax can meet all of these requirements and raise all the revenue governments need. Consequently, governments use a variety of methods of taxation, which tends to even out some of the inadequacies of some of them. A key source of debate is whether direct or indirect taxation is more appropriate.

The main advantage of direct taxes is that the rate charged can easily be changed or varied for different circumstances. For example, the overall rate of income tax can be simply changed centrally by the government, and it is possible to have varied rates: income tax is generally charged at a progressively higher rate to the rich and, conversely, at a lower rate to the poor. The PAYE system ensures that income tax is not only relatively easily collected (employers do much of the work) but it also allows the taxpayer to make contributions in small regular payments.

The main disadvantage of direct taxes is that they are expensive to administer and collect; many civil servants are involved and complicated rules and paperwork persist. Direct taxation often results in disputes between taxpayers and tax officials over the amount of tax due. In addition, those who do not pay their income tax by the PAYE method can fall into the trap of not saving sufficient money to pay one or two large payments a year.

Indirect taxes have the advantage that they are relatively easy and cheap to collect, the amount to be paid is generally clear and unambiguous, and it is difficult to evade paying them. In addition, indirect taxation collects money from foreigners (e.g. tourists) whereas they do not pay direct taxes.

The main disadvantage of indirect taxes is that they are regressive, in that poorer people tend to pay a higher proportion of their income in tax than those on higher incomes do. For example, payment of purchase tax or GCT is at the same rate whether one is a high earner, a low earner, or even a non-earner.

23.5 Inflation

Earlier in this chapter we saw that one of the functions of taxation is to maintain economic stability. One of the main threats to this stability is inflation, and governments throughout the world are continually striving to offset the effects of it.

Inflation describes a situation when prices are persistently rising and the real value of money is declining, which means that the cost of living has increased. If people's incomes do not improve, then the money they earn will purchase less. Under such circumstances we say that real income has fallen, and this results in a fall in the standard of living unless some other factor changes.

Inflation is the result of many factors, but two broad types of inflation can be distinguished; **cost-push** inflation and **demand-pull** inflation.

Cost-push inflation

This form of inflation is caused by rises in the cost of factors of production such as raw materials or labour, e.g. oil prices and wages. For example, wage increases may not be matched by increased productivity. When such increased costs are passed on to the consumer in the form of increased prices, this results in cost-push inflation. The resultant increase in the cost of living encourages workers to press for further wage increases, causing a continuing inflationary spiral with rising wages chased by rising prices, or vice versa.

Fig. 23.1 Cost-push inflation

Demand-pull inflation

This type of inflation involves 'too much money chasing too few goods', that is, an excessive supply of money relative to the goods and services available for purchase. Upward movement of wages can be an explanation of this, but 'too much money' usually refers to excessive credit expansions, for example, easier bank loans and other borrowing facilities, which encourage people to spend money that they do not immediately have available.

The effects of inflation

Inflation has the effect of making us all worse off. If your country has more inflation than other countries this will mean that your prices will rise faster. Consequently, your exporters will find it harder to sell their products. Consumers both in your country and abroad will be less inclined to buy the more expensive home-produced goods, preferring the less expensive foreign products. This will lead to reduced output at home and job losses, further adding to the rate of inflation. The following summarises the main effects of inflation.

- Prices are persistently rising, resulting in a decline in the standard of living, especially for those on fixed incomes.
- Saving is discouraged because people recognise that money saved will buy less in the future.
- Exports become more expensive because of increased production costs. Consequently, there is a tendency to import more goods, since they are relatively cheaper than domestic production.
- People who owe money to others (debtors) gain from inflation, whereas those who are owed money (creditors) lose.

Controlling inflation

If a government believes that demand-pull is the cause of inflation it can put a number of measures into effect. The government can:

- reduce its own demand for goods and services
- encourage increased productivity
- try to reduce demand by consumers and producers
- make credit more expensive and more difficult to obtain
- take more in taxes than the government spends
- introduce controls, for example of wages, prices, imports.

Where cost-push inflation is thought to be the cause, the remedies are more complex, and often open to political argument. For example, the price of imported goods and raw materials is outside the control of the government. However, some control can be exercised over wage increases and the cost of home-produced goods through a firm prices and incomes policy, although the desirability of this is subject to political debate and there is no clear evidence that such a policy works.

The dashed line shows what would be the trend if inflation remained unchecked. The thicker line shows the possible effect of deflationary or reflationary measures.

SUMMARY

Inflation Persistent rise in the general level of prices of consumer goods and services.

Cost-push inflation Inflation caused by increases in costs to producers (e.g. higher wages or material costs).

Demand-pull inflation Inflation caused by more demand in the whole economy than can be supplied at existing prices.

Deflation Where the value of money is rising while prices are falling.

Deflationary measures Strategies used by the government in an attempt to reduce spending in the economy (usually through monetary or fiscal policies).

Reflationary measures Strategies used by the government to increase demand and encourage growth.

Hyperinflation When prices are rising so fast that generally people prefer to spend their money rather than hold on to it.

Fig. 23.2 Government intervention

23.6 THINGS TO DO

This section contains a variety of exercises to help you create revision notes, to test your understanding and to prepare you for examinations.

Search and find

Write out the question and the answer by referring back through the text to form revision notes.

1. Describe the principles upon which taxation should be based.
2. Explain the differences between the proportional, progressive and regressive forms of taxation.
3. Explain the five functions of taxation.
4. Define direct taxation and describe the forms it can take.
5. How does indirect taxation differ from direct taxation?
6. Explain the difference between the terms 'specific' and 'ad valorem' in relation to indirect taxation.
7. Describe the forms of indirect taxation commonly used.
8. Do you feel direct or indirect taxation to be the more appropriate form? Give reasons for your answer.
9. What is inflation? How does 'cost-push' inflation differ from 'demand-pull' inflation?
10. What steps might a government take in order to control inflation?

What do you know?

Write out the complete sentence and insert the missing words, which can be chosen from the list at the end of the questions.

1. Money taken in taxation is used to control and direct the . . . . .
2. A tax is a . . . . . money payment to the State.
3. Taxes should be based on the ability to . . . . .
4. The easier it is to understand a tax system the less incentive there is to . . . . . paying the amount levied.
5. A tax should be . . . . . for the taxpayer to pay and the tax collector to collect.
6. Taxes should be collected as . . . . . as possible.
7. Taxation can be used to influence the level of total . . . . .
8. Taxation can effectively . . . . . income.
9. . . . . . taxation is levied at source.
10. . . . . . taxes can be 'specific' or 'ad valorem'.

Choose the missing words from the following:

indirect	economically	redistribute	pay
evade	convenient	compulsory	direct
expenditure	economy		

Multiple choice

Select the appropriate answer, a, b, c or d.

1. A tax is said to be regressive if:
   a) it is both a direct and an indirect tax
   b) it is charged at a uniform rate irrespective of income level
   c) a smaller proportion is taken from lower income groups
   d) it takes a higher proportion from higher income groups

2. Which of the following groups of people would be likely to benefit most during a period of inflation?
   a) people on fixed incomes
   b) pensioners
   c) members of a strong trade union
   d) firms who allow customers interest-free credit

3. Which of the following could be used to combat cost-push inflation?
   a) an increase in income tax
   b) a credit squeeze
   c) creation of a budget surplus
   d) implementation of an incomes policy

4. Which of the following is least likely to suffer under inflation?
   a) home buyers
   b) unemployed
   c) old age pensioners
   d) those with savings

5. If inflation was 5%, how much extra would a household with a weekly expenditure of $200 need to maintain its standard of living?
   a) $5
   b) $10
   c) $15
   d) $20

6. The letters PAYE are associated with which of the following methods of taxation?
   a) capital transfer tax
   b) general consumption tax
   c) income tax
   d) capital gains tax

TAXATION AND INFLATION

7. Which of the following measures would not have the effect of redistributing income?
   a) providing rent rebates
   b) improving pension payments
   c) increasing unemployment benefits
   d) raising purchase tax

8. An ad valorem tax is based on:
   a) a set amount per item
   b) a contribution with each wage payment
   c) a percentage of the value of a product
   d) the profits of a business

9. Which of the following taxes would be levied on the estate of a person who has died?
   a) capital gains tax
   b) capital transfer tax
   c) corporation tax
   d) stamp duties

10. Which of the following is not taxed at source?
    a) purchase tax
    b) income tax
    c) corporation tax
    d) capital gains tax

Key words

Find out the business-related meaning of each of the following words. Write a separate sentence for each word to show your understanding.

taxation   taxpayer   revenue   redistribution   customs
threshold   inflation   levied   profit   incomes

Structured questions

1. Ms Wiltshire earns $92,455 a year as a managing director of a large multi-national company. Ms Wiltshire resides in the country of Noland which operates a system of income tax 'banding'. Taxpayers are charged different rates for various levels of income. A breakdown of Ms Wiltshire's income tax paid for the last year is given in figure 23.3. Answer the questions related to this data.

   a) What is income tax? (1)

   b) What was the total amount of income tax paid by Ms Wiltshire? (1)

   c) What is meant by taxable income? Calculate Ms Wiltshire's taxable income. (3)

   d) Ms Wiltshire pays income tax by the PAYE system. Describe this system of tax payment. (3)

   e) Use the data shown here to help you explain whether income tax is 'progressive' or 'regressive'. (4)

Income	%	Tax paid
$49 800 at	60%	$29 880
$7 900 at	55%	$4 345
$7 900 at	50%	$3 950
$5 200 at	45%	$2 340
$16 200 at	29%	$4 698
$3 000 at	40%	$1 200
$3 455	Tax Free	
Total $92 455		**$46 413**

Fig. 23.3 Ms Wiltshire's income tax breakdown

f) Bearing in mind the 'principles of taxation', explain fully whether or not you think income tax is a good tax. (8)

2. The data shown in figure 23.4 relates to the imaginary country of Noland. It records the general index of retail prices between the years 1968–94. This is the way that this country and many others measure inflation.

   a) What was the rate of inflation in 1973? (1)

   b) What was the highest rate of inflation between 1968 and 1994, and in which year did it occur? (2)

   c) The rate of inflation in 1994 was 3%. What does this mean? (2)

Fig. 23.4 Retail price index for Noland

d) Average earnings in 1978 were $29.30 per week; in 1992 the figure was $178.80 per week. Does this mean that the people were six times better off in 1992 than in 1978? (4)

e) In a period of inflation, which of the following in your opinion would be the best and which the worst forms of personal investment. Give your reasons.
  (i) Bank deposit accounts
  (ii) Solid gold coins
  (iii) House purchase (4)

f) 'The high rate of inflation shown in this data in the 1980s was the result of cost-push inflation, partly caused by imports. It was not a result of demand-pull inflation.' Explain this statement. (7)

3 a) Explain any situation where you would pay two taxes in making a single purchase. (2)

b) Explain the difference between capital gains tax and capital transfer tax. (4)

c) Describe how the government might use taxation as a method of redistributing income and wealth within the country. (6)

d) Explain the working of *either* income tax *or* general consumption tax in your country, and describe its merits as a form of taxation. (8)

4 Look at figure 23.5, and answer these questions.

General Consumption Tax (GCT)

GCT is a tax levied by central government on general expenditure. It is a tax added to many goods and services at every stage of production. When several traders are involved in the movement of goods from the producer to the consumer, each will charge GCT to the person to whom they sell. Each trader, however, only pays to the Customs and Excise Department the amount of GCT they have charged their customers less the amount of tax paid to their own suppliers.

Example GCT
10 items at
$20 = $200.00   Gross invoice value
Less 25%   50.00   Trade Discount

              $150.00   Net goods value
Plus 15%   22.50   GCT

Total $172.50   Invoice value

Fig. 23.5 General consumption tax (GCT)

a) Name the government department that collects GCT. (1)

b) Why is general consumption tax so called? (2)

c) How can one tell whether GCT is a direct or an indirect tax? (2)

d) State one advantage of GCT from the point of view of the government and one disadvantage for the consumer. (4)

e) A wholesaler sells 16 items at $25 each to a retailer, to whom he allows a 25% trade discount. GCT at a rate of 15% must be added to the transaction. Produce a breakdown similar to that in the data in figure 23.5 to show the way in which the eventual charge will be calculated. (5)

f) Explain the difference between an ad valorem tax and a specific tax, using examples to illustrate your answer. (6)

5 Refer to the data in figure 23.6. It compares the weekly expenditure of old age pensioners (OAPs) and a high-income family with the Retail Price Index.

a) What is the OAPs' total weekly expenditure? (1)

b) What percentage of the high-income married couple's income is spent on clothing and footwear? (2)

c) If food prices rose by 10%, how much extra would the two families quoted in this data have to spend to maintain their real standard of living, assuming no other price increases? Express your answer:
  (i) in $s. (1)
  (ii) as a percentage of their total expenditure (i.e. their personal rate of inflation). (2)

d) Why are the rates of inflation worked out in (c)(ii) both below 10%? (2)

e) If food prices rose by 20% and housing costs rose by 10%:
  (i) calculate the rate of inflation for each household. (2)
  (ii) account for the difference in the rate of inflation between the households. (2)

f) Describe and analyse the construction of the Retail Price Index and explain its use for measuring inflation. Explain clearly why it may not be a true reflection of individual households' personal rates of inflation. (8)

Research assignments

1 Why does any government need to redistribute incomes? To what extent do you feel taxation achieves this aim? Give specific examples to illustrate your answer.

TAXATION AND INFLATION

Weekly expenditure of old age pensioners (OAP's) Mr and Mrs Jones.

- Other goods and services $15
- Food $20
- Alcohol and tobacco $5
- Housing $20
- Fuel $10
- Durables $10
- Clothes and footwear $5
- Transport $15

Retail Price Index Weighting.

- Other goods and services 18.3%
- Food 18.5%
- Alcohol and tobacco 12.2%
- Housing 15.3%
- Fuel 6.2%
- Durables 6.3%
- Clothes/footwear 7.5%
- Transport 15.7%

Weekly expenditure of high-income couple, Mr and Mrs Dunton.

- Other goods and services $60
- Food $45
- Alcohol and tobacco $15
- Housing $45
- Fuel $15
- Durables $30
- Clothes/footwear $30
- Transport $60

Fig. 23.6 Comparison of expenditure of two households with Retail Price Index

2 Using data quoted from any reliable source, describe the effect of inflation on your country and explain how the government is attempting to control it.

3 Describe four taxes levied on individuals by your government. How far do you consider them to be either progressive or regressive? To what extent do you consider them fair?

4 Explain the difference between direct and indirect taxation. How, if at all, do they affect the rate of inflation as measured by the Retail Price Index? Use official data to support your observations.

5 Use a collection of newspaper articles and headlines, together with your own explanations, to show the difference between demand-pull and cost-push inflation. What policies might a government adopt to reduce inflation?

6 Investigate the following question over a six-month period. To what extent is your family's personal rate of inflation the same as the official government rate?

Chapter 24
THE ROLE OF GOVERNMENTS

24.1 The responsibilities of governments

In all countries, the government plays a crucial role because it has such a wide-reaching effect on the community. The level of government involvement in the economy or in the life of the country is influenced by the type of economic system that the country has — free, planned or controlled, or mixed (see Chapter 1). Most Caribbean economies are based on the 'mixed' system, that is, a mixture of the free and controlled economic systems. In other words, there is some government involvement in the economy and in the life of the country.

The responsibilities of governments can be categorised into four major areas. Promotion of law and order and defence, strategic planning, provision of social services, and management of the economy.

Promotion of law and order and defence

The government is the protector of the people. The general aim is to ensure that all persons in the community receive 'just treatment'. Law and order are important in society because they promote economic stability. For example, tourists are not likely to want to visit a country where there is unrest and instability. Similarly, investors will be less likely to invest their money in a country where law and order are not evident.

In order to meet this responsibility, the government must promote appropriate legislation and provide police and courts of justice to administer law and order in the country. The government also has to make provision for defence (e.g. armed forces) against external dangers, and to provide diplomatic representation abroad.

Strategic planning

The government will develop plans for particular sectors of the economy. It may want to promote development in particular industries, or in specific locations. To support such plans, the government may provide grants, subsidies or 'soft' loans, advisory services and other agencies to the industries or people it wants to influence.

As part of their strategic planning many Caribbean governments provide public utilities, such as water and telephone. Many aspects of public transport are also provided or regulated by governments. Public ownership of enterprises such as these is examined in Chapter 4, and transportation is covered in Chapter 14.

Provision of social services

The government will provide services which private enterprise would be unable or unwilling to supply at a price that all people could afford to pay, including education, health, welfare, culture and sanitation. The provision of social services is examined in more detail later in this chapter.

Management of the economy

The government is charged with overall control of the economy. It will aim to achieve a high level of employment and to encourage economic growth through sound productivity. It will want to manage the national debt and protect the country's balance of payments position, and maintain its foreign reserves.

The budget

In order to meet its responsibilities, the government needs to raise the necessary revenue and exercise control over the economy. In Chapter 23 we have seen the part that taxation measures play, and in Chapter 16 we saw how governments can influence the financial markets. The budget plays a key part in the government's strategies for managing the economy.

The government makes public its budget at the beginning of each financial year. The budget summarises what services the government intends to provide for its citizens, how much money is needed, and how it intends to raise the necessary revenue. The budget may also set out measures to be taken to stimulate or depress key areas of the economy and to encourage saving and investment.

24.2 Government assistance to entrepreneurs

It is in the interest of all governments to help businesses to achieve their full potential, because in doing so businesses contribute to the ideal of full employment and add to national prosperity. Most governments will try to support businesses in the following ways.

- By providing an environment that is conducive to economic growth. They will do this by setting rules for business operations, and providing utilities and other facilities which support business activities.

- By the promotion and maintenance of competitive markets. Governments will prevent companies from abusing their power by taking action against monopolistic activities. This benefits businesses that are not in a monopolistic position, as well as safeguarding the consumer.

Trade promotion

The governments of CARICOM countries provide various forms of assistance to encourage trade, particularly in respect of the export sector. The latter is recognised as of special importance in contributing to the balance of payments (see Chapter 12).

The following are typical examples of government assistance in promoting trade.

- Tax-free loans given to manufacturers involved in export trade, to help them buy imported machinery.

- Technical and professional training, e.g. in management and in information technology developments such as CAD/CAM (computer-aided design and computer-aided manufacture).

- Favourable low-cost ('soft') loans to manufacturers and farmers through institutions such as the Industrial Development Corporation.

- Subsidies and grants (see later in this chapter).

Foreign market intelligence

The government provides information about foreign markets and trading opportunities. For example, it will advise on the market potential of an exporter's goods, and provide details of regulations and other specific local requirements in the target market. The government will also assist in the process of advertising and marketing the country's products abroad, e.g. co-ordinating participation in overseas trade fairs.

Many foreign market intelligence operations are carried out by governments through their embassies and diplomats abroad. These officials also register protests on behalf of their country if free trade is unduly threatened by the import controls of foreign governments.

Export Credits Guarantee Department

Some territories in the Caribbean region have set up departments such as this to provide a special form of insurance against the possibility of non-payment of debts by overseas traders. This facility encourages exporters to participate in foreign markets confident in the knowledge that they will receive payment for their exports.

Industrial development areas

Governments set aside large areas specifically reserved for industrial development, sometimes accompanied by subsidies and grants. An example of such a development area is Point Lisas, Trinidad.

The government may even build factories and then lease them to businesses that could not have undertaken such developments alone, thus encouraging productivity and employment.

Technical assistance

Caribbean governments recognise the need to attract investment, and they take an active part in encouraging investment from sources which are locally based or regionally based, or from international sources.

Caribbean governments will provide a variety of technical assistance to these sources of investment to encourage them to participate. The form this assistance takes could include the following.

- Infrastructure support (e.g. road networks and public utilities).

- Tax concessions (e.g. tax exemption for a limited period).

- Supporting agencies to encourage exporting.
- Bureaux of standards to promote and develop standardisation.
- Tourism development boards to promote the tourist industry.
- Co-ordination facilities through government agencies (see later).
- Provision of factory spaces.
- Advice on investment opportunities.

24.3 Government intervention in business

Governments throughout the world intervene in business activities for a variety of reasons and to different degrees. Sometimes they might do so in order to support enterprises. In other circumstances governments might be motivated by a need to control or regulate enterprises.

Consumer protection

Consumer protection refers to the range of facilities that exist to help consumers to make a wide range of purchases and to protect them from exploitation.

Governments accept some of the responsibility for consumer protection, and demonstrate this in a variety of ways, including the following.

- Contributing to consumer education and advice.
- Establishing and enforcing appropriate legislation.
- Control of quality, and weights and measures.
- Monitoring and control of prices.
- Promotion of fair trading practices.
- Supervision of credit facilities.

Consumer protection is examined in detail in Chapter 10.

Price controls

The government may pass laws which give them the power to limit the price that can be charged for certain goods or services. It may wish to do this where the items are in short supply, or are seen as essential to ensure supply at an economic price to poorer sections of the community (e.g. rice and bread).

Price controls are difficult to enforce because they often result in less incentive to produce the items, because the profit margin is reduced. Price controls also encourage the development of 'informal markets' — unofficial or illegal sales at uncontrolled prices.

Subsidies

Subsidies provide a way of solving the problem of reduced incentive to produce, which is a difficulty with price controls.

Subsidies are cash grants given by governments to entrepreneurs to encourage them to provide goods or services at a price below that normally recognised as economic. For example, a grant might be given to farmers to encourage them to grow certain crops and sell them at a price lower than they would normally expect to receive. Such grants are administered in the Caribbean by officers of the Ministry of Agriculture, who ensure that the system is applied correctly.

Subsidies are not restricted to agriculture. Sometimes they may be given to industries during a difficult period (e.g. to avoid the need to shed their workforce), and to infant (newly formed) industries to help them to get established. Subsidies may also be given to importers to enable certain urgently needed products to be brought into the country at a more favourable price.

Import controls

Sometimes governments may feel it necessary to place controls on goods being brought into the country in order to protect industries in the home market, or to secure a favourable balance of payments position (see Chapter 12). There are two basic methods of import controls — **quotas** and **tariffs**.

- **Quotas** are a limit on the quantity of a product that is allowed to enter the country in a given period of time. Sometimes the government may implement an **embargo**, which is a complete ban on the import of certain goods (or goods from a specific country).
- **Tariffs** are a tax on imports which has the effect of raising the cost price of the import. The tax may be specific or ad valorem (for an explanation of these terms see Chapter 23).

Taxation

Taxation of income, goods and property can also be used to influence and to encourage industry and commerce. For example, increasing taxation on certain products can depress demand and discourage production, and vice versa. Taxation is dealt with in depth in Chapter 23.

Nationalisation

We have seen in Chapter 4 that sometimes the state will take over the ownership of certain industries. When a business is taken into public ownership in this way, it is said to have been **nationalised**. Sometimes enterprises are in state ownership but have not been nationalised. In other words, they are enterprises that were originally established by the government. State ownership of industries has become a prominent feature in the Caribbean region.

State control of industries allows the government to ensure that certain goods and services are made available at an economic price, and it also makes it possible to plan for particular sectors of the economy. You should refer again to Chapter 4 for wider examination of the state ownership of industries. Look particularly at the arguments for and against state ownership.

24.4 Social services

In modern society, the responsibilities of governments are now seen to include the provision of social services at a national and personal level, including social security, medical and health care, education, housing, roads and transportation, and welfare facilities including sanitation.

It is generally recognised that governments have an obligation to provide their citizens with social services, because without government intervention many in the community would be denied their basic material needs. In this regard the government takes a political decision to provide services either free or at a cost subsidised by funds obtained from taxation.

Education

The Caribbean region has a strong tradition of education. Governments fund nurseries for infants, basic schools, primary and secondary schools. At the post-secondary and tertiary levels, many institutions are sponsored by the governments. The University of the West Indies has campuses in Barbados, Tobago, Trinidad and Jamaica, and there are affiliate centres in many of the other islands in the region. Guyana has its own university.

In addition, there are other important institutions providing tertiary education, such as the College of Arts, Science and Technology in Jamaica, the Imperial College of Agriculture in Trinidad, and the College of Agriculture in Jamaica. There are also a number of teacher training colleges, and technical training is provided at youth camps, technical colleges and trade centres throughout the region.

The foregoing are just a sample of the many educational initiatives and institutions that exist as a direct result of the influence of governments in the Caribbean.

Health

A healthy population is important to all countries, and therefore promotion of healthy living and provision of medical care is an important responsibility of government. This will include not only the provision of medical facilities such as hospitals, but also broadcasting information on health-related matters, such as sensible diet, hygiene and contraception.

National insurance (NI)

National insurance, which is a system contributing to health care, is operated by many countries as a social service. It should be noted that national insurance is not only concerned with health care, although this is one of its main aims.

National insurance is an example of the way that some governments ensure that medical and health care and other support services are available for all members of the community. National insurance is a scheme which aims to raise money through premiums deducted from wages, with contributions (approximately two-thirds) from employers. The funds raised in this way are used to provide the following benefits.

1 Sickness
2 Maternity
3 Invalidity
4 Old age
5 Funeral grant
6 Survivors benefit
7 Employment injury benefit
8 Unemployment.

Recreational facilities

Recreation also plays an important part in the health, education and leisure of both citizens and tourists. Governments provide libraries, botanical gardens and recreational parks for the use of both local residents and visitors. Sport is also encouraged by the government, often with a sports minister to oversee it. In addition, there are national galleries of art, museums and zoos, all considerably influenced by government.

Summary

The foregoing are just some of the many social services that countries provide for their citizens. It would be impossible to include all of them here. But the importance of social services is demonstrated by the fact that most governments establish ministries with responsibilities for various areas of social services. For example, there may be a ministry of education, of transport, of health and so on.

24.5 The role of government agencies

Government agencies are sub-sections of the government which assist it in running its affairs. Some of these agencies may be created by legislature and charged with specific functions, others may be less formally organised but still exist as a part of the government machinery. We have chosen a selection of these agencies to examine here, but there are many more than could be contained in one book.

The Industrial Development Corporation (IDC)

The IDC in Jamaica, Trinidad and Tobago, and Barbados is an example of the way that governments can assist commerce and industry. The IDC has operated for a number of years to assist the general development of industries in the following ways.

- Publicise the local industrial and business climate to overseas clients.
- Provide factory accommodation.
- Administer fiscal (taxation) incentives legislation.
- Assist in training workers through grants to employers.

The Management Development Centre (MDC)

This government agency offers advice, provides facilities for lectures, and operates seminars for business executives and managers and those being prepared for management positions. Although the MDC is based in Trinidad, it draws participants from throughout the Caribbean region. The centre publishes bulletins and newsletters which are distributed to interested parties. These publications often contain summaries of management studies carried out in other parts of the world (e.g. the United States and Europe) that are of interest to our own industries, managers and executives.

Both the IDC (examined earlier) and the MDC will sometimes co-operate to the benefit of businesses. For example, the IDC might provide a business with a loan to help it set up a manufacturing plant, and the MDC will advise the firm on the best ways to carry out its operations.

Tourism Development Board (TDB)

Tourism is a major industry in the Caribbean region and most of the islands have established a TDB to monitor, co-ordinate and develop tourism. The TDBs will provide technical assistance to those involved in the tourist industry, such as hotel owners, travel agents, tour operators and airlines.

Government Statistical Office

All of the Caribbean islands have a need for the provision of statistical information. Governments need statistics such as those referred to in Chapter 22, to show how the economy is performing. **Census statistics** are also needed to show any changes in population, e.g. growth or decline of population, and employment statistics. Data such as these are important to governments because they contribute to strategic planning, but they are also of interest to business people both locally and overseas.

Various statistical reports are published annually by the Government Statistical Office, although businesses also compile their own data banks from a wide variety of sources.

Export consolidation and investment

We have acknowledged earlier in this chapter and elsewhere in this book that governments are keen to encourage export trade, and there are a variety of agencies that support this. State corporations such as the Jamaica National Export Corporation have done much to promote the acceptance of some of Jamaica's products in the United States, Europe and Japan.

Agreements such as the Caribbean Basin Initiative which provides tax concessions and other incentives to encourage United States companies to invest in the Caribbean Basin, and also made it possible for certain Caribbean products to be exported into the U.S. duty-free for a period of 12 years (1983–95), have been influenced by governments. So have trade agreements such as the LOME Convention with the European Union. All these initiatives provide important support for industrial development and investment in the Caribbean.

24.6 Governments and the labour force

Unemployment

One of the biggest problems of the Caribbean region is unemployment. In Chapter One we saw that there are many types of unemployment, and many reasons why unemployment persists.

The obvious solution to the problem of unemployment is to create more jobs (employment). Whilst the majority of the opportunities to create jobs lies in the private sector, governments also have an important role to play. The government can create more jobs by directly employing more people to deliver the services it is responsible for. However, a better long-term strategy is to take steps which will make the labour force more employable. This is done through making workers more efficient and thereby more mobile.

Raising the efficiency of the labour force

An obvious way to raise the efficiency of labour is through education and training, and this is clearly an area where the government has a major role to play. Education must embrace the technology needed by commerce and industry. It must not only be able to provide the initial skills training that are needed by industry, but also play a part in re-training people as the need arises for them to change jobs or update their skills. By raising the efficiency of the workforce the government can contribute to the reduction of unemployment as well as make the workforce more effective.

Mobilisation of the labour force

Self-help and community groups do much to organise labour for productive activity. Community self-help organisations such as the Red Cross, Kiwanis, Jaycees, Lions and Leo clubs, Business Women's Associations, and church-based organisations engage communities in productive work. Often the persons being served are persons who lack the skills required for jobs, or who are unemployed. These self-help and community groups are non-governmental organisations (NGOs) that raise funds and establish skills training programmes combined with productivity for people who are in need, especially the young. By providing people with greater skills, we are making them more mobile in terms of employment.

Although the organisations we have examined here are independent of the government, there is an important role for governments to play. The government can encourage such organisations in their endeavours by providing community centres, perhaps in schools and other public places, that can be used by self-help groups. Governments can make a further contribution by providing tutors to train people directly or raise the skills of other tutors so that they can help others. The government also has an important part to play in funding such organisations through funding agencies, and encouraging the private sector to also provide funding. Businesses can be encouraged by the government to provide 'on the job' training for people.

Migration and the labour force

Migration refers to the movement of people from one geographic area to another on a permanent basis. Some people migrate from one part of the country to another, whilst others go to another country. If the person is moving from one country to another, then the person is referred to as an **emigrant**. When that person arrives in the recipient country, the person is referred to as an **immigrant**. Migration is a term used to represent both immigration and emigration.

Migration affects a country's labour force, because the country loses persons who would have been available for employment or would have been gainfully employed. Therefore, economic growth is affected by migration. Where skilled and competent persons as well as professionals migrate, then a '**brain drain**' is the result.

Persons may migrate:

- to find a better or more prosperous life
- in order to find or change employment
- to study and work
- for political reasons.

The effects of internal migration on the labour force:

- Communities lose qualified people who could have participated in the development and economic growth of the community, and could have helped to raise the standard of living of the community.
- The labour supply in the community is reduced. A sector such as agriculture may suffer from a shortage of labour which could have been solved by those who have migrated.
- The community or area to which persons migrate is often overcrowded, since many persons gravitate to the same economic centres seeking work. This brings

pressure on the local amenities. This has the effect of causing funds to be diverted from economic development in order to take care of social developments and social welfare demands (e.g. overcrowding, unemployment, social disorder, inadequate housing and insufficient supply of utilities services).

The effects of external migration on the labour force:

- Skilled and competent persons emigrate and so the country experiences problems in achieving its goals of economic growth and development.
- The labour force is reduced, often considerably.
- The country is required to continually put resources into training and re-training. If a community lacks the resources to do this, then a shortage of skilled and competent persons occurs. This leaves countries/governments with a need to recruit people from overseas with the skills required, often at considerable costs.

The effects of migration on the recipient country

- The recipient country receives skilled as well as unskilled persons who are added to the labour force.
- If the migrants move to overcrowded areas, then the country will have to divert funds from other targeted areas for development of social services needed to meet the demands caused by internal migration.
- Cultural differences could lead to many social, political and economic problems.

Although migration can have a serious social and economic effect on a country or a region, there are major benefits to be derived. For example, in the Caribbean where unemployment is a major problem, migration provides an avenue through which the unemployment problem can be eased. Persons who migrate support their families who are left behind, and so inflows of foreign currency classified as gifts from abroad add to Gross National Product and thus, National Income.

24.7 THINGS TO DO

This section contains a variety of exercises to help you create revision notes, to test your understanding and to prepare you for examinations.

Search and find

Write out the question and the answer by referring back through the text to form revision notes.

1. Describe the four main areas of responsibility of governments.
2. What is the purpose of the government budget?
3. How can a government assist the promotion of trade?
4. Why should a government be keen for a business involved in exporting to be successful? How could it help such a business?
5. How does an Export Credits Guarantee Department encourage foreign trade?
6. What is an industrial development area?
7. How does technical assistance provided by government encourage investment in the Caribbean region?
8. Why do governments intervene in business activities?
9. What are price controls and what kind of problems can they create?
10. How might subsidies be more effective than price controls?
11. Why would a government impose controls on imports and what form might these controls take?
12. For what reasons might a government want to own certain industries?
13. Describe some of the social services that your government provides.
14. How do government agencies assist business?
15. Why is it better to make the workforce more 'employable' than just providing them with employment?
16. What is the main effect of raising the efficiency of the workforce?
17. Explain the difference between the terms 'emigrant' and 'immigrant'.

18 Give reasons why people migrate.

19 What are the effects of migration on the workforce?

20 How might migration affect the recipient country?

What do you know?

Write out the complete sentence and insert the missing words, which can be chosen from the list at the end of the questions.

1 As protector of the people, the government must promote appropriate . . . . .

2 A government might want to promote . . . . . in particular industries or locations.

3 Governments often provide . . . . . that private enterprise would be unwilling to supply at a price everyone can afford.

4 The government is charged with overall control of the . . . . .

5 The . . . . . summarises the government's expected income and expenditure for the year ahead.

6 Successful businesses contribute to the ideal of full employment and add to national . . . . .

7 . . . . . trade is seen as of special importance in contributing to the balance of payments.

8 The government will advise on the market . . . . . for an exporter's goods.

9 The government may build factories and . . . . . them to businesses to encourage industrial development.

10 Consumer . . . . . refers to the range of facilities that exist to help people to make wise purchases.

Choose the missing words from the following.

export	economy	lease	legislation
services	potential	protection	prosperity
development	budget		

Multiple choice

Select the appropriate answer, a, b, c or d.

1 A government would use subsidies to:
   a) build cheap factories
   b) increase the cost of imported goods
   c) redistribute incomes
   d) reduce the cost of home produced goods

2 A government wishes to encourage industry to move into an area which has traditionally been predominantly agriculture-based. Which of the following measures would be least effective?
   a) provision of relocation grants
   b) pay subsidies to farmers in development area
   c) build factories and lease them to businesses
   d) make cheap loans available in development area

3 Which of the following is concerned with the provision of health care?
   a) GCT
   b) PAYE
   c) NI
   d) IDC

4 Which of the following is not a sound reason why a government would want ownership of some industries?
   a) enables large sections of the economy to be planned
   b) profits benefit the whole nation
   c) ensures the provision of essential services
   d) reduces competition

5 A price control is:
   a) a government limit on the price of something
   b) the minimum a company will allow someone to sell their products for
   c) a method used to curb imports
   d) a grant given to farmers to reduce their prices

6 Which of the following statements is untrue?
   a) governments provide diplomatic representation abroad
   b) all state enterprises are nationalised industries
   c) taxation can be used to depress demand
   d) governments provide many public utilities

7 A quota is:
   a) a government ban on foreign imports
   b) a quantity limit on imports
   c) a tax on imports
   d) a grant paid to importers

8 A business wishes to safeguard against the possibility of non-payment of debts by overseas customers. Which of the following organisations would be most helpful?
   a) Industrial Development Corporation
   b) Government Statistical Office
   c) Export Credits Guarantee Department
   d) National Export Corporation

9 A company in your country imports computers. The government charges $20 import duty on each computer, irrespective of its value. This is an example of:
   a) a specific tax
   b) a quota
   c) general consumption tax
   d) an ad valorem tax

THE ROLE OF GOVERNMENTS

10 Your government wants to improve its balance of payments situation. Which of the following measures is least likely to contribute to this aim?
   a) payment of subsidies to exporting producers in the home market
   b) establishment of embassies in many foreign countries
   c) formation of a Tourism Development Board
   d) sending Caribbean students to study overseas

Key words

Find out the business-related meaning of each of the following words. Write a separate sentence for each word to show your understanding.

census   legislation   diplomats   utilities
citizens   prosperity   concessions   lease
infrastructure intervention

Structured questions

1
WORKING HOURS
Trade unions have been trying for many years to reduce the working hours of employees, and governments have from time to time attempted to restrict the hours a business can operate. This has particularly been the case with regard to the times shops can open.

Unions and the Government do not necessarily have the same objectives in mind, and in any case it seems that there are always workers who are willing to work unsociable hours.

a) What do you consider as 'unsociable working hours'? (1)
b) Give two examples of ways that the government might try to restrict business operational hours. (2)
c) State two reasons why the government might want to influence the hours a business can operate. (2)
d) State two ways in which the reasons why unions try to influence working hours might differ from the reasons of the government. (2)
e) Give three economic or social reasons why some workers would be more willing than others to work unsociable hours. (3)

f) Allowing all businesses to operate unrestricted hours can affect different groups of people in varied ways. Describe the ways in which it could affect each of the following:
   (i) the employee
   (ii) the employer
   (iii) the government
   (iv) religious groups (4)
g) Write a report that argues against allowing businesses to operate unrestricted hours. (6)

2
THE BUDGET
The Chancellor of the Exchequer presents the main Budget once a year, and occasionally mini-budgets in between. Sometimes a budget *surplus* is achieved and sometimes a *deficit*. The Chancellor may prefer a deficit at a time of high unemployment but a surplus to check inflation.

a) What is 'The Budget'? (1)
b) Explain the terms *surplus* and *deficit* used here. (2)
c) State two examples of sources of government income as a result of measures contained in The Budget. (2)
d) List three major elements of central government expenditure. (3)
e) If there was high inflation because consumers were spending too much money, the government could create a budget surplus by increasing taxation and lowering its own spending. What could be the effect of this on business? (3)
f) Describe four circumstances where business organisations would want to influence government budgetary measures. (4)
g) Describe two examples of ways that individuals, and three examples where businesses, are affected by government fiscal policies. (5)

3

> **MONOPOLIES**
>
> Throughout the world there are many examples of industries that are dominated by a few very large firms. Even where there are a lot of firms the competition between them may not be particular effective.
>
> When the supply of a product is controlled by one or a group of firms acting together we say that a monopoly exists.
>
> Monopolies can be granted by law. For example, if you invented something you would be given the right (by patents) to have complete control of the production and sale over a given period of time.
>
> Sometimes the advantages of a monopoly outweigh its disadvantages and for this reason governments have sometimes not interfered, and may even encourage it. But the disadvantages of monopoly, particularly from the point of view of the consumer, have generally caused governments to exercise some control over it.

a) Define the term 'monopoly'. (1)

b) Why do monopolies occur? (2)

c) Give three examples of how a monopoly can occur. (3)

d) Explain how a monopoly can bring advantages and disadvantages for the public. (4)

e) In what ways might the government try to restrict mergers and monopolies? (4)

f) What are the reasons for saying that monopolies should be the subject of state control? (6)

4

> **NOLAND NEEDS NEW LIFE**
>
> Business activities in the country of Noland are slowing down. Many people are being laid off work and each week reveals substantial numbers of businesses going bankrupt. There are over-populated areas where unemployment is abnormally high and there is insufficient industry. The government has an important part to play in reviving economic activity.

a) State two reasons why business activities in a country might be 'slowing down'. (2)

b) What could the government do to influence consumer behaviour particularly in order to help increase economic activity? (2)

c) In what ways could a government relieve the pressure of industry and population in congested areas? (3)

d) Describe two social problems and two economic problems that could result from the situation described above if the government did not intervene. (4)

e) What strategies could the government use to increase employment in areas in which unemployment is abnormally high? (4)

f) Governments sometimes give tax relief and other incentives to small firms. Describe how such a policy could help to solve the situation described above. To what extent do you agree that the government is justified in interfering in business activities in this way. (5)

Research assignments

1 To what extent do you agree or disagree with the view that the provision of social services by the State is too generous in your country and, therefore, taxation is higher than necessary? Provide examples to support your views.

2 Design a questionnaire which concisely states the social welfare services provided by the State, and then present a series of questions aimed at identifying the social services which residents in your locality use most frequently. Present your findings using tables and charts and present a summary.

3 "Cigarette smoking has a private cost to the individual and social cost to the economy". Investigate this statement including data obtained by personal survey to establish private costs and data from government departments to identify social costs. Present your discussion of the statement in the form of a report that aims to raise awareness of the real cost of smoking to the economy.

4 What evidence can you find to support the view that there is a difference in living standards between the various parts of the Caribbean region? What influence can the government have on this?

5 Make a collection of newspaper articles from your local press related to matters of local concern, and related to business activities. Divide your articles into issues that you feel could be solved by local government and those that

are central government responsibility. Write a summary report, in two parts, to say how you feel the issues should be tackled:
(i) by local government
(ii) by central government.

Chapter 25
THE SCHOOL-BASED ASSESSMENT (SBA)

The Caribbean Examinations Council has expanded its assessment of Principles of Business by including a School-based Assessment (SBA) component. The following components comprise the assessment of Principles of Business at the General and Basic Proficiency levels:

1 Paper I — Multiple-choice items
2 Paper II— Essay or structured questions
3 Paper III — SBA (Research Project)

The SBA attracts 20 per cent of the overall examination mark. For example, the total number of marks for the Basic Proficiency Examination is 150. Therefore, the SBA will attract 20 per cent of the 150 marks which is 30 marks. The total marks for the General Proficiency Examination is 200. Therefore, the SBA will attract 20 per cent of 200 marks which is 40 marks. This means that the SBA component is a very important part of the Principles of Business course.

The SBA

The SBA is carried out as a research project. It requires the candidate to identify and investigate a public or private organisation of the Caribbean. This gives the candidate an opportunity to gain some practical experience in business. It also gives the candidate a chance to apply in practice some of the concepts, principles, procedures and methods learnt in the Principles of Business course.

The PROFILES of the Research Project

The three (3) PROFILES of the research project are:

Profile 1:   Organisational Principles
Profile 2:   Production and Marketing
Profile 3:   Finance and Introductory Economics

All three Profiles must be investigated and reported on in the research project, since the SBA marks will be distributed according to how well the candidate has dealt with *each* of the three Profiles. For example, if a candidate chooses to study a manufacturing firm, the candidate will need to investigate and report on issues relating to the organisational principles, production and marketing, and finance and economics of the firm.

The Principles of Business syllabus, especially Units 2 to 13, will prove invaluable in helping you to investigate these three Profiles. By reading the syllabus, you will get ideas about the kinds of questions you need to be asking to cover the three Profiles. You will also find the guidelines below very useful in your efforts to meet the requirements of the SBA.

Starting off the project

1 Choose the type of organisation you want to study and investigate.

   OR

   If you prefer, you could develop an imaginary business, since you may be thinking of starting your own business when you leave school. In this case, it would be wise to visit the Small Business Association office in your community or city, or a related non-governmental organisation (an NGO that handles small business affairs), to get some firsthand information on the subject.

2 Read through the syllabus units to ensure that the structure of the organisation or business idea you have chosen is sufficiently broad to cover the three Profiles.
   Make notes to show how the three Profiles will be covered by your investigation.

3 Clearly state why you want to study your chosen organisation or, if you want to develop your own ideas for a business, why you want to do that instead.
   What have you observed or learned about the organisation/business idea that interests you? Why has this made you want to investigate/start it?

THE SBA 'STEPS'

Fig. 25.1

*in relation to the 3 'Profiles'

1. Select a business to study
2. State the purpose of the study*
3. Decide on a data-collection strategy
4. Collect the data
5. Analyse the data
6. Interpret the data
7. Present findings in SBA Report

4 Then discuss your topic with your teacher. She/he will be supervising your SBA and will therefore confirm whether or not the topic is suitable for the SBA.

5 Once the topic is confirmed, formulate purpose/problem 'statements' – what are you going to investigate and why? You must formulate statements to cover each of the three Profiles.

Example (area of investigation: Marketing)
Purpose statement: The purpose of this part of the research is to determine whether there is a relationship between the advertising medium used by a firm, and the income of a firm.

Problem statement: What is the difference, if any, between income generated from electronic-media advertising, and the income generated from other forms of advertising used by a firm?

Hypothesis: A greater amount of revenue is generated by a firm advertising through the electronic media, than by a firm using other advertising media.

Once you have completed the above exercises, you will then be ready to begin your research paper.

Carrying out your research

The essential tasks you will need to undertake to complete your research are:

1 **Decide what your data collection strategy will be.**
2 **Collect the data.**
3 **Analyse the data.**
4 **Draw conclusions based on the data.**
5 **Plan the report.**
6 **Write the report.**

To help with your project, these six important steps are described in more detail below.

Data collection

This is a fundamental part of the project. If data is not collected, then your research questions and hypotheses cannot be adequately answered and confirmed.

Data can basically be defined as:

- *Primary data*: meaning that no other researcher has collected this data before you

- *Secondary data*: meaning that in the past a researcher collected and used data for some purpose, but that the data can still be reused (by you) in a different way. In other words, you can examine the data from a different perspective.

Data consists of such things as:

- responses to a questionnaire or an interview, or both

- reporting on events observed or experiments observed

- documents or records or physical materials.

In your study of the organisation, you may use a combination of the various data-collection methods outlined above. However, it is important to ensure that the data is relevant to your study. Never collect data for the sake of collecting data.

Let us now examine in more detail some of the data-collection methods just described. It is up to you to decide (possibly with guidance from your teacher) which of the following instruments will be useful to your particular research.

Questionnaire

This is one of the most common instruments used in the collection of data for research projects. A questionnaire is a method of collecting data and information from a sample of people. These people are often representative of a particular segment or group in society.

For example, a sample of shoppers in a supermarket could be questioned to determine their opinion of its products and service. The questions to be posed must be pre-formulated, put into a certain order, and written down, so that each shopper is faced with exactly the same questionnaire. This makes your analysis of their responses easier.

You need to be clear in advance about what you are trying to find out. Target your questions to obtain the information you want. Avoid leading questions. These are questions that suggest answers, an example being, 'This is a good supermarket, isn't it?'.

The questions you ask may be either '**open-ended**' or '**closed**'. If they are closed, the person responding gives a simple answer without making comments. Thus, the answer could be a straightforward 'yes' or 'no' (to a question like, 'Do you think the service in this supermarket is good?'). The answer could also be given by ticking a box (for example, if you are rating the service of the supermarket as 'good', 'fair' or 'poor'). Closed questions invite a limited response, but they make the questionnaire easier to complete. If, on the other hand, the question is open-ended (for example, 'What aspects of the service in this supermarket appeal to you?'), then the person is being asked to give a full answer. This allows them to explain themselves more, but at the same time it makes your analysis of their response less straightforward.

A questionnaire is easy to use if carefully formulated. People can complete it themselves, or the researcher can ask questions and fill in the appropriate sections him/herself. However, you may find that some people do not like to answer questionnaires that are too long. For this reason, you must ensure that the instructions and questions are clear, simple and precise. They should only have one possible meaning. Also, make the questionnaire itself as short as possible.

Often the questionnaire has to be left for the respondent to fill out, so you may need to visit them or call them by phone in order to retrieve it.

Once you have developed your questionnaire, ask your teacher or supervisor to check it.

Interview

An interview is another common method used to collect data. This involves questioning people about their opinions of certain topics or issues. In this sense, it is very similar to a questionnaire.

But there is a subtle difference — an interview is less formally structured than a questionnaire, taking the form of questions *and* discussion with the person being interviewed. This allows the interviewee to respond in a more natural way. The interviewer, in turn, may ask a more varied range of questions. The questions asked need not necessarily be the same for all interviewees, but instead can be formulated to suit the person being interviewed. This allows the interviewer to investigate more deeply the interviewee's particular views. The questions asked will also probably change as the interview goes on, for example if the interviewee raises an interesting point and the interviewer decides that she/he would like to investigate that point further.

The interviewer may need to tape-record the interview in order to transcribe and analyse the responses later. Before any attempt is made to tape-record an interview, always seek the permission of the interviewee. In the absence of a tape recorder, the interviewer will need to make full notes of the interviewee's responses.

Interviews may be conducted face-to-face or via the telephone.

Observation and participation

Some researchers find that observing an event taking place, or actually participating in an event, is also a useful way of collecting data.

Observation is designed to help the observer get information about an organisation, or a group of people, by simply watching how they go about their business and listening to their conversations and interactions. The observer records what she/he sees and hears by positioning him/herself in a particular location in order to monitor events. Tape-recording and video-taping are therefore useful observational tools, if available. The essence of observation is that the observer does not interfere in events — she/he watches and listens from the sidelines.

The advantages of observation are that you can make judgments about how an organisation or group works based on what *you* see. The conclusions you draw will be entirely your own — whereas with an interview or a questionnaire your conclusions are based on what other people said to you.

Participation is another way of observing, but this time you observe the actions and behaviour of a group/organisation from within. In other words, the observer assumes a role inside the group or organisation being observed. Participation gives the researcher the opportunity to learn, from practical experience and a 'hands-on' approach, the working methods and behaviour of those being studied.

Points to remember when undertaking an observation or participation:

- Record as much as possible of what you see and hear.

- If you do not clearly understand what you have observed or participated in, seek clarification from someone within the group or organisation.

- In participatory observation, the observer could become so involved that she/he forgets the aim of the exercise. Be on the alert if you choose to gather data in this way.

Documents and reports

Gathering data from documents is common to all types of research studies. Documents may be able to answer some of the questions you want to ask, without the need for you to deal with people in the organisation directly. In the study of an organisation the following documents can all be useful sources of information:

Company year books; manuals used in the organisation (such as procedures manuals, policy manuals, staff manuals); reports of all types, e.g. financial, sales and marketing, and production reports; company journals and magazines; minutes of meetings.

Additionally, library resources and computer-based information can also be useful.

If a government department, ministry or agency is being studied, you may also be able to consult government statistical reports and policy documents.

Documents are **secondary** sources of data, i.e. the researcher has not collected the information within the documents him/herself. However, they are still useful for SBA-type projects, especially if you are finding it difficult to collect primary (original) data.

Accounting for the '3 Profiles' within your research methods

Once you have decided on the data-collection methods you are going to use, you will need to think how these can be applied to discover information about the three Profiles for the organisation you are going to study.

You will find the exemplar questions listed below useful in the preparation of your data-collection methods. Some of these questions can be 'built in' to your research, i.e. put directly into questionnaires, interviews, etc. Otherwise, they can be used as 'background thinking' for you to decide on the approach you are going to take in collecting your data (for example, the type of questions that will be in your mind during an observation).

You need to be aware that the exemplar questions are just a few examples to get you going. The questions you formulate for your particular research should be carefully thought out in relation to the overall aims of your investigation. You can get ideas for questions by looking at the syllabus, and from what you have learnt in class during the year.

Exemplar Questions for Profile 1: Organisational Principles

Basic structure and rationale for the organisation

1. What is the official/legal name of the organisation?
2. How long has the organisation been in operation?
3. In what line of product or service is the organisation involved?
4. Has the organisation formulated a Mission Statement?
5. What is the mission of the organisation?
6. Does the organisation have a structure?
7. What organisational structure has been adopted by the organisation (Line, Line and Staff, Committee structure)?
8. Why has the organisation adopted this structure?
9. What is the size of the management team?
10. What categories of managers are employed in the organisation?
11. How many employees are employed in the organisation?
12. What is the span of control of managers to employees?

Working conditions

1. Are all managers provided with job descriptions?
2. Are all employees provided with job descriptions?
3. Do all managers sign employment contracts?
4. Do all other employees sign employment contracts?
5. Are job specifications provided for all categories of employees?

6 Indicate the hours of work adopted by the organisation:
   a) shift work
   b) flexible working time
   c) fixed hours of work.
7 Have workers been provided with a copy of the health and safety regulations of the organisation?
8 Are health and safety regulations displayed in a prominent place in each department or office?
9 Are all workers covered under a health scheme?
10 Do workers in 'high risk' areas have insurance coverage?

Exemplar Questions for Profile 2: Production and Marketing

Production
1 Where is the organisation located?
2 What factors influenced this location?
3 What product is being produced?
4 What is the scale/size of production?
5 How do products reach the consumers?
6 Products' packaging:
   a) Is labelling appropriate?
   b) Is the product appropriately packaged?
   c) Is information provided on weights?
   d) Is information provided on measure?
   e) Is information provided on product usage date?

Marketing
1 What market research is undertaken by the organisation, and what market research methods are used?
2 What is the purpose of the research?
3 What specific questions are asked by the researchers?
4 How often is market research undertaken?
5 What marketing strategy has been adopted by the organisation?
6 How do branding and packaging relate to the marketing strategy?
7 How have the outlets for distribution of the organisation's product(s) helped to determine the marketing strategy (e.g. point-of-sale displays, etc.)?

Exemplar Questions for Profile 3: Finance and Economics

1 How is the organisation financed?
2 Is the organisation insured, and what are the implications if it is not?
3 What level of profitability has the business been able to achieve over the past five years?
4 To what would you attribute the level(s) of profitability the organisation has been experiencing?
5 If the organisation is experiencing difficulty in its operations, what factors might be contributing to this difficulty?
6 Suggest ways the business could improve profitability.
7 What measures would you use to indicate whether or not the organisation is contributing to the social and economic development of a country, e.g. trade or exports?

Analysing the data you have collected

Once you have completed all your data collection, it is time to analyse the data. This will involve presenting the data in easily-readable and easily-interpretable form, which will make it easier for you to draw conclusions based on the data.

The data from **questionnaires** can sometimes be presented in graphic form (such as a pie chart or a bar graph), or as a table. For example, if you have asked 'closed' questions where only a 'yes' or 'no' answer is possible, or questions where the respondent is asked to tick one of three boxes, you can easily show this kind of data in a table or graph. You could show how many people replied 'yes' and how many replied 'no', or you could show how many people ticked each of the three boxes.

You should then be able to arrive at conclusions based on the graphic presentation of your questionnaire data. The data presented in graphic form will 'tell you' what you have found overall.

Data from **'open-ended' questionnaires**, or **interviews**, or **observation** and **participation**, is likely to be a little harder to analyse. This is because the answers/results recorded will be very descriptive. They will not be a simple 'yes' or 'no' answer – instead, they will be more in-depth, because individuals will have had more of a chance to express to you their own very particular views.

When analysing this type of data to draw conclusions, you need to look for overall patterns – did several individuals give the same kind of answers? It may be that no pattern emerges, and you should acknowledge this in your conclusion if that is the case (for example, every person interviewed may have given a completely different answer).

Based on all your research and the conclusions that have come out of it, you should now be able to give an indication of whether your original hypotheses or expected outcomes were correct. You may also like to make some recommendations. Remember, the conclusions you draw and the recommendations you make are not a place to include personal opinions about the organisation you are studying. Everything you say must be supported by the data from your research.

The report

Finally, having analysed the data and drawn your conclusions, you will be in a position to plan, then write, your report. Here are some ideas for organising the report:

I – Introductory section

A Title page

B Abstract
This is a one-page to one-and-half-page summary of the report. It gives the busy reader information on what was studied, why and how the study was carried out, and the major findings, conclusions and recommendations.

C Acknowledgement
This is a statement of 'thank you' to those who provided assistance with the research.

D Table of Contents
This gives clear and straightforward information on what the report contains. The following example illustrates a possible format for a Table of Contents:

Contents

	Page
Abstract	i
Acknowledgements	ii
List of Tables and Figures	iii
Description of the organisation investigated	1
Purpose of research/hypotheses	2
Description/justification of data-collection methods	3
Presentation of data collected (graphically where possible)	4–10
Analysis of data collected	11–14
Overall conclusions and recommendations	15–16
Bibliography	17
Appendix	18 onwards

E List of Tables and Figures

II – Main body

A Description of the organisation investigated
The type of organisation, its name, size, basic history and its reason for existing.

B Purpose of the research and hypotheses investigated
Example (area of investigation: Marketing)
Purpose statement: The purpose of this part of the research is to determine whether there is a relationship between the advertising medium used by a firm, and the income of a firm.
Problem statement: What is the difference, if any, between income generated from electronic-media advertising, and the income generated from other forms of advertising used by a firm?
Hypothesis: A greater amount of revenue is generated by a firm advertising through the electronic media, than by a firm using other advertising media.

C Description/justification of data-collection methods
Outline the methods used. How do those methods relate to the purpose of your research, and the hypotheses you outlined earlier in your report? Show how you made sure your research was as broad-ranging and thorough as possible.

D Presentation of data collected
Present the data gathered. Wherever possible make the data interesting and easy to read by presenting it as graphs, pie charts, bar charts or tables. Where you are reporting on interviews, observations or participations, you may want to summarise what people said and what you saw in a few short, clear paragraphs. This is *not* the time to say what you think your data *means* — it is the time at which you report, accurately, the evidence and facts you discovered in your research.

You may want to present the data in sections relating to the three Profiles: Organisational Principles, Production and Marketing, Finance and Economics. You may also decide to indicate how a particular piece of data relates to a purpose/problem statement you have outlined at the beginning of your report.

E Analysis of data collected
What does the data you have set out in the last section suggest to you? Does it confirm or deny your original hypotheses? Write a few short paragraphs to say what you think each of the pieces of data you have collected means. You are now *explaining* what you think your data means, which is called analysis.

Note that in some instances the data you have collected may be inconclusive — neither confirming or denying your original hypothesis. If some of your data seems to be like this, you must be honest about that fact. Your recognition of this will add to the credibility of your work.

III – Final section

A Overall conclusions and recommendations

Present some final conclusions and recommendations based on your presentation and analysis of the data you have gathered. These should be short, two- or three-line paragraphs that sum up the essence of what you have discovered. Set these out logically in your report — they should relate to the hypotheses you originally started out with, and to the three Profiles.

All your conclusions *must* be based on the research you have carried out. Have the findings helped you to confirm or reject your original ideas or hypotheses?

B Bibliography

From what sources did you draw information for your research?

These may have been company reports, staff manuals, yearbooks, books, journals, magazines, government reports (e.g. economic surveys) and policy documents. Prepare a list of these in alphabetical order, following an accepted format.

Example

1 Adams, Stephen, *Economic Principles for CXC*, (pp. 30–40). Publishers of the Caribbean, Castries, St Lucia (1996).
2 Doublas, Robert, *Principles of Business for the Millennium*. SWIFT Publishers, Port Maria, St Mary, Jamaica (1997).
3 *Economic Survey*, (pp. 16–20). Planning Institute of Jamaica, Government Printing Office, Kingston, Jamaica (1966).
4 Fyffe, Marcus, *Marketing Strategies for the Small Business*. Journal of Marketing, 2nd Edition, The Association of Marketers, Bridgetown Headquarters, Barbados (1977).

C Appendix

Place in this section of the report copies of documents such as employment contracts, job descriptions, memorandum of association, your completed questionnaires and interviews, observational notes and any other relevant documents you used in your research project.

The authors wish you every success with your research and in your examination.

INDEX

Acceptance, 154, 155, 156
Acceptance house, 186, 187
Acceptor, 154
Accounts, 25
Accounts department, 38, 41
Acknowledgement, 146
Actuary, 232
Administration department, 38, 41, 48
Ad valorem duties, 134
Advertising, 8, 20, 83, 89, 93, 94, 96, 106, 108–112, 119, 122, 173, 213
  agency, 41, 111
  arguments against, 111–112
  arguments for, 111
  campaign, 93, 110, 111
  criticisms of, 111–112
  department, 38, 41, 94
  forms of, 109–110
  functions of, 108–109
  informative, 109
  media, 109–110
  persuasive, 109
Advice note, 146, 147
Advisory committee, 57
Advisory services, 255
After-sales service, 101, 119
Agenda, 175, 176
Agent, 122, 133, 187
Agreement, 155, 156
Agricultural credit banks, 187
Agriculture, 6, 22, 23, 243
Aims (see Business aims)
Airport requirements, 166–167
Air waybill, 151, 168
Alien, 157
Applications, 63, 64, 65
Aptitude test, 65
Arbitration, 81
Articles of Association, 49, 50
Artwork, 111
Assets, 133, 152, 208, 211, 241
Association of African, Caribbean and Pacific Countries (ACP-LOME), 138
Auction, 88
Automatic teller machine, 40
Automation, 17, 20, 24, 30

Balance of payments, 132–133, 135, 241, 242, 255
Balance of trade, 131–132
Balance sheet, 208–209, 211
Bank account, 191, 192–197, 202
Bank cards, 200–201
Bank draft, 151, 202

Banking, 89, 119, 130, 151, 185–197, 198–207
Banking services, 198–207
Bank loan, 124, 151, 201
Bank overdraft, 201
Bank rate, 186
Bankruptcy, 220
Banks, 11, 20, 25, 30, 52, 87, 185–187
Bank statement of account, 192, 194
Bar code, 18, 123, 153
Barter, 1
Bears, 222
Bill of exchange, 151, 187, 202
Bill of lading, 151, 168
Board of directors, 38, 41, 48, 54
Bonded warehouse, 134
Borrowing, 185, 201
Brain drain, 6, 17, 260
Brainstorming, 111
Branding, 95, 97, 97, 106, 118, 122
Brand loyalty, 106
Brand name, 95
Break-even, 96, 210–211
Bridging loan, 201
Broker, 88, 202, 223 (see also Stock Exchange)
Budget account, 191
Budget, government, 57, 241, 242, 255–256
Budgeting, 191, 210
Building societies, 88
Bulls, 222
Bureaux of Standards, 112, 257
Business account, 192
Business aims, 31, 174
Business contracts (see Contracts)
Business documentation, 143–162
Business growth, 30, 41, 53–54, 96
Business location (see Location of business)
Business organisation, 29–44
Business reply service, 176
Business risk (see Risk)
Business, role and functions of, 29–30
Business size, 19–24, 36, 38–40
Business, types of, 45–62
Buyer, 87, 88, 123, 143, 144, 146, 150, 151, 223
Buying department (see Purchasing department)

Capacity, 156–157
Capital, 18, 30, 49, 50, 50, 96, 163, 187, 208, 210, 211–212, 219
  categories of, 211–212
  market, 187
  reserves, 209
  return on, 214
  sources of, 211–222
Capital consumption, 240
Capital gains tax, 248
Capital market, 88, 186
Capital transfer tax, 248
Caribbean Association of Industry and Commerce (CAIC), 135
Caribbean Basin, 244
Caribbean Canadian Agreement, 139
Caribbean Community (see CARICOM)
Caribbean Congress of Labour (CCL), 80,
Caribbean Development Bank (CDB), 136–137, 187
Caribbean Examinations Council, 7
Caribbean Investment Corporation, 136
Caribbean Market structure, 100–101
CARICOM, 7, 15, 16, 23, 80, 135, 136, 220, 256
Carriage arrangements, 144–145, 168
Carrier, 163
Cartels, 100
Cash discount, 144
Cash dispenser card, 200–201
Cash flow, 20, 152, 209–210
Cash flow forecast, 209, 210
Cash on delivery, 150
Catalogue, 122, 144
Catalogue shops, 122
Caveat emptor, 112
Census statistics, 259
Central bank, 11, 185–186, 187
Central government (see Government)
Centralised filing, 41
Certificate of Incorporation, 49
Certificate of origin, 152
Certificate of Registration, 56,
Chain of command, 34, 36, 40
Chain of distribution, 117
Chain store, 119
Chairperson, 32, 48, 175

Chambers of commerce, 7, 101–102, 135
Channels of distribution, 88–89, 94 (see also Distribution)
Charge cards, 124
Charging, 146–151
Charter party, 165, 168
Charts, 175
Cheque, 72, 150–151, 186, 192, 192–194, 198
Cheque card (see Cheque guarantee card)
Cheque clearing, 25
Cheque guarantee card, 194
Choice, 4, 106, 119
Citrus Growers Association, 101
Claim, 232–233
Clients, 88
Clock card (see Time card)
Closed circuit television (CCTV), 33
Closed shop, 82
Codes of practice, 101
Collateral, 201, 211
Collective bargaining, 81
Commerce, 11, 12, 89, 257
Commercial banks (see Banks)
Commission, 122
Committees, 58, 175
Commodity market, 88, 136, 138
Common market, 89, 139
Communication, 21, 30, 31, 33, 37, 40, 89, 89, 155, 163, 173–183
Community affairs, 57,
Companies Act, 49, 227
Company magazines and newspapers, 33
Company registers, 25
Company secretary, 38, 40, 41
Comparative advantage, 131
Comparative costs, 131
Compensation, 41, 227, 233
Competition, 100–101
Competitions, 123
Computer aided design (CAD), 256
Computer aided manufacture (CAM), 256
Computerised stock records,
Computers, 8, 17, 24–25, 30, 40, 41, 72, 153
Conciliation, 81
Conglomerate, 54
Consideration, 154, 155, 156
Consignee, 146, 163
Consignment note, 146, 168

273

INDEX

Consignor, 146, 163
Consultants, 57, 187
Consumer, 11, 30, 51, 83, 88–89, 93, 96, 97, 117, 119, 250, 256
Consumer Affairs, Ministry of, 113
Consumer durable, 212
Consumer education, 257
Consumer price index (CPI), 237
Consumer protection, 83, 112–113, 257
Consumers, 87, 94, 95, 100, 106, 112, 113
Containers, 167–168
Contract, 41, 153–158, 232
Contract of Employment, 66, 67, 74
Contribution, 229
Controlling, 31, 143
Co-operative Credit Union League, 52
Co-operatives, 50–52
Co-ordinating, 30, 33, 174
Corporate identity, 45,
Corporation tax, 248
Costing, 93,
Cost of living, 237–238
Costs, 30, 99, 210, 211, 258, 261
Cottage industries, 22,
Councils, 58
Courts of Justice, 255
Cover note, 232
Credit, 20, 49, 117, 118, 121, 122, 123–124, 150, 151, 198, 210, 211, 231, 257
Credit card, 18, 124, 200
Credit note, 149
Creditor, 151, 212, 250
Credit sale agreement, 123–124, 156
Credit transfer, 198–200
Credit union, 51, 88
Credit Union League, 52
Currency issue, 186
Current account, 187, 192
Current value, 233
Curriculum vitae, 64–65,
Customer, 31, 88–89, 93, 97, 99, 101, 106, 112
Customer concept, 93, 94
Customs and Excise, 249

Data base, 40
Data processing, 41
Debenture, 211, 220, 221
Debit note, 149
Debt interest, 241
Debtor, 151, 198, 211, 212
Debts, 210, 211
Decision-making, 40, 41, 54, 108
Decision-making support system, 40
Decisions, 36,
Deeds, 52, 211
Defence, 241, 255
Deficit, balance of payments, 242
Deflation, 133
Del credere agent, 88
Delegating, 31, 36
Delivery, 155
Delivery note, 146, 147
Demand, 30, 96, 97–98, 100, 250

Demarcation dispute, 82
Departments, 32, 38
Department stores, 121
Deposit, 123
Deposit account, 192
Depreciation, 240
Design, 30,
Desk research, 108
Despatch, 146
Devaluation, 133
Developed countries, 15
Developing countries, 15
Development (see Economic development)
Development banks, 88, 187
Differential pricing, 100
Direct debit, 198
Directing, 31
Direct selling, 122
Direct services, 11, 89
Direct tax, 248
Discharge, 155
Discounts, 20, 144
Dismissal, 41, 65, 67
Display, 97
Distribution, 5, 89, 93, 93, 94, 95, 117, 119
Diversification, 22
Dividend, 51, 202, 209, 220, 221
Division of labour, 2–4, 20
Documentary bill, 151
Documentary credit, 151
Documentation (see Business Documentation)
Documentation, business, 143–158
Dumping, 135
Durable assets, 241
Duties, 134

E & OE, 148
Eastern Caribbean Common Market (ECCM), 139
Economic development, 242
Economic dualism, 23, 243
Economic growth, 238, 239, 240, 242–243
Economic integration, 220
Economic objectives, 240
Economic planning, 239
Economic problem, the, 4–7
Economic resources, 6
Economic stability, 240, 247, 255
Economic systems, 7–9
 controlled, 8–9, 255
 free, 8, 255
 mixed, 9, 255
 planned, 255
 subsistence, 8, 11
Economies of scale, 9, 19–20, 24, 41, 53, 121
Economy, management of, 255
Education, 17, 18, 241, 247, 258, 258, 260
Efficiency, 31
Electronic funds transfer (EFT), 201
Electronic mail, 40, 178–179
Electronic Point of Sale (EPOS), 201
Embargo, 135, 257
Emigration, 260, 261

Employees, 31, 80
Employers, 21, 241
Employment, 6, 7, 9, 18, 22, 30, 247, 256, 260
Employment Act, 66
Employment Protection Act, 67
Endorsement, 232
Endowment, 230
Enquiry, 143–144
Entrepreneurs, 18, 30, 45, 123, 125, 208, 227, 256–257
Entrepreneurship, 16, 21
Environment, 19, 31, 83, 241
Equality, 247
Equilibrium price, 98–99
Equities, 220 (see also Ordinary shares)
Estimate, 144, 210
European Union, 136, 138–139, 259
Executive support systems, 40
Exchange control, 133, 135
Exchange equalisation account, 185
Exchange rate, 134
Exchange value, 98
Executives, 36
Exhibitions, 110
Expansion (see Business growth)
Expenses, 30, 209, 213
Expenditure, 191, 209 (see also Government, expenditure)
Experiments, 107
Export agent, 133
Export consolidation and investment, 259
Export Credits Guarantee Department (ECGD), 256
Exporters, 11, 89, 95, 131, 133, 134, 151, 250
 difficulties faced, 134
Export house, 133–134
Export licence, 152
Export merchant, 133
Exports, 130, 250, 256
Expressed rejection, 157
Extractive industries, 9, 10

Facsimile transmission (FAX), 178
Factor, 210
Factories Act, 66, 75
Factoring, 210
Factors of production, 8, 16–18
Factory, 146, 148, 259
Fair trading practices, 257
Family planning, 6
Farming, 9, 15, 22, 51, 87, 243
Fast food, 52, 123
Finance, 29, 30, 40, 51, 89, 101, 187, 208–218
Financial market, 87–88, 255
Financial projections, 209–210
Fishing, 9, 22
Fixed assets, 211
Fixed costs, 210
Flexible working time, 74–75
Foreign currency, 11, 202
Foreign exchange, 23
Foreign market intelligence, 256
Foreign reserves, 255

Foreign trade (see Trade, foreign)
Foreign trade documents, 151–152
Franchisee, 52
Franchise shops, 123
Franchising, 52
Franchisor, 52
Free enterprise, 8
Free gifts, 122
Freepost, 176
Free trade, 134–135
Free trade agreements, 137
Freight, 163
Freightliner, 167
Freight note, 151
Fringe benefits, 73
Funding, 57
Funding agencies, 57
Futures market, 88

General Agreement on Tariffs and Trade (GATT), 137–138
General Consumption Tax, 149, 249
Generalised trade preference, 138
General office, 41
Giffen goods, 97
Globalisation, 9
Goals, 33, 51, 57
Good faith, 157
Goods, 17, 241
Goodwill, 101
Go slow, 82
Government, 19, 54, 56–57, 100, 101, 185, 241, 255–264
 agencies, 56, 259
 assistance to entrepreneurs, 256–257
 borrowing, 185
 central, 56, 57, 241
 departments, 56–57
 expenditure, 241, 242–243, 248
 intervention in business, 19, 100, 257–248
 labour, and, 260–261
 local, 56, 57, 241
 owned businesses, 54–56
 policies, 17, 101
 responsibilities, 255–256
 revenue, 241, 247
 role of, 101, 255–264
 Statistical Office, 259
Grading, 88
Grants, 58, 241, 255, 256, 257
Graphs, 175
Grievance, 67, 74
Gross domestic capital formation (GDCF), 241
Gross domestic product (GDP), 240
Gross national product (GNP), 240–241, 261
Gross pay, 72
Group dynamics, 32
Groups, 32
Growth, business (see Business growth)
Growth, economic (see Economic growth)

274

INDEX

Guarantees, 39

Handbooks, 33
Heads of Government Conference, 136
Health, 259
Health and safety, 75
Health and Safety at Work, 66
Health services, 17
Hidden economy, 239
Hidden persuaders, 106, 109
Hierarchy, 31
Hierarchy of needs, 71
Hire purchase (HP), 123, 124, 156, 187, 211
Holding company, 52–53
Home market (see Market, home)
Hospitality, 23
Hours of work, 73, 74–75, 81
Housing, 258
Human relations, 31
Human resources department (see Personnel department)
Hypermarkets, 122

Immigrant, 260
Immigration officials, 167
Implied rejection, 158
Import control, 133, 257
Import licence, 152
Importers, 89, 95, 257
Imports, 7, 15, 130, 131, 250, 256
Income, 98, 106, 191, 237, 248 (see also Wages)
Income tax, 72, 237, 248, 249
Indemnity, 227, 228, 229
Independent shops, 120
Indirect tax, 248
Induction, 41, 66
Industrial development, 240
Industrial development areas, 256
Industrial Development Corporation, 259
Industrial Disputes Tribunal, 67, 81
Industrial inertia, 19
Industrialisation, 5
Industrial legislation, 81
Industrial relations, 31, 80–86
Industrial waste, 5
Infant industries, 135, 257
Inflation, 249–254
Informal economy, 239
Information systems, 40
Information technology, 40
Infrastructure, 7, 256
Inland Revenue, 239
Instalments, 123
Insurance, 11, 39, 88, 89, 119, 125, 130, 156, 177, 211, 227–236
Integration, 30, 39, 53–54
Inter-American Development Bank, 137
Intercom, 33, 175
Interest, 192, 201, 209, 210, 211, 238
Intermediaries, 89, 119
International Bank for Reconstruction and Development (IBRD), 137
International Labour Organisation (ILO), 80

International Monetary Fund (IMF), 133, 137
International trade (see Trade, foreign)
Internet, the, 108, 123, 178–179
Interviews, 65–67, 107, 174
Investment, 187, 202, 221, 242, 255
  banks, 187
  trusts, 88, 221
Investors, 45, 208
Invisibles (see Invisible trade)
Invisible trade, 130
Invoices, 94, 146–149
Issuing house, 88, 186, 187

Job applications, 63, 64–65
Jobbers, 222 (see also Stock Exchange)
Job description, 73, 74
Job satisfaction, 71, 73
Job specification, 73, 74
Joint account, 192
Joint stock company, 48

Labour, 6, 17–18, 19, 23, 40, 49, 240, 249, 260
  mobility of, 17
  quality of, 240
Labour-saving equipment, 20
Land, 19
Land titles, 211
Large businesses (see Business size)
Law and order, 241, 255
Leadership, 32–33
Lead time, 96
Lease, 156
Legal department, 38
Legality, 157
Legal tender, 151
Legislation, 31, 255, 257, 259
Lender of last resort, 186
Lesser Developed Countries (LDCs), 136
Letter of credit, 151
Letter of enquiry, 143–144
Letter post services, 176
Letters, 33, 87
Liabilities, 208, 212
Life assurance, 229, 230
Life expectancy, 237
Lifespan, 237
Limited liability, 45
Limited liability company, 124, 202
Linkage industries, 19, 22–24
Living standards (see Standard of living)
Liquidity, 208, 209
Loan, 6, 22, 88, 133, 187, 201, 209, 210, 211, 255, 256
Loan capital, 211
Local area network (LAN), 40
Local government (see Government)
Location of business, 6, 19, 124
Logos, 123
LOME Convention, 259
Loss, 18, 45, 47, 52, 209, 211
Loss adjusters, 233
Loss leaders, 99, 121, 122

Lotteries, 123
Luxuries, 131

Mail order, 39, 122
Mail shot, 94
Machinery, 30
Management, 30–34
Management Development Centre, 259
Management information systems, 39–40
Managers, 31, 32, 33, 34, 35
Managing director, 38, 38, 48
Manifest, 151, 168
Manufacturers' associations, 101, 135–136
Market, 8, 87–92, 99, 130, 142, 222
Market forces, 8
Marketing, 29, 89, 94, 107, 163
  campaign, 32
  concept, 93–94, 106
  department, 87, 93–105
  director, 94
  function, 94
  mix, 94–96
  strategy, 93, 94
  team, 34
Market-orientated pricing, 99
Market pull, 19
Market research, 93, 94, 106–108, 110
Market share, 40
Market traders, 120
Mark-up, 99, 124, 210
Maslow, Abraham, 71
Mass production (see Production)
Maximisation, 210
Medical care, 241, 247, 258
Meetings, 174, 175
Memorandum, 33, 174
Memorandum of Association, 49–50
Merchandising, 97
Merchant, 88, 133
Merchantable quality, 112
Merchant banks, 186–187
Merger, 53, 187
Metrication Board, 112
Migration, 17, 260–261
Mining, 9, 22
Ministries, 57, 257, 259
Ministry of Agriculture, 257
Minors, 157
Minutes, 174
Misdemeanour, 67
Mixed economy, 45
Money, 1–2, 239, 241
  card, 200
  market, 87–88, 186
Monopoly, 100, 101
Mortgage, 52, 156
Mortgage debentures, 221
Motivation, 31, 32, 33, 71–79, 112
Multinational company, 54
Multiple, 119, 120–121, 122, 174
Municipal authorities, 57–58

National accounts, 237–246
National cake, 240–241
National debt, 241–242
National expenditure, 241

National income, 238–240
National insurance, 72, 258
Nationalisation, 258
Nationalised industry, 56
National prosperity, 256
National wealth, 240–241
Needs, 1, 15, 31, 71, 89
Net pay, 72
Night safe, 202
North American Free Trade Agreement (NAFTA), 139
Notice, 67
Notices, 33, 174

Objectives, 32, 35, 36, 58
Observations, 107
Offer, 155, 156
Offeree, 154
Offeror, 154
Office automation system, 40
Office workers, 30
Oligopoly, 100
Ombudsman, 113
Open market operations, 186
Opportunity cost, 5
Order, 41, 94, 145–146
Organisational structure, 34–38
  charts, 34–38
  committee, 37
  functional, 36–38
  informal, 37–38
  line, 35–36
  staff, 36
Organisation of American States (OAS), 137
Organisation of Eastern Caribbean States (OECS), 87, 137
Organisation of Petroleum Exporting Countries (OPEC), 100, 136, 138
Organising, 30
Orientation programme, 66
Output, 21
Overdraft, 192, 201, 211
Overheads, 213
Over manning, 213
Overseas market (see Trade, foreign)
Overseas trade (see Trade, foreign)
Overtime ban, 82
Owners, 31, 36

Packaging, 95, 97, 107, 118
Paging, 175
Partnership, 46, 124
Par value, 221
Pay (see Wages and Rates of pay)
Pay advice, 72
Pay As You Earn (PAYE), 247
Payment of debts, 150–151
Payroll, 25
Payroll department, 72, 73
Pension funds, 88
Per capita income, 239
Perfect market, 99
Perks (see Fringe benefits)
Personal budget, 191
Personal identity number (PIN), 201
Personal records, 41, 65, 67

275

INDEX

Personnel, 29, 30
   department, 38, 41, 65–66, 67
   manager, 38
Picketing, 82
Pilferage, 121
Pipelines, 167
Place, 95, 96
Planning, 30
Plough back, 5, 23, 30, 31
Point of sale (POS), 18, 40, 109, 153
Policy, 33, 40, 57, 83, 138, 174, 232
Pooling of risks, 227–228
Population, 6, 98
Port requirements, 165
Postal services, 89, 176–178
Poste restante, 176
Premises, 97
Premium, 88, 227, 232
Pressure groups, 83
Price, 20, 95, 96, 97–100, 122, 148, 211, 212, 221, 249, 250, 257, 258
Price controls, 257
Price index, 237
Price list, 144
Price plateau, 99
Primary data, 108
Principal officers, 175
Private enterprise, 45–53
Private expenditure, 241
Private limited company, 39, 47, 49
Private treaty, 88
Producers, 11, 87, 93, 117, 118, 119, 123
Product, 94–95, 96, 210
Product development, 93
Production, 1, 2–4, 5, 6, 7, 9–11, 12, 15–28, 22, 25, 29, 30, 87, 93, 112
   aims, 15
   department, 38, 41
   direct, 11
   domestic, 15
   indirect, 9, 11
   levels, 15–16
   line, 25
   manager, 38
   mass, 20, 21
   primary, 5, 9, 10, 12, 22
   secondary, 6, 9, 10, 12, 22
   subsistence, 15
   surplus, 15–16
   tertiary, 6, 9, 10–11, 12, 22
Production line, 25,
Productivity, 1, 31, 40, 249
Product life cycle, 96
Product mix, 97
Product performance, 106
Product range, 97
Professional associations, 56
Profit, 18, 29, 45, 47, 50, 51, 52, 53, 54, 55, 56, 94, 95, 96, 208, 209, 210, 211, 213–214, 220
Profit margin, 124, 257
Pro-forma invoice, 149
Progress chasers, 30, 41
Promotion, 95–96, 256–257
Property tax, 249
Proposal, 33, 229, 232

Prospectus, 49, 50, 219, 232
Protective services, 241
Prototype, 30
Proximate cause, 229
Psychological pricing, 99
Public enterprise, 255
Public expenditure, 241
Public image, 101
Publicity campaign, 101
Public limited company, 39, 47–49
Public relations, 20, 31, 101
   officer, 101
Public sector borrowing requirement (PSBR), 242
Public utilities, 54, 100, 255
Purchase tax, 248
Purchasing, 145–146
Purchasing department, 38, 41

Quality controllers, 41, 257
Quantity discount, 144
Questionnaires, 107
Quorum, 175
Quota, 133, 134, 257
Quotation, 41, 144–145

Rates, 58, 213, 249
Rates of pay, 72, 81
Rationing, 100
Raw materials, 11, 19, 23, 24, 30, 88, 163, 174, 209, 210, 249, 250
Receipt, 112
Recorded delivery, 177–178
Recreation, 258
Recruitment, 63–65
Redistribution of income, 248
Red tape, 49
Redundancy, 67
Redundancy Payments Act, 67
Referees, 64, 65
References, 41, 65
Regional cooperation, 135
Regional economic institutions, 135
Regional trade, 135
Registered office, 50
Registered post, 177
Registrar of Business Names, 49
Registrar of Companies, 49, 50, 56
Reinvestment, 211
Relocation areas, 6
Remittance advice, 151
Reports, 33
Representatives (see Sales representatives)
Representative sample, 107
Requisition, 41, 146
Research agencies, 36
Research and development, 20, 30
Reserves, 211
Resignations, 41, 65
Resources, 15, 20, 23
Responsibility, 31, 58
Restrictive practices, 21, 82
Retail business, setting up, 124–125
Retailers, 11, 89, 95, 101, 117, 118, 119
Retail trade (see Trade, retail)

Retained earnings, 211
Return on capital invested, 214
Revenue, 210, 241, 247
Reward, 213
Risk, 25, 228
Roads, 241, 247, 258
Robotics, 39
Royalties, 52
Rules, 175

Safe deposit box, 202
Salaries (see Wages and Rates of pay)
Sale of Goods Act, 112
Sales, 40, 94, 96, 107, 209, 211, 212
Sales concept, 93
Sales department, 38, 41
Sales growth, 96
Sales leaflets, 94
Sales manager, 38
Sales promotion, 95–96
Sales representatives, 41, 94, 117
Sampling, 88, 107
Savings, 124, 250
Scale of preference, 98
Scanner, 18
Scarce resources, 23
Scarcity, 4
School-based assessment, 266–271
Screw-driver industry, 22
Sea port (see Port requirements)
Secondary data, 108
Secretary, 175
Securities, 87, 88, 219, 220, 221
Self-help, 6, 17–18
Self-service stores, 121
Seller, 87, 88, 143, 144, 146, 150, 151, 223
Selling abroad, 133
Selling on credit, 123–124
Service provider, 123
Services, 17, 87, 89, 94, 101, 241
Shareholders, 25, 39, 48, 50, 83, 209, 211
Shares, 30, 49, 124, 187, 202, 219, 220, 221, 222 (see also Stock Exchange)
Shift work, 74
Shipping agent, 168
Shopping precincts, 122
Shop stewards, 80
Short list, 65
Sit-in, 82
Size of business (see Business size)
Skills, 23, 37
Sleeping partner, 46
Small business (see Business size)
Small business incubator, 21–22
Smith, Adam, 247
Social costs, 6
Social needs, 89
Social problems, 6
Social services, 241, 255, 258–259
Sole proprietor, 45–46, 124
Space buying, 111
Span of control, 34–35
Span of management, 34–35
Special business relationships, 50–53

Specialisation, 1, 3–4, 8, 9, 12, 20, 36, 119, 131
Specialists, 36, 39, 87
Speculation, 222
Spot market, 88
Spreadsheet, 153, 153, 210, 211
Staff orientation, 66
Staff training (see Training)
Stags, 222
Stamp duty, 249
Standard of living, 237–238, 239–240
Standing order, 198, 199
State corporation, 54–56
Statement of account, 94, 150 (see also Bank statement)
Statutory body, 56
Stock Exchange, 88, 219–226
   brokers, 202, 222, 223
   jobbers, 222, 223
   new shares, 219
   share certificate, 222
   speculation, 222
Stock, 152, 210, 213
Stock level, 152
Stock market, 87, 219
Stock records, 123, 152–153
Stocks, 202
Storage, 30
Strategic planning, 255
Strike, 82
Subordinates, 31, 32
Subrogation, 229
Subsidies, 8, 100, 134, 241, 255, 256, 257, 258
Subsistence economy, 1, 8
Suggestion schemes, 33, 174
Supermarkets, 121
Supervisors, 32, 67
Suppliers, 41, 48
Supply, 16, 53, 72, 97, 98
Surplus, 1, 132, 242
Surveys, 33, 107–108

Takeover, 49, 53, 54, 187
Target market, 48, 94, 117
Tariff, 133, 134, 138, 257
Task force, 57
Taste, 106
Taxation, 58, 100, 149, 212, 239, 247–254, 256, 256, 257, 258, 259 (see also General Consumption Tax)
Teamwork, 31, 33–34
Technical assistance, 256–257
Technical progress, 242
Technological change, 24–25
Technology, 18, 54, 243
Telecommunication, 30, 39, 87, 89, 100, 175, 178
Teleconferencing, 40
Telegraphic money transfer, 185
Telephone, 33, 100, 107, 108, 175, 178
Telephone credit card, 200
Telephone interviews, 107
Telephone order trading, 122
Telex, 178
Tender, 143
Terms, of payment, 148
Testimonials, 65
Test marketing, 107

INDEX

Time card, 72
Tourism, 7, 11, 23, 130, 243, 257, 259
Tourism Development Board (TDB), 257, 259
Trade, 8, 89, 101, 117–129, 151–152, 256–257 (see also Free trade)
  associations, 101–102
  credit, 20, 123, 211
  foreign, 9, 89, 117, 130–142, 187, 241
  gap, 132
  invisible, 130
  local, 117–129
  mark, 95
  promotion, 256–257
  restrictions, 134–135, 138
  retail, 89, 101, 119–123
  services to, 89
  visible, 130
  wholesale, 89, 117–119
Trade discount, 144
Trade fairs, 24
Trade practices, 31
Trade promotion, 256
Traders, 11, 119
Trade unions, 80–81
Trading Certificate, 49
Traditional, 106
Training, 17, 20, 21, 23, 31, 40, 41, 54, 66, 260
Transaction, 143
Transaction processing systems, 40
Transport, 11, 19, 20, 38, 89, 95, 101, 118, 119, 130, 163–172, 210, 241, 258
  air, 166–167
  choice of, 163
  containers, 167–168
  department, 38, 39
  methods of, 163–167
  pipelines, 167
  rail, 163–164
  river, 165
  road, 164
  sea, 165
  water, 164–165
Traveller's cheques, 202

Treasurer, 175
Treasury bills, 186
Turnover, 212–213
Typing pool, 41

Underground economy, 239
Undistributed profits, 211
Unemployment, 6, 9, 21, 23, 25, 54, 260, 261
Uninsurable risks, 228–229
Union busting, 82
Unions, (see Trade unions)
Unit trusts, 88, 221
Utmost good faith, 229

Vacancies, 63
Vandalism, 122
Vending machines, 122
Visible trade, 130, 131–132
Video conferencing, 40
Visual promotion, 95
Visible trade, 130, 131–132

Wage differentials, 71–72
Wages, 30, 32, 71–73, 72–73, 81, 93, 210, 213, 237, 238, 241, 249, 250, 258
  deductions, 72
  payments, 72–73
  rates of, 72
Wants, 15, 30, 87
Warehouse, 117, 146, 148
Wealth, 1, 238, 239
Weights and measures, 257
Welfare, 66, 258
What-if scenarios, 210
Whispering campaign, 110
Wholesalers, 89, 117, 119, 123
Wholesale trade (see Trade, wholesale)
Word processing, 25
Working conditions, 66, 73–75, 81
Working relationships, 21
Work-to-rule, 82
World Trade Organisation (WTO), 138

Yield, 221

Answers to tests

CHAPTER 1

WHAT DO YOU KNOW?		MULTIPLE CHOICE	
1	DIRECT	1	(b)
2	SURVIVE	2	(a)
3	EXCHANGE	3	(c)
4	MONEY	4	(b)
5	BORING	5	(d)
6	EXPERT	6	(c)
7	CHOICE	7	(d)
8	PRIORITY	8	(b)
9	GOVERNMENT	9	(b)
10	PRICES	10	(d)

CHAPTER 2

WHAT DO YOU KNOW?		MULTIPLE CHOICE	
1	NEED	1	(d)
2	WANT	2	(a)
3	SUBSISTENCE	3	(c)
4	IMPORTS	4	(c)
5	SURPLUS	5	(d)
6	LABOUR	6	(d)
7	PROFIT	7	(a)
8	SITE	8	(c)
9	ECONOMIES	9	(b)
10	AUTOMATION	10	(a)

CHAPTER 3

WHAT DO YOU KNOW?		MULTIPLE CHOICE	
1	PROFIT	1	(b)
2	WANTS	2	(c)
3	FINANCE	3	(a)
4	MARKETING	4	(c)
5	PERSONNEL	5	(d)
6	MANAGERS	6	(d)
7	CO-ORDINATE	7	(c)
8	LIMIT	8	(a)
9	INFORMAL	9	(c)
10	FORMAL	10	(b)

CHAPTER 4

WHAT DO YOU KNOW?		MULTIPLE CHOICE	
1	MIXED	1	(b)
2	FAIL	2	(a)
3	DEED	3	(b)
4	PRIVATE	4	(d)
5	EXTERNAL	5	(b)
6	INTERNAL	6	(c)
7	WORKER	7	(a)
8	FRANCHISING	8	(c)
9	CONGLOMERATE	9	(a)
10	PUBLIC	10	(d)

CHAPTER 5

WHAT DO YOU KNOW?		MULTIPLE CHOICE	
1	HANDWRITTEN	1	(d)
2	HISTORY	2	(b)
3	PERSONNEL	3	(a)
4	INTERVIEWED	4	(a)
5	ACQUAINTED	5	(d)
6	ORIENTATION	6	(c)
7	SKILLS	7	(b)
8	NEWSPAPER	8	(a)
9	CONFIDENTIAL	9	(c)
10	UNFAIR	10	(d)

CHAPTER 6

WHAT DO YOU KNOW?		MULTIPLE CHOICE	
1	SATISFACTION	1	(c)
2	WAGES	2	(b)
3	ACADEMIC	3	(c)
4	BONUS	4	(a)
5	GROSS	5	(c)
6	NET	6	(a)
7	ADVICE	7	(d)
8	COMPUTERS	8	(b)
9	DESCRIPTION	9	(b)
10	CONTRACT	10	(a)

CHAPTER 7

WHAT DO YOU KNOW?		MULTIPLE CHOICE	
1	EMPLOYEES	1	(b)
2	CONFLICT	2	(d)
3	EMPLOYERS	3	(b)
4	CONDITIONS	4	(a)
5	NEGOTIATIONS	5	(c)
6	CONCILIATION	6	(d)
7	ARBITRATION	7	(b)
8	DEMARCATION	8	(d)
9	PRESSURE	9	(c)
10	STRIKE	10	(a)

CHAPTER 8

WHAT DO YOU KNOW?		MULTIPLE CHOICE	
1	PRODUCTION	1	(b)
2	TRADE	2	(d)
3	DISTRIBUTION	3	(d)
4	MONEY	4	(a)
5	CAPITAL	5	(c)
6	ECONOMIC	6	(b)
7	COMMODITY	7	(a)
8	COMMISSION	8	(c)
9	CONSUMER	9	(b)
10	COMMERCE	10	(d)

CHAPTER 9

WHAT DO YOU KNOW?		MULTIPLE CHOICE	
1	BUYERS	1	(d)
2	MARKETING	2	(a)
3	RESEARCH	3	(b)
4	SELLING	4	(c)
5	DIVIDE	5	(a)
6	REPRESENTATIVES	6	(d)
7	TARGET	7	(a)
8	FALL	8	(b)
9	HIGHER	9	(c)
10	EQUILIBRIUM	10	(a)

CHAPTER 10

WHAT DO YOU KNOW?		MULTIPLE CHOICE	
1	NEEDS	1	(b)
2	DECISIONS	2	(a)
3	QUESTIONING	3	(d)
4	REPRESENTATIVE	4	(c)
5	PRIMARY	5	(a)
6	SECONDARY	6	(a)
7	AWARE	7	(c)
8	INFORMATIVE	8	(b)
9	TARGET	9	(d)
10	AGENCIES	10	(c)

CHAPTER 11

WHAT DO YOU KNOW?		MULTIPLE CHOICE	
1	MIDDLEMAN	1	(c)
2	BREAKING	2	(a)
3	PRODUCTION	3	(d)
4	CREDIT	4	(c)
5	BYPASS	5	(a)
6	LINK	6	(d)
7	MARKET	7	(b)
8	MULTIPLE	8	(a)
9	DEPARTMENT	9	(b)
10	BRAND	10	(d)

CHAPTER 12

WHAT DO YOU KNOW?		MULTIPLE CHOICE	
1	INCOME	1	(c)
2	IMPORTS	2	(b)
3	EXPORTS	3	(c)
4	SPENDING	4	(c)
5	FAVOURABLE	5	(a)
6	ADVERSE	6	(d)
7	HOUSE	7	(b)
8	RESTRICTIONS	8	(b)
9	CURRENCY	9	(a)
10	WORLD	10	(c)

ANSWERS TO TESTS

CHAPTER 13

WHAT DO YOU KNOW?
1. ENQUIRY
2. QUOTATION
3. ORDER
4. ESTIMATED
5. DISCOUNT
6. ACKNOWLEDGE
7. ADVICE
8. INVOICE
9. SUMMARISES
10. CREDIT

MULTIPLE CHOICE
1. (b)
2. (c)
3. (d)
4. (a)
5. (b)
6. (d)
7. (b)
8. (a)
9. (c)
10. (c)

CHAPTER 14

WHAT DO YOU KNOW?
1. CAPITAL
2. TASKS
3. VALUE
4. RAIL
5. ROAD
6. SEA
7. FIXED
8. TRAMP
9. WAY
10. AIR

MULTIPLE CHOICE
1. (c)
2. (d)
3. (a)
4. (a)
5. (a)
6. (b)
7. (d)
8. (c)
9. (a)
10. (d)

CHAPTER 15

WHAT DO YOU KNOW?
1. CONTACT
2. ADVERTISING
3. TRANSPORT
4. INFORMED
5. SPEECH
6. PIE
7. MEETINGS
8. CHAIRPERSON
9. REPLY
10. PRINTED

MULTIPLE CHOICE
1. (c)
2. (d)
3. (b)
4. (d)
5. (c)
6. (b)
7. (c)
8. (a)
9. (a)
10. (c)

CHAPTER 16

WHAT DO YOU KNOW?
1. GOVERNMENT
2. TREASURY
3. CURRENCY
4. BANKERS'
5. CLEARING
6. COMMERCIAL
7. MERCHANT
8. REPUTATION
9. INTERMEDIARIES
10. ECONOMIC

MULTIPLE CHOICE
1. (b)
2. (c)
3. (c)
4. (b)
5. (b)
6. (d)
7. (a)
8. (d)
9. (b)
10. (a)

CHAPTER 17

WHAT DO YOU KNOW?
1. BUDGET
2. TASTES
3. LUXURIES
4. EVEN
5. DEPOSIT
6. CURRENT
7. OVERDRAWN
8. CHEQUE
9. SAFER
10. BOUNCED

MULTIPLE CHOICE
1. (c)
2. (a)
3. (d)
4. (b)
5. (a)
6. (d)
7. (c)
8. (b)
9. (a)
10. (d)

CHAPTER 18

WHAT DO YOU KNOW?
1. SAME
2. VARIES
3. DIRECTLY
4. MULTIPLE
5. GUARANTEES
6. CREDIT
7. DISPENSER
8. OVERDRAFT
9. LOAN
10. NIGHT

MULTIPLE CHOICE
1. (c)
2. (a)
3. (a)
4. (d)
5. (c)
6. (b)
7. (d)
8. (b)
9. (a)
10. (c)

CHAPTER 19

WHAT DO YOU KNOW?
1. ENTREPRENEURS
2. SNAPSHOT
3. CAPITAL
4. PAYMENT
5. WORKING
6. TURNOVER
7. OLD
8. PROFIT
9. FIXED
10. VARIABLE

MULTIPLE CHOICE
1. (b)
2. (d)
3. (c)
4. (d)
5. (b)
6. (a)
7. (a)
8. (a)
9. (d)
10. (d)

CHAPTER 20

WHAT DO YOU KNOW?
1. MARKET
2. EQUITIES
3. PROSPERITY
4. DEBENTURES
5. RISK
6. FREE
7. MEMBERS
8. BROKER
9. JOBBERS
10. TURN

MULTIPLE CHOICE
1. (b)
2. (d)
3. (a)
4. (a)
5. (c)
6. (b)
7. (b)
8. (a)
9. (a)
10. (c)

CHAPTER 21

WHAT DO YOU KNOW?
1. MARINE
2. ASSURANCE
3. ACCIDENT
4. COMPENSATION
5. POOL
6. PREDICT
7. INTEREST
8. CLAIM
9. LOSS ADJUSTER
10. CONTRIBUTE

MULTIPLE CHOICE
1. (a)
2. (d)
3. (c)
4. (b)
5. (d)
6. (a)
7. (a)
8. (c)
9. (b)
10. (d)

CHAPTER 22

WHAT DO YOU KNOW?
1. QUALITY
2. INCOME
3. WEALTH
4. INFORMAL
5. LIVING
6. OUTPUT
7. DEBT
8. GOVERNMENT
9. ADVANCED
10. TECHNICAL

MULTIPLE CHOICE
1. (b)
2. (d)
3. (c)
4. (a)
5. (c)
6. (a)
7. (c)
8. (b)
9. (d)
10. (a)

CHAPTER 23

WHAT DO YOU KNOW?
1. ECONOMY
2. COMPULSORY
3. PAY
4. EVADE
5. CONVENIENT
6. ECONOMICALLY
7. EXPENDITURE
8. REDISTRIBUTE
9. DIRECT
10. INDIRECT

MULTIPLE CHOICE
1. (b)
2. (c)
3. (d)
4. (a)
5. (b)
6. (a)
7. (d)
8. (c)
9. (b)
10. (a)

CHAPTER 24

WHAT DO YOU KNOW?
1. LEGISLATION
2. DEVELOPMENT
3. SERVICES
4. ECONOMY
5. BUDGET
6. PROSPERITY
7. EXPORT
8. POTENTIAL
9. LEASE
10. PROTECTION

MULTIPLE CHOICE
1. (d)
2. (b)
3. (c)
4. (d)
5. (a)
6. (b)
7. (b)
8. (c)
9. (a)
10. (d)